HARVARD EAST ASIAN MONOGRAPHS

130

Exhausting the Earth
State and Peasant in Hunan, 1500–1850

Exhausting the Earth
State and Peasant in Hunan, 1500–1850

PETER C. PERDUE

PUBLISHED BY
COUNCIL ON EAST ASIAN STUDIES
HARVARD UNIVERSITY

Distributed by
Harvard University Press
Cambridge, Massachusetts and London, England
1987

The Council on East Asian Studies at Harvard University publishes a mono-
graph series and, through the Fairbank Center for East Asian Research and
the Reischauer Institute of Japanese Studies, administers research projects
designed to further scholarly understanding of China, Japan, Korea, Vietnam,
Inner Asia, and adjacent areas.

Library of Congress Cataloging in Publication Data

Perdue, Peter C., 1949–
Exhausting the earth.

(Harvard East Asian monographs ; 130)
Bibliography: p.
Includes index.
1. Agriculture and state—China—Hunan Province—
History. 2. Land use, Rural—China—Hunan Province—
History. 3. Hunan Province (China)—Population—
History. 4. Agricultural productivity—China—Hunan
Province—History. 5. Peasantry—China—Hunan Province—
History. I. Title. II. Series.
HD2100.H86P47   1987   338.1'0951'215   87-5067
ISBN 0-674-27504-7

To my parents and the memory of Joseph Fletcher

Contents

Contents

Tables

Figures

Acknowledgments

This book has taken so long to produce that it would be impossible to thank everyone who had a part in it. Like many others, I began my studies of Qing history at Harvard under John K. Fairbank. Alexander Woodside first suggested to me the ideas that led to this study and by his own example encouraged my forays into Qing socioeconomic history. Joseph Fletcher provided continual inspiration by his enthusiasm, his broad-ranging intellect, his great generosity, and his devotion to scholarship. Benjamin Schwartz's constant stress on the importance of intellectual history has always been a valuable reminder when I have been tempted toward an excessively materialistic outlook. Long, intense discussions with R. Bin Wong during our graduate school days molded my approach more than I can imagine. Philip Kuhn supervised the final stage of the dissertation and has provided criticially needed support many times over. I owe an intellectual debt to the great French historians Fernand Braudel and Emmanuel LeRoy Ladurie, whose grand works inspired the fond hope that it might be possible to study the *longue durée* in China. A year spent studying social theory and European history at the University of Michigan with Charles Tilly and his students stimulated my excursions into comparative history.

Research in Japan and Taiwan was supported by Fulbright and Social Science Research Council fellowships. In Japan, I am particularly grateful for the warm hospitality of Professors Tanaka Masatoshi, Saeki Yuichi, and Yamane Yukio, and to the students in their seminars at Tokyo University and the Toyo Bunko, especially Hamashita Takeshi, Yamana Fuio, and Nakayama Mio-Kishiyama. In Kyoto, Fuma Susumu was most helpful in guiding me through the

Jinbun Kagaku Kenkyujo collection. I was fortunate to meet Morita Akira in Osaka, because his excellent work on water conservancy has been indispensable to this study. I also owe much to Oh Keum-sung's work on Dongting Lake in the Ming, so I was very glad to be able to see him during the year he spent at Harvard.

In Taiwan, Zhang Pide and Zhuang Jifa made the Qing archives accessible to me, while a group of us American scholars—Kent Guy, Bob Jencks, Jean Oi, and Beatrice Bartlett—collectively probed the mysteries of the Qing bureaucracy. Liu Shiji, of the Institute of Three People's Principles of Academia Sinica, constantly amazed me with his devotion to Western social science and its application to China.

Research in the Qing archives in Beijing was supported by the Committee on Scholarly Communication with the People's Republic of China. I owe much to Bob Geyer and Leon Slawecki for eventually negotiating my way into China past numerous obstructions, and to Ji Shaolin, of the Chinese Ministry of Education, for sponsoring my research stay. At the archives, Ju Deyuan and Wei Qingyuan were generous with their knowledge and most supportive. Kong Xiangji, of People's University, was a good companion on the long bike ride to the archives and made possible a short visit to Changsha.

My colleagues in the History Faculty at M.I.T. have created a congenial, enjoyable environment for both teaching and research. I owe a particular debt to Philip Khoury for his constant encouragement, and to Richard Douglas for his sagacious advice. Pauline Maier, as chair, has done her best to provide the time and money to support this work. Will Watson and David Ralston deserve thanks for their fellowship. Kathleen Bielawski heroically saved me from technological disaster by retyping the entire manuscript after the computer tape had been lost.

Others who have, by their comments, contributed to some version of what eventually went into this book include Elizabeth Perry, Lillian M. Li, Mary Backus Rankin, Joseph Esherick, Linda Grove, Steve Averill, James Lee, Hue Ho Tam-Tai, Benjamin Elman, Jonathan Ocko, and Timothy Brook. None of them is, of course, responsible for anything that has gone into it or been left out.

Families traditionally come last in acknowledgments, because their contributions to scholarly work are less direct, but more profound. Without the support of my parents, I could never have made it through the fifteen years leading to the completion of this book. And without the cheerful diversions demanded by my wife, Linda, and my children, Kay and Alex, this book might have been finished much sooner, but I would have been far less happy.

ONE

Introduction

C'est le pays le plus peuplé et le mieux cultivé qu'il y ait au monde.
—Encyclopédie *(1784), "Chine."*

Ever since the Enlightenment, foreign observers of China have been impressed by the apparent durability and effectiveness of its imperial bureaucracy. By contrast with the inefficient and burdensome mechanisms of taxation in absolutist Europe, many saw the Chinese bureaucracy as a model of correct government. The French physiocrat François Quesnay admired above all the beneficial attitude of the Chinese emperor toward his rural subjects:

> I have concluded from the reports about China that the Chinese constitution is founded upon wise and irrevocable laws which the emperor enforces and which he carefully observes himself.[1]

Quesnay and other physiocrats felt that the Chinese state served as a model of "enlightened despotism" that European rulers should imitate. Montesquieu, however, regarded the Chinese state as a pure

1

despotism, whose emperors ruled by fear. In his view, only the fear of losing his throne motivated the emperor to act benevolently so as to relieve famine.[2]

The Enlightenment observers of China produced two contrasting models of the relationship between the imperial state and the rural society it ruled: the "Light Government" and the "Oriental Despotism" model. To a large extent, these two paradigms still characterize modern views of the relationship of the Chinese state to the economy. It is, of course, an oversimplification to describe the great variety of approaches to China's economy under these two headings. Still, classifying a range of outlooks under these categories highlights the common assumptions shared by many scholars of China and demonstrates that our most general conceptions of Chinese society have their roots in the eighteenth-century observers of the empire.

ORIENTAL DESPOTISM

Proponents of the "Oriental Despotism" model stressed the lack of any limitations, legal or customary, on the absolute power of the emperor.[3] They traced the sources of this absolute power to the absence of a hereditary nobility or independent clergy and the lack of free, independent cities. In this view, China, lacking the representative institutions of the West and its dynamic urban economy, was ultimately doomed to stagnation. Montesquieu, for example, used this model of China to promote reform in the West. He warned that France too would suffer stagnation if it did not reform its absolutist institutions and respond to the needs of its people.[4]

The model of Oriental Despotism has had a pervasive influence on Western thinking about non-Western peoples. It formed the basis for Hegel's distinction between the West and the East.[5] Karl Marx's concept of the Asiatic mode of production elaborated on Hegel's abstract scheme and filled it in with information from European observers of China and India. Max Weber highlighted the contrast between China and the West by stressing the dominance of the official class over political and economic life, and by arguing that Chinese cities never achieved the economic centrality and political autonomy found in the medieval West.[6]

Karl Wittfogel's *Oriental Despotism* extended the concept to cover a vast array of societies, from imperial Russia and China to modern Communist states. The concept also underlies the model of the Chinese state held by a Sinologist like Etienne Balazs. He shares with Wittfogel the idea that the unlimited power of the imperial bureaucratic state stifled the development of both the rural and urban economies. Arbitrary confiscation of profits, lack of contract protection, and lack of prestige discouraged merchants from productive investment. Peasants, too, were powerless to prevent oppressive rents, high surtaxes, and abusive corvée levies. China failed to produce capitalism and Western science because there were no constraints on the state bureaucracy.[7]

Joseph Needham rejects the use of the term *Oriental Despotism*, but his *bureaucratic feudalism* has many points in common with it. He sees the imperial Chinese state as an all-powerful mandarin bureaucracy resting on top of a multitude of autonomous village communities. While the state did not try to interfere with the daily affairs of the villages, it ensured its dominance over society through the management of public works.[8] Although the bureaucratic state was responsible for great achievements in science and technology, its agrarian bias and hostility to commerce prevented the emergence of modern Western-style science and industry.[9]

The Oriental-Despotism model of China has been even more influential in Japan than in the West. There, its presuppositions were similar, but it served other functions. For Pan-Asian ideologists, the "stagnation" and "backwardness" of modern China justified the intervention of Japan on the Asian continent in the interests of modernization. Many historians and political writers asserted that it was Japan's mission, as Asia's most advanced nation, to bring China into the modern world. Since China's "despotic" imperial state had prevented her from developing democratic institutions and a modern economy by herself, Japan's duty was to introduce these essential features of a modern state—by conquest if necessary. The Oriental-Despotism, or "stagnationist" (*teitairon*) model of China became an essential element in justifying Japanese imperialism.

After World War II, the Oriental-Despotism model lost favor in both Japan and the West. In Japan, a new generation of scholars attacked it on ideological grounds. Because they rejected the legitimation of Japanese imperialism and because they were impressed by the radical modernization program undertaken by the People's Republic of China, they insisted that the rejection of the stagnationist model of China had to be the central focus of Japanese scholarship on China.[10] They argued that the development of commerce and the struggle of the Chinese peasants to free themselves from the burdens of heavy taxation and rent were dynamic forces transforming the mode of production before the arrival of the West.

Oriental Despotism still had its advocates in Europe and the United States, but its empirical flaws began to show. Many Sinologists and specialists on other parts of the world criticized Wittfogel's all-inclusive theory.[11] They attacked it for ignoring historical change in the Chinese empire, since the autocratic power of the emperor fluctuated depending on the emperor's personality and the institutions of his dynasty. Furthermore, despotic rule by a strong centralizing emperor did not necessarily hinder economic growth. For example, Ming Taizu, one of China's most brutal autocrats, encouraged considerable investment in the reconstruction of the agricultural economy.[12]

Historians discovered much evidence of vigorous economic growth, especially in the Song, late Ming, and early Qing eras. These three periods saw the growth of large urban centers, the rise of extensive marketing networks, and the accumulation of considerable merchant capital. In the countryside, the rapid development of rice cultivation in the lower Yangtze during the Song, the spread of New-World crops in the Ming and Qing, or the rapid spread of commercial cotton cultivation in eighteenth-century North China all testified to the dynamic potential of Chinese agriculture.

The imperial state seldom interfered with commercial or agricultural growth during these periods. For all the laments by Confucian traditionalists over the disappearance of old rituals or the rise of unruly *nouveaux-riches* merchants and peasants, many officials cooperated in mercantile ventures, while others devoted their efforts to the advancement of agriculture. Studies of Chinese agriculture have shown that Chinese peasants responded rapidly to market incentives to introduce new cash crops.[13] The recognition of the possibilities for growth in the commercial economy and the ability of peasants to respond to market incentives posed the old question of China's inability to develop capitalism in an intensified form: Why, *despite* China's considerable commercial development, did she *still* not develop an industrialized capitalist economy? As new answers were sought, it was the weaknesses and limitations of the imperial state, rather than its excessive strength, that seemed to provide the answer.

Paradoxically, as Western and Japanese scholars have turned away from Oriental Despotism, Chinese scholars have turned toward it. The developers of Marxist historiography in China in the 1930s seldom applied the Asiatic mode of production to China. Scholars and political organizers debated whether imperial China belonged to the "capitalist" or "feudal" stage, but they rarely assigned it to the "Asiatic" mode.[14] The stagnationist implications of the Asiatic mode were hardly congenial to Marxist nationalists organizing an anti-feudal and anti-imperialist revolution. If China belonged to the Asiatic mode, she could not progress on her own; she would have to rely on imperialist penetration to bring her into the modern world and make a revolution possible. That this was what Marx himself thought was conveniently ignored. After Stalin outlawed the Asiatic mode as a legitimate Marxist interpretation of history and imposed a unilinear model of evolution on the world Communist movement in 1931, little was heard about the concept in China for four decades.

In recent years, however, the Asiatic mode has returned to Chinese historical discussion.[15] Its advocates are still a small minority, outweighed by both the competing schools of "feudalism" and "sprouts of capitalism," but the concept has features attractive to theorists trying to explain China's economic development in Marxist terms. The main question for recent studies of Chinese economic history has been: "Why was China's feudal stage so prolonged?"[16] Promoters of

China's modernization, recognizing China's economic and techno-logical backwardness in the contemporary world, now find the source of the obstacles to modernization in the "feudal legacy" of the past. Many of the historical discussions of this issue find the causes of the "prolongation of feudalism" in the structure of the rural economy and its relationship with the imperial state. Some stress geographical fac-tors, others stress the small peasant economy, while others have con-centrated on the retarding effect of the autocratic feudal state. China's past is seen only as a source of obstacles, not as a positive resource. The progressive functions of peasant rebellions, which Mao Zedong stressed as China's distinctive source of anti-feudal movements, are now played down in order to emphasize the limitations of the peasant mentality. Even those, like Fu Yiling, who advocated "capitalist sprouts" now recognize that these sprouts were limited and failed to develop into capitalism.[17] The officials of the imperial state are blamed for obstructing technological progress and for their lack of interest in modern science. In the 1980s, China's intellectuals have pressed toward the most radical rejection of China's past since the May Fourth Movement. Viewing the past as a unified, unchanging presence seems to them to be the only way to reject it entirely.

The reaffirmation of the Asiatic mode also involves the unfreezing of the unilinear Stalinist model of historical development. It allows diversity of evolution for different societies, free of the Procrustean six stages (primitive communism—slavery—feudalism—capitalism—socialism—communism) leading all societies everywhere inevitably toward communism. Thus, it provides for creativity, and a welcome relief from cramming historical facts into an ideological straitjacket. Some of the historians who have revived the Asiatic mode show an unusual familiarity with European history and an interest in broad comparative history. Ultimately, their model of the Chinese imperial state echoes all the basic features of the Oriental-Despotism model, stressing the fundamental differences between the evolution of West-ern societies and the rest of the world. Just like Montesquieu, they find the causes of China's current backwardness in the lack of free cities, lack of an independent church, and lack of a hereditary nobility in the traditional society.[18] The Western concept that asserted the inevitable superiority of the West and the backwardness of the East is now fervently adopted by young Chinese themselves to overcome their own backwardness.

From the Western historian's point of view, the recent embracing of Oriental Despotism by some Chinese does not validate the concept. It does, however, illustrate the importance of the issues raised by the concept for contemporary China. The degree of power of the imperial state; the control of the state over the peasants it ruled; the attitudes of the state officials toward economic progress and technological change—these historical issues deeply concern young Chinese interested in their country's future. For all the inadequacies of Oriental Despotism as a historian's tool, it does provide a plausible explanation for China's current predicament. Those who use it are, by implication, boldly criticizing the bureaucratic power of the current regime, equating it with a recurring Oriental Despotism which is stifling the people's energies. A study of the real capabilities of the Qing state should provide a better understanding of what contemporary China can become.

THE LIMITED STATE

In contrast to Oriental Despotism, the second school stresses the limitations of the imperial state. This model derives from François Quesnay, who believed that "natural law" limited the Chinese emperor's powers and ensured that he would act in the interest of his subjects.[19] In Quesnay's view, the observance of rituals worshiping the supreme deity, Shangdi, encouraged emperors to carry out their obligations to relieve the sufferings of their subjects in time of drought.[20] Because agriculture was venerated, landowners held secure property rights and thus worked to improve the productivity of the soil. Quesnay particularly praised the low level of taxation in China.[21] He believed that limited tax rates demonstrated the emperor's concern for the welfare of the peasantry and encouraged the peasants to produce without fear of having their surplus confiscated. Like Montesquieu, Quesnay had France in mind, where agriculture was retarded by arbitrary taxation, the corruption of tax farmers, and landowners' insecurity about their property rights. While he praised the productivity of Chinese agriculture, he also recognized that the huge and growing population which consumed the wealth of the country accounted for the presence of great poverty.[22] Quesnay, in fact, was one of the first to recommend that the Chinese adopt birth-control policies by raising the age of marriage.[23]

Despite the superficiality of his information about China, many of Quesnay's insights agree with those of modern scholarship. The high yields of agriculture and the low level of taxation, as well as the burden of overpopulation, remain the characteristic features of our view of Qing China. Quesnay, of course, exaggerated the beneficence of the emperors and ignored the corruption, tax farming, and disorder in Qing administration, but he correctly recognized that the Chinese bureaucracy was much more systematically organized than the European states of his day. The recognition of agriculture as the foundation of society and the need for rulers to encourage and protect peasant cultivators were new ideas in Europe, but they had long been part of Chinese state ideology. Sinologists and theorists, like Max Weber, who describe the Chinese state's economic policies as "laissez-faire" are unwittingly elaborating the essential points of Quesnay's analysis.[24]

After the eighteenth century, admiration for the Chinese empire waned. Nineteenth-century British observers often agreed on the limited powers of the Qing state, but they saw these limitations as weaknesses. The reform movements of the late nineteenth century failed because the state did not have the strength to enforce its reforms against conservative gentry opposition. Explanations of China's failure to industrialize in the nineteenth century usually focus on the limited impact of the state bureaucracy on the economy. Many modern scholars consider the only effective functions of Qing administration to have been tax collection and maintenance of order.[25] They blame China's backwardness on the inadequacies of the "traditional Confucian state" to organize modern industrial development.

Recently, Ramon Myers and Thomas Metzger have revived the positive evaluation of the imperial state. They propose that the declining influence of the dynastic rulers on private economic activity from the Song to the eighteenth century did not necessarily mean declining effectiveness of government.[26] Metzger argues that the "dynamism of the private sector" was reinforced by state fiscal policies and changes in the property and class structure.[27] A major transformation in the organization of the economy occurred from 1500 to 1800, which made possible the enormous population growth of the period. Myers and Metzger sharply reject the predominant focus on corruption, inefficiencies, and abuses characteristic of most studies of Qing administration. Metzger points out, for example, that salt smuggling should not be seen merely as an abuse of the salt monopoly but as a practice that was tolerated by Qing officials because it was necessary to relieve shortages.[28] Qing officials contributed to economic growth by encouraging merchant participation in military and grain-supply markets, by regulating prices, and by participating in joint ventures with merchants.[29] Taiwan's economy in the post-World War II period has flourished despite the persistence of many of the particularistic traditions said to have prevented growth in the nineteenth century.

Advocates of the "proto-capitalist" functions of the eighteenth-century state are also found in China. Peng Zeyi has recently argued that early Qing rulers actively encouraged the growth of handicraft industry, and Wei Qingyuan and Lu Su have pointed to the emergence of merchant entrepreneurs in the mining industry.[30]

The recent work of Myers, Metzger, and others adds a refreshing perspective to the old question of China's backwardness. Instead of merely blaming China's failure to industrialize in the nineteenth century on the inadequacies of a reified "traditional Confucian state," we must recognize the major contributions of the Qing state to economic growth. It is time to turn away from focusing on what China's rulers failed to do by the criteria of twentieth-century economic development theory. Before condemning Qing bureaucrats for failing to meet the standards of two centuries later, let us examine closely what they could do in their time.

THE DYNAMICS OF STATE
AND SOCIETY IN MING-QING CHINA:
STATECRAFT AND AGRICULTURE

Whatever the differences in the opinions described above, they share a relatively static view of Chinese state-society relationships. Oriental Despotism, of course, takes for granted the unchanging nature of the Chinese state. The Limited-State theorists may recognize variations in the impact of the state on the economy over time, but fundamentally they stress that its impact was slight. "Proto-capitalist" proponents concentrate on those periods, such as the eighteenth century, when state involvement was most favorable to economic development, saying little about other times when it was not.[31] A resolution of the contradictions between these approaches requires a dynamic view of the nexus of state and society. Furthermore, it requires making distinctions among different levels of the polity. Central, provincial, and local officials, along with yamen runners and local gentry, each had their roles to play. Each group inside and outside the bureaucracy had vested interests which deflected policies enacted by the center. Only by investigating in detail the local impact of state policies toward the rural economy can we clarify the ultimate effect of the imperial state.

The shifting attitudes and capabilities of state officials over time interacted dialectically with long-term transformations of the economy. The founding years of the Ming and Qing dynasties offered the greatest opportunities for vigorous rulers to take charge of rural society in order to revitalize a devastated economy. Ming Taizu and the early Qing emperors actively intervened in the countryside to restore tax collection and social order. They also invested state funds heavily in the rural infrastructure, particularly in restoration of waterworks and clearance of abandoned land. The recovery of the economy stimulated by the state led to a decline in state control. As landlords and merchants became wealthier, they invested their own capital in agricultural production, and the relative share of state capital declined. In the eighteenth century, especially, the active development of commercial agriculture and urban markets gave local producers considerable autonomy from state control. They found their profits in the private market, not in government demand, and they acted to maximize private profit, not merely to obey official directives.

As the population grew and markets spread, officials faced new challenges to inherited precedents. Some clung to past policies and lamented change, but others sought to alter time-honored practices in order to meet new conditions. Of particular importance were those literati and officials of the "statecraft school": men like Gu Yanwu, Chen Hongmou, and Wei Yuan, who aimed to reform local administration in changing times. What stands out from their essays on local administration is a pervasive belief in the active role of the imperial state in shaping rural society. The Classics, however, prescribed no single policy for all places and times. The ancient texts provided the statecraft writers with a repertory of experience in grappling with agrarian problems, ranging from the radical Utopianism of Wang Anshi to the moral mobilization of Zhu Xi.[32] A brief examination of the proposals on agriculture of the major writers included in the *Huangchao Jingshi Wenbian* (Collected Qing essays on statecraft) will indicate part of the intellectual legacy that Qing officials inherited.

For statecraft writers in the seventeenth and eighteenth centuries, agricultural production was both a moral and an economic activity. They regarded prosperous fields as a sign of peasant "diligence" and abandoned fields as indications of "laziness." Agriculture also ensured social stability. Officials expected to eliminate banditry, beggary, and vagrancy once every peasant household had enough land to support itself.[33] Bare subsistence, however, was not their goal. They not only approved of improving peasant welfare but saw no contradiction between individual pursuit of gain and preservation of social and moral order. The character for "profit" (*li*), after all, is composed of the characters for "sickle" and "grain."[34] Classical strictures on pursuit of "profit" did not apply to increasing the output of the fields. As Qiao Guanglie recognized: "Using the people's pursuit of profit is more effective than having officials teach them. Where there is profit, they will rush in, with no concern about the labor involved. How can they then abandon cultivable land and leave it fallow?"[35]

The primary concern of statecraft writers in the seventeenth and eighteenth centuries was to "exhaustively use the resources of the land" (*jindili*). This meant both increasing yields and developing cash crops.[36] As the economy became more commercialized in the eighteenth century, statecraft writers recognized the positive values of market involvement. Textile production was particularly valued, since it kept women occupied in productive labor.[37] In fact, officials played a positive role in commercial integration of the empire by transmitting successful techniques from one region to another. Often these efforts failed, as in the series of efforts to transfer silkworm and mulberry production from Shandong to Shaanxi, or the continual attempts to promote rice cultivation in Zhili.[38] Nevertheless, Qing officials continued to promote overall advances in agricultural technology by urging peasants to transplant rice seedlings, fertilize them heavily, pay close attention to water supplies, and work diligently at weeding and pest control.[39]

The pursuit of individual gain, however, could not proceed at the sacrifice of broader social objectives. Writers and officials regarded the local peasantry as short-sighted seekers of immediate gain. The official's role was not to discourage the pursuit of profit, but to harmonize private and public good. Officials could provide peasants with a wider temporal and spatial perspective, urging them to plan for future generations by establishing reservoirs, for example, or encouraging adoption of promising techniques from other regions. Through exemplary leadership, local officials could turn peasant greed into social welfare. "The common people covet immediate profit and ignore the causes of long-term damage," noted He Changling, explaining why landowners failed to dredge waterways. "They are not willing to abandon a foot or an inch of land to provide drainage for water." He instructed them: "You must not look for petty profits and willfully cause obstruction. I, your *daotai*, will definitely carry out [the policy of dredging waterways]. You must not sit back and watch. You must know that I truly intend to act for your own benefit (*li*) and not to harm you."[40]

There are, however, interesting signs of ambivalence in the statecraft writers' attitudes toward agricultural progress. They certainly encouraged improvement of peasant welfare, but not indulgence in "luxury."

Some condemned crops, like tobacco, that did not contribute to basic needs.[41] Others repeatedly denounced making liquor from grain, calculating that major famines could be prevented simply by banning all liquor production. In writings like these, there is a clear tension between the survival of a moralist subsistence ethic and the realities of commercial agriculture. Efforts to ban liquor production reflect the legacy of moralistic, radical Confucianism—the wing of the neo-Confucian movement that advocated the overriding importance of morally correct behavior.

The contradiction between Utopian schemes taken from the Classics and the realities of diverse local production led to conflict between empirical practice and uniform, rational plans for agricultural reform. The persistent reappearance of the "small squares" method of grain cultivation (*qutianfa*) testifies to the enduring appeal of classical precedent.[42] This method required the division of each *mou* of rice paddy into 2,650 small squares, one and one-half feet on a side, separated by small ridges (see Figure 1). Created in the Han dynasty by the agricultural expert Fan Shengzhi, the technique was described in handbooks such as the Yuan dynasty *Nongshu* of Wang Zhen. Seeds would be planted thickly in one quarter of the squares and intensively cultivated, fertilized, and weeded. Proponents of the method claimed that it could produce enormous yields, up to 30 *shi* per *mou*, using very little seed. They also claimed that the method conserved water, allowing good harvests during drought years. When Zhili Governor Li Weijun proposed to clear land for poor people using this method in 1724, the Yongzheng Emperor was delighted to hear that someone was actually trying out the technique.[43] Pan Zengqi, a *juren* degree-holder in Wu county, Jiangsu, convinced Governor Lin Zexu that this cultivation method would relieve the local peasants of a serious famine in 1833.[44]

Despite the grand claims and official promotion, very few peasants adopted the *qutian* method. Pan Zengqi admitted that few people in his county were willing to try it. Wang Xinjing, when he discovered that real yields were only 5 to 6 *shi* per *mou*, accused earlier writers of exaggeration.[45] Lu Shiyi found from conversations with local people that one of the main objections to the method was its tremendous

Figure 1 The Qutianfa Method of Cultivation

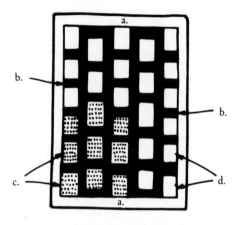

a. Irrigation trench
b. Ditches (black areas)
c. Seeded sections
d. Unseeded sections

Source: Amano Motonosuke, *Chūgoku Nōgyōshi Kenkyū,* p. 365.

labor demands. Yet, he still tried to convince the peasants that the benefits of the method outweighed its costs. In the twentieth century, several Hunanese officials continued to promote the technique as a means of preventing famine.[46]

Although this abstract, rational scheme of planting in small squares was unsuited to the varied conditions of local rice cultivation, many officials continued to try applying unrealistic formulas from the classical agricultural texts to the countryside. Still, such efforts could have beneficial consequences. Attempting to implement recommended techniques led officials to consult with the local peasantry and gain their cooperation, and thus made them better acquainted with local agriculture.

On the other hand, most officials did not rush into the fields with ready-made reform plans. One official described how he first consulted with elderly farmers in his area on the feasibility of a new practice, then encouraged them to try it out on experimental plots, with official guarantees of relief if the new method failed. Some officials even planted new seeds themselves on government land. They asserted that, after the success of the new method had been demonstrated, other peasants adopted it. Several writers urged that experienced peasants be designated to supervise experiments with new cropping techniques.[47]

Thus, while some writers on agriculture claimed great success for the abstract plans of ancient texts, others carefully pushed forward with small improvements based on the experience of local peasants. Attitudes toward agriculture exhibit both the "radical" and "moderate-realist" poles of Confucian thought described by Thomas Metzger.[48] In effect, the advocates of the *qutianfa* represented a transformation of radical Confucianism in the eighteenth-century context. As Metzger notes: "From the radical standpoint, one sought to act on society from the center of the political arena . . . political action, once based on the right principles, was easy and quick, because society was malleable . . . Political programs were formulated in general, macroscopic terms and they were seen as according with either the principles of ancient dynasties or some abstract program."[49] Proponents of the *qutianfa* did not try to overcome private property rights, and they were not aiming at fundamental political reforms. Their only concern was for rationalized agriculture. But they shared the radical focus on the activism of the officials, here transferred from the empire to the county scale, and the belief in the possibility of implementing models from the classic texts in their own time. Although Metzger considers all the statecraft writers to be advocates of "moderate realism," the persistence of ideal schemes for agricultural improvement indicates that the radical legacy continued to influence the statecraft school.

Most of the writers on agriculture, on the other hand, followed closely the principles of "moderate realism," which recognized the limited powers of the state, the diversity of local conditions, the need to work through mediating elites, to respect local customs, and to use remunerative instead of moral or coercive sanctions. Yet they did more than simply "umpire the activities of a populace openly given to the selfish competition for profits"; in many cases, they themselves actively encouraged the pursuit of profit.[50] Myers, in particular, goes too far when he implies that the Qing officials merely stood back and allowed economic actors to pursue profit freely. There was always tension between the urge to use bureaucratic intervention to remedy social problems and the recognition of the desirability of avoiding interference in the economy. The alternation of bureaucratic activism and a more liberal approach characterized economic policy throughout the dynasty.

Qing officials did not envisage radical social transformation of the land. The drastic redistribution of land à la Wang Mang or the pervasive interventionism of Wang Anshi were not on their agenda (although some did approve of some of Wang Anshi's policies). Some, like Huang Dan, proposed limitations on the size of landholdings, but they were a minority.[51] The Qianlong Emperor especially opposed efforts to redistribute wealth by bureaucratic intervention. When Guzong, the Governor General of grain transport, proposed in 1743 to limit the property of every household in China to 3,000 *mou* of land, the Emperor decisively rejected even this modest attempt to equalize rich and poor landholdings.[52]

In general, the Qing approach to agrarian problems was more technological than redistributionist.[53] Tacitly accepting the early Qing compromise, which confirmed the land rights of major landowners and restored the tax quotas of the early Ming, the statecraft writers relied mainly on encouragement of voluntary efforts. They fully accepted the rights of landlords and the unequal distribution of property in the countryside. Although they urged district magistrates to inspect the fields frequently, they expected leading farmers to be the main agents of reform. Writers who recommended the appointment of "supervisory peasants" to oversee improvements in crop yields expected district magistrates to reward or punish these local representatives appropriately. Increasing aggregate production served to ensure harmony in the countryside without undermining landlord interests.

Official policies responded to changing economic conditions. In the seventeenth century, the main problem was to resettle uprooted people and reopen abandoned land. During the eighteenth century, once it was recognized that most cultivable land had been exhausted, their main efforts turned to increasing yields on existing land. By the nineteenth century, although it became ever more difficult to accommodate the burgeoning population within an agrarian economy, even the most progressive reformers recognized the need to promote agricultural production while also developing industry. Writers and officials who recognized the transformation of the rural economy tried to draw on the repertory of the past for new methods to ensure peasant prosperity. Eighteenth-century developments, however, raised the serious possibility that traditional policies would be inadequate to save the dynasty from ultimate collapse.[54] The exploding population, combined with tremendous floods of migration into frontier areas, produced violent conflicts over land rights and a burgeoning class of landless poor. The rise of commerce undermining customary restraint led to luxury and extravagance on an unheard-of-scale. Contemporaries recognized these trends, and the most perceptive writers of the period accurately predicted future social cataclysms, but the inherited repertory of measures could do nothing to prevent the major rebellions of the nineteenth century. Ultimately, the Qing rulers and officials were the victims of the successful transformation they had helped promote in the early years of the dynasty.

THE DYNAMICS OF CHANGE IN THE MING-QING RURAL ECONOMY: THE CASE OF HUNAN

Recently, economists and scholars of contemporary China's economic development have recognized that understanding China's current economic problems requires study of the historical background.[55] The perspective included, however, usually extends no farther back than the nineteenth century, arguably the century in which state economic policies were least effective. We must instead examine longer-term trends in the economy extending over several centuries. The eighteenth century is particularly important for assessing the full potential of the imperial state in guiding the economy, as it was that period during which the maximum possible achievements of a traditional Chinese state were attained. The mid-Qing rulers followed precedents from the classical past, but they had more resources available to enact their policies than any previous dynasty. They had large tax surpluses and faced no major internal rebellions or foreign invasions until the end of the century. The factionalism that marred reform efforts in the Song and late Ming was relatively subdued, and the dominant statecraft officials took an active interest in local administration and economic regulation. Deep social and economic strains, however, masked by Qianlong's self-aggrandizing propaganda, lay beneath the façade of prosperity. These tensions reveal important divergences of interest between local officials and the central government. Local officials recognized early in the century that the growing inadequacy of land resources demanded active measures to encourage agricultural production and deal with the population problem. An examination of this period in a local context provides us with a picture of the best that the traditional Chinese state was able to do.

The policies of the Qing rulers toward agriculture fall into two broad categories: those that affected agricultural production, and those that influenced the distribution of the product. Qing writers on famine relief often made a similar distinction between short-term policies, designed to relieve immediate shortages, and long-term policies designed to raise overall production. The most important state efforts to influence distribution concentrated on the implementation of an empire-wide system of granaries. These granaries collected surplus grain after the harvest and sold it during times of shortage in order to level out the fluctuation of prices during the year. In times of severe dearth, the state mobilized grain supplies from other sources to provide extensive relief to famine-struck populations. A number of recent studies have investigated this famine relief and grain distribution system in detail. This one, however, concentrates on measures that affected production over the long term.[56] These included tax incentives, resettlement of migrants, promotion of new cropping techniques, and construction of waterworks. The distribution of relief forced officials to pay close attention to the structure of the grain market to make sure that grain reached the people for whom it was intended. Raising agricultural production, on the other hand, required close attention to the rural economy. Implementing both distribution and production policies required Qing officials to work through particular local social and economic structures.

Hunan is an excellent place to study the potential of the Qing state, because, during the eighteenth century, it experienced the three most significant economic trends of the period: population growth, commercialization, and ecological exhaustion. Population expanded throughout the empire, but its growth in Hunan was particularly significant, because Hunan desperately needed new immigrants in order to recover from the devastation of the Ming-Qing transition wars. Commercialization was also especially important in Hunan because it meant the development of new markets. The development of the grain export trade changed Hunan from a frontier region to one of the major granaries of the empire, fully incorporated into empire-wide grain markets. Han-sheng Chuan and Richard Kraus estimate that, in the eighteenth century, Hunan regularly shipped 5 million *shi* of grain per year down the Yangtze to Jiangnan.[57]

In certain ways this change parallels the transformation of the Jiangnan region into China's major rice producer during the Song. The development of the textile industry in Jiangnan during the Ming-Qing period, however, transformed the region from a grain surplus to a grain deficit area dependent on the middle and upper Yangtze for food. State policies toward both regions reflected a concern with regulating the rise of commerce, but in Jiangnan they focused on the problems of laborers in textile factories and peasants who abandoned grain production for silk and cotton. In Hunan they focused on the effects of a booming export trade in grain. One of the key issues, for example, was whether or not local officials had the right to prohibit the export of grain by merchants from districts facing shortages. Often local consumers staged riots to prevent the loss of local grain supplies. These food riots, like their counterparts in eighteenth-century Europe, represented efforts to preserve local control over food in the face of increasing penetration by external market forces.[58] They also aggravated conflicts between local and central officials. Local officials who yielded to local pressure to block external sale of grain clashed with provincial and central officials who aimed to ensure the free flow of grain supplies around the empire. Qing policies in Hunan exhibit reactions to agricultural commercialization distinct from the issues posed by proto-industrial commercialization in Jiangnan.

Finally, ecological problems—the shortages of resources highlighted by Mark Elvin as the essential features of China's "high-level equilibrium trap"–emerged in Hunan at the end of the eighteenth and beginning of the nineteenth century.[59] Early in the Qing, local officials saw clear signs of excessive use of land, overbuilding of water-works, and soil erosion. We can test the validity of Elvin's assertions about surplus resources remaining in imperial China by examining Hunan's condition in the mid-nineteenth century.

The chapters that follow examine the capabilities and limitations of Chinese officials in directing change in the agricultural economy of Hunan. Chapter 2 outlines the basic geographical features of the prov-ince. The divisions between the Dongting Lake region, the four major river basins, and the mountainous periphery defined different types of agricultural production and different types of settlement. Although soil and climatic conditions made Hunan a very favorable place for agriculture, crop production everywhere faced risks from flood and drought. Paddy-rice farmers in the lowlands around the lake did have the resources to protect themselves by building dikes, but even they could be seriously harmed by very large floods. River basin cultivators who could build fewer dikes were correspondingly more vulnerable to flash floods. Dry-land mountain farmers suffered the greatest dangers from both droughts and mountain floods. All the Hunanese peasants had means of protecting themselves from natural disasters, but their defenses were limited by their own poverty and by the caprices of nature.

The discussion of population and land clearance emphasizes the sparse settlement of the province in the Ming dynasty. Paddy-rice cultivation, with its great demands for labor, could not have been the dominant form of production. Hunting and fishing, dry-land farm-ing, and mountain crops were easier to pursue with small investments of capital and labor. Significant progress in land clearance was made in the Ming, especially in the lake districts, where an export grain trade began, but Hunan as a whole remained a frontier area during most of the Ming dynasty. Rebellions, which broke out at the close of the Ming, continued to make life uncertain until the suppression of Wu Sangui's rebellion in 1679. Rapid population growth during the eighteenth century stimulated the recovery and expansion of agricultural production. Peasant and merchant immigrants added new dynamism to the province's economic growth, but, by the end of the century, the tensions of overpopulation had become apparent.

Chapter 3 discusses the relationship between clearance of land in the province and state policies in the Ming and Qing. The rulers of both dynasties were ambivalent about land clearance: While it would increase food production, it usually encouraged migration of unruly people into loosely controlled frontier regions. Ming rulers did try to prohibit settlement in designated mountainous regions, but, for Qing officials, the increasing pressure of population on available land made the benefits of land clearance outweigh the losses. Excessive and unequal taxation in the late Ming also reduced peasant incentives to clear land. The Qing rulers arrived with a determination to equalize tax burdens and restore the devastated agricultural economy. As in Jiangnan in the same period, however, local gentry interests prevented Qing officials from enacting a thorough land survey. The result was a compromise which eliminated the abusive surcharges of the late Ming, surveyed some counties, but left most registered land quotas the same as in 1582. Illegal clearance and concealment were apparent even in the seventeenth century, but they were tolerated as necessary to gain the cooperation of the local elite in restoring the economy. The vigorous effort of Zhao Shenqiao in the early eighteenth century to revitalize Hunan still concentrated on elimination of surtaxes and promotion of grain production. Even so, he offended enough powerful interests to get himself impeached.

By the end of the century, the situation was quite different. Nearly all the available land had been cleared. Provincial governors no longer worried about encouraging people to clear land; instead they recognized the beginnings of serious overpopulation. The ecologically sensitive discovered that excess dike-building aggravated the threat of flood, while overcutting of forests exacerbated erosion, raised silt levels in rivers, and thus further increased flood damage. As arable land became scarce, social conflict changed in character. In the seventeenth and early eighteenth centuries, serious conflicts such as kinship feuds and banditry were rooted in the frontier nature of the region. By the end of the eighteenth century, conflicts expressed themselves as lawsuits over control of land, disputes of tenants with landlords over rent deposits, or defiance of official prohibitions on clearance and dike-building. Conflict was more "civilized" and less violent, but it indicated the serious consequences of oversettlement.

As supplies of new land ran out, the only remaining method of raising food production was to raise yields. Qing officials put great efforts into the promotion of double-cropping and the introduction of new seeds, as described in Chapter 4. Their achievements were limited but significant. Yields did rise, and the cultivation of wheat and early rice gradually spread. It was the combination of official promotion efforts and of the incentives offered by market production that stimulated Hunanese peasants to shift their cropping patterns. Utopian schemes derived from agricultural handbooks that were inappropriate to local farming conditions simply failed. The state could not and did not compel farmers to grow what was not in their interest.

On the other hand, Hunanese farmers did not simply respond as individuals to the presence of an abstract market. They made decisions on crop production within the constraints set by the imperial state. The officials provided resources, in the form of tax breaks, new seeds, and information, to encourage experimentation. They set up experimental plots to allow farmers to try out new seeds without risk. Some officials even invested their own funds in agricultural experiments. Qing agricultural experimentation compares favorably with the efforts of eighteenth-century European nobles to improve agriculture according to "enlightened" principles. The limits to Chinese agricultural production lay not in the blindness to the threat of overpopulation or lack of interest in improving productivity by officials and landowners but in the ecology of rice cultivation.

The growing conflict in Hunan in the late eighteenth and early nineteenth centuries focused on control of land. Chapter 5 describes the ways in which population growth and commercialization transformed the social relations between landlord and tenant. With increasing immigration and decreasing available land, tenancy inevitably rose. At the same time, tenancy contracts shifted from sharecropping to fixed rents, and landlords withdrew from direct involvement in production. Trends in eighteenth-century Hunan paralleled developments that had begun in Jiangnan in the sixteenth century. Conflicts arose as landlords raised rent deposits and ousted tenants in order to realize gains from increasing productivity. Likewise, independent landowners fought with each other over the ambiguities in land contracts. These conflicts drew officials into the world of customary land transactions in order to reduce lawsuits and ensure steady tax income. They tried to enforce two partly contradictory policies. (1) By stressing the mutual obligation between landlord and tenant they aimed to restore a harmonious rural society torn apart by litigation. (2) By clarifying the forms of land contracts they accepted a greater role for the state as adjudicator of property claims arising out of mistrust. Nevertheless, these efforts were limited by the ideal of "respecting local custom" and by the scarce resources available to the typical local magistrate for resolving an avalanche of lawsuits.

Conflicts over water control, described in Chapters 6 and 7, reveal even more sharply the limitations of the Qing state. Here, too, officials who previously had not paid much attention to water control on the Yangtze River were forced to concern themselves with it as the dangers of flooding became more and more threatening. The prohibition of dike-building around Dongting Lake could not succeed, because it brought the Qing authorities into direct conflict with the most fundamental interests of local producers. But, as the 1788 flood at Jingzhou, Hubei, demonstrated, the problem of overbuilding was real. Officials were aware of the dangers, and, when real disaster struck, they could punish the culprits. In the long run, however, the creeping growth of dikes, eliminating reservoirs and overflow basins, would prove more damaging to the environment than the dramatic blocking of the Yangtze by sand bars.

The ultimate causes of the failure of the Qing state to restrain excess clearance lay in its inability to create a national consciousness. It could not persuade or compel local peasants to sacrifice immediate gain for common benefit. Its failure should not be too surprising; the record of the most powerful modern states on environmental protection is quite mixed. The PRC itself faces extremely serious environmental problems which it has only very recently begun to address.[60] The early awareness of the impending crisis by Qing officials proves their insight into the rural environment; their inability to solve the environmental problems demonstrates the state's limited impact on the society.

TWO

Geography and Population

In every Chinese region, physiographic features of the landscape—topography, climate, water supply, and soil quality—condition the forms of agricultural production. Hunan lies at the southern end of the temperate zone, between 24 and 30 degrees latitude, with its southern border only 1 degree above the Tropic of Cancer. It covers an area of 210,334 square km., almost as large as than the United Kingdom and two-fifths the size of France.[1] Fairly high mountain ranges surround it on three borders: the Nanling range on the Guangxi-Guangdong border in the south, reaching peaks of over 1,500 meters; the lower Jiuling and Luoxiao ranges on the Jiangxi border to the east; and the Wuling range and Yun-Gui plateau on the west. To the northeast, it opens out into the large plain of the central Yangtze.

The average temperature of over 17 degrees centigrade varies little throughout the province.[2] Variation throughout the year, however, is rather wide. Summer temperatures average 28 to 30 degrees centigrade, while winter temperatures in January, the coldest month, average 4 degrees centigrade. The mountains ringing the province trap Mongolian high-pressure zones coming from the north, making the winters cold and dry, but the Nanling Mountains are not high enough to block the southeastern monsoon winds, which bring a long period of hot and moist weather in summer. Temperatures only briefly fall below freezing in the winter. The freezing of Dongting Lake was a rare enough event to be mentioned in gazetteers whenever it occurred, and snowfalls were regarded as auspicious phenomena presaging a good harvest.[3] The warm temperatures give Hunan a long growing season, with 170 to 220 days over 18 degrees centigrade, the best temperatures for growing rice. Sudden, severe fluctuations in temperature, however, such as occur in early spring, can be very harmful, especially in March and April, when early and middle rice crops are sprouting.[4]

The total annual rainfall of over 1,500 mm. per year is quite favorable for agriculture. Most of the rainfall, however, is concentrated in the spring and summer months: 40 percent of the annual total falls in the "plum rains" period from April to June. The amount of rainfall can vary widely from year to year. For example, from 1909 to 1954, the rainfall in May at Changsha averaged 209.3 mm., but the average monthly rainfall ranged from a peak of 359.9 mm. to a low of 94.0 mm.[5] The timing of the rainfall, too, is not well synchronized with the cropping cycle. The rains peak from April to June and are followed by many clear days, while the major rice crop ripens from May to August. Many upstream areas would suffer drought if they did not store water in reservoirs. Conversely, torrential rains come frequently in midsummer. Up to 100 mm. can fall in one day, and these downpours easily cause swollen mountain streams to flood.

The pattern of rainfall over the entire province indirectly produces other floods. The normal rains usually arrive first in the south of the province and move northward, causing the rivers to accumulate water upstream and increasing the difficulties of drainage further downstream. When the high water peak of Hunan's rivers coincides with the high water of the Yangtze River in June and July, water backs up from the Yangtze into Dongting Lake, blocking the drainage of

Hunan's basin and producing floods. The ever-present threats of floods and droughts were the main factor in guiding the evolution of cropping patterns of Hunan's peasantry. Compared to other provinces of China, Hunan was endowed with climatic conditions that were very favorable to high-yielding, intensive agriculture, but it was never free from the risk of crop failure. Peasants and officials together had to be prepared to overcome these risks.

Besides sun and water, soil is the third crucial factor in agriculture. Hunan was not nearly so well endowed with soil as with the other two elements. The natural soils of Hunan, like all of South China, are yellow and red forest soils.[6] These contain plant nutrients as long as they are covered by forests. After the forests are cleared, these soils may be highly productive for a short time, but yields will drop drastically after two or three years unless the nutrients are replenished. The red earths are particularly vulnerable to erosion by violent rains. Thus, in the mountains of Hunan, slash-and-burn agriculture cleared the forest but yielded crops for only two to three years. After that, the fields were either abandoned or, later on, kept in cultivation by the addition of fertilizer, both human manure and wood ash. To produce wood ash in turn required the burning of more forest. With increasingly dense settlement of the province, as more and more of the forest cover was removed and eroded, barren hills became prominent.[7] By 1957, only 20 percent of the Xiang River Basin was forested and over 20 percent was barren land.[8] Erosion, besides depriving the uplands of soil, increased the problem of flooding downstream by adding to the silt content of the rivers. Today, reforestation has become an important priority.[9]

The majority of Hunan's population, however, did not have to contend with such poor, eroded soils. Most of the Hunanese lived in river valleys and on the lowlands around Dongting Lake, where the red earths were covered by rich alluvial soils washed down from the mountains. The migration of nutrients from the mountainous peripheries to the core areas provided the densely settled valleys with some of the most fertile soil in the country.[10] Here dense human and animal populations provided abundant fertilizer, making it possible to grow high-yielding rice instead of upland crops. Soil and water conditions combined to make the alluvial plains the most attractive region for settlement. Population densities have been historically, and remain today, highest around the shores of Dongting Lake, diminishing progressively as one travels upstream on Hunan's four major rivers (Xiang, Yuan, Zi, and Li), and dropping more sharply as one leaves the major rivers for the highlands.

Administratively, Hunan benefited from being a compact, well-defined region (see Figure 2, and Appendix 1). The mountain barriers on its three borders effectively cut off interference from neighboring provinces. The entire province lies within the Middle Yangtze macro-region defined by G. William Skinner.[11] In the south and west, the provincial boundaries are nearly coterminous with the macroregional boundaries, except for small parts of Guangxi and Guizhou which lie in the upper watersheds of the Xiang and Yuan Rivers beyond the provincial borders. On a smaller scale, Skinner has divided the Middle Yangtze macroregion in 1893 into four Regional Trading Systems: the Yangtze corridor, the Han River Basin (upper Hubei and southern Shaanxi), the Xiang River Basin (including the Zi River Basin), and the Yuan River Basin (including the Li River Basin) (see Figure 3). The Xiang and Yuan River Basins defined by Skinner comprise nearly the whole of Hunan, and the provincial boundaries with Jiangxi in the east and with Hubei in the north are coterminous with the watersheds of the river basins. Skinner places most of Dongting Lake in the Yangtze corridor, but, because here the dividing line runs through lowlands and not mountain ranges, the boundary must be rather blurred. The Dongting Lake region, in fact, faced two ways: As the core area of Hunan it collected goods from all over the province, and as the key transit route to the Yangtze River it served as the supplier of exports for Hankow and the lower Yangtze Basin.

One other difference between Skinner's map and Hunan's position in the Qing dynasty should be noted. Until the mid-nineteenth century, the provincial capital of Changsha did not have nearly the size or importance that it had achieved by 1893. Nearby Xiangtan, the major collecting point for all production of the Xiang River Basin, far outweighed it in commercial importance. Changsha lagged behind

FIGURE 2 Hunan Province in the Qing

Sources: *Hunan Mingxi Ditu* (Wuchang, Minguo); *Zhongguo Lishi Dituji* (Beijing, Zhonghua Ditu Xuexshe Chuban, 1975); *Hunan Quansheng Tu* (late Qing).

FIGURE 3 The Middle Yangtze Macroregion ca. 1893, showing component regions, river systems, and the approximate extent of greater-city trading systems

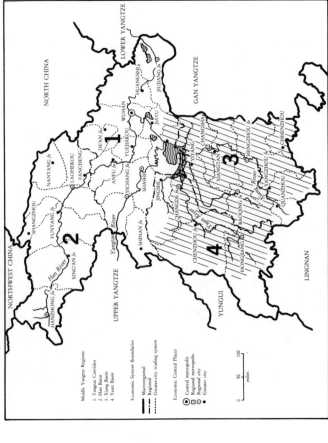

Source: G. William Skinner, "Regional Systems in Late Imperial China," reproduced with the permission of the author. Adapted to conform with map in G. William Skinner, "Presidential Address," p. 273.

Xiangtan mainly, it seems, because it lacked a deep-water port suitable for large ships. Qing officials made several efforts to build a port for Changsha, but the city did not succeed in overtaking Xiangtan until the mid-nineteenth century.[12] Still, on the whole, Skinner's map accurately depicts Hunan's regional divisions in the Qing period. The major administrative capitals of Changsha and Changde either coincided with or were close to the important regional metropolises. Further upstream, prefectural capitals like Baoqing and Hengzhou served as secondary administrative and commercial centers for the highlands and upstream river basins. An examination of the four river basins will illustrate features distinguishing each sub-region of the province.

RIVER BASINS OF HUNAN

The dominant river of the province is the Xiang River, which drains 44 percent of the land area (see Table 1).[13] In fact, the Xiang ranks tenth in length among the rivers of interior China and eleventh in drainage area. Originating in the uplands of northern Guangxi, it passes through steep mountain valleys to Lingling. Below Lingling the river widens out and remains a calm stream for the rest of its course, flowing through low hills and wide valleys. Near Hengyang, it is joined by several important tributaries, which not only widen the river but also add a good deal of silt from the mountains. Rapid erosion of the red sandstone cliffs in the Hengyang area further increases the silt load. As the river slows its rate of flow, deposited silt creates more sand bars. The stretch from Changsha down to Dongting Lake is the area of maximum sand-bar formation. Over 10 billion kgms. of silt were carried to Changsha in 1952. When the Yangtze flood waters fill up Dongting Lake, the lake often rises high enough to cause the Xiang River waters to back up as far as Changsha and Xiangtan, creating great flood danger. The yearly variation in water level is large, an average of 10 to over 12 meters per year at Xiangtan and Changsha. Heavy rainfall can cause sudden changes in the river; at You *xian* in 1955 the water rose 4 meters in one day.[14] The peak levels are usually

TABLE 1 Major Rivers of Hunan

Name	Length (km.)	Drainage Area in Hunan (sq. km.)	Population, 1959 (millions)
Xiang	811	92,500	16.8
Zi	650	25,180	5.0
Yuan	1,055	88,900	3.6–4.2
Li	300	17,775	2.3

Source: Hunan Nongye, pp. 8–19.

reached in June, after which the level declines to its minimum from December to February. By the twentieth century, the sharp peaks and sudden changes in river levels were certainly connected with deforestation and erosion in the highlands, plus sedimentation in the lowlands.[15] In the early Qing, when there was more forest and less silt, these changes may have been more gradual. Because the Xiang runs smoothly for most of its course, it was easily navigable throughout the entire province and served as Hunan's main commercial artery.[16]

The basin of the Zi River, to the west of the Xiang, is less than one-third the size of the Xiang Basin, because the Zi has few major tributaries.[17] It is separated from the Xiang only by scattered low mountains. The upper third of the river, down to Shaoyang, contains broad valleys where rich agriculture is possible because of over 100 major embankments lining the river. From Shaoyang down to Anhua, the river passes through narrow gorges with little usable agricultural land, but tea cultivation is possible on the steep slopes, especially at Anhua, the largest tea-producing county in the province. Below Anhua, the river broadens again as it reaches Dongting Lake at Yiyang.

The Yuan River is actually longer than the Xiang, and its basin is nearly the same size, but the land available for cultivation along it is much less. The high Xuefeng mountain range separates it clearly from the Zi Basin. The high mountains upstream cause frequent flooding, and, except in Zhijiang and Xupu, there is little flat land and few waterworks. Deforestation has caused serious erosion, so both droughts and floods are common. The area is much less densely populated than the Xiang and Zi River Basins, except in the lowland areas near Changde around the lake.

The northwest corner of Hunan, on the upper Li and Yuan Rivers, has several features that distinguish it sharply from the three major river basins. While the lower reaches of the Li River join the lowlands around the lake, nearly the entire upstream portion consists of steep mountains and rugged terrain ranging from 400 to 1,000 meters in elevation. The cultivation index in 1958 was only 10 percent, the lowest of all the regions in Hunan, and forests covered three to five times the area of cultivated land. Irrigation and intensive cultivation are difficult. In 1958, 60 percent of Hunan's maize came from this region, and slash-and-burn agriculture remained in use on the higher slopes. This is the region where most of Hunan's minority peoples are concentrated. They numbered 1,999,640 in 1957, or 3.3 percent of the province's population.[18] The Miao and Tujia peoples, the most numerous, are now contained within an independent sub-prefecture covering the counties of Jishou, Fenghuang, Huayuan, Guzhang, Lüxi, Longshan, Baojing, Sangzhi, Dayong, and Yongshun. This area is still the most remote and backward part of Hunan, as it was in the Qing era. Historically, it has been the source of the most unrest, as the Miao tribesmen who refused to assimilate to Han Chinese ways repeatedly staged uprisings together with their fellows across the border in Guizhou. The largest of these uprisings lasted from 1795 to 1806. Its origins sprang from increased immigration to the area in the eighteenth century by Han settlers seeking land, as they were doing in the rest of the province. This immigration in turn was an outcome of the coercive enforcement of the *gaitu guiliu* policy in the 1720s, which brought Qing garrisons to the area to enforce state power and protect Han settlers and merchants. Thus, the Miao region essentially was subjected to the same two basic forces that affected the rest of the province: a strong administration encouraging agricultural settlement and land clearance, and a wave of new immigrants to occupy the newly cleared land. Hunan's northwest corner deserves a separate study, but we shall point out here only those aspects in which its experience paralleled that of the rest of the province.[19]

MOUNTAIN AND PLAIN

Although each of the four river basins of Hunan had its own distinctive features, the chief influence on agriculture in Hunan was the opposition between mountain and plain. Mountain ranges with peaks over 1,500 meters high delineated three sides of the province. Within the province, too, mountain ranges divided the four major river basins from each other. Particularly conspicuous were the Xuefeng range dividing the Zi and Yuan Rivers, and the Wuling Mountains separating the Yuan and Li Rivers. Every county in Hunan, except for a few located entirely on the lake flatlands, contained some mountainous or at least hilly land. On the other hand, even the most mountainous counties had at least a small amount of relatively level land along a river bank that could be cleared for cultivation. Thus, all counties contained varying proportions of two different agricultural systems.

Agriculture was far more productive in the lowlands than in the highlands. The lowland farmers grew paddy rice predominantly, assuring themselves of an abundant water supply by building dikes and reservoirs. The mountain farmers, who relied primarily on dryland crops, depended mainly on rainfall, although they were encouraged by the government to build reservoirs to protect against drought. Districts like Huarong included both highly productive diked land on the border of Dongting Lake and hilly lands away from the lake. In Huarong in the nineteenth century, it was said:

> In a good year the harvest of the diked lands equals several years' harvest in the hills. The people of the diked lands are glutted with fine grain and meat, while the people in the hills usually eat bitter cabbage. Recently, many people from the hills have moved to the lowlands because their land is poor and the area small, while the lowlands have rich, broad fields.[20]

The situation was the same in Yongzhou in the far south of the province, where 70 percent of the land was mountain land and 30 percent paddy fields. Rice was grown in the lowlands and irrigated by waterwheels, while "miscellaneous crops" (*zaliang*) were grown in the mountains.[21] These miscellaneous food crops were the main diet of the mountain people; lowlanders ate primarily rice. Mountain households might grow rice, but they usually sold the rice for money and subsisted on other grains.[22] Mountain farmers always faced the threat of drought, as the lowland farmers constantly faced floods.[23] Ten days without rain could ruin a crop.[24] The only protection against drought was to build large reservoirs (*ba*) to store water, but these were not always sufficient.[25] In desperation, peasants dug up bracken roots (*jue*) in the forest, pounded them into powder, and made it into gruel. Bracken powder was an important local product of many mountain districts and was traded with other areas over long distances at very low prices.[26]

Farming on the lowlands was profitable, but there was always the risk of flood. Near Dongting Lake, flooding was almost certain somewhere every year. In Changde prefecture, "every summer the low areas near the lake become a big swamp. If the farmers are lucky to get a full harvest, the yield exceeds that of the highlands."[27] Here, too, safeguarding the harvest required the construction of waterworks, for the opposite reason: too much rather than too little water. Dike-building in eighteenth century Hunan created polder lands ringed by dikes along the shores of the lake, high embankments along the major rivers and tributaries, and reservoirs in the dry mountain areas. All these construction projects demonstrated an intense effort to provide security for agriculture in both the mountains and plains.

Growing crops successfully required not only a reliable water supply but also a supply of fertilizer. For the lowlands, there was no great problem supplying adequate nutrients to the crops. The dense human population in the cities of the plains supplied large amounts of human manure, and the rivers washed down fertile sediments from the hills upstream, depriving the mountain areas of their best soil. Replenishing the nutrients in the mountain soils, on the other hand, required continual applications of fertilizer, more than the sparse population of the area could provide. In Yuanzhou, only the fields near the city could use manure on their fields. Fields farther away had to depend on dead grasses. In the deep woods of Yongzhou, where wood could not be easily shipped out as timber, lumbermen burnt whole hillsides down to ashes with fires covering several tens of *li* in order to sell the ashes downstream.[28] Large boats carried quantities of ash to mountain regions in the second and third months of the year. Merchants collected payment in the form of a portion of the crop after the harvest, called "ash grain" (*huigu*)[29]

The limited yields of the mountain lands were not enough to feed the population, but fortunately the mountain population did not depend solely on food crops. Marketing of forest products, including timber, edible tree fungus (*mu-er*), bamboo, wax, and *tong* oil, was another important source of income.[30] There were also textile crops such as hemp, ramie, and *ge* fiber. Officials encouraged native tribes-people in western Hunan to sell tree fungus and lacquer to their Han overseers in exchange for salt and cloth.[31] In Qiyang, merchants tied together fir timbers into rafts, floated them down the river to Dong-ting Lake, and exchanged them for supplies of salt, sugar, and grain.[32] Peasants in Hengyang cut down bamboo and soaked it in water to make paper, which yielded "several ten thousands of *jin*" per year.[33] Qiyang and Hengyang also produced rice, but their mountain areas clearly depended on cash crops to trade for grain. Payment of taxes was another motivation. *Tong* oil and other commodities were sold to merchants simply to make it possible to pay taxes which were levied in money.[34] Tobacco, cotton, and tea would become important crops in the nineteenth century, but in the eighteenth century they were still of only secondary importance.[35] The exploitation of the forest economy grew progressively more intense as the population grew, and signs of deforestation began to appear by the nineteenth century. Local writers noted "hillsides stripped bare of trees," and fire-wood became scarce.[36]

Both mountain and plain, then, contained a variety of forms of agriculture, including both subsistence and cash cropping. The major types of production can be classified on a scale from least to most pro-ductive, or from least to most intensive labor input. As the popula-tion increased, agriculture tended to shift to more intensive forms of production, until it reached a limit defined by the ultimate capacities of the soil and climate; but at any point in time an entire range of forms could coexist in the same region. The following list includes the main forms of agriculture in Hunan:[37]

(1) *Hunting and Fishing.* These were the primary activities of the people of Chu, the early inhabitants of the Hunan region, up until the Han dynasty.[38] They also remained important secondary activities long after intensive agriculture had spread. When flooding made farming imposssible, lowland cultivators had the option of going fishing.

(2) *Slash-and-Burn Agriculture.* This was the simplest form of cultivation. Burning down trees and vegetation in the forest both cleared the fields and supplied nutrients to the soil. A plot could be cultivated for three or four years before yields fell drastically; then it was time to move on to clear a new patch. This, too, was an ancient practice of the people of Chu, but native tribespeople were still practicing it in Hunan in the twentieth century.[39] Crops like millet, sorghum, beans, sesame, and corn could be grown by this method, but it was possible only in sparsely populated areas with abundant land. References indicate that, in Hunan, slash-and-burn was practiced only by native tribes and never by Han Chinese. Groups of up to several hundred people cleared the land collectively, and men and women worked side by side in the fields, arousing the concern of moralistic Confucians.[40]

(3) *Forest and Lake Products.* The gathering of tree fungus, bamboo, *tong* oil, and so forth required no preparation of the soil, but it yielded significant returns to areas in contact with larger markets. Similarly, the collection of wild grasses from the swamps around the lake yielded products that required no investment in cultivation and could be sold for making rush mats.[41] In its simplest form, this required simply gathering the products of the earth without laboring to produce them, but investment in cultivation of forest products could often be a source of great wealth. In the Kangxi reign (1662–1722), for example, Liu Zhongwei moved to a deep valley in Hengyang county still inhabited by tigers. Together with his brothers he cut down several thousand trees, created several tree farms, and founded a wealthy family, whose descendants farmed tens of thousands of *mou* by the end of the eighteenth century.[42] Wealthy households in Chengbu, realizing that "one cannot raise a (wealthy) household from agriculture," put all their efforts into selling wood and bamboo. Officials warned

the poorer households not to imitate the rich and abandon agriculture for this more profitable but less secure trade.[43]

(4) *Miscellaneous Grain Crops (zaliang).* These included primarily sweet potatoes, corn, and buckwheat, but also sorghum, millet, pearl barley, beans, and other food crops. By the eighteenth century, these were the main food crops of the mountain cultivators. They were also important second crops, grown after the rice harvest, for the lowland peasants. Ping-ti Ho has described how the introduction of new food crops like corn and sweet potatoes from the New World in the sixteenth century allowed peasants to cultivate increasingly marginal lands.[44] The new food crops were an important factor in China's unprecedented population growth, but they were not grown in Hunan in significant quantities until the eighteenth century, and it took time to exploit their full potential. Qing officials exerted strenuous efforts to urge peasants to plant more crops and to clear more barren land in order to meet the demands of an increasing population.

(5) *Rice Cultivation.* Rice was, of course, the main crop of Hunan, but it could be grown in a variety of ways. In hilly areas, far from water supplies, it was (a) sown as a dry-land crop. Where irrigation was available it was grown in paddies. When a region was first settled, (b) only a single crop was harvested each year. Later, particularly in the eighteenth century, (c) double-cropping of rice followed by a *zaliang* food crop became most common in lowland areas, facilitated by the introduction of early rice seeds. (d) True double-cropping of rice—an early rice crop followed by a second rice crop—did not become common even in the most productive areas of Hunan until the twentieth century.

This list provides an overview of the main forms of agricultural production in Qing Hunan. Each form of production would serve a variety of purposes. There was not necessarily a simple progression from a less to a more advanced stage. For example, in the case of fishing, when fishing was the primary occupation of the Hunanese living around the shores of Dongting Lake, they were regarded as "poor and simple" people who did not engage in trade.[45] In Huarong county in the late Ming, 70 to 80 percent of the population lived on boats or "lived by nets."[46] As cultivated agriculture progressed, fishing became secondary, but it remained an important supplement for lake dwellers. In times of flood, when it was impossible to cultivate the fields, peasants took to their boats to make a living by fishing.[47] On the lands along the Xiang River in Hengshan, where it was said that "of ten plantings, nine are not [fully] harvested," peasants frequently abandoned their fields to go fishing. It was customary for many to rely on fishing to supplement the inadequacy of the harvest.[48] At the same time, fishing became a commercial activity to satisfy the demands of "buyers from a hundred *li* around."[49] The demands of fishing and agriculture began to conflict. Farmers built barrier dikes into rivers to irrigate their fields, while fishermen illegally broke the dikes that interfered with their nets.[50] The Hunanese continued to engage in fishing throughout the development from the most primitive to the most advanced stage of their economy, but fishing changed its function. From a main subsistence activity, it became first a supplement to grain crops and finally a commercial occupation.

On the whole, the increasing density of settlement drove peasants into progressively more intensive forms of cultivation. Increasing demands on the food supply arose from both commercial and local needs. The extension of the grain market in Hunan occurred in the eighteenth century, but, before commercialization became prominent, Hunan had already developed a high productive potential, based on a rapid increase in its population and cultivated land area in the Ming dynasty.

POPULATION GROWTH AND LAND
CLEARANCE IN THE MING DYNASTY

Topography provided the structure within which cropping patterns developed, but the evolution of successive stages of agricultural production in Hunan depended on the growth of its population. This section discusses the course of development of Hunan's population and land insofar as reliable quantitative data are available. The population of Hunan and Hubei combined at the beginning of the Ming

TABLE 2 Registered Population of Hunan and Hubei,
A.D. 140–1982
(hu [households] and kou *[persons] figures in thousands;
parentheses indicate estimates)*

Year	Huguang		Hunan		Hubei		Source
	hu	*kou*	*hu*	*kou*	*hu*	*kou*	*Source*
140	736	3,325	515	2,312	221	1,013	C&W; Durand
609	504		54		450		C&W; Durand
742	467	2,578	221	1,223	246	1,355	Perkins
1080	1,400		811		589		C&W
1102	1,992	4,254	1,195	2,612	797	1,642	C&W[d]
1280	2,347	7,972	1,819	5,650	528	2,322	Perkins; C&W
1381	786	4,593					C&W; vdS
1391	739	4,092		(2,082)		(2,010)	Durand; vdS[a]
1393	776	4,703	(1,874–2,393)		(2,310–2,829)		Ho; Wei[a,b]
1578	541	4,399	276	1,917	265	2,482	C&W;vdS[e]
1600			(5,082–6,485)				[c]
1749				8,672			Durand[e]
1771		17,614		9,082		8,532	Durand[e]
1776		29,805		14,990		14,815	Durand
1812		46,023		18,653		27,370	Durand
1851		54,458		20,648		33,810	Durand
1912		57,207		27,617		29,590	Durand
1928		58,196		31,500		26,696	Durand
1953		61,017		33,227		27,790	Durand
1982		101,872		53,958		47,914	10-percent sample

Notes: [a]See Table 3.

[b]Ho and van der Sprenkel date this figure to 1393, following *Gujin Tushu Jicheng, juan* 16, *hukoudian,* but Wei points out that this figure must be derived from the Yellow Registers of 1391, as no further surveys were done within 10 years of this date. The 1391 figure may be the result of an incomplete compilation of the registers, and the "1393" figure is probably more reliable than those of either 1391 or 1381 (vdS 298; Wei 247, n.2).

[c]The 1600 figure is a rough estimate assuming that population increased at the same rate as land area from 1393 to 1582. Cultivated land area of Hunan (1582) = 282,782 / Cultivated area (1393) = 104,280 = 2.71× 1,874 = 5.082; 2.71 × 2,393 = 6,485.

[d]*Kou* figure refers only to male adult taxpayers.

[e]The 1578, 1749, and 1771 figures clearly understate the real population.

dynasty is given as from 4.5 to 4.7 million people (see Table 2). This is a significant decline from the Yuan dynasty figures, which indicate 5.65 million for Hunan alone. The Yuan figures are suspiciously high, especially considering the considerable devastation inflicted on the province by the Mongol armies. It seems plausible to assume, as Perkins does, that these figures were copied from Song records preceding the Mongol invasion.[51] It is also generally agreed that the figures from the 1393 census, referring to the year 1391, represented less than the entire population.[52] The native areas ruled by tribal chieftains, in particular, were deliberately excluded from the Yellow Registers. Tribal areas constituted a large percentage of Hunan's area in the early Ming. The early Ming figures thus considerably understate Hunan's actual population in the late fourteenth century. Nevertheless, the population figures established by 1393 were the result of a thorough census ordered by the Hongwu Emperor, and they are the most accurate figures until 1776. They reveal fairly accurately the distribution of Hunan's population in the early Ming (Tables 2 and 3).

By combing through local gazetteers, I have been able to reconstruct the Hunanese population in 1391 in 37 counties, half the total number. These counties contained a total of 1.3 million people. By establishing the correlation between the number of *li* units in the early Ming era and the local population, we arrive at an estimate of the total Hunanese Han population in 1391 of 1.87 to 2.08 million people (see Table 3).[53]

Clearly the density of population in the early Ming was very low. The average of Huguang (including both Hunan and Hubei) was 32.4

TABLE 2 *(continued)*

Sources: C&W: Michel Cartier and Pierre-Etienne Will, "Démographie et institutions en Chine: contribution à l'analyse des recensements de l'époque imperiale (2 A.D.–1750)," pp. 161–245; Dwight Perkins, *Agricultural Development in China, 1368–1968,* pp. 195–200; John Durand, "Population Statistics of China, A.D. 2–1953;" Ping-ti Ho, *Studies on the Population of China, 1368–1953;* vdS: O. B. van der Sprenkel, "Population statistics of Ming China"; Wei: Wei Qingyuan, *Mingdai Huangce Zhidu,* p. 247; 10-percent sample: Guowuyuan Renkou Pucha Bangongshi, ed., *Zhongguo 1982 Nian Renkou Pucha 10% Chouyang Ziliao* (Beijing, 1983).

TABLE 3 Hunan Population Data, 1391

Place	hu (households)	kou (persons)	Source
CHANGSHA *fu*	86,684	509,100	FZ 1534.3 (a)
Changsha	7,952	46,853	
Shanhua	3,852	22,996	
Xiangtan	4,653	20,053	XZ 1889.6 (b)
Xiangyin	8,666	58,210	
Xiangxiang	11,063	74,097	
Liling	5,152	31,600	XZ 1743.5
Ningxiang	3,721	31,581	(c)
Yiyang	5,070	25,210	
Liuyang	12,680	71,950	XZ 1561 *xia* (d)
Anhua	2,561	18,348	XZ 1545;
			1872 (*hu:* 1561)
You	8,770	55,313	
Chaling *zhou*	12,568	56,563	ZZ 1817.7
BAOQING *fu**	20,584	134,918	FZ 1567.4
Xinning	2,600	12,180	XZ 1823.9
Shaoyang	1,652	10,828	FZ 1685.17 (g)
Xinhua	6,500	30,312	XZ 1759.8
YUEZHOU *fu*	70,867	282,224	FZ1567–1572.6 (h)
Huarong	8,527	43,099	XZ 1760.4;
			FZ 1567–1572
Pingjiang	15,047	19,265	FZ 1567–1572 (i)
Baling	17,510	84,850	FZ 1567–1572
Linxiang	3,701	21,478	FZ 1567–1572
CHANGDE *fu*	29,277	128,895	FZ 1671.4
Wuling	13,276	48,469	FZ 1671.4
Taoyuan	9,371	49,265	FZ 1671.4
Longyang	5,939	27,091	FZ 1671.4;
			XZ 1875.11
Yuanjiang	691	4,070	FZ 1671.4
HENGZHOU *fu**			
Hengshan	4,164	22,240	XZ 1774.7 (f)

TABLE 3 *(continued)*

Place	hu (households)	kou (persons)	Source
Leiyang	5,288	32,852	XZ 1725.3
YONGZHOU *fu*	25,006	113,590	FZ 1495 (e)
Lingling	5,920	29,199	FZ 1495;
			XZ 1684, 1876
Qiyang	1,696	10,953	FZ 1495
Dongan	1,573	6,588	FZ 1495;
			XZ 1752 (6598 *kou*)
Dao *zhou*	4,629	23,862	FZ 1495
Ningyuan	8,492	29,363	FZ 1495
Yongming	2,124	11,134	FZ 1495
Jianghua	562	2,491	FZ 1495
LIZHOU *zhilizhou*			
Lizhou *benzhou*	7,783	33,113	Yuezhou FZ 1567–1572
Anxiang	3,887	15,210	Yuezhou FZ 1567–1572;
			XZ 1748.3 (j)
Shimen	6,310	27,670	FZ 1567–72
Cili	8,100	37,709	FZ 1567–72
GUIYANG *zhilizhou**			
Linwu	12,841	63,811	XZ 1817
CHHENZHOU *zhilizhou**			
Yongxing	3,679	21,075	XZ 1762.5;
			1883 (k)
TOTAL 1		1,422,407	Totals of prefectures
TOTAL 2		1,230,681	Totals of counties

* indicates data are not given for all *xian* within the prefecture

Total *li* units: Hunan, 1,555.5, Hubei + Hunan, 3,057; Units listed above: 1,086.5. Estimated total population (1): Total = (Huguang population) × (*li* in Hunan) / (Total *li*) = 2,393,000 *kou* (1393). (2): Total = (population in list above) × (*li* in Hunan) / (*li* in list above) = 1,873,622 *kou*. If the Huguang population total for 1391 is used instead of 1393, Hunan's estimated population is 2,082,000.

Notes: XZ: *xianzhi;* FZ: *fuzhi.*
(a) The acual sum of the *xian* units is 512,774.
(b) XZ 1553 *shang* gives 4,620 *hu*, 25,053 *kou.*
(c) XZ 1682.3 gives 3,072 *hu*, 21,571 *kou.*
(d) XZ 1967 gives 7,810 *hu*, 271,950 *kou*, clearly an error.
(e) FZ 1383 gives 73,005 *hu*, 411, 616 *kou*, which seems too large. The figures above are more consis-

persons per square mile, or 7.8 persons per 1,000 *mou*.[54] Huguang, the third largest in area of the 15 provinces in the Ming, next to Sichuan and Shaanxi (which then included Gansu), ranked eleventh in population density, above Shaanxi and the southwestern provinces of Sichuan, Yunnan, and Guangxi.[55]

Mapping the distribution of this population in 1391 for the counties for which we have information displays the settlement pattern characteristic of Hunan (see Figure 4). The highest densities of settlement are found around the borders of Dongting Lake, over 15 persons per 1,000 *mou* in Baling and Huarong counties. Some counties on the lake, however, like Yuanjiang and Yiyang, were quite sparsely populated, because most of the extensive dike network which contributed to clearing the area had not yet been built. Dense settlement is also found along the Xiang River Valley, especially on the eastern side of the river and in those counties bordering Jiangxi province. The numerous tributaries feeding the Xiang from the east created broad valleys suitable for agriculture, even in fairly remote areas like Chaling county, whose density appears aberrantly high. As one moves west of the Xiang, densities drop to much lower levels, showing that the other river basins had not yet been greatly populated, although Taoyuan, up the Yuan River, had made some progress. In the mountainous regions on the upper reaches of the rivers, including the Xiang River above Hengyang, population was very sparse. There are anomalies in these figures that are difficult to explain, such as the quite high densities in Linwu and Ningyuan, but in general they indicate that the settlement of Hunan had only just begun.[56]

Hunan also ranked very low in terms of the proportion of

TABLE 3 *(continued)*

tent with figures from 1552 and 1569 in FZ 1571.

(f) XZ 1488, 1924 give 32,415 *kou* (probably referring to 1488).

(g) Only the figure for households is given; the number of *kou* is calculated by multiplying *hu* figure by the average *kou/hu* ratio for Baoqing *fu* = 6.5.

(h) The actual sum of *xian* figures is 282,124.

(i) The number of *kou* is clearly too low; XZ 1875.16 gives 5,690 *hu*, 53,890 *kou* for 1465–1494. In the Yongle reign, the figure is 11,736 *hu*, 51,388 *kou*, which is probably more accurate, but the figure in the table accords with the prefectural total.

(j) Includes 960 military households.

(k) Figures refer to 1442.

FIGURE 4 Hunan Population Density, 1391
(persons per 1,000 *mou*)

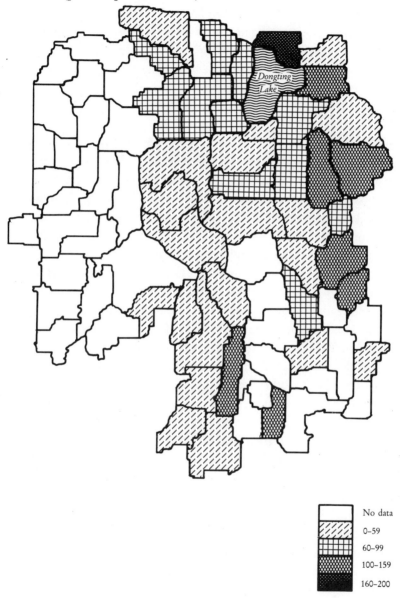

Legend:
- No data
- 0–59
- 60–99
- 100–159
- 160–200

Sources: Population data from Table 3; land areas from *Hunan Jinbainian Dashi Jishu,* pp. 350–352.

cultivated land. Fujii Hiroshi has shown that the total cultivated acreage given in the *Daming Huidian* of 220.2 million *mou* is impossibly high, due to errors in recording figures from local surveys. By adding up prefectural figures from local gazetteers, Fujii obtains a total of 10.428 million *mou* for cultivated land area in Hunan in 1472, or 24.0 million *mou* for Huguang.[57] Huguang ranked tenth in the percentage of its land that was cleared.

Local figures allow us to compute the ratio of registered land to total land area for some counties in 1391–1393. These are displayed in Figure 5. The pattern of distribution of cultivated land is quite close to that of the registered population. The highest percentages are found around Dongting Lake, the highest being Huarong, Anxiang, and Baling, while Yuanjiang's land clearance is very low. There is also some land clearance on the Jiangxi border in Pingjiang, Liuyang, and Chaling, while the other river basins are relatively little cultivated.

The low percentage of cultivated acreage meant that, even though the population was small, in many districts the cultivated land area per capita was rather small. Overall, the province averaged 5.1 *mou* per capita, only slightly greater than the major population centers of Jiangsu and Anhui.[58] Around the lake there was less than 5 *mou* per capita in Yuanjiang. In some districts, like Shaoyang, where the Zi River flows through a broad valley, cultivated land was relatively abundant, but in others, like Xinhua, where mountains pressed in close to the river, cultivated land per capita was quite restricted (Figure 6). This indicates that the sparse population of Hunan was clustered together in narrow strips of land along river banks and the lake shores. The marshes of the lake had not yet been drained and made into polders, and the mountainous lands upstream had not yet been cleared for upland crops. Limitations of water control and cropping patterns prevented the early settlers of Hunan from expanding the cultivated area.

Unfortunately, population registration deteriorated so markedly by the end of the Ming dynasty that it is impossible to estimate the total population in the sixteenth century, but the statistics on cultivated land area are fairly reliable, because of Zhang Juzheng's efforts to conduct a national land survey. Zhang succeeded in surveying nearly all

FIGURE 5 Registered Land as Percentage of Total Land Area,
1391–1393

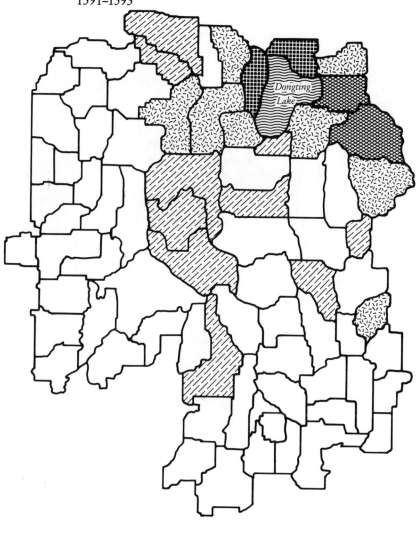

Dongting
Lake

No data
0.5–4.0%
4.1–8.0%
8.1–12.0%
Over 12%

Source: Table 4

FIGURE 6 Population Density per Registered Land Area, 1391
(persons per 1,000 mou)

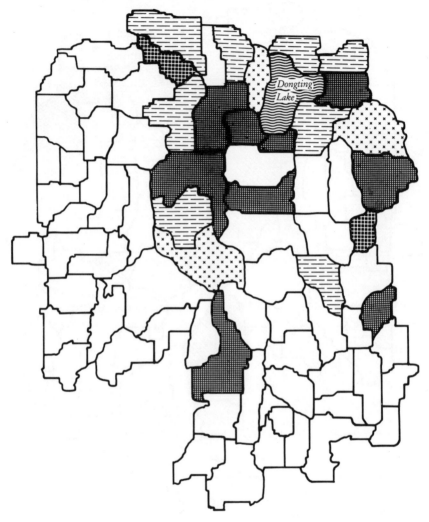

No data
10–80
81–160
161–240
Over 240

Source: Tables 3 and 4.

of China, and he uncovered large amounts of land that had been un-registered since Hongwu's time. The results are clearly evident in the large jump in registered land figures for the late Wanli reign (see Table 4). Wang Yeh-chien considers that the results of the 1578–1582 survey "are probably very close to the country's actual acreage at the end of the sixteenth century."[59]

There is a strong association between population and land clearance in the figures. If Hunan's population had increased at the same rate as its land area, the total population in 1582 would have equaled 5.1 to 5.6 million people. In fact, the real population was probably somewhat larger, because there are indications of crowding on the lowlands around the lake. Since the early Qing land-tax quotas were based on the Wanli figures, it is possible to reconstruct the amount of land cleared in 1582 on the basis of the quotas of the Qing period. In the cases where independent figures are given for the results of the 1582 survey and for the Qing quotas, the figures agree quite closely. The distribution of land clearance in 1582 is mapped in Figure 7 (see Table 5).

By 1582, the proportion of cultivated land in Hunan had risen con-siderably over 1393. Most of the districts bordering the lake had in-creased their cultivated land area to over 15 percent of the total land area. Land clearance had spread down the Xiang River along the main river valley and along the tributaries in the east. The Zi River Basin was also beginning to be cleared up to Wugang, and cultivation ad-vanced along the Yuan and Li Rivers as well. Only the northwestern corner of Hunan, including Sangzhi, Yongshun, Longshan, and Bao-jing, remained practically untouched by Han settlers. The mountain-ous borders with Guangdong, Guangxi, and Guizhou also showed very little settlement. The great boom in land clearance in Huguang raised it from near the bottom to the middle ranks of China's prov-inces in proportion of land cleared, with a provincial average of 13.9 percent.

But Hunan was by no means intensively settled. It was still referred to as a place where "grain is cheap, land is abundant, there are no peo-ple to cultivate it, and people do not set a high value on land."[60] Yet the province was already becoming known as a grain exporter whose bountiful production could feed the rest of the empire.[61] We have few

TABLE 4 Registered Land Area in Hunan and Hubei, 1400–1957
(in 1,000s of mou*); parentheses indicate estimates*

Year	Huguang		Hunan		Hubei		Source
	Qing mou	shimou	Qing mou	shimou	Qing mou	shimou	
1400	23,976	21,510	10,428	9,720	13,548	11,790	Perkins; Wang
1472	24,000		11,422				Fujii; *Huguang Zongzhi*
1512	24,400		12,027				Fujii; *Huguang Zongzhi*
1582	83,852		28,278				Wang (Wanli quota)
1661	79,335		28,114				Wanli quota; Huidian; Guo
1685	68,134		13,892		54,242		Otake; Guo; Huidian
1724	84,102		30,528		53,574		Huidian; Guo
1753	93,055		34,317		58,738		Otake
1766	93,000	102,000	(34,000)	(51,000)	(59,000)	(51,000)	Perkins
1766	88,153		31,308		56,844		Otake
1812	84,706		27,806		56,900		Otake
1872	91,184		31,740		59,444		Otake
1873	(117,000)		(66,000)		(51,000)		Perkins
1887	88,705		31,304		57,400		Otake
1893	(111,000)		(58,000)		(53,000)		Otake
1908	94,094		34,874		59,220		Wang
1913	(114,000)		(59,000)		(55,000)		Perkins
1933	(123,000)		(58,000)		(65,000)		Perkins
1957	(123,000)		(58,000)		(65,000)		Perkins

Sources: Dwight Perkins, *Agricultural Development in China, 1368–1968,* pp. 234, 236; Wang Yeh-chien, *Land Taxation in Imperial China, 1750–1911,* p. 24; Fujii Hiroshi, "Mindai Dendo Tōkei ni Kansuru Ichi Kōsatsu"; *Huguang Zongzhi,* 1591; Otake Fumio, *Kinsei Shina Keizaishi Kenkyū;* Guo Songyi, "Qingchu Fengjian Guojia Kenhuang Zhengce Fenxi," p. 36; *Daqing Huidian, juan* 20.

clues to the size of the population at this time, but it is possible to infer that the population-to-land ratio was in a relatively favorable balance: dense enough to stimulate land clearance and relatively intensive cultivation in some areas, but low enough to provide a grain surplus over local needs.

FIGURE 7 Registered Land as Percentage of Total Land Area, 1582

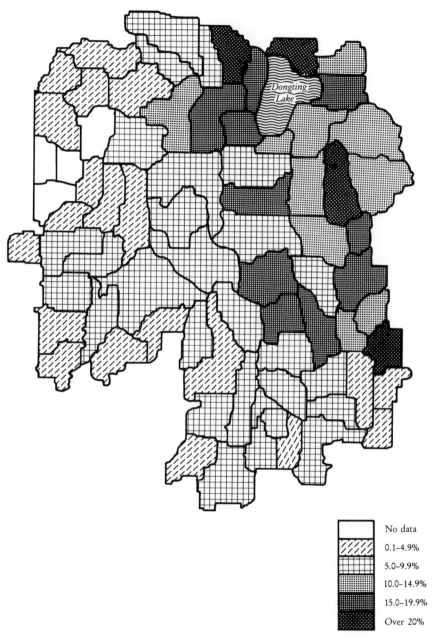

No data

0.1–4.9%

5.0–9.9%

10.0–14.9%

15.0–19.9%

Over 20%

Source: Table 5.

TABLE 5 Registered Land Area in Hunan, 1393–1582
(in 100s of mou)

Place	1393	Qing Quota
CHANGSHA *fu*		89,223
Changsha		7,618
Shanhua		3,812
Xiangtan		8,640
Xiangyin	3,663	7,855
Xiangxiang		13,365
Ningxiang	1,625	8,225
Yiyang		9,549
Liuyang	3,975	9,313
Anhua	834	2,849
Liling	1,162	6,366
You		7,210
Chaling	2,783	4,423
BAOQING *fu*	9,420	24,170
Shaoyang	3,550	8,592
Xinhua	2,008	4,784
Chengbu		885
Xinning		1,627
Wugang *zhou*		8,242
YUEZHOU *fu*	16,025	23,771
Baling	4,768	8,426
Linxiang	1,811	4,046
Pingjiang	4,475	6,600
Huarong	4,971	4,595
CHANGDE *fu*	6,704	23,513
Wuling	3,011	8,778
Taoyuan	3,772	6,896
Longyang	1,296	4,692
Yuanjiang	189	3,147
HENGZHOU *fu*		34,255
Hengyang		14,035

TABLE 5 *(continued)*

Place	1393	Qing Quota
Hengshan	2,509	8,007
Leiyang		5,590
Changning		2,374
Anren		3,158
Ling		1,090
YONGZHOU *fu*	20,532	22,853
Lingling	2,127	4,516
Qiyang		5,859
Dongan		2,753
Ningyuan		2,502
Yongming		1,663
Jianghua		745
Xintian		1,450
Dao *zhou*		3,366
CHENZHOU *fu*		7,214
Yuanling		2,717
Chenxi		1,117
Xupu		2,605
Lüxi		775
YUANZHOU *fu*		6,376
Zhijiang		2,782
Qianyang		2,609
Mayang		985
YONGSHUN *fu*		873
Yongshun		326
Longshan		296
Baojing		129
Sangzhi		122
LIZHOU *zhilizhou*		23,863
Lizhou	2,749	11,024
Anxiang	2,310	3,405
Shimen	2,150	3,386
Cili	1,240	4,025

TABLE 5 *(continued)*

Place	1393	Qing Quota
Anfu		2,023
Yongding		435
JINGZHOU *zhilizhou*		6,214
Jingzhou *benzhou*		1,630
Suining		2,263
Huitong		2,102
Tongdao		214
GUIYANG *zhilizhou*		9,001
Guiyang *benzhou*		4,010
Linwu		1,478
Lanshan		2,221
Jiahe		1,178
CHHENZHOU *zhilizhou*		10,868
Chhenzhou *benzhou*		2,341
Yongxing		2,957
Yizhang		1,466
Xingning		1,823
Guidong		727
Guiyang		1,555
HUANGZHOU, etc. *ting*		413
TOTAL		282,782

Sources: For 1393, county gazetteers; for Qing quota, *Hunan Tongzhi*, 1757, *juan* 26–37.

POPULATION TRENDS IN THE
EIGHTEENTH AND NINETEENTH CENTURIES

After the disruptions of the seventeenth century, Hunan began a second phase of rapid population growth accompanied by clearance of land. The indirect evidence in the following chapters bears this out: the proliferation of dikes, influx of immigrants, spread of new crops, and official concern about exhaustion of land. Unfortunately, we have no accurate data on population until 1776, and none at all on the amount of cultivated land.[62] The figures for cultivated land area

FIGURE 8 Hunan Provincial Registered Population, 1778–1880

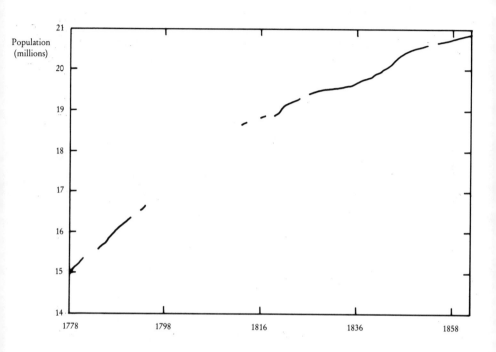

Source: Table 6.

merely repeat the quotas set in the early Qing era, with only small additions. The population data from 1776 to 1850, however, are the most accurate ever produced for an extended period of time by the traditional Chinese registration system. The yearly figures for total provincial population and annual rates of growth from 1745 to 1860 are given in Table 6 and in Figure 8. From 1745 to 1776, the population returns were quite incomplete; still, they indicate a progressive annual increase of 2 to 3 per 1,000. After 1776, the use of the *baojia* for population registration greatly improved the accuracy of registration and showed a clear trend of rapidly increasing population. From 1776 to 1860, Hunan's total population increased from 14.9 to 20.9 million people, an average rate of 4 per 1,000 per year. Within the

TABLE 6 Hunan Population Data, 1745–1860

Year	kou (persons)	Rate (%)	Year	kou (persons)	Rate (%)
1745	8,611,213		1812	18,652,507	0.6
1751	8,695,912	0.2	1813	18,688,755	0.2
1752	8,702,860	0.1	1816	18,823,541	0.2
1753	8,720,341	0.2	1817	18,847,893	0.1
1754	8,727,222	0.1	1819	18,891,743	0.1
1755	8,735,021	0.1	1820	18,928,865	0.2
1756	8,752,472	0.2	1821	19,118,210	1.0
1759	8,786,399	0.1	1822	19,186,119	0.4
1763	8,898,906	0.3	1823	19,243,052	0.3
1764	8,925,093	0.3	1824	19,292,504	0.3
1767	8,997,022	0.3	1825		
1768	9,018,662	0.2	1826	19,389,982	0.3
1772	9,086,641	0.2	1827	19,438,431	0.2
1773	9,092,328	0.1	1828	19,481,553	0.2
1774	17,896,007	—	1829	19,506,760	0.1
1775	14,854,834	—	1830	19,523,000	0.1
1775	19,880,577	—	1831	19,535,403	0.1
1776	14,889,777	—	1832	19,547,326	0.1
1777	15,111,161	1.5	1833	19,565,457	0.1
1778	15,219,603	0.7	1834	19,601,155	0.2
1779	15,352,359	0.9	1835	19,633,779	0.2
1782	15,584,609	0.5	1836	19,686,475	0.3
1783	15,676,488	0.6	1837	19,726,686	0.2
1784	15,785,866	0.7	1838	19,776,605	0.3
1785	15,934,528	0.9	1839	19,821,574	0.2
1786	16,067,630	0.8	1840	19,891,061	0.4
1787	16,164,887	0.6	1841	19,961,755	0.4
1788	16,261,505	0.6	1842	20,031,719	0.4
1789	16,347,798	0.5	1843	20,095,835	0.3
1791	16,556,174	0.6	1844	20,168,526	0.4
1792	16,667,227	0.7	1845	20,359,524	0.9

TABLE 6 *(continued)*

Year	kou (persons)	Rate (%)	Year	kou (persons)	Rate (%)
1846	20,439,678	0.4	1854	20,724,713	0.1
1847	20,504,482	0.3	1855	20,753,595	0.1
1848	20,539,560	0.2	1856	20,782,559	0.1
1849	20,575,952	0.2	1857	20,812,163	0.1
1850	20,613,885	0.2	1858	20,840,803	0.1
1851	20,647,752	0.2	1859	20,867,253	0.1
1852			1860	20,940,379	0.4
1853	20,700,153	0.1			

Sources: For 1776–1789, GZD-QL 33306 (1776–1777), 36927 (1778), 38906 (1779), 46448 (1782–1783), 52391 (1786–1787), 55626 (1788), 58705 (1789). For 1789–1860, *Quanguo Minshu Gushu Qingce.* I am grateful to James Lee for supplying me with these figures. The years 1786–1791, 1819–1820, 1830–1860 are also found in Yan Zhongping, ed., *Zhongguo Jindai Jingjishi Tongji Ziliao Xuanji,* pp. 362–374.

period, what is most noticeable is the change in the rate of increase per year. From 1776 to 1812, the growth rate was fairly constant, averaging 5.5 per 1,000 per year. After 1812, the growth rate fell off to a level of 2.6 per 1,000 per year until 1860, when the population figures show no further increase. Although it may be true, as Ping-ti Ho argues, that complete population registration was not carried out after 1850 because of the Taiping wars, the figures from 1850 to 1860 are consistent with the earlier trend, and it is only after 1860 that they become completely artificial.[63]

Even so, the rate of growth from 1812 to 1850 was only 2.8 per 1,000 per year, only slightly over half of the rate of growth from 1776 to 1812. This slowing of the growth rate is found in other provinces of the southwest, like Yunnan, whose annual growth rate dropped from a peak of 22 per 1,000 in 1775 to a low of 4 per 1,000 in 1848.[64] These trends indicate that the peripheral Han regions of China were reaching the limits of their potential for rapid expansion by 1800 and could no longer absorb large numbers of immigrants. Hunan's slow-down was more modest than Yunnan's, because Yunnan had already cleared most of its arable land by the end of the eighteenth century.

The population-to-land ratio, because of the limitations of the data, is only an imperfect indicator of the progress of settlement in the province. A closer understanding of the conditions under which the Hunanese lived requires an examination of the relationship between the Chinese state and local society. By the late sixteenth century, Hunan had greatly expanded its cultivated area and population. In some respects, it remained a frontier area, far from the economic centers of the empire, but it had developed considerably its productive potential. Natural conditions of soil, climate, and rainfall gave Hunan possibilities for greatly raising its yields of paddy rice and mountain crops. By the late Ming, the export grain market, which would bring extensive market penetration in the mid-Qing, had begun to develop. As Hunan rose in status economically, the officials who governed it became more interested in its potential resources. As the state became less concerned with security and more concerned with encouraging agriculture to develop to the fullest, state policies to encourage land clearance and improve agricultural productivity began to play a more important role.

THREE

The Resettlement of Hunan:
State Policies and Land Clearance

The rulers of every Chinese dynasty felt responsible for ensuring the welfare of their subjects. From ancient times, the Classics had stated that a large population and well-cultivated fields indicated a benevolent ruler.[1] Since extending the cultivated land area was the primary means of feeding an expanding population, every dynasty in its early years enacted policies to bring wasteland under cultivation quickly. Tax exemptions and loans of seeds, tools, and animals provided incentives for peasants to clear land. In frontier areas, where military colonists comprised the first wave of Han settlers, the state took a more direct role in resettlement. The military colonists were followed by merchants, artisans, and immigrant peasants moving out of overpopulated regions into areas where large supplies of land were available.[2] The state could directly move millions of settlers into uninhabited regions, and it could provide incentives and protection for settlers to clear large expanses of vacant land.

On the other hand, state policies did not always unambiguously favor land clearance. Officials realized that the influx of immigrants could easily cause unrest. Social conflict produced by immigration and land clearance could take several forms. In densely populated lowland cores, feuds and lawsuits broke out over the control of highly valuable land. In these areas, the high population-to-land ratio fomented intense struggles over rights to land, but these conflicts could at least be adjudicated by the civil bureaucracy. Conflicts in the periphery took a more militarized form. In areas inhabited by native tribes, there was continual strife, as Han settlers moved into valley lands, while tribesmen retaliated with ambushes, raids, and sometimes full rebellion. Even if there were no native tribesmen to resist new waves of settlement, the loose control of the bureaucracy over remote regions created a "wild West" frontier atmosphere, where conflicts were not settled by lawsuits but by use of force.[3]

Dynasties varied in their responses to the threat of disorder in remote regions caused by immigration and land clearance. The Ming dynasty attempted to seal off certain areas, such as the upper reaches of the Han River Valley, from further settlement. Such "prohibited mountain regions" *(fengjinshan)* were also established on the borders of Anhui, Henan, Hubei, Sichuan, Shanxi, Zhejiang, Fujian, and Jiangxi provinces. By doing this, the Ming rulers hoped to stop waves of settlement before they built up pressures that would lead to rebellious outbreaks.[4] This policy ultimately failed to prevent continued migration to the prohibited areas, and it failed to stop outbreaks of rebellion in northwest Hubei in 1464 and 1470.[5] After these rebellions, the policy shifted to allow clearance of land and immigration in Hubei, but mountain areas that were prohibited remained in the rest of the country.

The Qing rulers did not in general attempt to enforce a "prohibited-mountains" policy, but they shared the same ambivalent attitude toward settlement of frontier areas.[6] Manchuria, of course, was closed to Han immigration, although the Court was completely incapable of preventing illegal settlement there.[7] Qing officials also worried about conflict between Han settlers and native tribesmen. They attempted to avoid major conflicts by restricting contact between Han and native peoples as much as possible, allowing trade only at officially supervised markets. In western Hunan, they went so far as to construct a large pale whose intent was to keep Han and Miao totally separated.

At the same time, the overall thrust of Qing land policy worked to undermine the restrictions on land clearance. Tax exemptions and loans in the Shunzhi and Kangxi reigns encouraged clearance of wasteland. The Yongzheng Emperor's *gaitu guiliu* policy not only brought tribal chiefs into the regular bureaucratic administration but greatly accelerated Han immigration to native districts. Backed by civil and military authority, Han merchants and peasants inexorably pushed into Miao territory and obtained lands either by purchase or by force. From the Yongzheng reign on, as officials became more aware of the burdens of China's expanding population, they concluded that further extension of the cultivated area along with more intensive use of existing land was essential to producing an increased food supply. But, in the 1740s, half a century before Hong Liangji's famous "Essay on Livelihood," which warned that the population was increasing more rapidly than the means of subsistence,[8] officials were beginning to realize that a rapidly growing population was not an unmixed blessing and that there were limits to the extension of cultivated acreage. As nearly all usable land became cleared by the mid-eighteenth century, emphasis shifted to encouraging increased yields. Investments in irrigation, early rice seeds, and American food crops all played a role in raising food production, but, by the early nineteenth century, these new crops may have nearly reached the limits of their possible contribution. The resettlement of Hunan in the seventeenth and eighteenth centuries illustrates on a local scale the effects of population growth on agriculture and the role of official intervention in land clearance.

LAND CLEARANCE IN THE MING DYNASTY

There is not much information on land clearance in Hunan in the Ming era, but references to immigration from Jiangxi and the fact that many prominent Hunanese lineages came to the province in the early Ming indicate that there must have been considerable settlement during the course of the dynasty.[9] In the early Ming, however, most of Hunan remained a frontier. Dwight Perkins estimates the cultivated land at 10,428,000 *mou* in 1400, or about 3 percent of the total land area of the province.[10] Although some districts around Dongting Lake were fairly densely populated, there were few major waterworks, and the rest of the province was sparsely settled. By the late Ming, partly due to official encouragement, the cultivated acreage had more than doubled. For example, the assistant magistrate of Xiangyin county from 1457 to 1464 is said to have "personally cleared fields, taught people how to plant the five grains and how to relieve famine. For the first time, the people learned to reap the benefits of mountain land."[11] There was also some official investment in waterworks, like the Yongji dike built in Baling county in 1484–1486.[12] On the whole, however, private initiative accounted for most land clearance. In the late sixteenth century, Hunan's abundant land had already begun to attract immigrants from more densely settled areas. Changsha prefecture was described in 1591 as a "fine district, self-sufficient in food" to which many poor "roving people" were attracted.[13]

The positive attractions of Hunan were offset by the disincentives created by the Ming dynasty's inequitable tax policy. All over the country, the decline in effectiveness of the land registration system, the encroachment by large landlords, and the concealment of land by local power-holders resulted in the shifting of tax burdens from the strong to the weak, forcing the poor to abandon land.[14] Hong Maode, writing about Xiangxiang county some time in the late sixteenth or early seventeenth century, provided a detailed discussion of tax abuses in Hunan. He remarked: "Xiangxiang today is not what it used to be. In ten years land changes hands five or six times and then becomes barren. People disperse everywhere . . . there are now no *ding* (fiscal units) . . . without *ding* all the tax is laid on the land. The people see the land as poison and abandon it as quickly as possible."[15]

Hong described how land abandoned under the burden of heavy taxation was then taken over by powerful local families with enough influence to conceal their land from registration. He recognized that the process had begun with the disintegration of the *lijia* system. As the "lazy, wicked, and dishonest" took over control of the distribution of taxes and labor services, they "deceived the local officials, did not say whether land was barren or cultivable, or where it was located, and they forced poor taxpayers to supply corvée."[16] The result was the abandonment of land by the poor and the loss of tax income to the state.

It is difficult to judge how widespread the situation was in Hunan; since no land surveys were conducted after 1580, it is not possible to estimate the total amount of land abandoned. The incidence of inequitable taxation varied widely, depending on the laxity of the local administration and the power of the local elite. Hong claimed that Changsha prefecture, particularly Xiangxiang county, was the worst burdened with loss of registered land and heavy taxes, while Yuezhou, Changde, Hengzhou, and Yongzhou prefectures still kept their registers intact and had "rich land and light taxes."[17] A magistrate of Xiangxiang claimed that, while the county's neighbors paid taxes of 0.03 *shi* per *mou*, Xiangxiang had to pay up to 0.15 *shi* per *mou*, and in addition barren mountains and swamps were included in the tax quotas, so that each *mou* was counted as three *mou* for tax purposes.[18] Xiangxiang was, however, not the only county with heavy tax burdens. Minister of Personnel Li Tengfang wrote several essays describing taxation in his home county of Xiangtan, in which he noted that, despite the enactment of the Single Whip Reform, tax levies remained inequitable and people fled the land.[19]

Hong may have had an excessively local point of view, but Changsha prefecture does appear to have had unusually high tax burdens. In Liuyang county, on the Jiangxi border, taxes were not adjusted according to the quality of the land; there was one fixed tax regardless of yield. In bad years, the Hunanese fled across the provincial border to escape being pressed for payment. By the seventeenth century, up to 70 percent of the population had fled.[20] Wu Daoxing, of Changsha, claimed that Changsha produced one third of Hunan's taxes. He dated the worst tax burdens to the period following 1586, when many illegal surtaxes were added to the regular levies and when the Court refused to grant tax reductions.[21]

Other prefectures suffered from unequal tax burdens, too. In Huarong county, military garrisons illegally took over fertile lands on which they paid little tax.[22] In Shimen county, a local writer, appealing for tax reductions in 1583, outlined three abuses injuring the inhabitants: the takeover of lands by the military, soil erosion by mountain streams, and excessive corvée levies.[23] The confusion in tax levies and land registration in the late Ming era seriously limited Hunan's potential to attract immigrants to clear its fertile land. He Mengchun, writing around 1528, was the first to record the proverb "When Huguang has a good harvest, the empire has sufficient grain," but, at the same time as he noted the abundance of Hunan's grain production, he complained about heavy tax burdens, which, he claimed, were greater than those of Jiangnan.[24] Only after the establishment of a new dynasty could Hunan begin a new cycle of growth.

DESTRUCTION DURING THE
MING-QING TRANSITION

Before beginning the road to recovery, Hunan had to pass through the travails of the dynastic transition. From the 1640s through the 1660s, Hunan suffered great losses, even though the major centers of revolt in the late Ming were not in Hunan and the two main rebel leaders, Zhang Xianzhong and Li Zicheng, occupied the province only briefly. Li Zicheng moved into the Huguang area in 1643 and sent one unit to occupy Changsha, but he held the city for only a few days. Li did not return until 1645, when he occupied the Dongting Lake area briefly while being pursued by Qing troops.[25] Zhang Xianzhong occupied Wuchang on 15 July 1643, then moved south to take Xiangyin, Changsha, and Hengzhou. After occupying Changsha for three months, he then pushed south through Yongzhou across the Guangxi border. His control there, however, was also ephemeral. On 15 January 1644, he left Changsha, moving on to begin his notorious reign in Sichuan.[26] There was, on the whole, little resistance by government forces to Zhang's or Li's troops. Most of the local officials fled, while many people joined Zhang's army.[27] Zhang did destroy

Yuezhou in retaliation for resisting him and is said to have destroyed Changsha's walls and massacred the inhabitants of the city.[28] Passing through Ningxiang, he "left a trail of blood for a thousand *li*" and destroyed houses in Liuyang, Ningxiang, and Yiyang.[29]

Still, Li and Zhang alone cannot be held responsible for the devastation of the province. Although local observers tended to lump together all bandits as either *chuangzei* associated with Li Zicheng, or *xianzei*, associated with Zhang Xianzhong,[30] much of the destruction was caused by numerous independent attacks by smaller groups of rebels, like Ma Jinzhong, whose army plundered Baling, Linxiang, and Huarong in 1644.[31] Native tribesmen also took advantage of the confused conditions to rise up against Chinese, as in Wugang, where a local rebel in 1643 raised an army of several tens of thousands to attack the city.[32] On a smaller scale, bondservants rose up against their masters and ran off to join the military forces of the rebels. They relied on the military backing of the rebels to reclaim their contracts of bondage and to plunder their masters.[33] A great rebellion broke out in 1648, when dozens of groups of rebels invaded Hunan, and "every prefecture and county was occupied." Drought struck in 1652, causing the grain crop to wither. The provincial Governor noted that Hunan was especially vulnerable to natural disaster because, unlike other provinces, it relied on only one rice crop and lacked beans, wheat, and millet to provide insurance against crop failure.[34]

While the names of the rebel groups changed, for the local people it must have seemed like decades of continuous warfare. Descriptions of abandoned lands, ruined buildings, and desolate cities abound in the writings of seventeenth century observers. Censor Zhang Maoxi, traveling from Yuezhou to Changsha to take up his post in 1647, "slept in open fields and ate under trees" because the area was depopulated. He found Changsha, the provincial capital, practically deserted.[35] In Xiangxiang, 60 to 70 percent of the population was said to have disappeared by 1650.[36] In Guiyang *zhou*, the figure was 80 to 90 percent.[37] Chenzhou reported "no inhabitants for hundreds of *li*." An investigation of the tax registers found only 10 to 20 percent of the quota remaining.[38]

The sufferings of the people were increased by a spate of floods and droughts following upon the military activity.[39] All those who could escape fled the lowlands and cities to seek shelter in the mountains. Groups of refugees gathered in mountain fortresses or caves that offered protection from armed attack.[40] Those who could not escape were forced to adopt desperate survival strategies. Families sold themselves into bondage, and female infanticide became common among the poor.[41]

Restoration of the area progressed slowly, even after the Qing conquest. Even in the 1670s, much formerly cultivated land remained abandoned.[42] Then, in 1673, Wu Sangui once again raised the standard of revolt. He occupied Hunan in 1674 and established his headquarters in Changde. He proclaimed himself Emperor of China at Hengyang in 1678 but died in the same year. After his death, his son failed to hold on to the province, which was restored to Qing control in 1679.[43]

The revolt of Wu Sangui was the final major disturbance in Hunan in the seventeenth century. It left in its wake "empty markets, collapsed fences and wells, and fields occupied by wolves and thorns."[44] Agricultural implements had been melted down to make weapons.[45] The overall losses in land and population were less than during the transition period: Xiangxiang reported 60 percent of the population left alive in 1686, compared to 30 to 40 percent in 1650.[46] Liu Yingzhong, on the other hand, who took up his post in Chenzhou prefecture in 1680, succeeded in calling back 9,031 refugees, but he found that the total population was 41,564, less than one third of the old quota.[47] The compiler of the Linxiang gazetteer in 1685, looking at "empty markets, wind and rain blowing through official buildings, documents piled up in private houses, and empty fields in all directions," commented bitterly: "The officials in this area regard it merely as a wayside inn. They are concerned about tax collection and registers and have no time to ask about the people's problems."[48] At the same time, military disruption allowed repressed class tensions to surface. In 1682, a gazetteer writer noted that proper customs had lapsed during the years of military action, so that "people of the marketplace and clerks insulted the gentry; bondservants, hired laborers, and tenants raised lawsuits against their masters."[49]

MEASUREMENTS OF
LAND ABANDONMENT

It is difficult to measure exactly the amount of land abandoned during the seventeenth-century troubles, but some official surveys provide at least a rough guide. During the Ming and early Qing, taxes were levied on both land area and *ding* units. The *ding* originally corresponded to the number of adult male members of a household, but it was gradually transformed into an artificial fiscal unit. The early Qing rulers granted exemptions from the *ding* fiscal quotas to allow for people who had fled. Even though the *ding* figures represent fiscal units and not registered population, the distribution of *ding* exemptions provides some indication of the amount of destruction in the province (see Figure 9, Tables 7 and 8). Although the *ding* figures generally overstate the amount lost, there is also a correlation between the amount of *ding* exemptions and the amount of wasteland. In general, there was considerable damage around Dongting Lake and up the Xiang River Basin, forcing the population to flee the fertile lowlands for the hills. Farther upstream on the Xiang River, the proportion of *ding* lost is smaller. These more sparsely populated regions, located farther away from the main battle zones, may have been less damaged by rebellions. As Baoqing prefecture did not grant any exemptions, we cannot judge how great the losses were there; but the upper reaches of the Yuan River were relatively less damaged than the middle sections; Changde, on the lake, also seems to have had few losses.

Figures from Changsha prefecture provide a more detailed breakdown of wasteland created in each county by the Ming-Qing rebellions and by Wu Sangui's rebellions, respectively. They show that, overall, the prefecture lost 37.5 percent of its tax income during the transition period, and 23 percent after the Wu Sangui rebellion (see Table 7). More cultivated land was abandoned during the transition than during Wu Sangui's rebellion, but Wu's rebellion had a proportionately greater impact, since it came after a prolonged period of unrest. Thirty-six percent of the land was abandoned during the transition, but 41 percent of the remaining land had been abandoned

TABLE 7 Land Clearance and Abandonment: Changsha Prefecture
(in 1,000s of mou)

County	(1) Quota 1582	(2) Lost by 1667	(3) Cleared by 1667	(4) Waste 1679	(5) Falsely Cleared	(6) Cultivated 1680	(7) Cleared to 1681	(8) Cultivated 1685	Notes
Changsha	762	269	397	227	43	127	138	265	a
Shanhua	381	208	174	144	–	30	90	120	b
Xiangyin	770	306	464	192	–	272	143	415	
Liuyang	931	173	715	465	134	116	237	353	c
Liling	637	200	437	310	–	127	176	303	
Xiangtan	864	391	388	200	–	127	162	289	d
Ningxiang	784	586	197	198	–	177	197	374	e
Yiyang	955	232	613	238	93	283	177	460	c
Xiangxiang	1,336	611	725	214	127	384	177	511	f
You	721	251	470	–	68	–	–	402	
Anhua	285	15	270	–	–	270	–	270	
TOTAL	8,426	3,242	4,850	2,188	465	1,913	1,447	3,762	
Percent of Quota	100.0%	38.5%	57.6%	26.0%	5.5%	22.7%	17.2%	44.6%	

TABLE 7 *(continued)*

Total Tax Income: (taels)	Taels	Percent of Quota
Wanli reign (1573–1619) plus *jiuli* surcharges:	374,412	100.0%
Lost to wasteland and fled *ding*:	140,569	37.5%
Falsely reported cleared land:	22,815	6.1%
New wasteland (1674–1682):	86,138	23.0%
Total Collected (1685)	124,890	33.3%

Source: Changsha Fuzhi 1685.5 (does not include military colony land (*tuntian*) or land confiscated from Ming nobility (*gengmingtian*).

Columns: (1) Original registered land, 1582 (*tian, di, tang*); (2) Wasteland lost up to 1667 (except as noted); (3) Cultivated land area, 1667 (except as noted); (4) New wasteland (*xinhuang*) created, 1674–1679 (except as noted); (5) Falsely reported cleared land; (6) Cultivated land area, 1680 (except as noted); (7) Land cleared, 1680–1681 (for certain counties, 1682–1683). (8) Cultivated land area, 1685 (column 6 plus column 7).

Notes: a. Column (7) refers to 1682–1683.
b. Column (7) refers to 1681–1682.
c. Column (3) refers to 1664.
d. Column (3) refers to 1673.
e. Column (3) refers to 1671.
f. Column (3) refers to 1666.

FIGURE 9 *Ding* Exemptions as Percentage of Tax Quota, 1644–1685

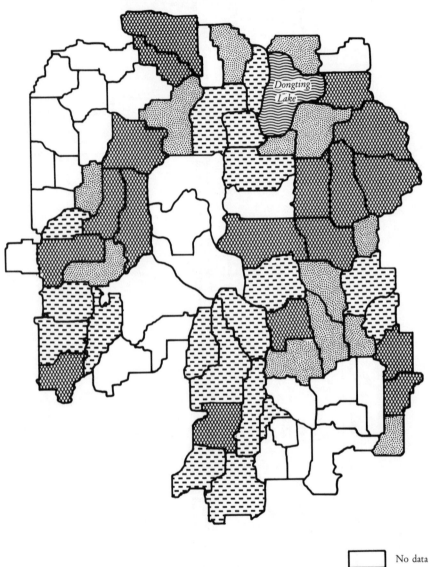

	No data
	10–40%
	40–70%
	70–90%

Source: Hunan Tongzhi, 1757, juan 24.

TABLE 8 *Ding* Exemptions in Changsha Prefecture

Place	(1) Quota	(2) Fled to 1674	(3) False Ding	(4) Newly Fled 1674–1679	(5) Remaining 1685	(6) % Land	(7) %Ding
Changsha	7,242	2,952	—	1,231	3,059	34.8	42.2
Shanhua	7,594	3,915	917	820	1,942	31.5	25.6
Xiangyin	15,705	3,519	—	1,279	10,907	53.9	69.4
Liuyang	9,195	—	1,102	3,503	4,590	37.9	49.9
Liling	5,588	1,514	—	1,469	2,605	47.6	46.6
Xiangtan	7,112	3,834	—	328	2,950	33.4	41.5
Ningxiang	11,230	8,281	—	334	2,615	47.7	23.3
Yiyang	11,310	4,196	1,068	2,758	3,288	48.2	29.1
Xiangxiang	21,033	11,492	129	1,370	8,042	38.2	38.2
You	6,115	1,978	—	—	4,137	55.8	67.7
Anhua	4,541	—	—	—	4,541	94.7	100.0
TOTAL	106,665	41,681	3,216	13,092	48,676	52.1%	45.6%

Source: Changsha Fuzhi 1685.6. Columns: (1) Original *ding* quota; (2) Number fled; (3) Falsely reported *ding*; (4) Newly fled 1674–1679 minus those returning 1680–1681; (5) Remaining *ding*, 1685 (= 1 − 2 − 3 − 4); (6) Cultivated land/original quota, in % (from Table 7); (7) Remaining *ding* / original quota, in % (column 5 / column 1).

71

by 1679. Only 27 percent of the land registered in 1581 was being cultivated in 1679. In effect, the agricultural settlement pattern of the late Ming had been inverted, leaving the prosperous lowlands desolate, while peasants sought protection in remote mountains.

RESETTLEMENT IN THE EARLY QING

After the military conquest of the Ming, the first task of Qing officials was to restore agricultural production. Local officials tried to call back refugees from other districts and encouraged peasants to return from remote mountain valleys to till the lowlands.[50] They enacted a two-pronged policy to bring wasteland back into cultivation and to reduce taxes on cultivated land. In some places, they first moved in military colonists to clear land. Troops collected surrendered rebels and refugees and settled them on abandoned military lands. In Ningxiang county, military officials were each given grants of land (*anchatian*) to settle in the county ranging from 50 to 150 *mou*.[51] For three years, from 1653 through 1655, the Qing rulers appropriated all non-taxed property to use for military settlement. They recruited cultivators, charging them heavy taxes, but promised that the land would become private land after three years. The policy was designed to produce revenues to support the Qing conquest of the southwest, but it was quickly abandoned when it became clear that the high tax rates were driving settlers off the land.[52]

Civilians, however, did most of the subsequent land clearance.[53] A variety of measures encouraged peasants to reclaim land. The *biao-chan* system in Xiangtan allowed anyone to claim land simply by planting bamboo markers on it and paying the land tax.[54] Liuyang county gave settlers on abandoned land, both natives and immigrants, tickets granting them permanent tenure after three years of cultivation.[55] In 1723, an edict announced a standardized program of land clearance, urging officials to invite in immigrants to clear land and to provide cattle, seeds, and tools to those who needed them. Paddy fields would be tax exempt for six years after clearance and dry fields for ten years.[56] Tax exemptions granted in times of famine also helped stimulate the recovery of agriculture. These exemptions were granted to individual counties on the basis of the degree of crop failure. From 1644 to 1701, in Hunan and Hupei combined, a total of 744 counties received such relief, an average of 13.3 counties per year.[57]

Tax exemptions were the main incentives offered by Qing officials to peasants who wanted to clear land. In addition, officials had to reorganize the complex Ming fiscal system. The inequities plaguing the Ming system persisted into the Qing, sometimes intensified by the confusion of the transition period. If a rational tax policy is one in which tax rates correspond to productivity, the late-Ming tax system represented the height of irrationality.[58] Some of the inequities dated from the beginning of the Ming dynasty. Because the Hongwu Emperor's rival, Chen Youliang, who had established his headquarters on Boyang Lake in Jiangxi province, supplied himself with grain from Changsha prefecture, Hongwu levied extra taxes on Changsha to punish the area.[59] Chaling *zhou,* for example, since it had supplied 40,000 *shi* of grain to Chen Youliang, was forced to provide the same amount to the Hongwu Emperor as its tax quota. The effect was to cause fertile land to remain uncleared and the population to decrease.[60] Taxes in Liuyang, unlike the rest of the prefecture, had been levied since the Yuan dynasty at a flat rate of 0.17 *shi* per *mou* regardless of the quality of the land, and Hongwu increased the rate to 0.214 *shi* per *mou.* The result was that, in fact, only one quarter of the tax quota was actually paid.[61] In Ningxiang county, "lower-middle" grade land was taxed the same as "upper-upper" grade land elsewhere, and "lower-lower" grade land as "upper-middle." Of the average lower and middle peasantry, 10 percent had fled, 20 percent served in the army, and 30–40 percent performed corvée labor, leaving fertile lands to turn barren.[62]

Local literati and officials continually made requests to have these irrational levies reduced. The Shunzhi Emperor refused to reduce them, saying that "surtaxes due to the revenge of the Ming emperors do not concern our dynasty."[63] The Kangxi Emperor also rejected requests by the provincial governor for general reductions, although Governor Zhao Shenqiao did achieve some partial reductions. Finally, after investigation revealed striking inequalities between the different counties of Changsha prefecture, the Qianlong Emperor in 1737 agreed to readjust all taxes in the prefecture so as to make them all equivalent to those of Changsha county. It had taken three and one half centuries for Hunanese taxpayers to recover from the Hongwu Emperor's spite.[64]

The Qing rulers took other steps to bring tax rates more closely in line with production. The Kangxi Emperor abolished the late-Ming surtaxes which had suddenly driven up the tax rates. Other efforts were made to adjust tax rates to the productivity of the land. On reed lands and silted lands around Dongting Lake, the tax rates were deliberately set in the lowest category. On other lands, tax categories were established according to yield. In Hengyang, for example, paddy land was classified as superior land (*shangtian*), which was defined as flat land with inexhaustible water supplies located near dense human settlements. Middle land (*zhongtian*) was land which yielded half a harvest when rains failed, and inferior land (*xiatian*) was rocky land which yielded no harvest without rain. Mountain lands (*shanxiang*), which yielded only one or two full harvests every ten years, were put in the lowest category.[65]

Although the new rulers did make some efforts to clear up the irrationalities of the Ming taxation system, the only way to have completely rationalized the tax system would have been to conduct a comprehensive national land survey. The early Qing rulers vacillated on this issue. The need for revenues and the urge to uncover concealed land drove them to order national land surveys in 1646, 1653, 1656, and 1663.[66] Yet, on each occasion, they drew back from such a survey and in fact undermined their own goals by stating that there was no need to resurvey the land if the amount cleared was equal to the quota of the Wanli reign in the Ming (1573–1615). After a few counties were surveyed in 1663, the idea of a national land survey was dropped. The abandonment of a comprehensive land survey represented a victory for the local gentry, who succeeded in allying with yamen clerks, large landowners, and local officials to frustrate any state attempts to discover their true landholdings. These coalitions were eventually able to win over provincial officials like Governor Zhou Zhaonan. He pleaded with the government to stop the land survey so as to spare his people the burden of supporting measurers, scribes, and yamen inspectors who would inevitably demand fees for their services.[67]

Henceforth, the Qing officials were forced to rely on the last reliable Ming survey, done from 1576 to 1580 by Zhang Juzheng.[68] They took the figures from this survey as the original quotas for land registration, deducted from them the amount of abandoned land, and added newly cleared land to arrive at the presently cultivated amount. For newly cleared land, they relied on the "self-reporting method," urging each landowner to report voluntarily the land he had cleared. Once the total land cleared reached the Wanli quota amount, however, very little further land clearance was reported.[69] Any land cleared beyond the Wanli quotas was effectively tax free. The Qing bureaucracy provided the greatest incentives for land clearance by tacitly agreeing not to tax any land cleared beyond the quotas of 1581.

The seventeenth- and early-eighteenth-century fiscal settlement had profound consequences. The failure to conduct an independent land survey and the reliance on local landholders to report their own cultivated land acreage left tax collection and assessment in the hands of the local elite. There was no drive by the central state to increase tax revenues and no effort to interfere in local collection. This left the imperial state with a relatively light grip on the collection of revenues. By contrast with seventeenth- and eighteenth-century Europe, where state-makers strove intensively to create rationalized bureaucratic systems of revenue collection, the Qing rulers remained satisfied with the status quo. The low level of tax collection did produce problems for local government, which was chronically underfunded.[70] A wide variety of extralegal surcharges developed to meet the costs of local administration, and the Yongzheng Emperor instigated an intensive campaign to incorporate many of these surcharges into the formal tax system. Yongzheng succeeded temporarily, but, after his reign, the same problem of inadequate tax levies producing informal surcharges reappeared. No further fundamental tax reforms were attempted.

The primary reason for this difference was the lack of military pressure. The demands of war were the primary force driving European states to create new forms of taxation.[71] Most new regular taxes originated, as in Brandenburg-Prussia, in "temporary" levies to provide for military needs. War stimulated both the creation of new levies and the growth of government apparatuses to assure their collection. Militarization, fiscal administration, and state bureaucracies were thus closely linked together.[72] From the defeat of the Three Feudatories in 1681 to the outbreak of the White Lotus Rebellion in 1796, the Qing rulers faced no external or internal military threats requiring major military reforms. China's revenues were based on relatively light taxation of a prosperous agrarian economy. European states, by contrast, had to extract greater levies from a more backward agricultural base. Brandenburg-Prussia, faced with creating a "first-rate state from a third-rate economy," relied on heavy agrarian levies which severely hampered the growth of the rural economy. England, on the other hand, was forced into innovative measures, particularly excise taxes and the creation of a national debt, to meet growing fiscal demands. The Qing rulers in the eighteenth century were fortunate in that they could meet the demands of the bureaucracy and military without unduly burdening the peasant, and they faced no pressure to tax commerce. On the other hand, the light hand of the state meant that the relative impact of state policies decreased as the economy grew.

The fiscal settlement of the early Qing reflected an established balance between local elites and the imperial state much closer to the English than the Prussian case. As in England, all landowners bore some share of the land tax and none were officially entitled to exemption. In fact, in both England and China, local assessment of taxes ensured that local gentry were highly favored in tax collection. Gentry authority in local government allowed part of the burden to be shifted to tenants and the landless. England, unlike China, derived much of its revenue from excise taxes levied both on luxuries and on necessities consumed by the poor.[73] China's nearly exclusive dependence on land taxes, and the merging of the poll tax with the land tax, meant that landowners nominally bore the entire tax burden. Surtaxes and customary fees, however, could be levied on all classes, and these provided the primary support of local government.

The structure of the Qing tax system indicates the relationship between the landed classes and the state. Shigeta Atsushi has argued that the merger of the land and poll taxes completed by 1712 meant the final establishment of "feudal" society.[74] Whereas the Ming system, which levied both poll and land taxes, implied that the state still had an interest in protecting the landless poor, the shift in the Qing to a purely land tax meant that the state had a strong interest in protecting the welfare of the landlord. This was reflected, Shigeta argues, in severe penalties in the law code for rent resistance and in tacit permission for landlords to pass on tax burdens to their tenants. From another point of view, however, the state secured the economic stability of the landowners by permitting under-registration of land and by not taxing gains from increasing productivity. Landowners in fact paid fixed tax quotas. Whatever surplus they produced was theirs to keep. Unhindered by state efforts to take more of their surplus, they could expand production to meet the needs of a growing population.

LOCAL SURVEYS AND LAND CLEARANCE

Although the Court rejected a national land survey, local officials did carry out their own surveys. Despite official claims that the purpose of these surveys was to equalize tax burdens, they almost always resulted in increased taxes. Huarong, for example, already suffered from high tax rates during the Ming dynasty, but these were not reduced by the Qing. In 1651, the district magistrate raised taxes by 3,000 *shi* to a total of 7,300 *shi*. A survey carried out in 1655 increased taxes again, while, over the next two decades, officials continued to encourage people to clear land. In 1691, another survey raised taxes by 3,700 *taels*, and, in 1700, another survey discovered 40,000 *mou* more of cleared land. As most of this land was low wetlands, it was taxed at a specially low rate. Nevertheless, from the local landowner's point of view, the district magistrate had "merely followed orders from above to increase taxes and did not consider the people's difficulties." Repeated requests for tax exemptions continued through the eighteenth century.[75]

While local landowners complained about heavy taxes, officials worried about concealment. They knew that, without thorough surveys, tax evaders could easily keep land off the registers. In the absence of a national survey, the Qing essentially relied on the landowner to report his own landholdings.[76] Many local officials rejected this approach, continuing to insist on the need for accurate surveys to uncover illegally concealed land or land that was deliberately placed in the wrong tax classification.[77] Owners of highly productive paddy land protected by dikes tried to register it as merely "superior land" (*gaotian*) for tax purposes.[78] The easiest places to conceal land from taxation were in the mountains and on the swamplands along the lake. Chen Changzhen estimated, in the 1750s, that 60 percent of the concealed land was mountain land (*shantian*) and 40 percent was lake land (*hutian*), while no land was concealed in the lowland areas (*pingtian*). He proposed to enact a system of land registration patterned on the *baojia* organization, dividing people into groups of ten who would be mutually responsible for reporting each others' landholdings.[79]

Although the central government had agreed not to press for discovery of all cleared land, local officials were in a different situation, as they were still under pressure from superior officials to meet their tax quotas. Even when the quotas were reduced to the level of 1581, this still caused problems in areas, like Hunan, where the cultivated land area had not yet recovered to the late-Ming level. It was in the local official's interest to bring the total registered land area back up to the 1581 level as quickly as possible, even if not all the wasteland had been cleared. Not only did the official gain a better tax base by clearing land, but, in 1658, rewards had been promised to provincial officials who cleared over 200,000 *mou*, prefectural officials who cleared over 100,000 *mou*, and county officials who cleared over 10,000 *mou* in one year.[80]

The zeal of these local officials, however, undermined the Qing government's efforts to encourage clearance of wasteland. Officials anxious to meet their tax quotas falsely reported much wasteland as having been cleared.[81] In Huarong, lands washed away by flood continued to be entered in the tax register despite local protests.[82] In Ningxiang, a magistrate gained 2,000 *shi* of revenue by the same means until the provincial governor stopped it in the 1660s.[83] The total amount of falsely reported wasteland amounted to 819,800 *mou* in 16 *zhou* and *xian*.[84] In the 1670s, edicts ended rewards to officials for clearing land and exempted taxes on falsely reported land.[85] Although these edicts did not end all abuses, they gave relief to land-owners and brought Qing land figures closer to reality. Table 7 shows that the amount of wasteland in Changsha prefecture was quite sub-stantial. In Xiangxiang county, also, 16 percent of the tax quota on registered land was first classified as wasteland, but 50,509 *mou* more, or 48 percent, was discovered by a subsequent survey and exempted as "new wasteland" before 1673.[86]

The late seventeenth century illustrates the conflicting goals of a new dynasty in a period of consolidation and reconstruction. The Qing rulers knew that restoration of agricultural production was a prerequisite to establishing stability. With a depleted population and a countryside filled with refugees, beggars, and bandits, the first prior-ity had to be placed on returning the peasants to the land. By pro-viding tax relief, the state could offer landowners strong incentives to put land into cultivation. Yet, at the same time, the new state needed a dependable source of tax revenues to finance its bureaucratic and military needs. In the early years of the dynasty, the Qing emperors had repeatedly offered tax exemptions of three to six years on re-claimed land, then withdrawn the exemptions as military campaigns like the defeat of the Southern Ming and the Three Feudatories de-manded more revenue. Efforts to promote land clearance were im-peded by illegal tax levies on newly cleared land.[87]

Qing tax policy was an outcome of these conflicting demands. Ulti-mately the state settled for collecting nearly the same amount as the Ming had collected in 1581, tacitly allowing powerful gentry land-owners to clear large amounts of tax-free land. Concern about con-cealment of land persisted, however, and edicts threatened to punish local officials who allowed taxable land to be reported as waste.[88] Local officials, however, were pulled between the twin objectives of restoring production and collecting revenue. The sporadic local sur-veys and efforts to uncover concealed land, or the false reporting of wasteland as cleared land, indicate that pressures to collect taxes persisted which could obstruct the extension of cultivation. In addition, many of the Ming surtaxes still remained, despite official prohibitions, since they were the only way to finance local government. Revolts against unequal taxes broke out in Wugang, Xupu, and Shimen in 1698.[89] By the end of the seventeenth century, Hunan had recovered significantly, but local surcharges still braked further production.

ZHAO SHENQIAO'S POLICIES
TO REVITALIZE HUNAN

The most effective policies to reinvigorate Hunan's production were carried out by Governor Zhao Shenqiao, who ruled the province from 1703 through 1710. In 1703, the Emperor instructed him to concentrate on reducing illegal surtaxes, particularly meltage fees (*huohao*), which were several times the regular quota (see Table 9). Arguing that the heavy taxes were causing many poor people to flee the province, he gave Zhao the responsibility of eliminating the tax surcharges and encouraging peasants to return to their fields.[90]

Hunan must have been a wild place when Zhao arrived. Throughout his tenure, he had to settle an extraordinary number of murder cases, fight bandits who infested mountainous areas, and protect merchant boats against attacks by pirates on Dongting Lake.[91] Frequent floods and droughts made life insecure, and families were still selling themselves into servitude.[92] Zhao arrived to find the province facing a drought, since no rain had fallen up to the middle of the 6th month. He distributed relief from the granaries and granted tax exemptions to those counties most in need. He made special efforts to ensure that grain loans and relief distributions at gruel stations actually reached the needy.[93] Finding that dikes destroyed in the Wu Sangui Rebellion still remained unrepaired thirty years later, Zhao provided funds to rebuild major waterworks and reestablish the dike administrators who had been responsible for their repair.[94] Zhao then moved to impeach officials guilty of collecting tax surcharges and abolished all surcharge collections.[95] At the same time, he exempted the people from payment of accumulated tax arrears.[96] By 1707, he reported that he

TABLE 9 Surtaxes Discovered by Zhao Shenqiao in Hunan, 1703–1710

County	Type	Charge
Xintian:	*lizhang* (tithing head)	10 *taels* / household
	changfu (servants)	12 *taels* / household
	zhishi (clerks)	1.2 *taels* / household
Xiangxiang:	surtax	0.3 *taels* / *shi*
	huohao (meltage fee)	2,700 *taels* total
	clerks' fees	0.12 *taels* / *shi*
		Total: 4,100 *taels*
	land tax surcharge	0.004 *taels* / *shi*
		Total: 2,793 *taels*
	haomi (wastage)	0.04 *shi* / *shi* tax
		Total: 990 *taels*
	collection expenses	0.05 *taels* / *shi*
		Total: 1,338 *taels*
Xinning:	*yabao* (guards) surtax	0.3 *tales* / *shi*
	(regular tax = 0.3 *taels* / *shi*)	
Yuezhou:	military grain *huohao*	0.56–0.70 *taels* / *shi*
	double wastage	2 *taels* / 50 *taels* tax
		1.1 *taels* / 30 *taels* tax
		0.9 *taels* / 20 *taels* tax
Chenxi:	wasteland tax	480 *shi*
	register fee	1.5 *taels* / *shi*
	Total:	720 *shi*

Source: Zhao Shenqiao, *Zizhi Guanshu*, 10.12a–24a, 14.5b; *Shenggao* 1.24b, 1.39a.

had eliminated all illegal surcharges, except in the areas controlled by tribal chieftains, who continued to collect taxes arbitrarily.[97] Zhao's claims were not literally true. In October 1710, the people of Liuyang county staged a revolt against excessive taxes by "surrounding the yamen, hanging out flags, and closing the market." They were protesting the actions of the assistant district magistrate, who had used his powers to send out 57 runners (*duchai*) to each of the subdivisions (*du*) of the county to collect a total of 200 *taels* of excess taxes which went into his gang's pockets. Zhao, recognizing the validity of the protest, impeached the assistant magistrate.[98]

Zhao also took measures to increase Hunan's grain supply. Knowing that the growing population was driving up the price of grain, he acted to ensure that granaries would be kept full and that merchants would not seek profits from hoarding. When he discovered large deficits in the granaries, he aimed to eliminate abuses in granary management by punishing collusion between large grain producers and granary officials.[99] He proposed to create additional granaries, called "publicly contributed charitable granaries" (*gongjuan yicang*), to supplement the activities of the ever-normal granaries in the cities.[100]

Zhao's study of Hunan's grain production indicated that the province, although still providing significant exports, was having difficulty satisfying both its own needs and those of other provinces. He pointed out that, while Hunan was known as an abundant grain producer, in actuality most of its territory was mountainous, and only Changsha, Hengzhou, and Changde prefectures were highly productive. Even these areas were vulnerable to frequent floods, and their populations lacked enough stored-up grain to last through a prolonged disaster.[101] When floods and droughts struck Hunan, it had difficulty feeding itself, let alone providing for the needs of other provinces. Hunan, in fact, at times even had difficulty sending grain out to relieve shortages in Hubei. Zhao sympathized with local officials who urged curbs on merchants exporting grain when these exports threatened to drive up the local price. When Changsha requested a prohibition on exports, Zhao approvingly remarked, "This is only storing up the locality's grain to supply the area's needs." Sometimes he was able to order prohibitions against "wicked merchants and outsider bullies who export grain," but at other times he was overruled by the Governor General's orders to "open up the blockages of grain" in order to supply the rest of the empire.[102] Zhao's actions indicate that the severe damage to Hunan's grain production had strained the ability of the province to supply both local and extra-local demands. The restoration of production temporarily relieved the tension, but the conflicting demands leading to blockages and food riots persisted. They would become more severe by the end of the century.[103]

Since Zhao's action earned him a good deal of unpopularity among those whose interests were damaged by his reforms, it is not surprising that attempts were made to remove him from office. In 1708, one of the local gentry named Song impeached him, claiming that every year had been a famine year since Zhao became Governor. Song blamed Zhao for the outbreak of a food riot in Changsha, when Zhao had forced grain merchants to keep grain in the province and sell it at a lower price to feed the hungry.[104] Song also claimed that Zhao had impeached 200 officials by "blowing on hairs and looking for scabs, overturning standards of right and wrong."[105]

It would be interesting to know more about the background of this impeachment effort, but the only sources available are Zhao's replies to the impeachment petition. Zhao survived the attempt to remove him and went on to attack further abuses in the province. In 1709, he found that false reporting of wasteland as already cleared still persisted, but he concluded that a more serious problem was the failure to report fertile land. Concealment of land meant either that the state lost revenue, or that more vulnerable taxpayers had to make up the missing amounts to fill up the quota (*baopei*). The burdens of *baopei* simply drove more people to abandon land, while powerful land-owners accumulated land and escaped taxation. *Baopei* also occurred when poor households were forced to sell land to relieve burdens of debt, and rich households took advantage of their plight by forcing the sellers to put falsely low tax rates in the sale contract. This allowed the rich households to buy lightly taxed land while leaving the poor sellers burdened with taxes on land they did not own. Zhao tried to enforce tax rates set only in proportion to the quality and amount of land, and he prohibited forcing sellers to set unrealistically low tax rates.[106]

Zhao distrusted the self-reporting method of land registration, because it allowed much fertile land to be reported as barren. He predicted, "A day will come when no more fertile land will be reported." Like other local officials, he insisted on the need for a land survey, but a province-wide survey was never conducted.[107] He was also aware that every investigation of land inevitably led to the levying of special fees, such as "expenses of the land register." He dismissed the magistrate of Chenxi county in 1707 for repeatedly collecting fees for making land registers. The total amount of tax on wasteland collected was 480 *shi,* and the magistrate levied a fee of 1.5 *taels* on each *shi* of tax collected.[108] Insistence on a land survey, however necessary to discover concealed land, would have completely undercut Zhao's efforts to eliminate tax surcharges. Although he ordered punishment of those concealing land, he concluded that it was better to encourage those concealing land to report it voluntarily by pardoning them.[109]

Zhao also tried to overcome the increasing disparities in land ownership produced by the disruption of the province. It was common for rich households to lend money to the poor in the critical period of early spring and collect the loan in kind after the fall harvest. For a loan of 1 *tael* they might receive 10 *shi* of grain in return. Eventually, the increasing debts would force the poor to sell their lands. Zhao tried to restrict the interest on loans to 3 percent per month and forbade the lending of silver for repayment in grain.[110] He also attempted to ensure that the benefits of tax exemptions reached the poor by requiring that landlords distribute three-tenths of every tax exemption to their tenants.[111] Zhao thus tried both to raise aggregate production and to alter the distribution of wealth.

The most drastic proposals for rectifying Hunan's administrative problems concerned the abolition of the post of *lizhang.* The *lizhang* in the Ming was a post held in rotation by the heads of members of a *li,* consisting of 110 households. The *lizhang* was responsible for delivering the taxes due from each *li,* and he had to make up personally any arrears. In the late Ming, increasing disparities of wealth, combined with land concealment, made the *lizhang* post ever more burdensome, driving many families into bankruptcy. The wealthy households who, as pillars of the local community, were supposed to act uprightly in performing the *lizhang* duties, were driven out by its burdens, and their place was taken by aggressive entrepreneurs who saw the *lizhang* as a source of opportunity for gaining wealth by practicing *baolan,* or tax engrossment.[112] Governor Zhao himself recognized that the worst of the illegal tax surcharges were the result of *baolan* practiced by the *lizhang.*[113]

In the late Ming and early Qing periods, reforms in Jiangsu and Zhejiang aimed to replace the *li* based on households by *li* based on territorial units and to replace the *lizhang's* responsibility for tax payment by individual household responsibility.[114] Many counties in Jiangsu and Zhejiang had carried out these reforms by 1670. By the 1700s, district magistrates in Hunan demanded similar reforms modeled on Jiangnan. The magistrate of Jiahe county complained that his district had no city walls and no granaries and was being burdened with levies double the ordinary amount for military needs as well as illegal surcharges. He noted that many households were concealing land and resisting tax payment, while the *lizhang* was still being held responsible for tax arrears. The *lizhang* either had to bear the burden himself, or, more commonly, raise more surcharges to pay the missing taxes. The Qiyang and Hengyang magistrates, pointing to the advantages of the Jiangnan system, urged shifting the *li* to a territorial basis and abolishing the *lizhang.*[115]

Governor Zhao was, however, ambivalent about the reform. He argued that, even if the *lizhang* were abolished, yamen clerks would have to be recruited for the same task. The basic fault lay in the inaccuracy of the land registers, which allowed landowners to conceal land. Although he admitted that earlier surveys in 1691 and 1705 had not solved the problem, Zhao called for further land surveys to discover the concealed land.[116]

The debate over the function of the *lizhang* in Hunan anticipated a national debate over the entire land-registration and tax-collection system (*lijia*).[117] Trends in the eighteenth century undermined the distinctive functions of the *lijia.* The freezing of the *ding* levy in 1712 and the merger of the *ding* with the land tax made the compilation of land registers useless. The quinquennial compilation of registers was abolished in 1772. The *lijia,* as a result, lost its distinctive function of land registration, but *lijia* leaders in many areas continued to abuse their powers of tax collection. Even though the Yongzheng and later emperors insisted that the established practice was that "the labor service imposts and land taxes are to be paid by the people in person," *lijia* leaders, along with yamen runners and local gentry, participated actively in *baolan,* the proxy collection and remittance of taxes.[118] Zhao's ambivalence about the reform of tax collection demonstrated penetrating insight into the fundamental problems of the Qing tax system.

Zhao's reforms greatly stimulated land clearance in Hunan. By 1724, the total amount of land had more than doubled over that registered in 1685 (see Table 4). From 1650 to 1717, the *Qingshilu* records the clearance of 11.4 million *mou* of new land in Hunan and Hubei, over one-quarter of the total amount recorded.[119] It did not take long for most areas to recover to the levels established by the quotas of the 1581 survey. Lizhou reported in 1713 that all its quota land was now cultivated.[120] Land clearance obviously did not stop at this point. Unfortunately, because land-tax quotas were fixed, the Qing officials were not interested in registering more land beyond the 1581 level, so we have little accurate information on later land clearance. There is evidence, however, that the limits of land clearance were nearly reached in the eighteenth century. Already by 1712, Hunanese were leaving the province for Sichuan, where land was more abundant.[121] The Qianlong Emperor's edict of 1766 indicated that he was aware that the supply of cultivable wasteland was running out. Recognizing that taxation was inhibiting the clearance of land in Hunan, he ordered the exemption of all taxes on "scattered bits of land" in mountain areas, which in Hunan amounted to less than 1 *mou* of paddy land per piece.[122]

By the middle of the century, local writers claimed that, "wherever there is the least bit of arable land, (the Hunanese) have cleared it."[123] Mountains were stripped bare and swamps were drained to produce the maximum amount of cultivated land. Forests that abounded in wood, bamboo, ramie, fiber, and charcoal exhausted their production as cultivated fields spread.[124] Local officials, while still under pressure to promote cultivation, began to report that there was no more arable land to be cleared.[125] Even wild areas like Sangzhi county, whose mountains were filled with tigers and leopards when the area was first opened to Han settlement by the Yongzheng Emperor in the 1720s, reported, by the 1760s, that the wild animals had disappeared and that "all the mountains have been turned into cultivated fields."[126] Around Dongting Lake, dikes proliferated to enclose new fields. By 1763, Governor Chen Hongmou reported: "All slightly high land is completely surrounded by dikes. They spread like fish scales all around the borders of the lake."[127]

Lacking precise figures, we must allow for exaggeration in these statements. Further clearance did proceed in the nineteenth century, but there was little good land left. Wei Yuan stated, in the 1830s, that "there was no more benefit to be had from clearing flat lands," and that landless peasants were moving out of Hunan to Guizhou, Guangdong, Sichuan, and Shaanxi.[128] By the Daoguang reign (1821–1850), the mountains of Hengyang county were bare, forcing local people to go into the city to buy imported firewood.[129] Deforestation of the mountains and clearance of all possible land was reported from Yiyang, Daozhou, and Qiyang in the 1870s.[130] The missionary Mortimer O'Sullivan, traveling through the province in 1897, was told that 90 percent of all available land had been cleared.[131] By that time, many Hunanese were turning away from agriculture and returning to boating or fishing for a livelihood. While the exact timing of the clearance process is uncertain, it is clear that the continually increasing population, urged on by official encouragement, progressively extended Hunan's cultivated land area throughout the eighteenth and early nineteenth centuries.

LAND CLEARANCE AND SOCIAL CONFLICT

The early Qing land policies had succeeded almost too well. The devastated lands were brought back quickly into cultivation, but the peasants continued to demand more land. In the eighteenth century, local observers anticipated further increases in the population running up against limits to the total cultivated land area. They expected a future impoverishment of the population unless efforts were made to make the existing land more productive.[132] Zhao Shenqiao had already recognized in 1708 that even Hunan's abundant grain supply had its limits in the face of a growing population.[133] In 1724, the Yongzheng Emperor, as he exhorted his officials to promote agriculture, noted that, "in the last several decades, the population has grown daily, but the land is limited."[134] The author of the Ningxiang gazetteer, wondering why the local people were so poor, asserted clearly that the cause was overpopulation:

> When there are too many people (*renman*) there is not enough land to contain them, there is not enough grain to feed them, and there are not enough wealthy people to take care of them . . . Where one man used to cultivate the land, he collects several men to cultivate it; where a tenant used to rent land for ten *jin*, he now borrows one hundred *jin* to rent it . . . Water rushes down violently from the mountains and the mountains become bare; earth is dug out from and rocks and the rocks are split; there is not an inch of cultivable land left.[134]

Other officials were concerned about the long-term ecological effects of excessive land clearance. In the mountains, peasants cleared many small plots of land without constructing reservoirs and dams. Relying primarily on natural rainfall and uncertain mountain streams, these settlers remained highly vulnerable to drought. If they built any waterworks at all, they constructed only small diversion dams across streams (*yan*) and not the large reservoirs (*tang*) necessary to ensure an adequate water supply.[135] Worse, in their eagerness to clear mountain lands, the new settlers often filled in existing reservoirs.[136]

Clearance of the mountains posed another danger, in the form of erosion. With the forest cover gone, "the earth was loose; when the big rains came, water rushed down from the highlands and mud and silt spread out below. Fertile areas near the mountains were repeatedly covered with sand and were abandoned."[137] Solving these problems required major official efforts to promote waterworks construction in the mountains.

Another problem with mountain land clearance which was becoming apparent in the early eighteenth century was conflict between

Han settlers and native tribesmen. In 1710, Zhao Shenqiao enforced the drawing of clear boundaries between Han and Miao lands by prohibiting land transactions between the two peoples. Any land sold by a Miao to a Han person had to be redeemed at its sale price and made into government land. Both the parties to the sale and the mediators were to be punished.[138] Despite all official efforts, commercial contact between Han and Miao continued to increase, because Han settlers persisted in encroaching on Miao territory. The great Miao Rebellion of 1795 was the ultimate outcome of this process, but the first signs were apparent as early as 1710. The Miao were no longer simply the wild peoples who conducted raids on the Han from impregnable mountains but were now becoming objects of commercial exploitation.

Indeed, it is striking how many of the tensions in the land market which were to grow during the eighteenth century had already appeared under Zhao Shenqiao's tenure. Military colonists' land became the focus of contention over claims to redeem land that had earlier been sold or mortgaged. In Tonggu garrison, the Ming military colonists were allowed to mortgage land but not to sell it. Because of their poverty, they had mortgaged over half their land in the Ming and early Qing eras. By the early eighteenth century, with the return of peace and the growth of population, the descendants of the Ming soldiers were claiming the right to buy back at the original sale price the land their ancestors had sold. They claimed these rights even if the land had already passed through several hands, or if the direct line of descent had died out. The mortgage-holders resisted, claiming that, since there was no written proof of these land transfers, no redemption rights existed. Zhao settled these disputes by affirming the right of military colonists' descendants to redeem the land, except in cases where the family line had died out.[139] The same kind of lawsuits occurred after 1709 over the *anchatian* settled by troops in Ningxiang, so that, in 1738, all of this land, which also was not allowed to be sold, was declared to be the same as ordinary private land.[140]

The effort to exercise redemption rights is a clear indication of the rising value of land in Hunan. It became worth the time and expense of a lawsuit to acquire land at its price of a century earlier. Governor

Zhao could recognize such customary claims, even though they were unwritten, because they applied to a limited group, the military colonists, who by law were not allowed to sell land. His successors would have to deal with a much wider range of conflicts over private land in cases where the law was not so clear (see Chapter 5).

As the pressure to find land increased, newly cleared land became the focus of intense competition. Struggles over rights to land became the main source of lawsuits in Hunan, some so severe that they lasted for over a century. When construction of a dike in Xiangyin county in 1747 created 667 *mou* of new land, the district magistrate anticipated a profusion of lawsuits over this fertile property. He solved the problem by declaring it to be government land to be used for the support of schools.[141] A land case brought to the governor in 1829 concerned land claims in Yuanjiang county dating back to the Kangxi reign.[142] Li Xiuxi's ancestors had occupied over 5,000 *mou* of silted land along the Wanzi Lake since the Kangxi reign. By the 1800s, 900 *mou* of this land remained in the possession of Li and his lineage. Next to his land was uncleared marshland which no one used, except to collect grasses and to fish in the lake. In 1818, Deng Chaoqun, hearing that the county was encouraging landowners to report their newly cleared land for taxation, took advantage of this policy to claim the marshland falsely as his own. He duly received a receipt granting him title to the land in 1823. Deng then built dikes around his land, drained out the water, and recruited tenants to cultivate the newly created land.

In 1824, Li Xiuxi raised his first lawsuit against Deng, but they were able to settle the suit by drawing a boundary line between their landholdings. Subsequent events proved that the boundary was not a very clear one. In 1826, Deng began to encroach by giving some land on the boundary to tenants to cultivate, and the tenants built shacks on Li's land. Li brought a suit a second time and succeeded in getting an official decision that the land was his; but the shacks were not torn down. Finally, at the end of 1826, Li and his lineage relatives took matters into their own hands and burnt down the shacks. This time the tenants together with Deng brought suit against Li. Meanwhile,

Li had sold the disputed land to Shi Jingguo, who put up his own shacks and hired guards to defend his crops. A disgruntled hired laborer, who was dissatisfied with what Shi was willing to pay him for clearing the land, led an attack on Shi's crops which provoked a battle in which four men were killed. The governor then had a murder case as well as a land suit on his hands. He settled it by dividing the land on the border into equal parts between Li and Deng, declaring any remaining wasteland to be government land, and forbidding further construction of dikes in the area, while ordering the destruction of those built by Deng.

The silting up of wasteland along Dongting Lake brought similar results in Baling county. The ancestors of Xu Guoru had owned land along the lake on which they paid a fish tax of 64.5 *taels*. They called in fishing households to fish for them. Nearby, the ancestors of Chen Weizhi had cut grass along the lake. The Chens and Xus had been feuding over land claims since the Kangxi reign, each accusing the other of plotting to take over his land. Their conflicts came to a head in 1823, when Xu's tenants tried to cut grass forcibly on Chen's land. They ended up fighting with Chen's tenants, and in the struggle one man died. In this case, the governor declared the disputed land to be government lands and made Chen and Xu each tenants on it, dividing the land equally between them.[143]

Such conflicts as these were the outcome of a growing population in the province looking for increasingly scarce cultivable land. Because landowners of even marginal lands along Dongting Lake were able to gain profits by recruiting tenants to clear land for them, it was worth fighting for rights to newly cleared land. Since, in theory, all silted-up lands along lakes and rivers belonged to the state, one solution to these land struggles was simply to confiscate the land. Qing officials, however, increasingly lost the ability to control the disposition of such lands during the eighteenth and nineteenth centuries, as more and more dikes were built by private landowners in defiance of official prohibitions. Only in drastic cases, where land quarrels led to murder, would officials intervene to take over disputed land.

As the succeeding chapters show, the successful recovery of

production in Hunan, which the seventeenth and early eighteenth century officials had tried so hard to promote, stimulated a variety of social conflicts which the Qing administration found increasingly difficult to settle. The fuel for these conflicts was the growing pressure of population on a province that was exhausting its supply of readily cultivable land.

FOUR

Immigration and Agricultural Productivity

Hunan's evolution from underpopulated periphery to densely settled core depended on a rapid increase in its population. The new settlements relied on a steady stream of immigrants from provinces downstream, drawn by the promise of easily available land and by the attractions of commercial activity in the new towns. Jiangxi, in particular, was the major source of migrants to Hunan. The clearance of hillsides and lake land, the development of export agriculture, and the opening of mines all attracted laborers from outside the province. Qing policy encouraged this new settlement, but the mobile population looking for a livelihood in the province could pose serious problems of social order. As Hunan filled up in the eighteenth century, easily cultivable land disappeared and mines were exhausted, but people continued to flood in from the even more crowded provinces downstream. Many were forced to leave Hunan for other areas to the south and west, or they turned to banditry when they could not make a living on the land.

Recognizing that cultivable land was being used up, local officials had to decide how to accommodate the ever-growing population. On the national scale, too, the Emperor and his advisers grew increasingly concerned about the uncontrollable movements of millions of peasants, laborers, and refugees, but they recognized that it was impossible to force them back to the villages forever. In the pre-industrial empire, commerce could absorb only a fraction of the labor force. The clearance of new land had been the classic answer of previous dynasties, but expansion of the land area alone was insufficient. As the population to land ratio increased, the promotion of greater yields from existing lands became the primary means of providing for the people's livelihood.

STATE-DIRECTED COLONIZATION

Hunan, because of its abundant quantities of uncleared land, had attracted immigrants from North China and the lower Yangtze Delta ever since the beginnings of the Chinese empire. Rebellions elsewhere in the empire were a major impetus driving refugees into Hunan. The first migration of Han Chinese to the province occurred around A.D. 12, when peasants moved from Xiangyang and Nanyang south into Hunan to open land.[1] A second wave came in A.D. 306, this time from the west, as rebellion in Shu drove refugees into the Huguang region. The Five Dynasties period (A.D. 907–960) brought another wave of migrants fleeing rebellions elsewhere.[2]

Military colonization was the other major form of migration to the region in early times, impelled by the strategic objective of controlling a sparsely populated frontier region. For example, in A.D. 1197, over 9,000 men were settled on garrison land in Chendingli, "scattered among uncultivated frontier lands and taught the use of arms."[3] The early Ming brought a second wave of military colonists, as garrison members were moved into Hunan in the Hongwu reign.[4] Added to the aboriginal populations, then, were two types of immigrants:

military colonists and civilian refugees, and these two groups often struggled with each other over control of land. In the late Ming era, officials frequently had to settle complaints about encroachment by "crafty" military colonists on civilian lands.[5]

Hunan, then, drew in immigrants, military and civil, both because of its strategic location controlling the corridor leading to the southwest and because of its relatively unpopulated fertile lands. Local officials, in order to increase their tax base and provide greater security, actively encouraged immigrants to come in and clear these lands. For example, in the early sixteenth century, after Magistrate Hu Mingshan of Ningxiang county, working for two years and spending several thousand *taels,* rebuilt the yamen, "people all knew of it and came in from other districts." Similarly, in the early Qing era, the assistant prefect in Lizhou "hired people" to clear mountainous garrison land which had gone to waste. After four years, he was able to build an office on Xiangyang Street (the name indicates the Hubei origin of the migrants), collect people there, and create a market town.[6]

AGRICULTURAL IMMIGRANTS

While officially encouraged immigration played a role, especially in the first years of a new dynasty, it was not essential to repopulating the region. Hunan's reputation as a fertile region alone was sufficient to draw in hordes of immigrants seeking new land. At first, apparently, people were attracted not so much by commercial profit as by the image of rich, self-sufficient lands. Areas like Liling county were described as having "land that is broad and fertile," where "the residents do not depend on the outside for anything. Many wanderers from all directions seek food and come there."[7] When there was drought or flood in the vulnerable districts of Mianyang and Jianli, just to the north in Hubei, crowds of up to several hundred people formed "teams" (*dui*) and went to the county offices in Hunan crying for loans of grain. Officials in charge of relief had to feed these refugees, and, despite their best efforts to send the migrants home, many stayed to settle in the south.[8] There was even a slave trade running human traffic between Hubei and Hunan, in which Hubei people sold themselves to slave traders (*maizhu*), who drew up contracts of personal bondage and brought the victims on boats to Hunan, bribing customs officials along the way, to provide women and laborers in the south.[9]

Immigrants spread all over the province, from the most fertile lake lands to the most remote forests and mountains. The highly productive lowlands around Dongting Lake and along the Xiang River had, of course, great drawing power both to outsiders and to Hunanese from poorer mountain lands. In the late Ming period, fertile Xiangtan was flooded with people migrating from more remote land in Changsha prefecture. Local official Li Tengfang's efforts to enact the Single Whip Reform in Xiangtan were in vain, because the local elite there successfully resisted the incorporation of the poll tax into the land tax and profited from the failure to register the new migrants.[10] The diked polders in Huarong county drew in people from the surrounding mountains, because "one year's harvest for the polder peasants was equal to several years' harvest in the mountains." While there was danger of flooding in the lowlands, it was less than the danger of drought in the highlands, and during floods one could always go fishing on the lake while waiting for the waters to subside.[11]

In the mountains, too, away from the lake, immigrant laborers were essential for promoting agricultural production. In Liuyang and other areas along the Jiangxi border, the "shack people" (*pengmin*), in the case of Liuyang mostly from Guangdong, settled the mountains as tenants and engaged in rent disputes with their landlords. All over South China these mountain settlers were the first to respond to state encouragement to clear wasteland. Unlike uprooted refugees, they brought their own tools and animals with them, the men and women worked together in the fields, and the women did not bind their feet. The mountain people also pioneered in the introduction of New-World crops.[12] Local people or earlier immigrants profited from the influx of laborers to relieve themselves of the need to work in the fields, as in Wugang *zhou*. Wugang had better soil than other counties in Baoqing prefecture, but the farmers there were said to be "somewhat lazy" because immigrant workers from Qiyang and Xiangxiang toiled in the fields.[13] The evolution of settlement in Yongzhou prefecture in the early Qing era indicates a similar pattern probably typical of many areas. The first immigrants arrived in the depopulated region after a period of upheaval (in the case cited, the Miao Rebellion of the late eighteenth century; in other cases the Ming-Qing transition), setting themselves up as independent farmers by clearing the wasteland. Later on, they were able to entrust farming to immigrants who served them as tenants. The new landlords, now wealthier than before, remained on their lands and did not put their profits into commerce. As a result, "the advantage increasingly fell into the hands of immigrants from outside," that is, a second group of immigrant merchants who took control of trade.[14]

Besides the merchants, to be discussed below, there were new arrivals who took advantage of the profits from growing cash crops. In the mountainous parts of eastern Yuezhou prefecture, especially Pingjiang county, immigrants from Jiangxi developed a trade in forest products, cutting trees and planting new food crops like sweet potatoes, tobacco, and sorghum. Jiangxi immigrants also dominated the trade in "wood ears," an edible tree fungus, which was particularly important in this area. As tenants, they cut down the withered trees on which the fungus grew and in the winter opened shops to sell the wood ears they had harvested.[15] Immigrants also gathered the *ge* fiber and sold it for making cloth, as well as producing ramie (*ning*) and indigo.

In You county, further south on the Jiangxi border, immigrants from Fujian, Guangdong, and Jiangxi all "lived in the mountains and not in the lowlands, cutting down the hillsides with hoes." These foresters, "arrogant by nature" with "rough customs," were difficult for local officials to include in the population registers, but excluding them, "treating them like wild beasts," would have meant burdening the lowland people unfairly. The policy adopted toward them was to "transform their nature so that they learn civilization and their fierceness disappears." In other words, these Han immigrants were to be treated just like non-Han tribesmen or barbarian tributary states.[16]

In fact, all the immigrants, as they spread over the province, constituted a difficult problem of registration and local control, precisely because they, like tributaries and native tribespeople, were beyond the pale of settled Chinese peasant society. While officials encouraged immigration with grants of tax-free land, and loans of seed, tools, and animals when it was urgent to restore wasteland to production, sooner or later local people (who may themselves have been the product of an earlier wave of immigration) were bound to resent the excess tax burden forced on them because of immigrant exemptions, and officials suffered loss of tax revenues. In Changsha county, for example, where migrants with "bare hands and open jaws" went to seek food, "production was not completely done by locals, and people did not perform corvée, so households grew accustomed to being in arrears on taxes."[17]

The problem was worse in the case of immigrant merchants and students, who were legally exempted from corvée. In Xiangtan in 1553, "the city population was dense, but most were immigrant merchants who do not bear corvée, so the rest of the people were burdened" with their taxes.[18] In Xiangyin county, charitable land was established to support examination candidates for the first time in 1563, and in 1564 two immigrants were selected as students, but "others protested, saying, 'How can these two as outsiders be exempted while local people take over their corvée duties?' so the students were each ordered to pay a fee of 30 *taels*."[19]

Besides tax evasion and exemption, immigrants posed a threat to social order. Even the lowlands and swamps around Dongting Lake served as excellent hiding places for pirates with swift, light boats, who dashed out and plundered merchant and passenger traffic across the lake.[20] The most dangerous regions, however, were the mining districts of southern Hunan. Coal, iron, lead, and tin were produced abundantly there since at least the late Ming dynasty. In Hengzhou prefecture in the sixteenth century, merchants gathered from all around and opened over 30 tin mines, employing "several hundred thousand men." But the miners were regarded as "unreliable refugees" who committed all kinds of crimes and conspired to form "death squads" (*sidang*), so it was proposed to establish a police office (*xunjiansi*) there.[21] Miner refugees collected in Guiyang *zhou* and Chenzhou, often turning to banditry and mingling with minority tribes.[22]

The mines flourished in the late Ming, but, by the early eighteenth century, formerly productive mines in Leiyang and Guiyang had been exhausted, while the 48 mines in Maogang in Yongding county, which had been so dominated by Jiangnan traders that the area was called "Little Nanking," yielded decreasing returns by the end of the Qianlong reign.[23] At the same time, local officials moved to shut down the mines in order to stop the flow of migrants to these regions. The time of closing varied from place to place. Some of Dongan's mines were closed in 1694, and others in 1709. In Leiyang *xian* and Wugang *zhou*, local officials tried to subvert some closing orders by giving out unauthorized licenses to mountain landlords to run mines.[24] Coal mines in Shanhua ordered closed in 1795 by the district magistrate were reopened by members of the Zou lineage in 1814. When the local official repeated his prohibition, "masses collected" to reopen them in 1817. Finally, the prohibition had to be carved in stone.[25] An edict of 1735 allowed mines to remain in 68 places, including Anhua, because they were not in frontier regions, but it tried to enforce mining by local people only, forbidding immigrant miners from coming in and prohibiting merchants from selling the ore outside the county.[26]

From these policies we can conclude that Qing officials were by no means biased against profits from mining. Their main concern was to ensure that profits from mineral pursuits flowed into the local communities that possessed the ore and not into the hands of vagrants, floating miners, and outside merchants. In this aim, the interests of central and local officials worked in tandem with those of the Hunanese, who felt entitled to their share of local production and found opportunity to express their resentments at being deprived of it by commercial outsiders.

MERCHANT IMMIGRANTS

While probably fewer in number, ultimately of greater significance in overall social impact were the immigrants who came to work in trade and crafts. As the example of Yongzhou above indicates, the Hunanese generally did not participate in commerce. Although Hunanese migrated within the province in search of new land, once settled securely on the land they did not care to move.[27] Even if they migrated temporarily, they often returned to their home counties, and they put all their surplus wealth into land.[28] Nor did they excel in crafts. While local artisans produced some crude articles for daily use, refined articles of bamboo, wood, stone, textiles, and trades like house repairs were mostly handled by skilled artisans from outside the province.[29] In Xiangtan, native and immigrant artisans recruited by the government collected in two separate workshops (*chang*), although both worshiped the same deity, Lu Ban, at the same temple.[30] Some of these artisans came in originally on contract to perform a specific job and returned home when it was done, but gradually more artisans came to settle in Hunan.[31] By the nineteenth century, the Hunanese also gradually began to learn certain crafts from the immigrants, such as the making of cotton paper and hide boxes, or they developed new crafts on their own, as in Yuanzhou in 1790, when some workers began to quarry a special local stone and widely sell refined carved inkstones.[32]

The largest profits, however, were to be found in commerce, both small-scale local trade and large-scale interprovincial trade. Non-Hunanese dominated both spheres. Trading had begun to develop in certain areas in the late Ming, and local literati complained about the spread of customs of extravagance undermining an idealized rural simplicity,[33] but most of the province remained relatively untouched by interregional commerce in the sixteenth century. It was in the eighteenth century, particularly the Qianlong reign, that commercial prosperity spread widely over Hunan.[34] Boats run by guild merchants plied the major rivers, carrying oil, wax, iron, salt, wood, cloth, paper, and drugs.[35] By the 1740s, the market had begun to transform even remote regions like Ningyuan, where in the early eighteenth century many people were said to have lived seventy years without entering a city.[36] Although tea and cotton did not become major export items until the nineteenth century, certain areas, like Anhua county in Changde prefecture, were already in the eighteenth century attracting tea merchants from Guizhou, Sichuan, Fujian, Guangdong, Guangxi, Jiangsu, Zhejiang, Shaanxi, and Henan.[37] In areas like Yuanzhou, which did not have a great export trade or large-scale guild merchants, many immigrant shopkeepers participated in rural marketing.[38]

In major commercial centers near Dongting Lake, some Hunanese did set up shops for local trade, but there they were overpowered by the highly capitalized export merchants. In the rice trade at Changsha, Hunanese served as local millers and operated local rice shops, while outside merchants controlled the bulk of the export trade.[39] In addition, the hired laborers and porters servicing the wholesale merchants were outsiders, guaranteed near monopoly of the labor market by their fellow provincials.[40]

JIANGXI IMMIGRANTS AND COMMERCIAL CONTROL IN HUNAN

Immigrants poured into Hunan from all directions: from the lower Yangtze Valley, from Jiangxi, from Hubei and sometimes Sichuan, and from Guangdong, Guangxi, and Fujian. There was, to some extent, regional specialization in the occupations and motivations of the different groups. People from the south and southeast were either shack people in the mountains or artisans and petty traders, mostly in southern Hunan. Those from the lower Yangtze came looking for fertile agricultural land, or they were involved in wholesale interprovincial trade. Many migrants from Hubei were refugees forced out by floods of the Yangtze, seeking relief grain and, if possible, new land. But of all the groups, the people from Jiangxi had the most longlasting and pervasive impact on the province. Jiangxi people had begun arriving in Hunan at least as early as the Song and Five Dynasties period,[41] but the classic text on this immigration pattern comes from the Ming, written by the noted scholar Qiu Jun (1420–1495), author of the famous administrative manual *Daxue Yanyibu* (Supplement to *The Great Learning*).[42] He noted that Jiangxi people were moving to the Huguang region because of the excess population and lack of food supplies at home, and that the "people of Huguang feel different from the people of Jiangxi and the Jiangxi people feel separate from the people of Huguang."[43] Since the immigrants, who paid no tax in Huguang, meant a loss of revenue for the government, Qiu proposed a "policy of assimilation" which involved registering new immigrants as tax-paying households, including information about their origins, their status, their masters (if they were tenants or laborers), their military units, and their occupations. Qiu intended to have tenants as well as landlords pay tax or contribute labor according to their ability, and he ordered single men and women to marry according to their local customs, bringing in spouses from Jiangxi. His goal was to encourage the increase of population in Huguang and to open up uncultivated land, while maintaining careful registration of the population and ensuring tax revenues for the government. It is noteworthy that he recognized the distinctiveness of the immigrants' customs from those of their hosts and that he did not expect any intermarriage between the two groups.

While some assimilation must have occurred, an awareness always persisted among the Hunanese that the Jiangxi people, despite being neighbors and fellow Han, were basically foreigners. The perceptive German traveler Baron von Richthofen in 1870 noted the persistence of these distinctions. He observed that the Hunanese, who had turned to soldiering as a profitable profession during the Taiping Rebellion, were characterized by honesty, a strong sense of self-reliance, but also a certain crudity, while the Jiangxi people were basically non-military, excelled in petty commerce, and "held a large part of the middle and lower Yangtze in their hands."[44]

Besides the scattered references to Jiangxi immigrants that appear in local gazetteers, the predominance of Jiangxi people in Hunan also appears in genealogies of local Hunanese lineages. Tan Qixiang used some of these genealogies extensively in his pioneering study of immigration to Hunan.[45] Ping-ti Ho has criticized the use of such genealogies, pointing out that they do not provide an accurate record of the pattern of immigration over time, because it required a long period of time for a family to establish itself and become prominent enough to produce a genealogy. Thus, Ho argues, although most of the lineages recorded in the genealogies migrated in the Ming dynasty or earlier, this does not necessarily mean that immigration slackened or that Hunan became a net emigrating province in the Qing.[46]

Ho's admonition on the use of genealogies, however, does not invalidate their use as a source. While the picture they give of immigration over time may be inaccurate, there is no reason to believe that they give inadequate information about the origins of the migrants. Furthermore, several sets of genealogies compiled in the Republican period, not used by Ho or Tan, do include a considerable number of Qing immigrant lineages. In fact, they show a greater number of immigrants arriving during the Qing than during the Ming. The data from the genealogies is presented in Tables 10 through 13, which clearly illustrate the overwhelming predominance of Jiangxi immigrants in the settlement of Hunan. In addition, the immigrants are not randomly drawn from all over Jiangxi, nor are they found predominantly in the counties nearest the provincial border. The practice of chain migration, in which new arrivals in Hunan drew in more relatives and fellow countrymen from home, is clearly illustrated by the linkage of certain Jiangxi counties as suppliers to Hunanese receptors—for example Taihe to Xupu, Fengcheng to Liuyang, and Lüling to Rucheng. These links between counties further increased the distinctive character of the Jiangxi migrants.

Migration routes are difficult to trace, but occasionally there is information on the path the migrants took, especially when they made several moves in succession. Many people did not go directly west over the low mountains into Hunan but went north first, following the river systems, sometimes stopping in Hubei for a period of time, then moving gradually south along the major rivers. This was not true of the officials stationed in Hunan who later settled there, but even in those cases there seems to have been a certain amount of prospecting around before they picked a place to settle. They did not necessarily settle in the county or prefecture in which they had served.

In some districts, Jiangxi people are said to have constituted "all" or "nine-tenths" of the total population.[47] When Xinhua was repopulated after the suppression of a tribal rebellion which had caused the Han population to flee to neighboring counties, over half the new registrants came from Ji'an prefecture in Jiangxi. Even allowing for exaggeration by literati writers, there is no doubt from the figures

TABLE 10 Origins of Hunanese Migrants

Origin	Present Abode							Total	Percent
	Baoqing fu	Jing zhou	Liling xian	Liuyang xian	Rucheng xian	Xiangyin xian	Xupu xian		
Anhui	5	5	4	–	4	3	2	23	1.3
Fujian	5	2	51	3	5	7	–	73	4.0
Guangdong	–	–	75	22	58	–	–	155	8.5
Guangxi	3	2	–	1	1	–	–	7	0.4
Guizhou	–	–	–	–	–	–	9	9	0.5
Hebei	7	1	–	–	1	–	–	9	0.5
Henan	13	2	6	–	1	7	4	33	1.8
Hubei	6	–	8	2	2	12	1	31	1.7
Hunan	40	3	81	21	55	12	323	535	29.5
Jiangsu	22	6	12	–	6	11	1	58	3.2
Jiangxi	168	14	309	71	52	142	78	834	46.0
Shaanxi	–	–	–	–	1	1	–	2	0.1
Shandong	2	2	1	–	–	2	2	9	0.5
Shanxi	1	–	2	–	–	–	1	4	0.2
Sichuan	1	1	4	2	–	1	4	13	0.7
Yunnan	–	–	1	1	–	–	–	2	0.1
Zhejiang	2	2	6	3	1	–	3	17	0.9
TOTAL	275	40	560	126	187	198	428	1814	100.0

Sources: Xupu Xianzhi, 1921, shizu; Liuyang Xianzhi, 1967.6; Rucheng Xianzhi, 1932.28–30; Liling Xiangtuzhi, 1926; Tan Qixiang, Table 2.

TABLE 11 Origins of Hunanese Lineages from Jiangxi

Origin	Abode			Total
	Xupu	*Liuyang*	*Rucheng*	
Jiangxi (unspecified)	18	10	5	33
1. NORTH JIANGXI				
Nanchang *fu*	–	8	–	8
Nanchang	3	–	–	3
Xinjian	1	1	–	2
Fengcheng	4	18	1	23
Jinxian	3	–	–	3
Fengxin	2	3	–	5
Ruizhou *fu*	1	–	–	1
Gaoan	1	3	–	4
Shanggao	–	4	–	4
Xinchang	–	4	–	4
Nankang *fu*	–	–	1	1
Xingzi	1	–	–	1
Xiushui	–	4	–	4
		TOTAL:		63
2. CENTRAL JIANGXI				
Fuzhou *fu*	–	1	–	1
Dongxiang	2	4	–	6
Xiajiang	4	1	–	5
Fuzhou	–	1	–	1
Jinxi	2	1	–	3
Linchuan	–	2	2	4
Linjiang *fu*				
Xin-gan	2	–	–	2
Qingjiang	–	1	–	1
Ji-an *fu*	8	1	2	11
Lüling	–	2	16	18
Taihe	12	1	5	18
Jishui	11	1	7	19
Yongfeng	1	–	–	1
Lianhua	–	–	1	1
Yongxin	1	–	–	1
Jianchang *fu*				
Nanfeng	–	3	2	5
Xincheng	–	1	–	1
Yuanzhou *fu*	–	1	–	1

TABLE 11 *(continued)*

Origin	Abode			Total
	Xupu	Liuyang	Rucheng	
Wanzai	–	1	–	1
Yichun	–	–	1	1
Pingxiang	–	2	–	2
		TOTAL		103
3. SOUTH JIANGXI				
Ningdu *zhou*				
Ruijin	–	1	–	1
Nan'an *fu*				
Nankang	–	–	1	1
Shangyou	–	–	3	3
Chongyi	–	–	1	1
Ganzhou *fu*				
Gan	–	–	2	2
Xinfeng	–	–	1	1
Longnan	–	–	2	2
		TOTAL		11
TOTAL				210

Sources: Same as Table 10.

above that a substantial majority of the Hunanese could trace their origins back to Jiangxi. The period of greatest predominance of Jiangxi migrants seems to have been the early Ming. Tan is probably correct in stating that the Qing period saw a greater diversification of migrant origins, with a rise in prominence of migrants from Fujian and elsewhere.[48] In Yizhang, in 1756, it was said that "the military people sound like people from Chaling *zhou* (in Hunan), the merchants speak like Jiangxi people, and the newest immigrants like Fujianese."[49]

The abolition of the autonomy of native chieftains by the Yongzheng Emperor opened up many tribal areas to Han settlement, producing a new wave of immigration to southern and western Hunan. Ho may be correct in asserting that Hunan did not become a net emigrating province in the Qing era, but there was an outflow of migrants to Sichuan in the eighteenth century, as Wei Yuan noticed,

TABLE 12 Hunanese Intraprovincial Migration

County	Destination		
	Xupu	*Liuyang*	*Rucheng*
CHANGSHA *fu*			
Changsha	–	6	–
Shanhua	–	1	–
Xiangtan	–	–	1
Xiangxiang	14	–	–
Liling	1	–	–
Ningxiang	1	–	–
Yiyang	1	–	–
Anhua	10	–	–
Chaling	1	2	1
BAOQING *fu*	13	–	–
Shaoyang	20	–	–
Xinhua	55	–	–
Wugang	3	–	–
YUEZHOU *fu*			
Pingjiang	1	10	–
CHANGDE *fu*	3	–	–
Wuling	–	1	–
HENGZHOU *fu*	–	–	1
Qingquan	–	–	1
Hengyang	–	–	1
Hengshan	–	1	–
Ling	–	–	1
YONGZHOU *fu*			
Ningyuan	–	–	1
CHENZHOU *fu*			
Yuanling	158	–	–
Chenxi	24	–	–
Lüxi	7	–	–
YUANZHOU *fu*			
Qianyang	1	–	–
Mayang	2	–	–
LIZHOU *zhilizhou*			
Lizhou	2	–	–
JINGZHOU *zhilizhou*			
Huitong	2	–	–
Tongdao	1	–	–

TABLE 12 *(continued)*

County	Xupu	Liuyang	Rucheng
		Destination	
CHHENZHOU *zhilizhou*			
Chhenzhou	–	–	3
Yizhang	–	–	24
Xingning	–	–	10
Guidong	–	–	10
FENGHUANG *ting*	1	–	–
Total	321	21	54

Sources: Same as Table 10.

TABLE 13 Hunanese Migrants: Dates of Migration

Time	Xupu	Liuyang	Rucheng	Total
		Abode		
1. Year Undesignated				
Tang (A.D. 618–906)	–	3	2	5
Five Dynasties				
(907–959)	1	5	4	10
Song (960–1278)	32	17	30	79
Yuan (1279–1367)	23	20	12	55
Ming (1368–1643)	75	13	15	103
Qing (1644–1911)	16	–	–	16
2. Year Given				
1360	3	25	9	37
1380	–	–	4	4
1400	23	2	4	29
1420	1	–	–	1
1440	3	3	1	7
1460	–	3	1	4
1480	–	1	6	7
1500	–	–	3	3

TABLE 13 *(continued)*

Time	Abode			Total
	Xupu	*Liuyang*	*Rucheng*	*Total*
1520	1	5	6	12
1540	2	2	4	8
1560	1	–	–	1
1580	7	–	8	15
1600	–	1	–	1
1620	5	1	13	19
1640	27	2	7	36
1660–1680	95	31	25	151
1700	1	–	–	1
1720	11	2	5	18
1740	5	–	–	5
1760–1780	35	2	17	54
1800	7	1	1	9
1820	12	–	–	12
1840	5	–	–	5
1860	3	–	–	3
1880	3	–	–	1
Total	395	139	177	711

3. Totals by Dynasty	*Number*	*Percent*
Tang	5	0.7
Five Dynasties	10	1.4
Song	79	11.1
Yuan	92	·12.9
Ming	250	35.2
Qing	275	38.7
	711	100.0

Sources: Same as Table 10.

and a tide of migrants leaving Hunan or passing through on the way to open up the southwest.[50] Nevertheless, the Jiangxi migrants, old and new, still retained their relative predominance because of their commercial wealth and strong local associations. The first brick house in Xinning county was built by members of the Liu lineage from Jiangxi, as was the first charitable granary after the Taiping

Rebellion.[51] City streets named "Jiangxi Street" or "Migrants' Street" (*yourenjie*) indicate that Jiangxi people and other migrants clustered together with their fellow provincials. In so doing, they kept alive their distinctiveness from the surrounding native population.

IMMIGRANTS AND LOCALS: CONFLICT AND COOPERATION

This description provides only a sketch of the immigration process in Hunan, many of the contours of which still remain unknown. There are only a few fragmentary figures on the total number of immigrants to a district at any point in time, and these vary greatly, so it would be rash to extrapolate any overall estimate from these data. What stands out most of all is the diversity of the immigrants. They came to Hunan as cultivating peasants (both lowland farmers and shack-building mountain dwellers), agricultural laborers, fishermen, miners, skilled craftsmen, woodcutters, famine refugees, small peddlers, and large wholesale merchants. They covered the entire province, adapting their activities to the requirements of diverse local economies. In so doing they contributed greatly to the revival of the Hunanese economy in the Qing period. They brought in seeds of early-ripening rice which stimulated agricultural productivity (see Table 15).[52] They opened up barren hillsides and wasteland to new cultivation. They opened mines in remote regions. They raised the standard of living in backward areas and introduced new customs, like brick houses, along with new opportunities for trade.

The Hunanese certainly benefited along with the immigrants from the new opportunities. Their overall welfare may indeed have improved.[53] But this does not mean that benefits were equally distributed, or that there was not resentment at the disproportionate share of the new prosperity taken by the outsiders, particularly the astute traders from Jiangxi. Very conservative literati had one ax to grind, as they complained about the moral degeneration produced by the spread of "lavish customs," seen most plainly in the proliferation of lawsuits, for which the Hunanese were notorious. John Watt has plausibly suggested that litigation became more frequent in the eighteenth century because of continual disputes over use of arable land by an expanding population.[54] Local gazetteer writers tended to blame this litigation on the corrupting effects of commerce and, by implication, on the immigrants who had brought in new lifestyles and new opportunities for wealth.[55]

It was not only reactionary Confucians looking back to the virtues of rural simplicity who had reason to resent the influx of outsiders. As mentioned above, local officials feared an excess influx of laborers to mining and forest regions, people who were "arrogant by nature" and likely to turn to banditry. In Daozhou, over half the population settling there after the Ming-Qing rebellions consisted of immigrants, who engaged in trade, crafts, and clearance of mountain lands. A local writer had no objection to those who lived there peacefully, but he attacked woodcutters and miners without families, who gathered there in the thousands moving to and fro, hiding in deep forests beyond the reach of *baojia* officials. When the price of grain rose, they harassed local producers and merchants, provoking the local people to attack them and causing great conflict.[56]

In the north of the province, on the Hubei border, the hordes of refugees fleeing Yangtze River floods to seek food in the south threatened local order. Refugees colluded with local bandits to extract grain coercively. "If they got slightly angry, they destroyed people's houses, and there were many cases of killing." The local writer recognized the need to relieve these vagrants (*liumin*) if they were truly in need, but he also emphasized the burden they placed on Hunan, and he tried to urge Hubei officials to take measures to bring the refugees home. He stressed that "the local people (in Hunan) are accumulating great resentment" and urged that measures be taken before the two groups harmed each other.[57]

Thus, it was not only literati and local officials who feared or resented the newcomers. There is some evidence that popular attitudes were similar. It was common to note that merchants prospered from the increasing trade in the eighteenth century, but that the peasants remained poor.[58] In Huarong, it was said that local people got only

20 to 30 percent of the profits from the fertile lake lands, because outside landlords from Lizhou, Jingzhou, Longyang, Yuanjiang, and Yiyang controlled the land and rented it out.[59]

The role of immigrants in Hunan, then, was double-edged. Immigrants were welcomed when they were needed to resettle devastated lands and when they brought in scarce skills and promoted trade, but there was always an underlying awareness of their separateness and latent anxiety about their disruptive potential, combined with resentment at their greater economic success. Officials concerned about the exhaustion of cultivable land after the mid-eighteenth century recognized that tensions were growing as the population increased and the Hunanese found fewer resources available to them. In 1819, Hunanese resentment burst out in a major riot against Jiangxi domination of the commercial economy.[60]

One solution to the problem was emigration. As people flowed into Hunan, Hunanese began to leave for richer territories. Many migrants moved through Hunan into as yet uncultivated lands in the southwest (Guangxi, Guizhou, and Yunnan), but Sichuan seems to have been particularly attractive.[61] The Yongzheng Emperor had already noticed this pattern in 1728, when he complained that labor contractors were enticing people to Sichuan from Hunan and other provinces with false promises of cheap land and low prices.[62] Some Hunanese could make a go of it in Sichuan, but others, unsuccessful there as well, turned to preying on the boat traffic up and down the Yangtze. The Hunanese emigrant population proved to be as troublesome outside the province as the immigrants within it.

The careers of Liu Laoshi, Luo Tianfu, and their followers, are instructive in this respect. Luo was originally from Shaoyang county in Hunan, until he followed his father to Chengdu to open a food shop, where he came to know his fellow shop-owner, Liu Laoshi. When his father died, Luo went to work in Liu's shop. In July 1778, Liu ran out of capital and closed his shop. Along with Luo and five other men, he discussed turning to banditry. Together they attacked and plundered travelers along the Yangtze, expanding their band and setting up a lair in the mountains, attracting recruits from other migrants to Sichuan. They, along with many other similar bands, became known as "*guolu* bandits" or *guofei*.[63] Soon, pursued by government troops, they moved back into Hunan to plunder in Changde prefecture, until they were finally captured and executed while stealing from the Jiangxi provincial guild hall in Longyang county. The court decided that in the case of *guofei* there was no need to distinguish between leader and follower and sentenced all the members to execution.[64]

This episode (which is not an isolated one) sheds light on the mysterious *guofei* who infested Sichuan in the late eighteenth century.[65] The *guofei* were not a single band but a large number of scattered small bands without any elaborate organization, composed predominantly of immigrants to Sichuan. The *guofei* did not confine their predations to Sichuan but were apt to spill over into adjacent provinces or return to their home provinces in search of loot. Much more could be said about these groups, but with our focus on Hunan it is worth stressing these points: that some of the immigrants to Hunan did not succeed in establishing themselves there and turned to banditry, and that they ended up returning to Hunan to prey on their fellow provincials or on Jiangxi immigrants. In light of the discussion of Jiangxi merchants above, it is particularly interesting that Liu and his confederates ended their criminal career with an attempt on a Jiangxi guild hall. Like all good Hunanese, they knew who owned the wealth in the province.

INCREASING AGRICULTURAL PRODUCTION IN THE EIGHTEENTH CENTURY

The social problems caused by the immigrants were fundamentally a result of the growing scarcity of agricultural land. As the supply of cultivable land was used up, officials had to look for other ways to stimulate increased production in the province. By 1773, they had concluded that, while there was land to be cleared in Xinjiang and the remote frontiers, in interior China "there may be wasteland here and there, but in very small amounts."[66] Recognizing that there was little more to be expected from further land clearance, they turned to promoting higher yields on existing fields. They encouraged both double-cropping on fertile rice paddies and the planting of more productive New-World crops on marginal hill lands. Qing officials aimed to help peasants overcome obstacles to the spread of double-cropping and early rice seeds.

The main cropping systems in Qing Hunan were those producing rice on the lowlands and "miscellaneous grains" (*zaliang*) in the highlands. With the growth of population and market demand in the eighteenth century, both types of agriculture became progressively more intensive. Two trends stand out: the clearance of nearly all possible mountain land to plant grain crops, and the spread of double-cropping on the lowlands, facilitated by early rice seeds. The meaning of "double-cropping" must be made clear. For the most part, it was not double-cropping of rice, that is, an early rice crop followed by a late rice crop on the same plot. A few references indicate that this form of production did exist on some of the lowlands around the lake in the nineteenth century, or possibly the eighteenth century, but it cannot have been predominant (see Table 14).[67] In 1949, double-cropped rice was planted on only 2 million *mou*, or 7 percent of the total amount of land planted in rice. By 1957, over 10 million *mou* were double-cropped with rice, but only in the Xiangtan special district was slightly over half (53 percent) the cultivated-rice area double-cropped.[68]

Officials had made several ineffective efforts to promote double-cropping of rice in the early eighteenth century. In 1733, Governor Zhao Hongen reported on the possibility of planting a late rice crop in areas near the lake in Huarong. In 1743, Governor Jiang Pu again tried to encourage double-cropping, but he met with little response.[69] Most references to "double-cropping" in gazetteers appear to mean either successive planting of early and late rice on different plots of land, or alternation of rice with other crops (see Table 14). Seldom is there an unambiguous statement that two crops of rice were grown on the same plot of land. Jiang Pu had proposed to command one or two households to plant a late rice crop in the middle of the 6th month, after harvesting the early rice crop, but the Emperor

TABLE 14 Single- and Double-Cropping in Hunan

	Single-Cropping		
Place	*Year*	*Crop*	*Note*
Xiangxiang	1587	rice	90% of land is rice, one crop per year
Yongzhou *fu*	1670	rice	Grown by Yao in mountains; if crop fails they beg for food outside
Xiangxiang	1685	rice	No *zaliang* grown
Liling	1745	rice	Cattle let into fields after harvest
Dao *zhou*	1745	rice	Official efforts to encourage double-cropping rejected by peasants because "water is too cold"
Changsha *fu*	1747	rice	One crop per year
Hunan	1752	all	One crop followed by fallow
Xiangtan	1756	rice	One crop per year; other crops encouraged but people fail to respond
Xiangtan	1781	rice	Same
Changde *fu*	1813	rice	Single crops in mountains; in north and east areas bordering lake, beans and wheat grown after rice
Xiangtan	1818	rice	Only one rice harvest per year
Hengshan	1823	rice	Peasants on plains grow paddy rice
Chengbu	1868	*zaliang*	Peasants lazy, cattle let into fields
Qiyang	1870	rice	No second crop as land not suitable for wheat; peasants urged to plant auxiliary crop
Xiangtan	1889	rice	Rice the only crop, vulnerable to flood
Yongxing	1906	rice	Single-crop rice in valleys, buckwheat, etc. in mountains

TABLE 14 *(continued)*

	Double-Cropping		
Place	Year	Crop	Note
Xiangtan	1553	early/late rice	
Yongming	1716	early/late rice	Not on same plot, "people seldom work hard"
Jianghua	1729		Double-cropping, rice dominates
Hunan	1733	early/late rice	Possible to replant late rice after flood
Hunan	1743	early/late rice	
Yizhang	1756	rice/rice, millet, wheat	
Yuanjiang	1810	early/late rice	On same plot?
Liuyang	1818	rice/*zaliang*	On low wet, lands
Xiangyin	1818	early/late rice	Lowlands
Xiangyin	1818	rice/*zaliang*	Highlands
Wuling	1868	rice/rice	Level land two crops; hilly land one crop
Liling	1871	rice/rice	Lowland only good for rice
You	1871	rice/buckwheat	
Baling	1873	rice/*zaliang*	Dry land
Baling	1873	rice/rice	Land west of river
Yiyang	1874	early/late rice	Lower districts
Yiyang	1874	rice/buckwheat	Upper districts
Liuyang	1880?	rice/rice	
Leiyang	1885	rice/wheat-buck-wheat	Profit very low; most land only one crop
Liling	1926	rice/rice	Late rice planted between rows of early rice

Sources: Xiangxiang Xianzhi 1825.10.25, Yongzhou Fuzhi 1670.24.42, Xiangxiang Xianzhi 1673.15.41b, Yongxing Xiangtuzhi 1906.1.58, Changsha Fuzhi 1747.14.6a, HNSLCA hu 8.6 (1745), GZD-QL #1872, 1752.5.26, Xiangtan Xianzhi 1756.13.5a, Xiangtan Xianzhi 1781.14.4b, Changde Fuzhi 1813.13.1, Xiangtan Xianzhi 1818.39.3b, Hengshan Xianzhi 1823.18.7b, Chengbu Xianzhi, 1867.10.33b, Qiyang Xianzhi 1870.22.5b, Xiangtan Xianzhi, 1889.6.8b, Xiangtan Xianzhi 1553.1.14, Yongming Xianzhi 1716.2.3a, Jianghua Xianzhi 1729, Zhupi Yuzhi 1733, QSL 1743.8.7, Yizhang Xianzhi 1756.4.5, Yuanjiang Xianzhi 1810.18.2, Liuyang Xianzhi 1818, Xiangyin Xianzhi 1818.17.2b, Wuling Xianzhi 1868.28.1a, Liling Xianzhi 1871.1.24, You Xianzhi 1871.18.2a–3a, Baling Xianzhi 1873.11.10, Yiyang Xianzhi 1874.2.66, Liuyang Xianzhi, 1967.13.26B, Leiyang Xianzhi 1885.7, Liling Xiangtuzhi, 1926.6.24.

discouraged him, saying, "You should not harm the people by attempting to get quick results."[70]

The main form of double-cropping in eighteenth-century Hunan was rice followed by another food crop, usually sweet potatoes, wheat, buckwheat, maize, or beans. Many different forms of crop rotation were practiced—over 100 types were in use in Hunan in the 1950s.[71] The most important forms depended on planting an early rice crop, which was harvested in the 6th lunar month, and following it with the second crop harvested in the 10th month. The early rice depended on the Champa rice seeds first introduced into the lower Yangtze Valley from southeast Asia in the Song dynasty.[72] Early rice seeds had spread rapidly in Changsha prefecture from the eleventh through thirteenth centuries, but double-cropping systems made little headway in the Song because of the scarcity of labor.[73] Early rice seeds do not seem to have made their way to other prefectures in Hunan until the late Ming era. There is evidence of early rice in Baoqing and Hengzhou prefectures in the late sixteenth century. The distribution of early-rice seeds shows them spreading up the entire Xiang River Valley during the mid-eighteenth century. By the early nineteenth century, the seeds had spread farther, up the Yuan River to the western periphery. Jiangxi was the source of the fastest ripening and most widely used seed, the "Jiangxi early" (*Jiangxi zao*), which ripened in 60 days (see Table 15).[74]

The primary reason for the spread of the seeds was not to increase grain production but to protect against disaster. Provincial Treasurer Bulaichao noted in the 1760s that "over half" of the Hunanese planted early rice because of their concern about flooding.[75] In lowland areas, peasants could hope to harvest an early rice crop in the 6th or 7th month before the summer flood waters arrived; then, even if the floods arrived before the harvest was over, at least part of the crop could be saved.[76] The development of special late rice seeds allowed farmers to plant another rice crop after the flood waters had subsided.[77] In 1733, Governor Zhao Hongen, fearing that floods in the end of the 5th month had damaged crops in Baling, Linxiang, and Huarong counties, urged that late rice seeds be planted after the flood waters subsided. These examples show that planting a second rice

TABLE 15 Early Rice Seeds in Hunan

Place	Latest Date Not Mentioned	Earliest Date Mentioned	Notes
Changsha *fu*			
Changsha	1685	1747	1817, early, middle, and late rice found
Shanhua		1747	
Xiangtan		1553	
Xiangyin		1756	
Xiangxiang		1673	
Ningxiang		1682	
Yiyang		1874	
Liuyang	1680	1818	
Anhua	1545	1872	
Liling	1744	1871	
You		1871	many varieties
Baoqing *fu*		1567	(location not specified) many varieties
Shaoyang		1877	
Xinhua		1549	
Xinning		1823	
Wugang		1746	
Yuezhou *fu*	1736	1746	(location not specified)
Linxiang		1685	
Pingjiang		1680	
Huarong	1760		
Changde *fu*	1671	1813	(location not specified)
Wuling		1873	
Taoyuan	1685	1821	
Yuanjiang		1810	
Hengzhou *fu*		1593	(location not specified)
Hengyang		1761	

TABLE 15 *(continued)*

Place	Latest Date Not Mentioned	Earliest Date Mentioned	Notes
Hengshan	1488	1774	seeds arrived in 1746
Leiyang		1725	
Yongzhou *fu*	1495	1694	(location not specified)
Lingling		1828	
Qiyang		1765	
Dongan		1752	
Ningyuan		1754	
Yongming		1716	
Jianghua		1654	
Chenzhou *fu*	1765		
Yuanling	1708		
Xupu	1684		
Yuanzhou *fu*			
Zhijiang		1839	
Yongshun *fu*			
Yongshun	1874		
Sangzhi		1764	
Guzhangping		20th century	very little rice grown
Lizhou		1750	(location not specified)
Anfu	1667	1869	more than 10 varieties of seeds
Chhenzhou			
Chhenzhou	1665	1772	
Yongxing		1762	
Yizhang		1756	

TABLE 15 *(continued)*

Place	Latest Date Not Mentioned	Earliest Date Mentioned	Notes
Qianzhou *ting*	1739	1877	
Fenghuang *ting*	1758	1824	
Yongsui *ting*		1909	

Sources: see Chapter 4, note 74.

crop was not yet a common practice in these areas but only an expedient to be adopted in emergencies.

It was, however, in the highlands that the new seeds became most widely used, since early rice seeds were more important for protection against drought than against flood. In 1694, three counties of Yongzhou prefecture (Lingling, Qianyang, and Dongan) were said to have no worries about drought in the fall, while four other counties (Daozhou, Ningyuan, Yongming, and Jianghua), which lacked early rice, still faced that danger.[78] One or two decades later, Yongming and Jianghua acquired the early seeds from Baoqing.[79] The early-rice crops in the highlands were important not so much in themselves, since their yield was very low, but as insurance against a drought which could destroy the more important fall crop.[80] Some areas, like You county, that had a large percentage of hilly land planted early rice on up to 60 to 70 percent of the cultivated area, while in Changsha county, which was mainly lowland, there was very little of it.[81]

Although several studies have highlighted the contribution of early-rice crops to China's food supply, it is also important to recognize that local conditions limited the spread of the new seeds.[82] Most of the native Miao area in western Hunan did not really have early-rice seeds at all in the eighteenth century. Seeds called "early" rice there were harvested in the 8th month, much later than early crops in other areas of the province. What was called "early" rice in western Hunan corresponded to "middle" rice in the rest of the province.[83]

Still, the spread of early-rice seeds is an important illustration of how Chinese peasants sought to improve the security of their crop production by adapting cropping patterns to local conditions. This process of adaptation involved not simply raising agricultural output but finding the combination of seeds and crops that would maximize protection against natural disaster. There were "iron-foot" varieties of seeds with long, tough roots for hard soil, "cold-water-red" seeds which could endure the water from mountain wells, and "flat-sand rice" which could withstand wind and rain. Fifty, 60, and 70-day varieties were valued for their rapid ripening times. Names like "save-from-famine early rice" (*jiuhuangzao*) and "rescue-from-hardship grain" (*jiuqongliang*) indicate the subsistence value of the new seeds.[84] The process of crop adaptation in rice production culminated in three basic types of rice crops: early rice, grown on high lands, giving low yields but providing insurance against full drought; middle rice, the highest-yielding variety, grown as a primary food and export crop on secure plains and well-diked lowlands; and late rice (*chongyang nuo*), grown only on the lowest and wettest lands after the summer floods had receded.[85]

The calendar of cropping in Hunan was remarkably similar all over the province and over a long period of time (see Table 16). Early-rice seeds were soaked in water and planted in seedbeds in the middle of the 2nd lunar month, around the vernal equinox. After sprouting in the 3rd month, they were transplanted to the fields. The grain was always harvested in the 6th lunar month. Middle rice followed the same schedule with a delay of half a month to a whole month, and was harvested at *chushu* (16th day of the 7th lunar month). Late rice was usually soaked and planted in the third month. The traditional planting date was the *qingming* festival beginning in the 3rd lunar month. Some varieties were planted later, the latest possible date being *mangzhong* ("grain in ear"), the beginning of the 5th month. Seeds were transplanted in the 4th month, irrigated in the 5th and 6th months, and harvested in the 7th to 8th months. The latest variety, called *chongyang* (9th month) grain, grown only on low swamplands, was harvested in the 9th month.

Nearly the whole province followed this schedule, except for the Miao regions in the west. There, early rice was planted in the 3rd and

TABLE 16 The Agricultural Calendar in Hunan

Crop	Lunar Month											
	1	2	3	4	5	6	7	8	9	10	11	12
Early rice	planting	sprouting	transplanting		harvest							
Middle rice		planting	sprouting	transplanting		harvest						
Late rice			planting———				harvest———					
Chongyang rice					planting				harvest			
Other crops			planting———					harvest———				
Winter wheat				harvest					planting			
Granaries				Grain sales———			Restocking———					

4th months and harvested in the 8th month, while late grains were planted in the 4th month and harvested in the 9th to 10th months.[86]

Non-rice crops followed a less rigid schedule. Maize could be planted early in the 3rd month and harvested in the 6th month, or it could be grown as a fall crop. Gaoliang, millet, wheat, buckwheat, rapeseed, and sesame were generally planted in the 3rd to 4th month and harvested in the 9th or 10th month. The winter-wheat crop, where it was grown, planted in the 9th month, could be harvested in the 4th month of the next year, helping the peasant family over the hardships of what the French call the *soudure*, the difficult time in early spring when "the brown (winter crops) and green (spring crops) do not join" (*qinghuang bujie*).

Provincial officials kept watch on the progress of the harvest cycle by reporting monthly on the price and prospects for harvest of each crop. The schedules of restocking and selling of granaries had to be adjusted to the current supply and demand on the market.[87] By intervening at the appropriate time, selling grain particularly in the short period of the 4th and 5th months, and restocking in the 7th to 9th month, officials aimed to keep prices stable, and most of the time they succeeded. The available price reports of this period rarely give seasonal fluctuations of more than 2 or 3 percent per month. From a low point in the harvest season, prices rose gradually through the winter, reaching a peak in the early spring. This was the time when the granaries unloaded their stocks to damp down price rises in preparation for the early rice harvest. Usually, when the early rice harvest was good, prices leveled off and remained steady through the fall (see Figure 10).

Qing officials recognized the importance of new rice seeds for keeping prices stable, but they put the greatest emphasis on the second crop following the rice crop. Noting that population growth was outrunning the available food supply, they urged peasants to increase the cultivation of a variety of non-rice grains. They aimed to take advantage of the new rice strains to promote a crop of rice followed by a *zaliang* crop. While prices might be stable throughout the year, the long-term trend of rising prices increasingly concerned them.

FIGURE 10 Grain Prices in Hunan, 1801–1802
(high-grade rice, average price)

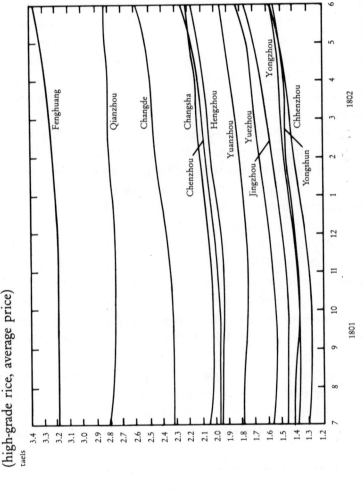

Sources: *GZD-JQ* (1801.8); #6104 (1801.9); #6331 (1801.10); #6705 (1801.11); #7260 (1802.1); #7691 (1802.3); #8476 (1802.5); #8306 (1802.6).

124

Governor Fan Shishou noted in 1752 that the highest price in Hunan used to be 1.5 to 1.6 *taels* per *shi,* but that now there were areas where the price was up to 2 *taels* per *shi.*[88] By 1801, prices averaged over 2 *taels* per *shi* in Changsha and Hengzhou, the most productive areas of the province, and over 3 *taels* per *shi* in remote areas like Fenghuang (see Figure 10).

The official strategy was deliberately aimed at satisfying the needs of the poor. The district magistrate of Chengbu noted that, because of population growth, "the price of grain has gradually risen. As the prices rise, the profit goes to the rich, and the poor who depend on a *sheng* and *dou* of rice daily are burdened." If more *zaliang* were planted, he argued, prices would be lowered and, even if the rich hoarded grain, they would be unable to raise the price.[89]

In encouraging new crops, officials often concentrated their efforts on promoting winter wheat, the widespread food crop of North China. Wheat, however, was not grown very successfully in Hunan. It was grown in some areas around Dongting Lake, but even there not too commonly; in Changde prefecture, it was planted on only one thirtieth of the land area.[90] At first, officials attributed the limited cultivation of wheat to peasant "laziness," but soon they were forced to admit that "it is not entirely due to the people's laziness but probably also because the soil is not suited" to wheat.[91] They had to recognize that objective factors of soil and climate thwarted the most earnest exhortations. They did, however, have some success in the long run. While only 10 counties reported a wheat harvest in 1752, 20 did so in 1755 and 33 in 1837.[92] Although wheat was grown in less than half of Hunan's counties, it did have a significant effect in easing the food shortages of the early spring. Governor Qian Baochen reported that it was a "great help" to have the winter-wheat crop come on the market at the critical *soudure* in the 4th month.[93]

Local administration ran into difficulties in places where there was no winter-wheat crop. Officials did not want to open the granaries until the beginning of the 4th month, since they knew that, if they distributed granary stores too early, the supply would not last until the early-rice crop arrived in the 6th to 7th month. This meant that the 3rd month of the year was the tightest period, when the Hunanese poor had to get by on stores from the winter, gentry contributions, and privately run soup kitchens.[94] The lack of wheat also meant that farmers had trouble paying taxes twice a year. They could rely on the fall harvest to pay the fall taxes, but they had few resources to pay in the 4th month when, in theory, one-half of the taxes fell due. In 1838, the provincial governor received permission to adapt tax collection procedures to fit the harvest cycle by allowing taxpayers to pay most of what they owed in the fall.[95]

Much more common than wheat was buckwheat, which was found in nearly every county of the province. It could be planted in both spring and fall. Maize, from the New World, was a more recent import which withstood drought well. Sometimes maize even replaced rice cultivation because of its hardiness.[96] It produced a large harvest with little labor, and it adapted well to newly cleared mountain land and areas still using slash-and-burn agriculture. Locally, it was called the "precious grain" (*baogu*).[97] At first, poor farmers went into the mountains and "planted maize wherever they found flat land," cooking it into a form of gruel which they ate themselves. Later, maize became a marketed product as well.[98] Although maize was widely planted, there were areas, such as Dongan and Yongshun, where it was not found in the eighteenth century. In most of the province, it had been introduced only recently.[99]

Sweet potatoes, brought in from Fujian, were another recent arrival which had the advantage of producing tremendous yields. One *mou* of land could produce a harvest of several tens of *shi*, enough to feed a family for a year. Their main disadvantage was their taste, disliked by Han Chinese. Native tribespeople and outsiders took to the new crop more readily than the Hunanese. Immigrants from Guangdong and Fujian, forced to occupy poor mountain lands, were the first to introduce sweet potatoes to Yuezhou prefecture.[100] Sweet potatoes began to spread in counties like You *xian* only in the middle of the nineteenth century.[101] By the end of the century, however, all the mountain dwellers made their whole diet out of sweet potatoes; they sold their rice for cash.

MOUNTAIN RESERVOIRS AND DAMS

Besides the introduction of new crops, the improvement of yields in the highland periphery depended on adequate water supplies. During the eighteenth century, officials were shocked to find how many peasants in the highlands relied solely on rainfall, and they put strenuous efforts into promoting the construction of reservoirs. In the seventeenth century, when taxes were unequally levied, peasants in poor regions lacked the capital to construct the reservoirs that would improve their livelihood. Nine-tenths of the population of Xiangxiang in 1673 depended on rainfall for irrigation, because taxes took away all the surplus they could have used to build reservoirs. The district magistrate requested the elimination of 9,904 *shi* of taxes levied on wasteland which had falsely been reported as cleared, in order to provide the people with the capital to build reservoirs.[102] The tax reforms of the early eighteenth century, which relieved much of the burden on the poor districts, made investment in waterworks possible.

During the first half of the eighteenth century, local officials actively encouraged the hill peoples to shift from complete reliance on *zaliang* crops toward more intensive cultivation by digging reservoirs and building dams.[103] Varieties of waterworks proliferated through the mountains in the eighteenth and nineteenth centuries. The terminology of waterworks is not entirely consistent, but several broad categories can be distinguished. *Ba* were the largest dams, built of huge stone blocks to dam up large mountain streams, diverting them to irrigate hundreds or thousands of *mou*.[104] *Pi* and *yan* designated dams built across smaller streams. *Zhen* and *qu* were long narrow channels which directed the water directly from the streams or from the dammed up holding areas to the fields.

Often, on the hillsides, many fields were located higher than the water source. The channels directed the rapidly flowing water into water pumps (*tongche*) which lifted the water up in buckets to the field level.[105] These pumps could irrigate several hundred *mou*. Where water pumps would not work, oxen were used to turn norias, made of a wheel on a wooden frame, with slots to lift the water onto the field. Where oxen were lacking, human labor was used.[106]

Tang, on the other hand, were reservoirs located in low places to collect water naturally for use in times of drought. The hill districts faced constant unpredictable threats of both flood and drought. Ten days without rain in Zhijiang county, for example, produced a drought, while three days of constant rain created floods.[107] As the dams and reservoirs spread through the mountains, they gradually made agricultural production more secure. Table 17 lists the number of different types of waterworks built in Chhenzhou in the eighteenth century.

As in other features of agricultural production, official promotion alone was not enough. Some private landowners put up capital for substantial waterworks. In the seventeenth century, the Li family in Chenzhou prefecture was able to produce three crops a year along the banks of a small mountain stream. They harvested winter wheat in the 4th and 5th month, after which they let water into the fields and planted paddy rice. After harvesting rice in the 7th month, they planted buckwheat, followed by winter wheat in the 9th and 10th months. A large dike built over a century earlier diverting the river water to the Li family's fields made such intensive cropping possible. When the family neglected repairs on the dike, it collapsed, and their fields were flooded.[108]

The construction of waterworks often determined settlement patterns. Each of the 27 dams listed for Changde prefecture in 1684 is directly associated with one village.[109] Waterworks construction was also critical to the penetration of native tribal areas by Han settlers. After the Miao Rebellion in Qianzhou, the prefect deputed soldiers to encourage settlers along the river to dam the streams and dredge the river. This both facilitated agricultural settlement and allowed boats to carry large numbers of troops into the Miao "nests."[110]

Despite official and private efforts, many counties, like Yuanling, still lacked reservoirs in the eighteenth century. The local populations, dependent on uncertain rainfall, could be self-sufficient only in good years. When the rains failed, relief supplies had to be brought in from more prosperous counties.[111] Many other mountain regions did not have well-developed irrigation works. In Yuanzhou in 1790,

TABLE 17 Waterworks in Chhenzhou, 1772

County	Type			
	Pi	Ba	Tang	Yan
Chhenzhou *benzhou*	17	44	44	
Yongxing	38		43	3
Yizhang	8	17	5	3
Xingning	60		29	
Guiyang	8		8	
Guidong	11			9

Source: *Chhenzhou Zongzhi*, 1772, *juan* 4.

the people were said to be "working hard at opening up new land but inept in irrigating the land." Peasants relied primarily on natural sources of irrigation and rarely built dams or irrigation ponds. Some peasants labored cooperatively on well sweeps but they regarded this as "hard work." The water wheel (*tongche*) had only arrived recently.[112] In Mayang, as late as 1873, yields were much lower in the northern and eastern parts of the county, which had few dikes or dams, than in the south and west, which had access to mountain streams.[113]

In fact, there were serious obstacles to rapid waterworks development. In the early stages of settlement, the most serious was the scarcity of labor. Accusations of "laziness" by local officials really reflect the fact that the population was too sparse to build large projects. The same situation obtained in the entire province during the Song, when the same accusations of "laziness" were common.[114] The increasing population in the eighteenth century provided sufficient labor, but lack of capital still prevented much construction. In the early eighteenth century, Hunanese officials encouraged "landlords to put up capital and tenants to put up labor," just as in Jiangnan. The state treasury gave assistance in large projects.[115] Even when the state or wealthy landlords could put up the capital, the transaction costs of negotiating agreements on reservoirs and mobilizing the labor remained high. There were strong incentives, as population pressure grew, to clear land for crops rather than sacrifice it for a reservoir of common benefit.[116] In the 1750s, governors Yang Xifu and Fan Shishou repeatedly had to prohibit the filling in of upstream reservoirs.[117] Water wheels along major rivers could obstruct boat traffic. Some local bullies used such obstructions to extort fees from passing merchants. Official policy supported the construction of all water wheels that were needed for irrigation and did not completely obstruct the river.[118]

Even after reservoirs were built, they had to be maintained. The failure to dredge ponds allowed many of them to dry up, if there was no official supervision.[119] Even in 1741, the Lingling magistrate found many old irrigation ponds that had been abandoned.[120] By 1851, Baoqing prefecture still had few reservoirs, and people neglected their repair. Lawsuits and feuds broke out every time drought struck. To overcome such "stinginess," prefects and governors offered special rewards to those who invested in reservoirs and wells.[121]

Struggles over control of important reservoirs produced serious conflicts. Polders in the lowlands tended to be dominated by large landlords, but reservoirs in the highlands were even more tempting targets for aggressive local power-holders. In Leiyang county, where most of the reservoirs were controlled by these rural bosses (*shihao*), crops frequently yielded poor harvests because the reservoirs had been filled in.[122] Most of the lawsuits in the highlands were a result of a landowner attempting to divert water supplies to his own lands, cutting off users downstream. Once nearly all the mountain land was cleared in the nineteenth century, the safety margin was gone. This left the local inhabitants to struggle over scarce supplies of water.[123]

In promoting waterworks construction, Qing officials made a significant impact in opening up mountain lands for settlement. They fell short of their goals, however, because of natural and social obstacles. The campaign for double-cropping similarly indicates that, while the Qing state could affect agricultural production, it had difficulty in fundamentally altering the structure of peasant society.

THE CAMPAIGN FOR DOUBLE-CROPPING:
SUCCESSES AND FAILURES

Qing officials made many efforts in the eighteenth century to encourage Hunanese peasants to grow two crops a year, yet they were often frustrated. Many districts still cultivated only one crop a year into the nineteenth century (see Table 14). In the lowland areas, the large demand for rice encouraged peasants to put all their stakes on a single rice crop. In Xiangtan, no one responded to official encouragement to plant a second crop of another grain.[124] The reason for clinging to a single crop in these areas may have been a fear that the second crop would lower the yields of rice. Even in the 1950s, government officials found Hunanese farmers reluctant to adopt a rice/wheat double-crop rotation because of fears that this might lower rice yields. Experiments conducted in 1957 found that this was true, if there was not a sufficient supply of fertilizer.[125] The high profits from commercialized rice production led Hunanese farmers to depend exclusively on a single rice crop. By throwing themselves on the mercies of the market, they prospered in good years but, when floods struck, were more likely to suffer than farmers with a back-up crop.[126]

A serious official effort to persuade peasants to grow two crops a year, launched in Hunan in 1745, indicates how harsh reality was for officials who had learned their agriculture from books.[127] Daozhou magistrate Duan Rulin, noting that "the population is growing daily while the land is not expanding," consulted old peasants in his district on ways of increasing production. They told him that both early and late rice were planted at about the same time, in the 4th month of the year. Early rice was harvested in the middle of the 7th month, and late rice in the beginning of the 9th month. This was essentially a single-cropping system in which different fields were planted with early- and late-rice seeds to spread out the risks. When told to try growing a second crop on the same plot after the early-rice crop, the peasants refused, saying that "the water is too cold."

Duan consulted the classical text on agricultural production of his time, the *Nongzheng Quanshu*, compiled by Xu Guangqi in the seventeenth century, which stated that in southern lands it was still possible to plant a second crop in the 8th month after the early-rice harvest. This could only be done in areas near the river, where the land was flat and water could be pumped up for irrigation. The magistrate of Lingling county, however, discovered that farmers had already tried out the successive planting of two rice crops by planting middle or late rice in between the rows of early rice. The result was that the later crops failed to grow, and even some of the early crops failed to sprout. After this failure, no one tried it again. The Qiyang magistrate was told by the local gentry that "the soil is not suited" to double rice cropping, but the governor ordered him to try planting for himself, admonishing him, "How can you believe the peasants' pretext that the land is not suited?" So the magistrate ordered a land-lord holder of a *jiansheng* degree and a local farmer to plant early rice, followed by late rice. They reported that ears of grain were produced, but failed to grow, and there was no harvest. Local farmers told the magistrate that they had tried in previous years to plant very early rice, before the *qingming* festival, and to follow this with a late-rice crop, but the yield had been so low that the total yield of the two crops was less than half that of one crop, so the effort was abandoned. Despite the best efforts of officials and local farmers, it proved impossible to grow two rice crops a year in these areas. The Jianghua magistrate concluded that the plan of the *Nongzheng Quanshu* was, frankly, "an absolutely impossible idea." The authority of agricultural handbooks had to bow before the realities of soil and water.

In more mountainous areas, other factors limited the spread of double-cropping or rice followed by a *zaliang* crop. While the quality of soil was one consideration,[128] probably more important was the local labor supply. As double-cropping required greater amounts of labor than single-cropping, the shift to more intensive cultivation could only be made after population density had crossed a certain threshold. The shortage of labor is probably what lies behind the frequent official statements that "peasants in the mountains are lazy" or that "people in double-cropping areas work harder than those in areas that grow only a single crop."[129]

Another limitation to double-cropping was the need to feed animals. In single-cropping, non-paddy areas, it was customary to let the oxen into the fields after the harvest to graze on the stubble. When the mountains were sparsely settled, there was no risk in letting the cattle roam freely to feed themselves.[130] This custom, however, made it impossible for anyone in the village to plant a second crop, because the cattle would trample his fields. Officials repeatedly prohibited this practice and urged the peasants to confine the cattle by fencing off the fields. Some thought that, if the rice stubble were allowed to grow, instead of being eaten by cattle, a second rice crop (called "grandson rice" *daosun*) could be produced.[131] Its yield would be small, only several *dou* per *mou*, but it could be obtained without much effort.

From the official point of view, there was no reason to waste the fields by letting the cattle trample them. Seldom did they see it from the peasant farmer's perspective. How was the farmer to feed his cattle if he kept them penned up? Clearly he would have to sacrifice some of his own grain reserves to feed his cattle, and he would need to have faith that the increased harvest from double-cropping would provide the necessary food. But for a second crop to be effective, everyone in the village would have to agree to surrender the right to let his cattle into fields and trample others' crops. The transaction costs of arriving at such a communal decision seriously delayed the introduction of a new cropping system which would have benefited everyone. In this sense, the introduction of double-cropping faced problems analogous to the maintenance of polders on the lowlands. In Qiyang, "diligent peasants," as the officials called them, did try to keep the animals penned up indoors all year round, but they found that they could not get a reliable *zaliang* harvest to compensate for the loss of gleaning the fields. Nevertheless, when drought threatened in 1760, the district magistrate strictly forbade letting cattle out to trample the grain, beat and cangued those who disobeyed, and urged the farmers to plant a second crop of buckwheat to save themselves from famine.[132]

Official prohibitions notwithstanding, the custom of letting cattle into the fields persisted. On the other hand, more farmers began suing their neighbors for allowing their cattle to trample newly sown lands.[133] In Lingling county, a fine was levied on those who allowed their cattle to trample another's crop. Some villages organized a system for neighbors to watch each other's cattle in rotation. One official proposed to give the duty of watching cattle to the *baojia* mutual-responsibility groups. This increase in local conflict and regulation indicated that a number of peasants were prepared to take the risk of change to more intensive production. In so doing they responded more readily to the incentives of population growth and market demand than to official initiatives. But local officials did facilitate the change by protecting the property rights of the innovators.[134]

Despite these obstacles, the *zaliang* food crops did spread widely through the eighteenth and nineteenth centuries, and they did make a significant difference in the food supply. One effect seems to have been to make some mountainous areas more self-sufficient, so that they no longer depended on downstream areas for their grain. Yuanling, Lüxi, and Chenxi counties used to depend on Taoyuan to provide grain for their granaries. By 1815, because of the spread of *zaliang* cultivation on "mountain tops and corners of land," they not only had enough grain to feed themselves but were able to export rice produced on paddy fields.[135] A gradual transformation was changing *zaliang* crops from a supplement to an inadequate rice crop to the major food crop, while rice became primarily an export cash crop.[136]

By 1800, it might be thought that the Hunanese had overcome the problems of too great a population on too little land which officials had anticipated in the early eighteenth century. Hunan appeared to be a prosperous grain producer, feeding its 17 million people and providing large quantities of grain for provinces down the Yangtze. The first phase in increasing the food supply had been marked by the extension of cultivable land area by large numbers of settlers from outside the province. When less and less new land could be cleared, producers shifted to working the existing land more intensively. In both stages, government officials played an important part, both by providing tax incentives to clear land and by encouraging the peasants to plant new crops.

Qing officials, however, do not deserve all the credit. Official policies succeeded only because they accorded with the economic needs of the local population. The abundance of fertile, unoccupied land in itself provided a powerful incentive for immigrants to settle in Hunan. As the export market in grain grew, the profits from grain production

for the market encouraged more intensive cultivation. The Qing policies only accelerated a process that would have begun in any case.
When officials tried to defy local conditions by urging inappropriate
cultivation techniques, their efforts failed. The Chinese state could
not despotically remold Chinese society to its own purposes independently of local custom and market forces. The rulers, particularly
Qianlong, did not even try to alter long-established trends, but
neither did they passively allow agriculture to go its own way. They
intervened extensively in the smallest details of cultivation in order
to ensure a reliable food supply for an expanding population.

Yet, all was not healthy with agriculture in the eighteenth century.
Agricultural production kept up with population growth, but the
potential for further improvement was shrinking, while the population continued to expand. Exhaustion of the local ecology, in the
form of deforestation, erosion, and excessive dike-building, threatened
to eliminate the impressive achievements. Rising conflicts over land
rights led to lawsuits and even murder. In the area of dike-building,
a crucial component of paddy agriculture, the imperial state had to
face a mounting challenge caused by social forces beyond its control.
The means by which officials attempted to halt the inexorable process
of dike-building around Dongting Lake and the growth of land conflicts reveal both the impressive strengths and fatal weaknesses of the
late-eighteenth-century Chinese state.

FIVE

Property Rights and Social Relations on the Land

Since, in Hunan, as in any agricultural society, local power centered on the ownership of land, property rights are a significant indicator of how local influence was recognized. In eighteenth-century Hunan, there was an active land market with frequent transactions in small pieces of property. Previous studies of Hunan have concentrated on the relationship between landlord and tenant, but we also need to consider the property rights defined by local custom, the interplay between local customary and official law, and the effects of both on the actions of landowners.[1] Landlord and tenant struggled over more than the level of rent or the ratio of rent to total yield; their relationship depended on customary expectations about rights to land and the proper behavior of landlords. These expectations were transformed in the eighteenth century by the increasing commercialization of the rural economy.

First, it will be useful to take a quick look at Chinese concepts of property rights in land.[2] The earliest Chinese land contracts date back to 140 B.C. In the Han dynasty, an official transfer of land required a written document, with witnesses, accompanied by a formal ceremony of transfer of property and money. Written contracts remained essential to the validity of a land transaction ever after. North China peasants in the 1930s stated that oral contracts were worthless; unless a contract was drawn up there was no recognized sale.[3] After the fourth century A.D., all contracts were supposed to be reported to the local officials and a tax paid equal to 4 percent of the value of the land. Officials had the responsibility of checking to see that the sale was valid, and they had the right to cancel a sale, even if the contract had been drawn up and the money paid. In the Song dynasty, officials first began to apply red seals to the contracts they approved, and, after the eleventh century, the state's contract tax rose gradually, up to 20 percent of the land value. The rise in the contract tax meant the proliferation of more "white contracts," or privately drawn-up contracts lacking an official seal. Both red and white contracts existed side by side through the twentieth century, and the average landowner would have several bundles of each. While only the red contracts had any validity in official eyes, landowners were clearly willing to put their trust in the white contracts. The lower cost of the white contracts compensated for their lesser security. Whether a given land sale produced a red or white contract depended on such factors as the amount of the contract tax at the time of the sale, the relative wealth of the two parties, and the degree to which they trusted each other.

The development of land contracts stimulated a wider land market, but the Chinese never achieved the absolute rights of individual ownership accompanied by total alienability characteristic of the modern West. Relatives, neighbors, and mortgage-holders all had rights of pre-emption on any sale.[4] Most important, the seller himself seldom surrendered permanently all his rights to the land, but implicitly or explicitly usually retained the right to repurchase the land within a given period of time. Studies of land contracts from Fujian province indicate the great flexibility of Chinese customary law in apportioning rights to land.[5] There was a spectrum of arrangements from permanent alienation (*duanqi*) to temporary pledges of land for cash (*dian*). In each type of contract, the seller surrendered some portion of his property rights in exchange for money, but there was no sharp boundary between irrevocable sales, mortgages, and land pawns. Most land contracts, however, did not stipulate absolute sale. The seller reserved the right to reclaim the land by repaying the sale price or, if the value of the land had risen, he claimed the right to seek an extra amount of money from the buyer as part of a share in the increased land value. This was called "seeking extra value" (*zhaojia*). In Fujian, the seller could claim extra value in three stages: *zhao* ("seeking"), *zeng* ("increase"), and *tie* ("additional"). In principle, after obtaining these extra funds, he should renounce all further attempts to get money from the land by drawing up an absolute sale contract (*duanqi*), but in fact many sellers continued to demand further sums after drawing up an absolute sale contract. There was, in effect, a gradient of claims to land ranging from absolute ownership to absolute sale, and landowners constantly attempted to extract cash in exchange for surrendering each degree of ownership rights.

The rarity of permanent sales, as opposed to land pawns, cannot be attributed to the desire to avoid paying the contract tax, since contracts were just as necessary in pawn transactions as in absolute sales. What it meant was that land was not yet solely a commodity to be bought and sold like any other. The owner of land held it in trust, and he was reluctant to alienate the property that would be passed on to his successors. Since land had use value as productive property, it could be held as security for a loan. Owners sold their land in order to obtain money for immediate use, but they always hoped to be able to recover the money and to buy back the land under favorable conditions. Even "dead-sale" contracts (*simai*), which explicitly stated that the seller permanently alienated his land, could be "brought back to life" (*simai huotou*) by the later addition of a clause permitting repurchase by the original seller. After a supposedly "absolute" sale surrendering all rights to land, the seller, if he faced destitution, could also ask the buyer for charity by drawing up a "grief contract" (*tanqi*) which entitled him to some extra cash based on his previous ownership of the land.[6]

Redemption rights, implicit or explicit, also perpetuated the seller's grip on the land. Many contracts stated that the owner was selling the land because of urgent needs for cash, but that he reserved the right to redeem the land by repaying the original price. As long as the seller had the right to reclaim the land, all land transactions, whatever their name, were really closer to being land pawns (*dian*) than true sales (*mai*). In effect, there was no sharp distinction between a sale of land with an implicit right of repurchase and a pawn of land as security for a loan. Both transactions conveyed only limited rights of owner-ship to the buyer and left the seller with the hope or intention of recovering his land.[7] Land pawns were distinguished from conditional sales with rights of redemption only by the time period involved. *Dian* contracts set a fixed time period, after which the land returned to the seller (unless the contract was extended). Conditional sales transferred the land for an indefinite period of time but always allowed for possible recovery of possession by the seller. The blurred boundary between sale and mortgage allowed landholders to raise capital from their land in a bewildering variety of ways. Fujian and other areas further complicated the matter by distinguishing between subsoil and surface rights, each of which could be sold or pawned.

The flexibility of customary law responded to the commercialization of the land market since the sixteenth century, facilitating market penetration and active trading in land. The official attitude toward customary law was ambivalent. Nominally, state law codes disapproved of the complications that customary law introduced into the land market. The Fujian provincial code of 1730 prohibited the use of "subsoil" (*tiangen*) and "surface" (*tianpi*) in Fujian land contracts, clearly without effect.[8] Likewise, even though Hunan provincial regulations prohibited the practice of rent deposits and "seeking extra value" (*zhaojia*) as early as the 1680s, Hunan land documents commonly used these terms.[9]

Aside from these ineffectual prohibitions, however, the state did not interfere with customary law. Magistrates, in fact, upheld contracts based on customary law in their courts.[10] From the eighteenth century on, local officials began to issue regulations in order to clarify ambiguities in land contracts. Contracts for absolute sales had to state expressly that no repurchase was allowed, else repurchase rights were understood by default. By the nineteenth century, most land contracts explicitly prohibited repurchase, but eighteenth-century contracts often did not clearly spell this out.[11] The conflict over the interpretation of "absolute-sale" contracts in Hunan during a time of rising land values provided an opportunity for the state to step in to regulate the private land market and to attempt to replace the private white contracts with officially backed, tax-producing red contracts.

LAND DISPUTES OVER CLAIMS
OF REDEMPTION RIGHTS

No amount of regulations and customs governing land transactions could eliminate all sources of dispute. Lawsuits over land could break out for any number of reasons. Although both parties would normally first seek to settle a dispute by mediation, sometimes the expense involved in going to the magistrate's court for litigation was unavoidable. It was easier to take a case to court in the eighteenth century than it had been earlier because of the proliferation of "pettifoggers" (*songshi*) who, for a fee, offered to take up a person's case.[12] Hunanese officials thought that many ordinary people with small disputes, who would normally have settled for mediation, were enticed by pettifoggers into blowing up their case into a large lawsuit.[13]

Eighteenth-century Hunanese seem to have been particularly prone to initiating lawsuits. This propensity was partly due to provincial peculiarities and partly to new eighteenth-century developments. The Hunanese, like nearly all the South Chinese, had long been regarded as a particularly litigious group, but local writers in the eighteenth century remarked on the recent increase in the number of lawsuits there.[14] In particular, new economic pressures of the eighteenth century meant a rise in litigation over land rights for which Qing officials were not prepared.[15]

In Hunan, the flourishing rice export market and clearance of valuable fertile lands around Dongting Lake offered new opportunities for aggressive and unscrupulous men to take advantage of ambiguities in customary law. Inevitably, as lawsuits proliferated, officials found themselves drawn into a welter of conflicting claims to land. They had to try to systematize a variety of cloudy practices with which they had never previously concerned themselves. The efforts of Qing officials to regularize land transactions in Hunan required further intervention by the state in the land market and created new tensions between official regulations and local custom.

The exercise of redemption rights provides the clearest example of the effects of economic change on land disputes. Although it was understood that most sellers of land had the right to buy it back, contracts often left unstated the time limit within which this right could be exercised and the price of redemption. As the growing population and the flourishing economy drove up the price of the land, more and more people sought to exercise their rights to buy back the land at the original selling price. In Changsha prefecture, sellers claimed the right to an additional share of the land value after three years and insisted on redemption after five years.[16] Prohibitions on reversing absolute sales by turning them into mortgages were ignored.[17] Buyers resisted by bringing suit before the magistrates. Hubei Governor Yan Sisheng reported in 1744 that, because of the recent rise in land prices, "only now are people claiming the right of redemption." During the early years of settlement, when tax burdens were high, many people had been anxious to sell their land. Now they tried to recover land that had been sold several decades ago. Sons and grandsons tried to reclaim the land of their fathers and grandfathers. In some cases, one person sold land and his relative sued to recover it. After ten years, the land might have changed hands several times, while the original owner was still seeking to recover it.[18]

Sometimes, as in Yuanling county in 1734, a dispute over land redemption led to murder. The grandfather of Cao Zongshu had either sold or mortgaged a piece of land to the ancestor of Cao Zongqi over two decades earlier. Zongshu, learning that the original price was lower than the present value of the land, claimed the right to redeem it. The case was brought to the Cao lineage, which decided to settle it by ordering Zongqi to pay Zongshu an extra 3 *taels*, but Zongqi refused to pay. On 21 April 1734, when Zongqi went to the land to pick tea leaves, he met Zongshu and his wife returning home. A quarrel broke out, both parties pulled out clubs, and the battle ended with Zongshu beating Zongqi to death.[19] Besides punishing Zongshu, resolution of the land issue hinged on whether Zongshu's grandfather had sold or only pawned the land. Zongqi's side claimed that they had bought it outright, while Zongshu and his children claimed that the land had only been pawned. Nothing could be proved either way, because a fire in 1710 had burned up the contracts.

A case in Hengyang county in 1808 provides another example.[20] In 1805, Wang Bolan and his older brother, Wang Bozhen, took property they owned in common and mortgaged it (*dian*) to a fellow lineage member, Wang Boshi, for a price of 17,600 cash. Wang Bolan and Bozhen continued to cultivate the land, paying a yearly rent in kind of 3.74 *shi* of grain. Wang Bozhen, in 1806, left the area to go out trading on his own. In 1807, Bolan defaulted on the rent because of a poor harvest. Boshi then threatened to exercise his right to take over the land by returning the rents paid. Bolan refused, and they quarreled. Boshi then threatened to destroy the grain in the fields if Bolan did not give up his rights to the land. Even though Bolan and another brother slept in a shack in the fields to guard the crop, Boshi succeeded in evading their guard and destroying the grain. Bolan plotted to take over the land himself by killing his brother Boming and throwing the blame on Boshi. When the plot was discovered, Bolan was sentenced to death by slicing, Boshi was given only 80 blows, and the title to the land reverted to Wang Bozhen after he returned from his business trip.

Although it was described as a dispute over redemption (*shu*), this case really involved an attempt by the mortgage holder, Boshi, to gain control of the land after default on the rent payment by the mortgagor. In each of the above cases, it was the rising value of the land that prompted those with claims to property to try to exercise them. Similar claims were made for similar reasons in the Miao frontier area in western Hunan. Land had been fairly cheap there before the abolition of the autonomy of the native chieftains by the Yongzheng Emperor, but, after the execution of the policy absorbing the native areas into the regular administration, the demand for land rose, and "crafty people" sought the right to redeem land, claiming that the contracts they had signed earlier were not complete sale contracts.[21]

Here, as elsewhere, officials tried to forbid redemption for all contracts that did not specifically allow for redemption rights. The key to resolving the disputes over redemption rights was to enforce a sharp distinction between mortgage contracts and contracts of absolute sale. Absolute sale required the seller to relinquish all future claims on the land, while mortgage contracts left open the possibility of future repurchase. The terminology and legal definitions of the two kinds of contracts had long existed, but customary law in Hunan had made no rigid distinction between the two. The rise in land values in the eighteenth century highlighted the ambiguities of customary law, and the land disputes forced officials to step in to clarify property rights.

Their job was made more difficult, however, by ambiguities in the contracts themselves. Some contracts explicitly stated, "No matter whether the time period is long or short, [the original owner] has the right to redeem the land if he can produce the money."[22] Some contracts of "absolute sale" stated "No redemption at all is allowed from this date on," but many contained no explicit provisions at all. In 1744, the magistrate of Huitong county, Yu Wenjun, proposed that all contracts drawn up before 1723 be regarded as absolute-sale contracts, with no claims for redemption allowed. After 1723, redemption would be allowed if the price of land had not changed drastically. If redemption was allowed in the contract, but the original owner lacked the money to redeem the land, a "re-mortgage" (*zhuandian*) was allowed which would preserve his rights. If, however, the land was resold to a third party, the first party no longer had any redemption claim. Even contracts called "sale contracts," if they set no time limit for redemption, were to be treated as pawn contracts and redemption claims allowed.

With this proposal, Yu aimed to prevent lawsuits by officially establishing limits to redemption rights that were not specified by local custom. The governor, however, rejected his proposal, noting that "people sell their land in an emergency, and they want to keep an opportunity to recover it. This proposal eliminates the people's intention not to abandon their land. It stops disputes by contradicting local custom (*duzheng yi lisu*)."[23] He rejected as well the idea of requiring all contracts to set time limits to redemption. The reluctance of provincial officials to take action was overcome only by an edict in 1752 which provided that all redemption rights be exercised within thirty years, unless the contract specified a shorter time limit.[24] Provincial officials had decided not to contradict customary usage in regard to redemption rights, despite the conflicts its ambiguities produced.

IRREGULARITIES IN LAND CONTRACTS

Besides disputes caused by the ambiguity in written contracts, conflicts arose from the failure to draw up any official contract at all.[25] Contracts were often concealed in order to avoid payment of taxes, and they could be lost when the original owner died. Then "evil elements" could take advantage of this situation by drawing up false contracts giving them title to the land, paying the tax, and obtaining a sealed document from an unwitting official. Even if the first owner or his descendants found the original contract, it would be judged invalid because no deed tax had been paid on it. To prevent this, officials tried to require that every new contract for land sale or land pawn be officially registered and the tax paid. They tried to ensure that only the officials could guarantee the title to land. Legally, transfer of possession (*tuishou* or *guoge*) occurred only after the buyer had gone to the magistrate's office, paid the deed tax, and had his name officially entered in the land register.[26] In Hunan, however, because of the large number of concealed contracts, land registration did not reflect ownership. "Crafty elements" could take advantage of such discrepancies to foment lawsuits. The governor ordered that clerks be selected to check on all land sales, investigating the borders and yields of the lands, and then to enter the phrase "X receives title, Y yields title" in the land register. In all land sales, the tax had to be paid within twenty days from the date of sale (later extended to three months).[27] There were punishments for failure to pay the tax on time. On pawn contracts, however, no tax was to be required.

Ideally, under these regulations, all lawsuits should have ceased, as all land transactions would be confirmed by official seal and recorded in the land register. In addition, it was necessary to make sure that the contracts were drawn up precisely and that the boundaries of the parcels involved in a transaction were clearly described. The grasslands around Dongting Lake produced many feuds, simply because it was impossible to define the boundaries of the land.[28] The local official was supposed to indicate the location of the land on a map, fill in the names of the neighboring owners on all sides, and attach the map to the contract after the tax was paid. In an effort to standardize the format of contracts, officials printed up "easy-to-understand forms" (*yizhidan*) for distribution by paper shops, at a fixed cost of 2 copper cash per form. These forms indicated all the required information, including blank maps. The buyer had only to fill in the blanks on the form.[29]

Besides regulating future land sales, officials tried to legitimize old "white" contracts by requiring landowners to bring in old contracts, pay the deed tax, and get them sealed. The tax was set at a low rate of 3 percent of the land value. But the main problem was not with the official tax but with surtax collections, "wastage money," and other fees collected by runners. In Mayang county, these fees raised the price to 7 percent of the land value, over twice the official amount.[30] Some people sued unsuccessfully to avoid paying the excess tax. Nevertheless, there was widespread compliance with the order. In Mayang, in the nine months of 1758, deed-holders paid tax on over 400 contracts.[31] In 1761, in Jingzhou, the magistrate had given out 1,500 forms by the 9th month and feared that he would not have enough forms to last the year. In this county, it is true, the official had made a special effort to enforce the contract tax by "sending deputies to the countryside to lead the people (in tax payment)," and he succeeded in collecting 1,146 *taels* of tax in six months.[32]

LIMITATIONS ON REGULATION
OF THE LAND MARKET

Vigorous action by local officials could successfully enforce tighter control over land contracts and bring in some extra tax income. Yet there were limits to this bureaucratic intervention in the land market. The basic aim of local officials was not to control every transaction or to collect the very small extra tax income from contracts, but to save themselves the trouble of hearing lawsuits. Strict enforcement of the policy would only give yamen clerks yet another pretext to squeeze extra fees out of landowners, causing further disputes. Considerations of convenience limited the drive to control the land market. In 1751, Governor Yang Xifu rejected a proposal to require that all the owners of land adjacent to a plot being sold be present in the fields when the boundaries were verified. He noted that the neighboring owner might live hundreds of miles away, in a different county or prefecture, or that a greedy neighbor might seek to buy the land at a low price by threatening to bring a lawsuit over the boundaries.[33] Still, without careful delineation of land boundaries, a seller might try to include adjacent fields in a contract, hoping to get a higher price, and the buyer would not question too closely, as he hoped to be able to encroach on these fields.[34]

Such practices could occur only when the neighboring landowners did in fact live far from their fields and where there was enough pressure on the land supply to make it worthwhile to risk a lawsuit in order to take over valuable land. The proposal to require verification of land boundaries by the neighbors indicates that there was indeed an increasing amount of absentee landownership and that rising land values offered greater incentive to cheat. Yang's rejection of the proposal, on the other hand, indicates a recognition by the provincial governor of the practical limits on the ability of officials to regulate strictly the terms of local land sales. He implicitly recognized that officials could not eliminate disputes over land boundaries.

Installment sales were another area in which officials could not alter local custom. In these sales, the buyer received tenure to the land but did not pay its full price all at once. The seller received an I.O.U. with the character "unpaid" (*qian*) on it. When the entire sum was paid off, the seller returned the I.O.U. to the buyer with the character "received" (*ling*) written on it. This type of sale, however, repeatedly provoked quarrels leading to beatings and deaths.[35] These quarrels usually occurred either because the buyer refused to pay the remaining sum once he held the property, or because the seller later demanded compensation for the increased value of the land. The magistrate of Suining county, saying that "by law there should be no debts in land sales," urged abolition of the installment sale system, but prefectural officials refuted him and confined their efforts to enforcing regular payments by the buyer.

Even where contracts were drawn up, certain local practices could still lead to disputes, as in the case of joint purchase (*hemai*) of land by relatives or friends. Often several members of one lineage, or even members of two different lineages, would pool their funds to buy a single parcel of land, drawing up one contract for all parties. This practice frequently produced conflicts among the sons and grandsons of the original buyers over who should pay the tax. When in Huarong, in 1747, a dispute between the sons of two joint purchasers led to a beating in which one man died, the magistrate ordered that all joint purchases be split apart, with the boundaries between the plots made clear, and he prohibited joint payment of the land tax by several households.[36]

In Anxiang county, on the borders of Dongting Lake, it was customary for all land sales to be made jointly. The rental income was divided between the owners, but the shares remained disputable, and sometimes supporters of the disputants gathered together in crowds to fight with each other. Officials tried to stop these disputes by refusing to allow purchase by an entire lineage or the use of several surnames in one contract. They also forbade joint petitions in lawsuits.

Joint claims to land were also the issue in Guidong county in 1808. Hu Yuanshen had five sons, who together contributed 1,000 *shi* of grain to purchase charitable land for the use of their lineage. In 1786, Yuanshen divided the land into five shares, drew up contracts and had them officially sealed at the county office. Eventually Hu Yuling, the eldest son, passed the examination for the *juren* degree. As an expectant district magistrate, he needed money to pay his debts, so his father sold Yuling's share of the land to the other four brothers, who contributed enough to compensate for its price. Hu Yuanshen stipulated that Yuling, when he had enough money, could redeem the land. Although Yuling did get the money, he never did redeem his share of the land, and later, when he again appealed to his brothers for financial aid, they refused. He then, in August, 1807, brought suit against his brothers in Peking, claiming that his share of his father's lineage land had been stolen from him and sold by his brothers. Yuling's suit was rejected as a falsification of the facts, but it was the concept of joint property rights that had led him to believe that he could demand that his brothers surrender their shares in the lineage land to him.[37]

A variant form of joint purchase which prevailed in Xiangxiang county was designed to prevent the breaking up of land into small plots. In several districts of Xiangxiang, Changsha, and Xiangtan counties, custom required a landowner who had bought land in a large block to sell it all in one piece. He was not allowed to sell off small pieces to pay occasional debts.[38] According to Peng Yangzhong, member of a prominent lineage in Xiangxiang, this custom produced unnaturally low land prices on such large plots, which made it difficult for large landowners to pay their debts. If they invited tenants to cultivate at reduced rents, the rents they received were not even enough to pay the taxes. The result was lawsuits between landlord and tenant, arrears in tax payments, and impoverishment of the large landowners. Peng proposed to tell all the lineages in the relevant districts of Xiangxiang county that they were allowed to cut up their land in pieces to sell it. In this case, a representative of local society, without any official intervention, was trying to alter local custom in order to protect the interests of the prominent lineages of his area.

These examples show eighteenth-century Hunanese officials attempting to intervene in local land markets in an effort to clarify ambiguous property claims resulting from local custom. The officials tried to apply uniform, clear standards of ownership, and they attempted to record all land transactions on officially approved contracts and land registers. Their goal was to eliminate conflicts over property rights produced by the lack of clarity in customary agreements. Land disputes were regarded as minor matters, but they were extremely time-consuming. Magistrates hoped to reduce litigation in order to keep their dockets clear. The weaknesses of the state and the persistence of variant local practices often limited the success of their efforts, but they did not always try to simply outlaw customs which conflicted with bureaucratic rationalization. They sometimes refused to "stop disputes by defying local custom."

Ramon Myers and Chang Fu-mei Chen have argued that the development of customary land law during the Ming-Qing period greatly stimulated the commercialization of the economy. Myers argues that "the increased volume of [resource] exchange in China after the seventeenth century was primarily a function (a) of customary law which greatly reduced transaction costs and (b) of the activities of the state which both permitted customary law to operate and adjudicated disputes over transactions by respecting customary law."[39] Myers's argument extends to China the thesis of Douglass North, who ascribes the transition from the manorial to the capitalist system in Europe to the emergence of well-defined and enforced property rights, beginning in sixteenth-century England and the Netherlands.[40] Clear definitions of property rights, by reducing the transaction costs of resource exchange, made possible the rapid development of markets for land, labor, and capital which were necessary for the growth of capitalism. In Myers's view, the Qing state, simply by recognizing the validity of a sophisticated system of customary law, whose principles can be traced in surviving land contracts, facilitated a period of rapid economic growth.

Myers's focus on land contracts, which by their very nature establish agreements, minimizes the role of dispute settlement in the land market and exaggerates the clarity of customary law. Qing officials did more than passively accept the standards of customary law in their courts; in some cases, they actively tried to reform it. They used written contracts as the basis for their decisions, but contracts alone did not eliminate ambiguity, and the Qing code did not provide for many individual cases. The development of provincial legal codes was a response to the diversity of local economic conditions. The cases in the Hunan provincial legal code indicate that local customs varied greatly from county to county within the province. Officials sought to devise universal rules for solving land disputes, but these efforts at standardization constantly produced tension with the diversity of local custom. The Qing state intervened sporadically, but actively, to alter the rules of the land market; it did not simply allow the invisible hand to reign.

On the other hand, the eighteenth-century state did not try despotically to replace custom with imperial law. Customary law aided the rise of the commercial land market, but commerce, in turn, undermined the authority of custom. When rising land prices increased incentives to manipulate the terms of redemption contracts, the state had to step in to clarify ambiguous agreements. The continual urge to rationalize customary agreements by bureaucratic supervision, however, was offset by the limited impact of the state on rural society and ideological approval of non-interference in popular customs. As a result, in contrast to Europe, thoroughgoing rationalization of property rights never took place, and absolute rights of ownership and alienation never came to predominate.

QING OFFICIALS
AND LANDLORD-TENANT RELATIONS

Hunanese officials not only had to clarify claims arising from land sales; they also had to clear up disputes in the much more difficult area of landlord-tenant relations. Like land sales, the terms of tenancy agreements were governed by local custom, but in Hunan these agreements were usually not written down. When disputes arose, either because the tenant refused to pay rent or because the landlord abused customary practices, officials aimed to restore "friendly relations" (*qingyi zhi jiao*) between landlord and tenant. Although they rejected the idea that the tenant belonged to a servile status (*pu*), they still recognized certain personal non-contractual obligations tying the two parties, described as the "relationship of master and guest" (*zhubin zhi fen*).[41] Once again, however, the pressures of commercialization and population growth undermined the paternalist ideals of "friendly relations." In intervening in the landlord-tenant relationship, Qing officials tried to adapt local custom to the new conditions of the time, while preserving the basic rights of the landlord to his land and the state to its tax.

Conditions of tenancy varied widely throughout the province, from the most commercialized to the most remote areas. In parts of Hunan and Hubei in the Song dynasty, tenants had been bound to the land in a form of serfdom.[42] Extreme subjugation of tenants into servile status had disappeared from most parts of Hunan by the mid-Qing, but it persisted in a few areas. In the 1680s, a district magistrate in Changsha attacked the practice of landlords turning tenants into servants, imposing corvée labor on them, and selling their women into servitude.[43] In Sangzhi county, in Miao territory, the native chieftains were said to own tenant households which "were people they had bought like slaves." The chieftains traveled in entourages with many guards, and all who saw them "lined the roads and prostrated themselves."[44] Here, children were still being sold into bondage, although these sales were disguised as adoptions in order to evade prohibitions on the sale of servants. The best that local officials could do was to order that adopted children should be treated as commoners (*liangmin*) and not as servants (*pu*).[45]

On the whole, however, the "feudal remnant" customs, which indicated nearly total dependency of the tenant on his master, were not prevalent in the eighteenth-century Hunanese countryside.[46] Qing regulations did impose penalties on landlords who mistreated tenants. It was illegal for gentry to beat their tenants, turn their tenants' wives into concubines, or to buy concubines. The punishment for beating a tenant was the same as the punishment for holding back rent: 80 beatings with the cane. Many of these prohibitions were, of course, ineffective, but they indicate a definite policy by Qing officials to treat tenants as commoners with equal rights before the law.[47]

The philosophy of paternalist benevolence embodied in Qing law was expressed in several ways in Hunan. By reducing rents and exempting arrears on government lands in time of famine the state ensured the welfare of its own tenants.[48] Officials also encouraged landlords to reduce rents in bad years. As mentioned above, Governor Zhao Shenqiao, in the early eighteenth century, had ordered landlords to pass on tax exemptions to their tenants. An edict of 1745 exempting tax arrears in Hunan specifically instructed that rents should be reduced as well.[49] When Hunan Governor Pu Lin relieved flooding in 1788, he declared that tenants need not pay the full amount of rent to their landlords.[50] These examples contradict Shigeta Atsushi's assertion that Qing officials never tried to reduce rents after the amalgamation of the poll tax and the land tax in 1713.[51] Nevertheless, officials and the Emperor himself were reluctant to force landlords to reduce rents. The Yongzheng Emperor noted in 1735 that it would only cause needless trouble if landlords were ordered to reduce rents every time they received tax exemptions, even though he knew that exemptions were seldom passed on to tenants.[52] He did, however, praise generous landlords who split the burden of bad years equally with their tenants, ordering rewards for the generous landlords, but no punishment for those who refused. The fear of encouraging rent resistance inhibited active state intervention in reducing rents. The Qing officials could not enforce the ideals of benevolence beyond the point at which they compromised landlord authority.

Where landlords still resided in the countryside, they were more likely to relieve tenant burdens, as in Pingjiang, where tenants and landlords investigated the land together after a flood or drought and agreed on rent reductions.[53] In general, however, economic trends separated the landowner more and more from his lands. Kuang Minben found it very difficult to "stimulate good will" (*fa qi shanxin*) of landlords in hard times by urging them to relieve their tenants. He found most landlords more interested in hoarding grain for profit than in passing on tax exemptions to the poor.[54]

Officials were reluctant to disturb most customary practices as long as they felt that the practices did not threaten to upset rural stability. An example is the prevalence of small "gifts" by tenants to landlords: chickens, eggs, and grain presented at New Year's, or carrying the landlord's sedan chair at weddings. Some Qing officials criticized these practices for putting the tenant in a servile status. Others, however, like Hunan Governor Yang Xifu, felt that an exchange of gifts was all right as long as the landlord responded in kind: "While the relationship of tenant to landlord is not one of the 'base' to the 'noble,' it is like the friendship of master and guest. If the landlord responds to these gifts with other items, there is no need to prohibit it [the exchange]."[55] Governor Yang did not, as a contemporary anthropologist might, concern himself with whether or not the actual exchange of gifts and services was an equal one, but he was aware that some exchange had to be conducted. As long as tenant-landlord relations were not yet fully contaminated by the cash nexus, these non-contractual gifts and services served to maintain rural stability.

All was not, however, peace and quiet in the villages. There is evidence that South China in the eighteenth century experienced a growing amount of landlord-tenant conflict.[56] The causes of these conflicts ultimately lay in the major trends of the period: immigration, land clearance, and population growth.

In many cases, in Jiangnan, Fujian, and Jiangxi, the disputes centered around tenant claims to hold "surface rights" in land. These claims were connected with a shift from share rents to fixed rents. Under the share-rent system, the landlord supplied most of the tools, seeds, and animals needed for production, while under the fixed-rent system these were the responsibility of the tenant. As the tenants put greater investment into their landholdings, they began to claim rights of ownership as well. By the Ming dynasty at the latest, these claims led to the establishment of two forms of land rights, "surface rights" and "subsoil rights." The outcome reflected in land contracts was a form of permanent tenancy. Tenants controlling surface rights had permanent rights to the land, but they could also rent out or sell their rights, while the original owner had similar rights to the subsoil. This "two-lords-to-one-field" (*yitian liangzhu*) system provided security for the tenant cultivator and offered him incentives to improve the soil. Nevertheless, when landlords in the eighteenth century sought to recapture surface rights from their tenants, further conflicts broke out.[57] Tenants who fought to preserve surface rights to land battled with landlords who sought to replace unruly tenants with others who would pay higher rents.[58]

The "two-lords-to-a-field" system was not prevalent in Hunan, but conflicts over rent appeared in other guises. With the productivity of land rising, landlords sought ways to raise rents. One common method was to collect rents in kind with an oversized grain measure, 20 to 40 percent larger than the official measure. This kind of effort at raising rent naturally aroused tenant resentment.[59] Again, the major fear of officials was that such abuses by landlords would destroy harmonious relations between landlord and tenant. "If landlords are too oppressive in such trivial matters as these, they will cause the relations between landlord and tenant to become unfriendly ... if landlords mistreat their tenants, we fear that they will make them 'get hold of Long and aim for Shu' and thus open the way to deception. Rent resistance will increase and this will not be the way to make landlord and tenant secure."[60]

In other words, if landlords could get away with petty exactions, tenants would in turn be encouraged to resist rent payments, and the ideal of "friendly relations" between landlord and tenant would be undermined. Officials repeatedly invoked the mutual dependency of tenant and landlord, urging them to cooperate for their common benefit in the face of economic and social pressures that were inciting them to conflict.

RENT DEPOSITS

Rent deposits (*jinzhuangyin*) were the most significant source of conflict between landlord and tenant in Hunan. It was common in Hunan to require tenants to pay a fee to the landlord for the right to take over cultivation of the land. The original purpose of the deposit was to insure the landlord against default on rent payment by the tenant. In fact, rent deposits came to serve the same function as the division of surface and subsoil rights in other South China provinces. Tenants came to regard the payment of a deposit as a guarantee of the right to hold the land.[61] Hunanese tenants did, in fact, sublet their land rights in much the same way that Fujian tenants sold surface rights, although lawsuits sought to prevent this.[62]

There were several different forms of rent deposit. The earliest mention of deposits in Hunan comes from Ningxiang during the Ming, but most sources do not mention the existence of deposits until the eighteenth century.[63] Later sources describe deposits of 1 to 3 *taels* per *mou* as the most common form. These amounts were paid only once by the tenant upon taking tenure. If the tenant defaulted on his rent at any time, the landlord had the option of returning the deposit to the tenant and forcing him to leave the land. In this form, called *daxie,* the deposits offered security to both landlord and tenant. The landlord held money to guarantee payment of rent, while the tenant knew that the landlord would have to pay the price of returning the deposit to evict him from the land. This system was best suited to fairly well-off tenants who could put up a large amount of capital. Other forms of deposits offered less security but were better suited to poorer tenants who lacked the capital for large deposits. Under the *xiaoxie* system, the tenant paid only one-tenth the amount he would pay under the *daxie* system, but the deposit would not be returned to him when he left the land. A third system, called "additional rent" (*jiazu*), allowed the deposit to be paid not in cash but in kind, and it too was not returned to the tenant. While the *daxie* system best served the aim of guaranteeing rent to the landlord and security to the tenant, the *xiaoxie* and *jiazu* systems were the most common among poor tenants, and it was the poor tenants who were most likely to default on rent payments.

The evolution of rent deposits paralleled a gradual change from share rent to fixed rent. Fixed rents in kind were the predominant form in Hunan. Of 48 incidents of conflict over rent in eighteenth-century Hunan, only 4 (8 percent) concerned share rents, 32 (67 percent) concerned fixed rents in kind, and 12 (25 percent) concerned money rents.[64] By the twentieth century, 75 percent of the lands around the lake paid fixed rents in kind.[65] Under a share-rent system, the landlord was still actively involved in agricultural production, providing the tenant with seeds and animals. As the landlord withdrew from active involvement on the farm, he needed the deposits to ensure continued payment of rent.[66] Tenants also had to invest more of their own resources in the land than they had previously done. For them, deposits guaranteed longer-term tenure rights, ensuring that they could occupy the land long enough to recoup their investment. Personal ties of dependency had been replaced by commercial contracts.

Landlords were free of the burden of sharing the costs of farm management and the risks of crop failure, but they surrendered the opportunities to gain in abundant years. Tenants had to put more resources into their plots and face risks without expecting relief from landlords, but they could keep the surplus remaining after the fixed rent was paid. Thus, they had strong incentives to improve the productivity of the land. Scanty information on agricultural yields in Hunan indicates that productivity did rise significantly during the eighteenth century.[67]

The balance of risks and benefits had shifted, but it is hard to argue that the outcome was *necessarily* unfavorable to tenants. As tenants tightened their claims to the land, they were more inclined to resist landlord efforts to raise rents. The local writer in Chhenzhou who was disturbed by outbreaks of tenant resistance cited the proverb "long-term tenants produce treachery" (*jiudian shengjian*). He recognized that tenant claims to security of tenure motivated the rent-resistance efforts.[68]

The economic changes of the eighteenth century transformed the function of rent deposits. They became less a guarantee of rent payments and more a source of money income for the landlord. The size of deposits tended to rise at the end of the eighteenth and into the nineteenth century.[69] The 1818 gazetteer of Liuyang county had stated that there still were generous scholars who did not raise rents or deposits, but the 1873 edition remarked that "now such cases are rare."[70]

Since agreements over deposits, unlike land sales, were not written down, there was ample opportunity for conflict and abuse. "The landlord [would claim] that no deposit had been paid, when in fact it had been; the tenant [would claim] that a small deposit was a large one; the landlord [would claim] that rent payments were in arrears [and keep the deposit], while the tenant claimed that they were fully paid."[71]

When landlords tried to evict tenants from their land, the tenants "squatted on the land" (*juzuo*) and refused to leave. They could resist more easily because the landlord's residence was far from the fields.[72] The development of absentee landlordism had reduced landlord control over the countryside. Since many of the tenants were immigrants from Guangdong or Jiangxi, they had little in common with their landlords.[73] Kinship ties, however, did not alleviate distrust.[74] Even lineage relatives paid deposits. On the other hand, landlords often tried to evict tenants by raising deposits deliberately in order to replace them with others who would pay the higher price. Then the old tenants battled with the new tenants who were brought in to replace them.[75]

THE QING VIEW
OF LANDLORD-TENANT COOPERATION

Hunanese officials, recognizing that rent deposits were the major cause of conflict between landlord and tenant, repeatedly pressed for abolition of the system. As one official remarked, "in the exploitation of the tenant, nothing is worse than rent deposits."[76] Officials conceived of the effort to eliminate rent deposits as protection of tenant rights against landlord abuse. Beginning as early as 1743, provincial governors successively prohibited rent deposits. Needless to say, simple decrees could not eliminate a custom so solidly rooted in local needs. Rent deposits persisted and even increased in Hunan and elsewhere through the early twentieth century.[77]

Governor Gao Qizhuo, in fact, had faced the problem more realistically in 1736. In response to a proposal to abolish all surcharges on rents, including rent deposits, he commented:

> The plan is very great and its benefits broad; it must certainly be enacted. But these practices have gone on in Hunan for a long time and have at least become local custom, so that, in planning adjustments, one must accord with human feelings and harmonize with local custom. We hope that the poor have virtuous feelings and that the rich do not speak resentfully; only then can the policy be enacted smoothly and permanently. If we bind up people with the law, it will not only frighten the property owners but also create obstructions and offer the chance to wicked tenants to make threats, which will obstruct the enactment of the laws.[78]

Gao concluded that rent deposits, like the other surcharges on the rent, were to be regarded as "gifts" from the tenants to landlords in return for being given land. As long as the surcharges were not excessive, he found it inadvisable to prohibit them.

Governor Gao's statements strongly stressed the ties of mutual responsibility binding landlord and tenant: "The poor people lack land and must rely on the landlords and the rich households. The rich households lack labor and must rely on the tenants to cultivate the land. Landlord and tenant fundamentally rely on each other, and they should naturally share a common fate." He stated most explicitly the official paternalist ideology urging landlord and tenant to cooperate in preserving a stable, harmonious social order of mutual obligations and clearly distinct statuses.

His successors had to face the obvious fact that this cooperation had broken down, if indeed it ever had existed. The commercialization of the economy and the new mobility offered by the export market opened up new opportunities to both landlord and tenant. Some writers, like Huang Dan, feared that the landlords would take all the profit. Huang, noting that land prices were over ten times what they had been in the Ming dynasty, lamented:

> The rich hoard grain for speculation and accumulate vast wealth. They get the profit from the land without suffering its losses. They do not begrudge a high price to obtain fertile land nearby, and the middle-ranking people cannot resist them. So [the rich] compete with each other and the price of land gets higher. The rents become heavier, while the tenants work diligently all year round but do not escape hunger and cold . . . The rich become daily richer and the poor become daily poorer.[79]

On the other hand, not all the tenants necessarily became poorer. Evelyn Rawski has argued that the gains to tenants from improved productivity and rising prices for rice sold on the market could more than offset losses due to increased rent deposits. Although her argument explicitly applies only to the "able and ambitious peasant" and to tenants located in districts able to improve agricultural productivity and take advantage of the export market, the description of "wicked tenants" in Yuezhou by Prefect Chen Jiuchang demonstrates that this type of aggressive tenant could be found in commercialized Hunan.[80]

Chen, who served in Hunan for nine years, from 1730 to 1738, was astonished to find that, in Hunan, "everything great or small followed the tenants' demands, and the landlords listened to their orders." Unlike Henan, where he had found that "the landlord was like a master and the tenants were like servants (*nupu*)," or Jiangnan, where tenants "always paid rent at the landlord's door and never resisted by force," in Hunan "the tenants, when they were angry, paid nothing at all." Another indication of the strength of Hunanese tenants was their ability to maintain claims to a plot of land after it was sold. "The land may have several masters, but the tenant household remains the same. This is called 'changing the master but not changing the tenant.'" Tenants were thus able to hold the same plot and pass on arrears in rent from generation to generation.[81] There were "tenants who called themselves landlords," tenants who sought to collect extra amounts of money from landlords (*zhaojia*), and tenants who brought suit against landlords for illegal sales. They took advantage of new officials who were unfamiliar with local customs to bring suit to get land for themselves. Chen's response was to reinforce landlord authority by ordering tenants to obey and by giving landlords the right to exchange bad tenants for good ones. The governor backed up Chen, but with the proviso that landlords also needed to be restrained from extorting excessive rent deposits and that they had to return the deposit to the original tenant before calling in a new one.

Thus, the picture of landlord-tenant conflict in Hunan is a complex one. It is possible to cite cases of landlords raising rent deposits, evicting tenants for monetary gain. It is also possible to find tenants resisting rents and defying landlord orders to leave the land. Shigeta Atsushi has pointed out that most of the former cases occurred in mountainous areas relatively distant from large markets, such as Daozhou, while the latter cases were characteristic of counties like Yuezhou, near Dongting Lake and strongly affected by commercialization.[82] He argues that the strength of the landlords in the mountainous regions was due to the remnants of servile paternalist relations from the Ming dynasty, and that commercialization gave the tenant greater freedom by undermining his dependency on the landlord. Shigeta's argument is only partially valid. Although it is true that most of the accounts of tenants squatting on the land and refusing to pay rent come from counties near the lake like Baling, Huarong, Shanhua, and Changsha, resistance also occurred in Hengyang, Chhenzhou, and Changning, in the south of the province.[83] In other peripheral districts, like Leiyang, tenants could "grab the harvest and flee" into the remote mountains to clear more wasteland.[84]

The spread of market relations transformed the entire social and political balance of power between cultivator and landowner. It is misleading to define "tenant welfare" simply in terms of per capita income level of rent in relation to productivity. As land grew scarcer, security of tenure became more important than the level of rent. Most of the conflicts broke out only when the tenant refused to leave the land, not when the landlord initially raised the rent. This problem continued into the twentieth century, when investigators recommended setting minimum time limits for tenancy contracts at twelve to eighteen years.[85]

Commercialization offered opportunities and risks to both sides. Both landlords and tenants played on the ambiguous function of rent deposits for their own benefit. Landlords aimed to profit from the grain market by raising rent deposits and exchanging old tenants for new ones. In so doing they changed the function of the rent-deposit system from a simple guarantee of rent payment into a form of usury. By raising the deposits they were, in effect, trying to collect a monetary income from the increased value of their land. The tenant, for his part, benefited from clinging to the "traditional" concept of rent deposits as a safeguard for rent payment. If rents remained fixed in cash, he gained from increased productivity and greater demand for his crops on the market. Both landlord and tenant were thus competing to take advantage of the new opportunities for gain offered by the market.

Madeleine Zelin's analysis of Sichuan land contracts confirms the trends found in Hunan.[86] In Sichuan, too, rent deposits became a major source of conflict as the practice spread through the province from the eighteenth to the nineteenth century. Deposits in Sichuan were clearly not a guarantee of permanent tenure but a source of capital for the landlord, since landlords frequently tried to evict tenants despite collecting deposits from them. On the other hand, tenants who paid deposits of over 100 *taels* clearly possessed substantial amounts of capital. They often sublet their tenancy rights to other tenants who did the actual cultivation. Poorer tenants had to pay lower deposits but higher rents. In Sichuan, landlords seem to have been more successful in evicting tenants without protest than in Hunan, but in both provinces it is clear that the growth of a commercial economy brought about an increase in conflict over rights to land.

The response of the Qing state to this struggle significantly affected its outcome. Qing officials had to decide how to resolve an increasing number of landlord-tenant conflicts. Fundamentally, of course, their sympathies were with the landlord. As state representatives, they were primarily concerned with tax collection, and they knew that rent resistance by tenants impaired the ability of landlords to pay taxes. "The landlord buys the land and depends solely on the rent, and pays his taxes out of this. How can wicked tenants willfully deceive him?" asked Yang Cang, acting local magistrate of Xingning county. He insisted that "the decision as to whether the tenant keeps cultivating the land depends entirely on the landlord . . . If the tenant refuses to leave the land or steals the harvest, the landlord, *after paying the tax,* may bring suit either to collect his rent or to force the tenant to leave the land."[87]

Officials did not, however, support landlord rights without qualification. They repeatedly insisted that rent deposits could not be raised arbitrarily, that tenants were to be treated as commoners and not as slaves, and that gentry who practiced such abuses as turning tenants' wives into concubines should be stripped of gentry status. They prohibited landlords from changing tenants during the spring planting season. This allowed tenants who were in arrears to continue to resist payment until the fall harvest was completed.[88] Some local officials tried to reduce landlord usury by enforcing a limitation of interest rates to 3 percent per month. They hoped thus to prevent the loss of land due to indebtedness.[89]

Legal cases demonstrate that Qing authorities would punish landlords for beating tenants who refused to pay rent. In 1750, Zhang

Rongchang invited Huang Dafu to clear cultivated land for him, offering him three years' rent free. This tenancy contract seems to have been modeled on the early Qing land-clearance policies which offered three tax-free years for land clearance. When Zhang tried to force his tenant to pay rent early, in 1752, Huang refused, beat Zhang, and was struck down by Zhang's hatchet. Zhang was sentenced to strangulation for killing his tenant. A similar killing of a tenant by his landlord occurred in 1761.[90]

On the other hand, powerful local gentry could evade control for some time. Duan Xingbang, a *jiansheng* degree-holder, in Chen-Yuan circuit, bribed the local district magistrate to confiscate the property of a tenant, Zhou Dexian, who could not pay his rent. He continued to persecute Zhou until he had forced Zhou and four others to commit suicide.[91] Duan obstructed imperial investigation with a trail of false depositions until he was finally punished as a "local bully" (*guanggun*).

Officials tried to restrain both sides by invoking images of the common good. The continual insistence on mutual dependency, harmony, and "friendly relations" between landlord and tenants shows that Qing officials were trying to resolve conflicts by invoking ideals of solidarity from an age gone by. These ideals were becoming increasingly irrelevant in a time of rapid mobility and economic growth. There were new opportunities for the "unbenevolent wealthy," the moneylending landlord, the aggressive tenant, the legal pettifogger, or the yamen clerk, none of whom were encompassed by the static norms of Confucian paternalism.

The struggles between landlord and tenant intensified in the early nineteenth century. Kojima Shinji has shown in great detail how tenants, as the spread of the export trade in Hunan and Hubei drew them into the market, broke out of paternalistic bonds of dependence to demand lower rents. Rent and tax-resistance movements turned into military struggles as secret society members extended their influence. When the Taiping armies passed through Hunan and Hubei, they attracted much support from peasants who had previously mobilized themselves in these small-scale incidents. The local rent resisters soon merged their energies with the broad Taiping revolutionary movement.[92]

The overall response of Qing bureaucrats to social conflicts over land in Hunan was a two-pronged attack, combining bureaucratic rationalization and paternalistic exhortation. When changes in social relations in the countryside produced lawsuits over property rights and conflicts over rent, Qing officials responded first by increasing government supervision over the land market. They created more registers, issued standardized land contracts, and issued uniform regulations to replace the ambiguities of local custom. When they could not settle a question with more regulations, they invoked ideals of cooperation for mutual benefit.

Both these approaches had their limitations. Bureaucratic intervention was constrained by the inability of the local official to control the habits of the hundreds of thousands of people he governed, and by a policy of leaving local customs intact as much as possible. Moral exhortation would be effective only if both parties saw the advantage of working together, but there were often incentives for personal gain that outweighed the benefits of cooperation. Qing efforts to resolve conflicts on the land in Hunan demonstrate both the impressive organizational capacities of the eighteenth-century Chinese state and its limited effectiveness in altering major social trends.

SIX

Waterworks Construction
and Official Intervention

The Song of the Dam-Builders

The clouds pass above the bridge.
Looking down below one sees
The dragon appear at the bottom of the sea.
When the Yellow Dragon appears
He will soon fly up to the Nine Horizons.
When the Evil Dragon appeared
He was bound to the high iron tree.
Only when this high, high iron tree blooms
Will the Duke of Ya release him.[1]

Of all the productive efforts of an agricultural community, irrigation
lends itself most naturally to cooperative labor. The building of dikes
is essential to protect crops from flooding and to enhance yields. As
dike works require large capital investments which are seldom within
the means of an individual peasant household, it is not surprising to

find various forms of cooperation in construction and maintenance of dike systems in rural China.[2] What is striking, however, is to find inequality, exploitation, and abuse of the cooperative organizations for private ends. Since village institutions were inadequate to check incentives for private aggrandizement, officials during the Ming and Qing were forced to step in and regulate waterworks projects simply to protect local areas from massive flooding. In so doing, their goal was to restore the ability of producers to maintain autonomously the dikes that protected them. Yet, each time officials tried to intervene, they ran up against fierce resistance from entrenched power-holders who defended local prerogatives against outside reorganization. When the state was restoring the foundations of an economy devastated by war, its initiatives were welcomed as contributions to order and prosperity, but, after one hundred years of peace, local power-holders preferred to use their autonomy in their own interests and to keep state authorities at a distance.

The following two chapters analyze the relationship between official intervention and the construction of waterworks in the Dongting Lake region, broadly defined as the area in Hunan surrounding the lake and the area in Hubei between the lake and the Yangtze River. This chapter discusses the evolution of the important post of *dizhang,* or dike administrator. The dike administrator, a member of the village community responsible for mobilizing labor for dike repairs under official supervision, represented the efforts of the imperial officials to promote self-regulating village control of agricultural production. In Hunan, the post was revived after the collapse of the Ming and remained an important function during the Qing. Debates over the abolition of the post indicate the dilemmas of Qing officials who tried to establish greater state control of agricultural production without committing greater state resources to its regulation.

Chapter 7 discusses the long-term process of encroachment on the lake surface by the progressive construction of polder dikes, which cut off and surrounded newly cultivable land. Despite numerous prohibitions against excessive dike-building, which was likely to increase the danger of flooding, Qing officials were unable to halt the continual erection of illegal dikes around the lake. Local conflicts between state authorities and local irrigators became aggravated in the late eighteenth century and led to serious flooding in the nineteenth.

WATERWORKS AND STATE CONTROL IN HUNAN

The promotion of irrigation was high among the concerns of the statecraft school of Chinese administrators and philosophers. Yang Xifu, Governor of Hunan in the 1740s and 1750s, wrote a notable essay in 1748 describing the long-term rise in grain prices in the eighteenth century, which he blamed on population growth outstripping the growth of agricultural production.[3] His main solution to the problem, besides adjusting granary regulations, was official encouragement of irrigation. He noted:

> Although barren lands have all been recently reclaimed, irrigation does not yet flourish everywhere . . . Irrigation in areas with cities and important roads has already been rehabilitated, but, among mountain villages and secluded regions, there are old dikes, dams, and embankments, not a few of which have fallen into the water and been neglected for a long time . . . Although channels can be dredged, the land has many owners and no one can organize the project.[4]

Yang had to face a basic social contradiction. The ideal community, in official eyes, could manage its own affairs and promote its own welfare with little direction and little claim on official resources, but in fact the villagers often failed to perceive their own best interests. Yang complained that "short-sighted" peasants refused to surrender any of their valuable cropland to build reservoirs for protection against drought. Thus, it was the responsibility of officials to persuade the people to act in their own best interests: "If officials point out the above situation and lead the people, all will be startled into awareness."[5] Effective promotion of waterworks, he concluded, depended on official leadership. Still, he envisaged no fundamental conflict between official and popular interests. Prefectural and circuit officials could lead magistrates in concentrating efforts on irrigation, checking written records, and interviewing gentry and commoners. Within the spectrum of policies designed to increase production, waterworks had the advantage that their benefits were immediate and the results easy to monitor. Yang does betray a certain skepticism about the sincerity of district magistrates when he notes that "building and rebuilding of dams, dikes, and embankments leave clear traces which can be investigated." In fact, he well knew that the conversion of irrigation reservoirs into land had been abetted by local officials; hence he called for impeachment of "local officials who listen to popular bullies and turn reservoirs into cleared land, plotting to gain profit from taxing the land and to claim achievements for encouraging land clearance."[6] He relied on circuit and prefectural officials to investigate and reward or punish magistrates for their success in preventing floods. Control was clearly to be exercised by upper echelons, but magistrates had the responsibility of encouraging voluntary participation by local elites and villagers.

Yang's discussion shows that he was aware of the fact that waterworks are collective goods. Yang, in fact, had perceived the same problems as modern theorists of collective goods, like Mancur Olson, who argue that, "unless the number of individuals in a group is quite small, or unless there is coercion or some other device to make individuals act in their common interest, *rational, self-interested individuals will not act to achieve their common or group interests.*"[7] Olson's analysis has been extended to peasant societies by Samuel Popkin.[8] A reservoir, polder, or dike is a good which provides benefits to all local peasants. None of them can easily be excluded from enjoying the protection from flood and secure water supplies it provides, whether they have contributed to its construction and maintenance or not. Although it is in the common interest of all households to have a reservoir, the individual interest of each household will lead it to clear the land for crops. Dike repair presents the same paradox. Even though all members of the peasant community benefit from well-maintained dikes, individually it is more profitable to let someone else do the repair work. Waterworks exhibit perfectly the classic "free-rider" problem common to all collective goods. The "short-sightedness" of the "ignorant people" perceived by Governor Yang was purely rational. Left to oneself, it was individually more benefi-cial to clear a small bit of land for extra grain production than to sacri-fice it for a reservoir which would benefit everyone equally.

There are, of course, several other notable examples of collective goods in Chinese society, such as corporate lineage endowments and school lands. Compared to these, reservoirs and dikes seem to be par-ticularly insecure. Lineage lands and school endowments did have a certain staying power, although even these were vulnerable to similar temptations: The lack of "selective benefits" for the largest contribu-tors reduced incentives to build up the endowment, and the tempta-tion for private gain led to selling off pieces of the estate in defiance of the strictest regulations. The prototypical charitable estate of Fan Zhongyan, founded in the 1040s, was constantly threatened with dis-integration caused by the lack of clan cohesion. Denis Twitchett con-cludes that the estate had no significant *economic* impact on the members of the clan.[9] What preserved the estate was the "sense of mutual responsibility" toward the clan as a ritual group. Reservoirs in general had no comparable justification, although there are some instances of reservoirs and dams owned by a lineage which may have served analogous functions. The prestige value that officials attempted to instill in waterworks by granting symbolic rewards could not equal the value of endowments of schools or lineage temples.

There are several conditions under which the general paralysis endemic to collective goods can be overcome. First, the state can decide to use its tax revenues for public benefit. In Olson's words, "A state is first of all an organization that provides public goods for its members, the citizens."[10] The Qing state did use its tax revenues to support large-scale irrigation projects, but it did not have enough funds to support every necessary project. Subsidies, loans, and tax incentives were significant means of stimulating water conservancy work, but, for most local projects, the officials had no choice but to encourage voluntary organization and contributions by local groups.

Second, if one member of the group gains significantly more from the provision of the good than others, he may be willing to shoulder the burden of providing the good by himself, and the fact that other free-riders benefit from the good is irrelevant to him. Olson classifies this as an extreme case of "the exploitation of the great by the small." Others may contribute "for reasons of ethic, conscience, or altruism."[11] Qing officials constantly appealed to the literati's conscience by invoking their duty to provide for the local people's welfare. But the "altruistic" large landowner who made major contributions to a dike that benefited many other landowners in fact reaped more than the purely economic benefits of the dike. The rewards in patronage, influence among the local elite, and prestige might be significant enough to outweigh a net loss on the dike itself. Thus Olson notes that "large organizations [cannot] support themselves without providing some sanction, or some attraction distinct from the public good itself, that will lead individuals to help bear the burdens of maintaining the organization."[12] It is no accident that so many large dike projects bear the name of the principal organizer and landowner, a local gentryman who ensured his local prestige by conspicuous contribution to an enterprise of public benefit.[13] When Qing officials offered symbolic rewards—medals, feathers, buttons for caps, sometimes honorary degrees—to local gentry who contributed to public works, they drew on local resources in exchange for the symbols of authority conferred by a centralized autocracy monopolizing legitimation of local power.[14] But these symbolic rewards could work only to a limited degree to draw the local elite into providing contributions that exceeded the tangible economic benefits, and they were effective only in mobilizing resources for new projects, not in discouraging inadvisable projects. After the mid-eighteenth century, officials in Hunan began to realize that it was now more important to discourage excessive dike-building than to promote further construction, but for this new task the earlier system of incentives proved inadequate.

Third, as Douglass North has pointed out, ideology significantly affects the incentives for people to contribute to collective goods.[15] If everyone sought to be a free-rider at all times, no public institutions or voluntary associations could ever survive. No one would pay taxes, people would commit crimes whenever they could avoid being caught, and no one would ever contribute voluntarily to charities or public works. Qing state officials, and statecraft writers in particular, understood that "the fundamental aim [of ideology] is to energize groups to behave contrary to a simple, hedonistic, individual calculus of costs and benefits."[16] Their constant exhortations for moral behavior aimed to overcome short-sighted temptations for private benefit in the interests of common security. In water conservancy, the role of the local official was not simply to use coercive means and material incentives to induce people to cooperate; he also was supposed to reinforce a sense of mutual obligation among gentry and peasants. Yang's program for water conservancy development demanded active official involvement in organizing projects in the early stages, but he believed that ultimately, "with the planting of good customs, even in areas not personally visited by officials, the people will rebuild irrigation works on their own. Then all the land will be fertile."[17]

The success of water conservancy was, therefore, tied to the legitimacy of the Qing state. Only if official ideology was accepted by local producers would the "good customs" flourish which would induce people to repair waterworks even without official direction. The growing crisis in waterworks repair during the eighteenth century signified not only difficulties in economic production but a serious compromising of the legitimacy of the state.

OFFICIAL INTERVENTION AND LOCAL AUTONOMY IN DIKE REPAIRS

Numerous studies have made us aware of the wide spectrum of alternative organizational structures which carried out waterworks projects in traditional China.[18] These ranged from large-scale complex autonomous organizations, like the Sangyuanwei polder in Guangdong, whose directors held regular meetings and independently planned waterworks policies,[19] to closely controlled official projects like the Wancheng dike in Hubei. "Autonomous" units could be directed by a single lineage, which held hereditary posts of supervision, as on Hainan island,[20] or by "gentry directors" (*dongshi*), as in Shanghai,[21] or by locally elected residents.

These waterworks could be classified on two axes according to (1) their total size, and (2) the degree of autonomy from government control:

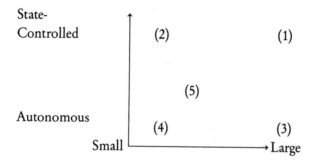

Contrary to the theory of Oriental Despotism, there is no direct relationship between size of project and degree of state control. There were, of course, (1) large state-controlled projects like the Yellow River Administration, with its hordes of bureaucrats and military troops responsible for maintenance, but there were also (2) smaller state-run projects in nearly every province, like the Jinshazhou works in Wuchang prefecture, Hubei, or the Hucheng stone bank in Jiujiang prefecture, Jiangxi.[22] Relatively autonomous works range from (3) the huge Sangyuan polder down to (4) the tiniest irrigation ditch in a peasants' field. Control varies along a continuum just as much as size, and it fluctuates over time with the waxing and waning of state authority and its articulation with local groups.

The Hunan polder organizations (5) fell between the extremes of autonomy and official control, but nearer the autonomous pole. They were smaller than the Guangdong polder, and they did not conduct regular meetings of their members or have a designated board of directors. Local officials did intervene to approve the selection of dike administrators and to register the amount of work to be levied per landholder, but the dike administrator was responsible for organizing the yearly repairs.

Mark Elvin has argued that "the geographical structure of water control systems . . . imposed a spatial pattern on social action that was distinct from that of the marketing system, though obviously not

TABLE 18 Prominent Lineages Associated with Polder Lands in Xiangyin County

Dike	Lineage	Date	Origin	Degrees			Posts	
				jinshi	juren	low	high	low
Jingtang	Li	1341–67	Jishui, Jiangxi	1	14	1	3	11
Gutang	Lin						3	
Hanwan	Wang	1692	Mianyang, Hubei		11	1	5	7
Shejia	Yang	Ming	Fengcheng, Jiangxi	2	22		2	
Dongzhuang	Jiang				1		3	
Hanwan	Luo		Nanchang, Jiangxi	1	1		4	1
Fuxing	Yi	Ming	Mianyang, Hubei	7	1		5	
Xifu	Wang	1662–1722	Jishui, Jiangxi				5	3
Wangtong	Wang	1341–1367		1	15		1	2
Renhe	Fu	1662–1722	Shanghang, Fujien		2		2	2
Gongyue	Zhou							
Gongyue	Yao	early Ming	Taihe, Jiangxi		2	2		2
Wenzhou	Li	1726	Putian, Fujien			1		1
Wenzhou	Huang	1663	Shanghang, Fujien	2	12		11	2
Wenzhou	Zhang			1	20		17	14
Wenzhou	Zhou						1	
Wenzhou	Tan	1600–1660	Nanchang, Jiangxi				1	
Wenzhou	He	1669	Jianli, Hubei		2		7	
Shunfeng	Ren				2		7	
Shunfeng	Lin						1	

TABLE 18 *(continued)*

Source: Xiangyin Xiangtuzhi 1881, *juan* 17–18. Many other lineages listed here are also named according to irrigation features, such as *tang* (16 lineages), *ba* (7), *duan* (12), and *chong* (9). The lineages on whom detailed information is given in *juan* 17–18 are not necessarily the same as those described as *daxing* in *juan* 1–5. *Juren* in the table includes both military and civil degrees and all the *gongsheng* degrees placed in "upper gentry" by Chang Chung-li, *The Chinese Gentry*, p. 9. "High" posts are all those above the rank of district magistrate (Rank 6B and above); "low" posts include district magistrate and below (Rank 7A and lower). When a person is listed as having an official post but no degree is given, it is assumed that he has a *juren* degree, except for posts obtained by "military merit."

unrelated to it."[23] The self-contained geographical units of the enclosures around Dongting Lake must have had a strong shaping effect on
the social communities they contained, particularly since the development of these polder lands made possible the growth of new
marketplaces. We can find out very little about the social structure
inside each of the enclosures, but the gazetteers do inform us that in
Xiangyin county each polder was dominated by one or two prominent lineages (*daxing*), each of whom was identified by the polder
with which it was associated[24] (see Table 18). Many of these lineages
had roots in Hunan reaching back to the early Ming. The development of these polder lands must have made it possible for them to
increase their prosperity by providing them with secure authority
over consolidated geographical units. Conversely, polders offered an
attractive opportunity for lineage investment in corporate property.
In Guangdong, clearance of alluvial soil in the Pearl River Delta produced even larger, more formally organized lineages, who hired "sand
guards" to protect their fields against neighboring clans.[25] The compact shapes of these enclosures may have slowed down the normal
scattering trend endemic to Chinese landholding and made it possible
for these lineages to maintain their local prominence into the late
nineteenth century, when they were recorded in the 1881 gazetteer.

The Hunan structure appeared to Yang Xifu to be an effective
compromise between excess local autonomy and excess official control. When pleading for the retention of the dike administrator, he
argued that there were far too many polders for one local official to
supervise personally and that deputing supervision to assistant runners and clerks would only lead to worse abuses than those committed by the dike administrator. He vigorously defended the right of
local people to conserve their own land by doing their own dike repairs. But the story of water conservancy in Hunan demonstrates that
local autonomy in dike maintenance was too vulnerable to the
incentives undermining collective goods to provide effective flood
prevention.

THE STRUCTURE OF
WATERWORKS IN HUNAN

Waterworks had always been essential to agricultural production in Hunan. Every local gazetteer describes Hunan as a "well-watered" region (*zeguo*), but this term had two meanings. It could mean that the abundant supplies of water from the four major rivers of Hunan, Dongting Lake, and the channels from the Yangtze made possible high-yielding paddy-rice agriculture. But *zeguo* also referred to an area that had been literally covered with water when inadequate waterworks gave way. In contrast to areas of North China irrigated by canals (*qu*), and hilly areas of Central and South China dominated by reservoirs (*pi* and *tang*), where conflicts over the ownership and distribution of scarce water supplies predominated, the main problems of water conservancy in the Dongting Lake region, as in the Jiangnan Delta, involved the drainage of excess water and the dredging of silted canals. Maintenance of a strong dike system was crucial, but the success of dike construction and repair depended on fluctuations in administrative capability and popular response.

Dikes in Hunan were mainly built to enclose agricultural land. Trade, of course, flourished on the Xiang River, and Yang Xifu stressed the importance of rebuilding a dike near Changsha which had been destroyed in the Yuan dynasty in order to allow merchant boats to moor near the city. But the richest paddy fields in the province were protected by round and square enclosures (*yuan*) ranging from 1 km. to 150 km. in circumference. In a good year, the harvest from *yuan* fields was equal to several years of harvests in the mountains.[26] The walls of the enclosures protected fields that lay below the water level of the lake itself.[27] Filling the fields with water was as simple as cutting a small channel in the dike, but draining the water out required intensive labor on human- and animal-powered pumps.[28] In Jiangsu, collective labor on pumping crews (*dapengche*) was an important focus of community organization.[29] We lack such evidence for Hunan, but it is reasonable to suppose that some such form of collective mobilization reinforced the autonomy of the polder communities.

The lakelands of Hunan were quite similar to the lowland area in Hubei between the Yangtze and Han Rivers. The major dikes in Hubei, however, were the long, straight dikes lining the Yangtze River. The largest of these was the Wancheng dike, which extended over 200 *li* (115 km.) from Dangyang to Jianli county, and attracted considerable government attention and resources.[30] Hubei also had enclosures similar to Hunan, but these tended to be smaller, only reaching about 30 *li* (17 km.) in circumference. The functions of dikes in the two provinces also differed. In Hubei, straight dikes were built primarily to prevent flooding from the Yangtze and its tributaries, while, in Hunan, floods were due to the seasonal rise and fall of the lake. In Hubei, there were often two lines of defense between the river and the fields: an outer barrier (*waidi*) and an inner enclosure. Governor General Wang Guodong reported in 1727 that these dikes were strongly built and well supervised.[31]

The Hunan polders created well-defined landed communities. Most of the plots held by a landowner were contained within one enclosure, or two or three neighboring enclosures.[32] The dikes themselves often defined villages with the same names as the dikes that enclosed them. Even as early as the Song dynasty, Longyang county's villages were organized according to the dikes containing them.[33] The areas cleared earliest tended to be occupied by small-holder peasants, but lands cleared later on were controlled by large landlords. In the 1930s, "old dikes" were 75 percent occupied by owner-cultivators, while "new dikes" were over 50 percent tenant land.[34]

Finally, the polder communities were distinguished by the predominance of outside immigrants.[35] Outside landlords, usually from Jiangxi, supplied the capital to build the new dikes, and immigrants from outside the province became the tenants who worked on dike construction and repair. These "wicked migrants" were the source of the illegal dike-building that spread around the lake through the eighteenth century.[36] The fact that the "people who clear land [illegally] are not the local wealthy," but rather "wicked people hoping for profit," in Kuang Minben's words, made local officials even more determined to end their illegal clearance.[37]

Differences in dike structures also significantly affected the kinds of floods liable to occur in each province.[38] Hunan floods in the lake region were generally an indirect consequence of excess rainfall either in the mountains at the headwaters of Hunan's four major rivers or in the tributaries supplying the Yangtze. Baron Richthofen found that the filling up of Dongting Lake in the summer was almost entirely due to the rise in the Yangtze River and not to the four smaller rivers of Hunan.[39] Flooding from swollen streams occurred regularly in the 5th month of the year, causing the level of Dongting Lake to rise. Some of the enclosures broke nearly every year, but the damage varied according to the significance of the dike affected. Floods in Hunan were frequent but limited in effect, usually damaging only a small part of the lowland crop area. Grain prices on the whole remained stable. The increased grain prices that worried Yang Xifu were not caused by flooding but by the imbalance of supply and demand when downstream provinces affected by natural disaster demanded increased grain exports fron Hunan.[40] Hubei floods, by contrast, were less frequent, but a break in one of the major Yangtze dikes could suddenly inundate large stretches of farmland.

Despite their differences, hydrographic features of the middle Yangtze region fundamentally united the two provinces. The seasonal floods of the Yangtze, produced by heavy rains upstream in Sichuan, brought high-water crests down the river annually. Dongting Lake, along with hundreds of smaller lakes in Hubei, served as the overflow basin for this excess water. It was, in effect, a gyroscopic regulator of flood peaks, moderating violent swings in total flow. This moderating influence in turn protected the lower Yangtze region from sudden flooding. From the mid-sixteenth century on, settlement in Hubei progressively filled in many of the smaller lakes. As Hubei gradually lost its ability to catch flood waters, Dongting Lake and the channels connecting the Yangtze to it became even more crucial for flood prevention. But as Dongting Lake's own surface area decreased in the eighteenth century, the flood danger mounted for the entire Yangtze river basin.

Dongting Lake, then, presents a distinctive complex of geographical, social, and economic features. Less commercialized than Jiangnan and intensively focused on high-yielding rice agriculture, its peasant economy relied on polder dikes to protect fields from flooding and ensure state supplies of water. This strategy had both benefits and costs. Fertile rice paddies brought prosperity, but the flood danger was ever-present. Since floods of the lake were not as dramatic as those of the Yangtze River in Hubei, officials allowed the Dongting residents great autonomy in maintenance of their own waterworks. This autonomy allowed the local peasants to prosper, but, by the nineteenth century, it led them into serious ecological difficulties.

SELF-REGULATED DIKE REPAIR:
THE ROLE OF THE DIKE ADMINISTRATOR

THE DIKE ADMINISTRATOR
IN LATE MING JIANGNAN

The dike administrator (*dizhang*) was a member of the local community responsible for organization of dike repairs and drainage. His post was established in the early Ming era, but the manifold developments in Ming society after the sixteenth century transformed his relationship to state officials. This evolution is made clearest by numerous studies of Soochow prefecture in Jiangsu province. While the evolution of the *dizhang* in Hunan in many ways parallels that of Jiangnan, it also has distinctive characteristics.

From the early Ming through the mid-fifteenth century, resident landlords in Jiangnan undertook dredging and repairs as part of their responsibilities as leaders of the *lijia* tax-collection system. The *liang-zhang*, or chief of the *li*, while nominally responsible for tax collection alone, in fact participated actively in dike repairs along with the *li* elders.[41] After the 1450s, the duties of *lijia* chiefs became more specialized to include only tax collection, and a separate post of "dike administrator" (*tangzhang*) was established, whose duties were codified by regulations in 1495–1496.

Although the *lijia* remained the unit for organizing dike labor, the amount of labor demanded from each landlord was allocated according to his frontage on the creeks along which dikes were built. The rationale for this "head-land" (*tiantou*) system was that the lands along the numerous creeks were mostly owned by the wealthy, while the more distant lands, which were the most difficult to irrigate and drain, were generally owned by the poor. All the members of the dike enclosure cooperated in certain activities, especially the practice of "collective pumping" (*dapengche*),[42] but the actual labor levies were designed to achieve rough equality by placing the burden only on the wealthy landowners bordering the creeks.

Defenders of the *tiantou* system recognized the importance of creating incentives to contribute to collective works. They argued that, if equal levies were placed on all lands within the dike, there would be no incentive for landowner A to contribute to the repair of B's dike. "Ultimately, if A takes care of B's land, or C repairs D's banks, A and C will not only not be willing to do it thoroughly, but there will also be no reward or punishment for them."[43] The principles of the *tiantou* system accorded with those of the *lijia* of the early Ming in that responsibility and control of waterworks, as of taxation, were not equally shared but entrusted to a class of relatively wealthy landowners residing in the countryside.[44]

With the growth of commercial relations in the countryside in Jiangnan in the sixteenth century, however, resident landowners moved to the cities and became absentee landlords, causing the *lijia* system to decay.[45] In Japanese terminology, the "resident landlords" became "gentry landlords," residing in the city, uninvolved in farm production, exempt from corvée duties, interested only in collecting rents and not at all in waterworks repair. Since the rich now escaped corvée duties, the dike-administrator post fell to poorer households, many of whom were bankrupted by its responsibilities. By the Jiajing reign (1522–1566), the inadequacies of the dike administrator resulted in increased neglect of waterworks repair, increased silting of canals, and increased flooding.

As Geng Ju, magistrate of Changshu country, stated, the reasons for this neglect were that (1) common people could not support the burdens of repair work; (2) the land of large landowners was mixed together with that of small landowners, and the large landowners contributed nothing toward repairs; (3) small landowners who became tenants of the large landowners would not repair dikes on land they did not own; (4) even if a landlord wanted to promote repair, his tenants feared that he would oust them and install new tenants at higher rents once the repairs were done, so they refused to work for him; (5) large-scale repairs required official aid.[46] Most repairs done in this period were done by officials. The waterworks projects undertaken from the Jiajing period on differed noticeably from the earlier ones in that (1) the number of projects increased; (2) there was greater involvement of lower-level officials in the projects; and (3) officials were involved in a greater variety of projects, from drainage of Lake Tai to dams along large rivers, down to dikes on the smallest creeks.[47] To build these projects, officials, faced with declining tax income because of the decay of the *lijia,* had to levy further surtaxes on the people.[48]

As the *lijia* crumbled in the late Ming, the tax collectors lost the original purpose for their existence. Widespread tax evasion eliminated the effective control of the *liangzhang* over the countryside, but the dike administrators remained, because someone still had to supervise the collection of levies for local dike repair. In fact, the dike administrators expanded their authority to fill the vacuum left by the decline of the *liangzhang*. In Soochow and Jiaxing prefectures, it was the dike administrators who conducted land surveys, compiled land and population registers, determined levies on newly cleared land, and allocated duties to pay taxes on lands whose title was disputed. The dike administrator became responsible even for local military organization.[49] In effect, the irrigation officials had usurped from the tax collectors whatever authority remained over local communities, and the organization of dike repair became the determinant of local power.

Some late-Ming officials in fact favored this usurpation. They sought to use the consolidated authority of the irrigation officials to reconstruct the fiscal structure on more solid foundations. They proposed to replace the old *tiantou* system by the system of "levies according to actual land" (*zhaotian paiyi*), which would require all landowners living within the dike's enclosure to contribute to dike repairs according to the size of their landholdings. The introduction of this new system of levies presupposed the increased authority of the dike administrator to handle the fiscal as well as strictly irrigation-related affairs of his community.

Introduction of the *zhaotian paiyi* system required further state intervention in the organization of the repair of waterworks. State officials now had to back up the dike administrators in ensuring that all the landowners paid their share of the levies. They were particularly concerned to eliminate gentry landlords' privileges of exemption from corvée duties. The series of local tax reforms known as the "Single Whip Reform" had commuted many corvée duties into silver payments. Commutation made it easier to insist that both gentry and commoners should be subject to corvée.

A new system, entitled "landlords supply food, tenants supply labor" (*yeshi dianli*), provided for tenants within a dike to supply the labor for dike repair, while their landlords provided the food or its money equivalent to support the laborers. In this way, the absentee landlords in the cities were forced to contribute to the protection of the lands they owned, while the tenants actually residing in the area were given support to do the necessary work.[50] The growing importance of cotton-textile handicrafts in the Soochow region also encouraged the adoption of the *yeshi dianli* system, because tenants had to be compensated for the opportunity cost of working on dike repairs instead of in the cotton industry. The increased independence tenants gained from working in the cotton industry led them to resist excessive landlord demands for rent.

Magistrate Geng Ju, of Changshu county, Soochow prefecture, succeeded in the early seventeenth century in enforcing the principle that all households using water on their lands, whether gentry or commoner, should take responsibility for dike repairs, a principle that persisted into the twentieth century. Geng Ju ensured that the landlords would provide for their tenants' labor by giving ration coupons to the tenants, who then presented them to officials to obtain food. Elsewhere, however, effective enforcement of the reforms had to wait for the Qing conquest. Landlord opposition had defeated reforms in the fifteenth and sixteenth centuries, but new district magistrates in the seventeenth century, backed by the new dynasty, were able to enact the reforms successfully. Songjiang prefecture introduced the same principle in the 1660s, and Huzhou prefecture in the 1740s.[51]

The *yeshi dianli* system, when effectively enforced, represented a significant intervention by the state in the local rural economy for the purpose of shoring up community organizations involved in water control and dike repair. It succeeded in eliminating gentry privileges in respect to water control and challenged landlord authority over the countryside. While there is some dispute among Japanese scholars about the extent to which autonomous community organization was significant independently of state initiatives in promoting the reformed system,[52] there is general agreement that the new system could not have been effectively instituted without official intervention.

Once established, with official backing, the system must have strengthened the corporate organization of the irrigation communities and increased the ability of their residents to fend off excessive extraction by city-resident landlords. The new dike administrators had to be residents of their dike area, and even tenants were allowed to fill the post. City-dwelling landlords benefited indirectly, in that their tenants were assured of subsistence, while the residents of the community, landowner and tenant, benefited from increased autonomy and a more stable organization of repairs. Jiangnan in the late Ming had been plagued by rent resistance revolts by tenants demanding that landlords fulfill their expected duties in contributing to local repairs, but, by the early Qing, the new system seemed to have effectively eliminated the threat of this type of rent resistance.[53] In Jiangnan, the urban gentry ceased to resist the new equalized levy system as applied to irrigation alone. They accepted the need to pay their share of the levies in return for the assurance by the state that their tenants' subsistence would be maintained and that they would collect their expected rents.

DIKE ADMINISTRATORS IN HUGUANG

The conditions for irrigated rice agriculture production on polder fields were very similar in the Dongting Lake area and in Jiangnan, and the general trend of evolution of the dike administrator's post was similar. Huguang did, however, have its own distinctive developments.[54] In the early Ming era, as in Jiangnan, irrigation was not a specialized responsibility but was subsumed under the duties of the *lijia* heads. By the mid-Ming, as both officials and people increasingly promoted waterworks construction, the special post of dike administrator appeared, variously known as *tangzhang, bazhang, yanzhang,* or *dizhang*. The "general dike administrator" (*dizong*) served as an overseer of several *dizhang*.[55] Under the supervision of the district magistrate, the *dizhang* could mobilize local people to repair dikes. In 1522, for example, magistrate Zhuang of Yuanjiang "had the *dizhang* lead the *baojia* and hundreds of laborers" in repairing major dikes after severe flooding.[56] The work was completed in three months. Magistrate Zhuang was rewarded by having a local bridge named after him, and the local scholars all remembered his generosity.

Nevertheless, the organization of repairs soon began to decline:

> In the villages there have long been official dikes, dike administrators (*tangzhang*), and dike laborers (*tangfu*) supervised by the assistant magistrates, who repeatedly inspected and ensured that the dikes were firm and the waterways deeply dredged. The dikes could irrigate over one hundred *mou*. If there was the smallest break, the blame fell on the *tangzhang*. Thus, through Chenghua and Hongzhi (1465–1505) there were no floods. After Zhengde (1506–1521) they neglected their duties and the reservoirs daily silted up, while the lands were taken over by local power-holders (*haoyou*). If there was a drought, they folded their hands and did nothing.[57]

Huguang, like Jiangnan, suffered the same processes of tax evasion, enlarged gentry privileges, neglect of repairs, and increased flooding up to the end of the Ming. Official efforts to rectify the system were, however, more limited. Just as later in the Qing, the straight dikes along the Yangtze River in Hubei were put under a rational bureaucratic structure. After major floods in Jingzhou, Hubei, in the 1560s, the prefect intervened to appoint a dike elder (*dilao*) for every 1,000 *zhang* of dike, a dike administrator (*dizhang*) for every 500 *zhang*, and a dike tithing head (*dijia*) for every 100 *zhang*, supervising 10 dike laborers (*difu*).[58] The Hunan polders, however, were not restructured under the *yeshi dianli* system. There was an increase in dike-building in the late Ming era, but, unlike Jiangnan, the proportion of officially built works declined. Huguang, a more remote region, was less commercially developed and of less vital concern to the state. As it had not yet developed a flourishing cotton-textile industry comparable to Jiangnan's, there was no handicraft industry to compete with agriculture for tenants' labor time and farmers' investment.[59]

Huguang, compared to Jiangnan, had more private initiative in dike construction and stronger local control over the polder organizations. A good illustration of this consolidated local power in the late Ming era is the fact that, in some places, the dike administrator posts were, de facto, occupied hereditarily by one family or lineage. As one writer noted, "The post of *yuanzong* (polder chieftain), unlike the *dilao* (dike elder) and *yujia* (polder tithe head) along the river, who are rotated yearly, is held by one surname, and it has been this way for generations."[60] There is also no evidence in Huguang in the Ming period of the rent resistance found in Jiangnan. In fact, conflicts over both rent and land rights and increased official intervention in the irrigation structure do not appear until the mid-Qing. Huguang, as a more backward region, had to wait two centuries before it experienced the conflicts Jiangnan had undergone in the late sixteenth and early seventeenth centuries.

Huguang's irrigation, however, faced difficulties similar to Jiangnan's in the late Ming and early Qing. The decline of the *lijia* led to tax evasion and misallocation of repair funds. This brought about major floods even before the revolts that brought down the dynasty broke out. The floods in Huarong county in 1600 were the worst in a century.[61] Unequal tax burdens produced deterioration in the dike network. In 1617, a local official in Yunyang county was impeached for going around to each of the residents of a dike and extorting payments of 20 to 30 *taels* from them.[62] The collapse of the Ming dynasty meant serious flooding and abandonment of land around the lake. Early Qing magistrates made some efforts to restore the irrigation network, but the Wu Sangui Rebellion destroyed it again.[63] Even in the early eighteenth century, reconstruction was only just getting under way. Violence was still prevalent. Households tried to avoid their duties to serve in the *dizhang* rotation, fearing that "violent types" would resist corvée levies by leading masses to plunder their houses. As long as officials could not punish these offenders, rumors spread that "official law is far away, the rebels' law is near."[64] There could be no regular allocation of repair duties until the turmoil of the transition period abated.

By the mid-eighteenth century, the *dizhang* had again assumed a dominant role in directing the activities of the agricultural community, unsupervised by official representatives. This loose control made it easy for *dizhang* interested in personal profit to engage in engrossment at the expense of dike repair. This engrossment was particularly easy in areas like Wuling county, where all contributions for dike repair had been commuted into levies in silver based on land holdings.[65] *Dizhang* also claimed the same rights as regular officials to gifts of food after the autumn harvest and at the New Year.[66] In Lizhou and Huarong, engrossment of commuted labor levies, bribes by "wicked gentry," and unequal burdens levied on the poor meant that actual laborers became fewer and "existed in name and not in reality."[67] As there were no registers stipulating the amount of labor to be contributed according to one's landholding, misallocation of labor levies was common.[68] The Changde prefect in 1688 found peculation of repair money so rampant that he petitioned to abolish the entire *dizhang* system. His desperate remedy anticipated by fifty years the conclusions of his superiors.[69]

EARLY QING TIGHTENING OF CONTROL OVER DIKE REPAIR

During the eighteenth century, there was a persistent tendency for officials to intervene in the dike-repair process to correct abuses and inequities. Yang Xifu had tried to single out certain dikes as particularly important "strategic works" (*xiangong*), subject to "major repairs" (*daxiu*) every three years under the supervision of local officials.[70] Given that the few local officials could not possibly survey the entire irrigation system, Yang tried to ensure official control over at least the most vital portions of the dike network. Yearly repairs would be carried out by tenants, who would only add several inches of earth to the dikes; the triennial repairs, on the other hand, were entrusted to landlords (*tianzhu*), who would heighten and widen the dikes by several feet. Yang found that in Yiyang and Xiangyin counties, the recently built "people's dikes" (*minwei*) were loose and thin; older official dikes were also in decay. Although several inches of earth were added each year, the next year's rains washed it away and caused much of the dike to collapse, so that "yearly repairs" existed in name only. Yang wanted to ensure the stability of those dikes which were to be preserved by establishing closer official supervision, but, instead of setting up a large network of official posts, as in Hubei, he left landowners in the diked lands responsible for their own repairs. "Each landowner household with resources will put up capital to repair dikes and make the land eternally fertile, but we cannot force them to do what is difficult."[71]

Yang's triennial repair schedule really only set goals for individuals to achieve. Yang did try to improve official supervision by making it a rule that officials solely responsible for irrigation could not be deputed to work on other tasks. Nevertheless, the regulation of Hunan dike-builders was much looser than the elaborate regulations for Jingzhou dikes in Hubei. Forms of management varied according to the structure of water control in each province.

Yang Xifu took other measures to increase official control in Hunan. All responsibility for waterworks around the entire lake had been previously concentrated in one circuit, Yue-Chang-Li *dao*, comprising the prefectures of Yuezhou and Changde, the independent department of Lizhou, and the two counties of Xiangyin and Yiyang. Because circuit jurisdictions were intended to embrace functional economic units, it made sense to have the entire lake area under one unit spanning several prefectures. In the 1750s, Yang Xifu pointed out the anomalous position of the two counties of Xiangyin and Yiyang.[72] Both were parts of Changsha prefecture and thus subject to Chang-Bao circuit in judicial and taxation matters, but to Yue-Chang-Li in waterworks. He argued that the circuit intendant in Yuezhou was too far away to be able to supervise these two counties effectively while the intendant in Changsha was nearby. Yang succeeded in having the Xiangyin and Yiyang dike works placed under Chang-Bao circuit, sacrificing the functional unity of the circuit around the lake for the sake of closer control.

Another effort of Yang's to increase control of dikes in the region was the reestablishment of the post of assistant district magistrate in Baling county.[73] Baling, the locus of the prefectural capital of Yuezhou on the northeast corner of the lake, had been quite important in the Ming era, possessing an assistant district magistrate (*xiancheng*), a register (*zhubo*), a jail warden (*dianli*), and a river police inspector (*hebosuo*). By 1698, after the rebellions of the Ming-Qing transition and the Wu Sangui uprising, the population had become so sparse and administration so much simpler that all these posts had been eliminated. By the 1740s, Baling had recovered so much that it was designated as a "four-character" (very important) post, yet it was one of only two metropolitan counties in Hunan to lack an assistant district magistrate.[74] Yang proposed to shift a *xiancheng* to Baling from Shaoyang county in Baoqing prefecture, which used to have rebellious minorities but was now quiescent. The new official in Baling would assist in tax collection but be solely responsible for dike works.

THE STATE STEPS IN:
THE ATTEMPT TO ABOLISH
THE POST OF DIKE ADMINISTRATOR

Up to the early Qianlong reign, Qing officials made no attempts to intervene in the *dizhang* system, but, in Qianlong 4 (1739), they seriously considered a proposal to abolish the post. The original proposal was made by the Guangxi Governor Antu, who requested a change from "levying labor according to landholding" (*anmou paifu*) to "collecting expenses according to landholdings" (*anmou zhengfei*). He proposed to eliminate all dike administrators and to give a seal-holding official responsibility for collecting the money and hiring laborers to work on the dikes.[75] Hunan provincial treasurer Zhang Can, after investigation, found that dike administrators collected fees from peasants who hoped to escape the corvée labor levy and that they acted in league with clerks to inflate the costs of repairs. As a result, the total paid by the people far exceeded the cost, while the hired laborers failed to tamp down the earth on the dikes securely enough to prevent floods. He recommended greater official involvement in dike repairs, based on regulations already adopted in Hubei. The official would estimate the work required each year and distribute the total cost among all the taxpayers by collecting the sum along with the regular tax.

Judging from the numerous protests against Zhang's proposal, local officials believed that the advantages of official intervention in dike repair were outweighed by numerous drawbacks.[76] First of all, each dike included a variety of types of land. Some polder land in high areas was never flooded, and people in these areas did not need to provide labor for dike repairs. Land located outside the dike enclosures also provided no repair labor. The land registers used for tax purposes recorded the location of land within a district (*qu*) but not its location with respect to a given dike. Tax levies and their associated land grades thus did not correspond to dike-labor levies. An accurate allocation of dike fees according to land area would require an entirely new land survey, creating special "land registers organized according to dike [location]." Not only would it take years of work, but "as soon as ignorant people heard the word 'survey' they would be greatly alarmed."[77] The Manchu rulers had already determined by the late seventeenth century that they would not force a comprehensive national land survey on a hostile local society. Giving up accurate knowledge of land ownership was part of the price for gaining gentry acquiescence to Manchu rule. By the mid-eighteenth century, local landlord interests were powerful enough to make even limited provincial or county-level surveys impossible.

Second, under the new system, yearly levies for repairs would not be uniform but would depend upon the estimated cost of repairs for the year. But the absence of a fixed tax quota would only make it more difficult for peasants to predict the amount they would have to pay, and it would open the way for clerks to conceal the true amount of the levy.

Third, any officially imposed levy would have to be standardized over a given area. Thus, it would pool contributions in order to use the surplus from one area where little work was needed that year to fill a deficit in another. The people, however, would not accept this, it was argued, and they would not want to give increased levies in order to help another dike area. If the levies were reduced in one year of little repair work, the people would fight against increases in later years. Here was a vivid illustration of the entrenched localism of the polder communities. Landowners could be induced to cooperate on the maintenance of polders in which they had a personal stake, but they strongly resisted surrendering funds to assist neighbors in a different polder. A sense of the common good only extended as far as the wall of the polder dike.

Fourth, laborers on the dikes would have to be drawn from the local area, since recruiting outsiders would mean extra costs for lodging. The local official could not recruit all the laborers personally, but, if he delegated the task to underlings, he could not prevent them from cutting the workers' wages for their own profit. This argument implied that laborers recruited from outside the county were preferable to the use of local laborers. If outside laborers were exploited, they could always go home; they would be unlikely to disturb the local magistrate. Local laborers, who already had to bribe yamen underlings to pay their taxes or settle lawsuits, would fall victim to yet another type of bureaucratic squeeze. Local labor kept costs down, but it would not ensure firm dikes.

Fifth, under the old system, local people had set up their own rotation system to watch over the dikes in the spring and summer highwater season and to stop breaks immediately. If officials took over collection of dike fees, the local people would become lax, leaving all the responsibility up to the official. The sense of collective responsibility depended on having the local residents personally interested in dike maintenance. If local landowners lost the power to manage their dikes, they were apt to surrender all interest in protection of their fields to the officials.

Finally, the rotation system aimed to elicit greater participation from large landowners than from small holders. Even higher gentry (*shen*) were subject to assessments for repairs. The *dizhang*, too, whatever their opportunities for enrichment, had a personal interest in protecting their lands within the dike. With the *dizhang* posts eliminated, the officials would be dependent on their clerks, "who are only interested in enriching themselves," and "the zeal of hired inspectors cannot equal the self-patrolling of the dike residents."[78] Although officials could be impeached for negligence if the dike broke, the people would have already suffered disaster.

Besides these abstract arguments, specific reports from Xiangyin, Yiyang, Huarong, Wuling, Longyang, and Yuanjiang counties, Lizhou, Changsha and Yuezhou prefectures all claimed that the levy of labor according to the landholding system worked perfectly well, that there were no abuses of commutation and engrossment, and that to change to a system of monetary contributions would only provide more pretexts for peculation and burden the poor unfairly. The magistrates stressed particularly the poverty of their districts and the inability of poor landholders to find the money to pay a new surtax. These reports portray a local economy still not greatly monetized and not yet highly productive. Changsha prefecture claimed that only one- to two-tenths of the landowners contributed money to hire laborers to do dike repairs; most of the landowners preferred to contribute their own family labor.[79]

Given what we know about the extensive commercialization of Hunan in the eighteenth century and the prevalence of corruption in the dike-repair organization, these reports must be regarded with suspicion. The unanimous local opposition to reforms indicates that local officials and gentry had vested interests in keeping things the way they were. The *dizhang* who profited from the system were successful in convincing county-level officials to side with them against proposals by their superiors for reform. In fact, this opposition did succeed in persuading Governor Yang Xifu to agree to preserve the dike administrator's post. He, in turn, pleaded their case with the Emperor, arguing that the villagers around the lake could effectively repair the dikes themselves.[80]

Hunanese officials, then, despite their concern about the lack of restraints on the *dizhang*'s activities, were forced to conclude that it was best to leave the old system alone. While they decided not to abolish the post, they still attempted to limit his powers with official regulations. In Qianlong 11 (1746), the assistant district magistrate of Yiyang county reported: "Every time I go to a dike, the landowners report to me in profusion, either talking about the injustice of levies by the general dike administrator (*dizong*) or about errors due to the sale of land and taking over dike work on it."[81] He blamed these abuses on the absence of an official land register for allocating labor according to landholding. While the *dizong* had their own private dike registers, it was impossible to know whether or not these registers had been altered. Furthermore, sales of land allowed the seller to transfer his excess dike levies to the buyer, so it was necessary to make careful registers of land sales and diked land-holdings, with one copy to be kept in the county and one to be held by the *dizong*.[82]

These regulations were part of a series of official attempts to establish more formalized control over dike repair organizations while preserving their essential autonomy. Officials tried to ensure that levies for repair were required from everyone owning lands within the dike, not only those adjacent to the dike.[83] They urged the *dizhang* to investigate all the people living within a dike and to report to officials "those with unclear backgrounds" so that unreliable people could be driven out.[84] They also urged the *dizhang* to conduct surveys of uncleared land within the polder, dividing these lands into uncultivable grasslands and potentially cultivable land. The owners of potentially cultivable land were to be assessed for dike-repair levies in order to prevent inequities if the land was ever cultivated.[85] At times, county-level officials conducted their own surveys to determine whether new lands had been cleared or lost to flooding, so that repair levies could be adjusted.[86]

Most important, official regulations formally defined the rotation of the *dizhang* post. Wang Yuandong, assistant district magistrate of Wuling, reported that, when he arrived at his post in Yongzheng 6 (1728), there were no formal regulations establishing the rotation of the *dizong* post; it was all left up to the dike people to "mutually replace each other" (*sixiang gengti*). Thus, only "crafty ones out for profit" were willing to take the post. In Yongzheng 11 (1733), Wang set up a yearly rotation of the post, which gained the governor's approval.[87]

In Qianlong 10 (1745), circuit intendant Yan Youxi laid down more specific regulations, establishing one *dizong* for every one thousand *zhang* of dike length, with two *dizhang* subordinate to him. Each year the responsibility for repairs shifted to a different section within the dike. Later Yan, deciding that one-year terms did not provide enough experience, altered the term to three years,[88] but some areas maintained a yearly rotation. He inscribed in stone regulations specifying the *dizong*'s responsibilities and posted them in each county.[89]

By establishing such regulations, officials aimed to reinvigorate the dike-repair organizations while at the same time instituting closer regulation. They hoped thereby to eliminate the endemic vice of engrossment, or *baolan,* which permeated Chinese society below the county level. Yamen clerks and local gentry could be involved in engrossment of repair funds, while dike administrators, like officials, felt entitled to collect customary fees for their services.[90] Yan Youxi learned that, in Yue-Chang-Li circuit, 60 to 70 percent of the land within a polder was owned by "gentry, large lineages, circuit officials, and clerks." When it became the turn of these people to serve in the labor rotation, some of them, "because the low-ranking irrigation officials cannot punish them, not only resist the repair of their own dikes, but engross their friends' dikes and take responsibility for them."[91] Frequent cases of resistance to performing repairs by local gentry, particularly *shengyuan* and *jiansheng,* required local officials to intervene to enforce performance. Ultimately, they decided that it was better to exclude degree-holders from the dike-administrator rotation and to have their brothers, sons, or servants serve in their place.[92]

Closer supervision could not prevent the gradual deterioration of autonomous dike repair. Besides the perennial peculation of the *dizhang* himself, the new proliferation of illegally built dikes around the dike seriously undermined the *dizhang*'s control over his polder. Just as, in the late-Ming period, the dikes had proliferated as the *lijia* system decayed, so in the Qing era the autonomous dike repair organizations collapsed while illegal dikes flourished. Governor Chen Hongmou found, in 1755, that the proliferation of private dikes was undermining the established system of local autonomy in organizing repairs:

People from other counties establish polders in this county, call in tenants to cultivate them, and, after sharing the rent from the fall harvest, each
returns to his home county. When they are responsible for repair work,
they entrust it to the tenants. The tenants are not able to do repairs, so the
dike chief (*dizong*) reports to the authorities to force the absentee landowner to take responsibility, but the officials in the other county [where
the landlord lives] refuse to concern themselves. Once they have urged [the
defaulters] to pay up, they are not in charge of the work. The dike chief
may put up funds on their behalf and deduct it from the rent in the fall,
but the landowners refuse to accept this and raise lawsuits every year, causing endless delay.[93]

Thus the dike-administrator system had once again broken down,
and again the officials tried to reconstitute it. They tried to cut back
the yamen clerks to four, appoint one dike administrator per polder
to serve in rotation and lead the landowners in conducting repairs,
and inscribed the new regulations on a stele.

Through the mid-eighteenth century, then, Qing officials did take
definite measures to increase official supervision of dike repair. They
were responding to a growing awareness of increased threat of flooding
which they felt required greater official control. Still, their achievements were relatively small. The dike administrator's post was not
abolished, both because of local resistance and because of limits on
local government funds. In 1728, a district magistrate in Xiangyin
county was dismissed for levying surcharges on the people to repair reservoirs.[94] When Huguang Governor General Ding Chang proposed,
in 1768, to levy a surtax to cover the cost of repairs, the Emperor criticized him for contradicting the empire's benevolent policy on taxation.[95] There were other ways to raise funds. In 1781, a small amount
of grain from community granaries, totaling 1,804 *shi*, was sold to raise
funds for irrigation work in Xiangyin.[96] Other sources were salt-
merchant contributions, "wastage fees" (*haoxian*), and interest from
loans.[97] There were no fixed procedures for deciding who would bear
the cost of repairs until 1788, when an edict declared that the people
would manage all repairs costing less than 500 *taels*, while officials
would finance repairs costing more.[98] But, as long as increased land
taxes were forbidden, provincial and local budgets lacked the funds to

conduct substantial repairs. They could only intervene on a large scale after a major disaster. The limitations of local finance meant that dike administrators continued to perform the essential duties of mobilizing repair projects.

The Hunanese peasants in polder communities successfully warded off attempts by state officials to regulate their lives more strictly. The compact structure of the polder communities made it easier for them to close ranks against state officials, seen as an intrusive force. Their experience sets them off particularly from their brethren in Hubei, where, after the major flood of 1788, the state did succeed in establishing an elaborate series of regulations to control dike repairs along the Yangtze River (see Appendix 2). There was a precedent for such close management of the dikes along the Yangtze River in Hubei. As mentioned above, in the late Ming dynasty, responding to another serious flood, local officials had already set up a detailed hierarchy of dike-repair management. The eighteenth-century regulations represent the ultimate extent of official intervention in dike repair in the middle Yangtze. The term "manage" (*jingli*) replaced the usual word "supervise" (*duxiu*) describing official duties. The new regulations insisted on fixed time limits, advance planning for funding, surtaxes on landowners, detailed division of responsibilities, and close personal inspection by the local magistrate. This tight control was a reaction to the worst flood the mid-Yangtze Basin had experienced in centuries.[99]

In fact, these bureaucratic reform efforts soon fell apart. In 1833, Huang Jueci distinguished three types of dike-building in Hubei: (1) direct conduct by officials, requisitioning materials and labor from local gentry; (2) completely autonomous repair by local people; (3) *guandu minxiu*, the method used along the Yangtze River, in which officials closely supervised privately conducted repairs. He found that the third type was the worst, because extortion by clerks in collusion with local power-holders bankrupted the local supervisors and siphoned off the funds.[100] *Guandu minxiu* was, of course, the same method used by reformers in the late nineteenth century to promote modern industry. The problems of dike repair in the late eighteenth century prefigured those which China's first industrializers would face a century later. Close official supervision was an alternative to autonomous repair, which was feasible on long, straight dikes, but, in the long run, it brought no better results.

The struggle between official reformers and local irrigators for control of dike repairs ended in a stand-off. Provincial reformers urging abolition of the dike administrator and more active intervention by the state in the local economy were defeated in Hunan by the opposition of the dike organization leaders and their allies among the county officials. In the seventeenth century, the urbanized Jiangnan gentry had been willing to strike a bargain with the Qing rulers, protecting their rent collection rights in return for allowing equalized distribution of levies for irrigation repair. In less commercialized Hunan in the early eighteenth century, local landowners tenaciously defended their rights to run the irrigation organizations independently of state control. The Qing officials achieved a modest degree of supervision over the dike-repair organizations, but no more.

In the early eighteenth century, the balance struck between official and local control seemed reasonable to both sides. Officials were willing to allow the irrigators their independence as long as repairs were made and floods prevented, while the irrigators accepted loose supervision along with the benefits of official subsidies. By the end of the century, after decades of unprecedented population growth and a new commercial boom, the Hunanese irrigators, more prosperous than earlier in the century, found themselves once again fending off successfully the meddling of Qing officials, but in a different context, including substantial immigration from outside the province and an increasing threat of disastrous flooding. Compared to the late eighteenth century, sources on the early Qianlong reign indicate that most Qing officials were content with a limited supervisory role over local irrigation repairs, and local irrigators were able to protect their independence while accepting gladly whatever bounty the new conquerors bestowed on them.

This discussion illuminates the fragility of one of the few communal institutions that existed in pre-modern Chinese rural society. Even in Hunan, where the round dikes surrounded a well-defined social and economic space, organized around dominant lineages, and where officials actively encouraged local autonomous irrigation communities, the forms of labor organization and revenue collection for repair of dikes tended to break down and needed to be propped up by repeated official intervention. Relatively speaking, the Hunanese were more successful in maintaining collective repair organizations than peasants in other irrigated rice communities of Qing China. The late arrival of commercialization, the compact shape of the polders, and the tolerant attitude of the authorities allowed collective dike repair to persist. Still, the free-rider problem was not definitively solved. Shirking by laborers and corruption by dike administrators always undermined the stability of dike repairs. The long-term transformation of the lake economy eventually led, in the nineteenth century, to serious damage to the lake's peasants, brought on by individual gains at the expense of long-term regional planning.

SEVEN

The Transformation
of the Dongting Lake Economy

When the mountain land is all cleared
And the flat land is all cleared
There will be no place to catch the water
And the water will struggle with the people for the land

—Wei Yuan, "A Discussion of Irrigation in Huguang"

The building of waterworks was critical to the transformation of
Hunan from a sparsely settled, frontier area to a densely populated,
highly productive rice-exporting province. Only the gradual extension of dikes into Dongting Lake and along major rivers made possible the conversion of malarial swamps into fertile paddies. In the
early stages, the imperial state played a crucial preparatory role. After
the wartime devastation of the province, only the state treasury had
the funds to invest in the major dike works necessary for recovery.
State officials also created the social order essential for economic

growth by suppressing banditry, building city walls, and regularizing local administration. Once the state had provided these prerequisites, however, it was private capital that promoted the dynamic development of waterworks in the province, raising agricultural productivity to new heights. By the end of the eighteenth century, officials at the provincial and central level worried about the damage to the environment caused by this aggressive pursuit of profit, but private interests in local grain production had grown so powerful that, to protect local producers, district magistrates subverted directives from their superiors.

THE HYDROLOGY OF DONGTING LAKE

Today, Dongting Lake is the second largest lake in China, with an area of approximately 2,700 square km. Archaeologists have discovered settlements dating back to the New Stone Age in the region between Dongting and the Yangtze and Han Rivers.[1] In Qin-Han times, in fact, there was no large lake in the region, but only a series of small lakes, marshes, and river junctions. Over a centuries-long time scale, the gradual subsidence of the lake bed increased its surface area and water volume by drawing in water from the Yangtze. During the Tang dynasty, poets described views of vast expanses of open water across the "800 *li* of Dongting."[2] In the Song era, as this expansion of the lake was accompanied by the increase in cultivation of the shores of the lake, the local inhabitants began to face the problems of water control (see Figure 11).

Large amounts of water flow into the region from the Yangtze and Han Rivers to the north and from the four major rivers of Hunan emptying into Dongting Lake from the south. The characteristic feature of this lowland area is its very small gradient, producing a very slow rate of water flow. To the west, north, and south, the rivers flow through mountainous highlands in narrow stream beds, but, when they reach the Dongting region, they slow down and spread out until their water drains to the east through the mountains on the Hubei-Jiangxi border.

FIGURE 11 The Expansion and Shrinkage of Dongting Lake

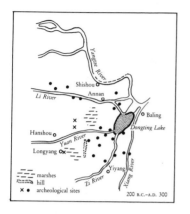

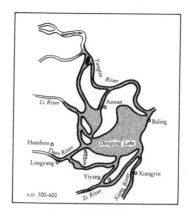

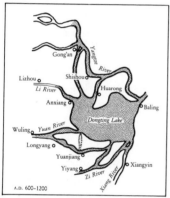

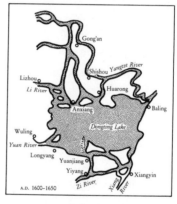

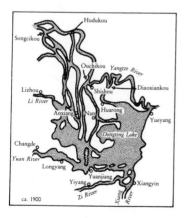

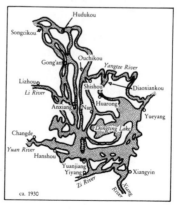

Source: Zhang Xiugui, "Dongtinghu Yanbian di Lishi Guocheng."

The flatness of the region and the change in rate of water flow creates a great drainage problem. The water level in Dongting Lake rises and falls extensively every year. The English traveler Dickson, who crossed the lake in May, found the waters always 10 or more feet deep, and concluded that the high water lasted all summer, but Baron Richthofen, passing through in February, was surprised to find "sand and nothing but sand in place of water."[3] The entire lake had dried up, and the outlets of Hunan's rivers had become mere canals in the sand.

The rise and fall of the lake depended more on the water level in the Yangtze than on the Hunanese rivers. The water level in all the rivers in turn depended on the timing of mountain rains in the south and west. Hunanese river waters usually rose to their peak in May through July, but they could drain out through the lake into the Yangtze when its level was low. The Yangtze began to rise only in June, peaking in August and September. These were the months when the lake reached its maximum level. The lake then began to decline after November to reach its low point in January and February. The total difference between high and low waters was more than 15 meters.[4]

The timing of rainfall upstream critically affected the ability of the lake to drain out surplus water. As Hunanese officials recognized, Dongting's dual role as catchment basin for the Yangtze and as outlet for Hunan's four rivers made its situation, and that of the peasant cultivators on its shores, much more precarious than that of the other great lakes of China—the Boyang in Jiangxi, or Taihu in Jiangsu. If heavy rains fell early in Sichuan or in the uplands of the Han River Basin, then in June, when Hunan's rivers crested, they met a wall of high water in the Yangtze, forcing the water to flow back and raise Dongting to critical levels. This "backflow" (*daoyang*) caused by the synchronization of flood peaks could cause serious flooding around the shores of the lake.[5]

THE HYDRAULIC CYCLE

The seasonal rise and fall of the lake defined an annual cycle of water flow determined by the interaction of rainfall and river levels, but long-term trends in agricultural cultivation and management of the dike network around the lake created a "hydraulic cycle." Pierre-Etienne Will has described the operation of this cycle in the lowlands of Hubei.[6] In Hunan, the hydraulic cycle developed very similarly, but the presence of the lake created significant variations.

The hydraulic cycle can, in fact, be detected in the core of all the regions of China that depend heavily on irrigated rice agriculture.[7] Its basic dynamic depends on the interaction between state initiatives to maintain the water-supply system and peasant cultivators' promotion of increasingly intense settlement near abundant water supplies. In the first stage of the cycle, the dike network has broken down because of maladministration and social disorder. Water covers abandoned lands and homes. Official grants of funds, seeds, and tools begin the restoration of agricultural production. In the second stage, once the initial infrastructure has been built, private incentives to clear land come to dominate. Investment by wealthy landlords and urban merchants recruits immigrants to build dikes and clear land around the lakes and rivers. The state withdraws to a supervisory role, and officials intervene with funds only when very large-scale repairs are needed.

As the population grows, however, maintenance of the waterworks becomes essential, and local officials attempt to encourage cooperation by the inhabitants in organizing repairs. On the other hand, the drive for profit, accompanied by increasing commercialization of agriculture, tends to undermine incentives to cooperate. The benefits of a given dike cannot be restricted only to those who contribute to its repair. Since everyone near the dike benefits from its protection, whether or not he contributes to it, it is natural to contribute less than the amount necessary. The state role becomes one of encouraging landowners to work together by invoking traditional ideals of harmony, even though market incentives stimulate the landowners to neglect repairs. Constant conflict between upstream and downstream users over water produces tensions which require official intervention, but the state is able to settle only local conflicts that lead to court cases. It cannot enforce any wider regional planning. Here, the failure of regional planning parallels the unsuccessful efforts of reform-minded officials in Wang Anshi's time to enact wide-scale plans for controlling the water flow in the lower Yangtze.[8]

Furthermore, denser settlement overburdens the ecology of the region. Not only does the clearance of land deprive surplus water of its outlets, but the stripping of highland forests by "shack people" immigrants increases erosion, which in turn raises the silt content of the rivers, further reducing the surface available for storing water. The turning point of the cycle occurs when the state attempts, without success, to prohibit dike-building and even to destroy illegally built dikes. By this time, however, state power has declined so much that it is unable to confront effectively local private interests in land clearance. Disaster strikes in the form of massive, continual flooding, but the officials have lost the resources to relieve it. Relief becomes increasingly dependent on private contributions, but these can at best resolve only local problems; they can never provide a wide-scale regional solution. Flooding, abandonment, and neglect once more afflict the region until a new, stronger state can intervene.

In Hunan, we can trace two complete hydraulic cycles, the first beginning in the early Ming, peaking in the sixteenth century, and declining into the seventeenth, the second starting in the late seventeenth to early eighteenth centuries, peaking around 1800, and declining until the 1950s. In each case, strong state intervention in the early stages was followed by the increasing power of private interests, which ultimately brought oversettlement, neglect of repairs, and disastrous flooding. Nineteenth- and early-twentieth-century reformers drew up ambitious plans for using Western technology to dredge the lake, but these remained unworkable because of the weakness of both Qing and Republican governments. Finally, in the 1950s, a new, powerful regime created a large overflow basin to capture the runoff from the Yangtze. It required the resettlement of 240,000 people to create a flood diversion area of 900 square km., but this policy at least temporarily resolved the chronic flooding problem of the middle Yangtze. Recent reports of serious flooding in the region, however, raise the question of whether there will be a third hydraulic cycle in the future.[9]

The Qing cycle, the main focus of discussion here, differed in several respects from that of the Ming. The recovery from destruction was more rapid in the early Qing than in the Ming, government resources were more abundant, and the demographic dynamism was greater. These factors brought about an earlier onset of the peak in the Qing: By the mid-eighteenth century, officials had already tried to meet the oncoming crisis by prohibiting further dike-building around the lake. On the other hand, because administrative effectiveness was far greater in the eighteenth century than in the mid-Ming, heavy relief grants could stave off disaster for some time. Qing decision-making was also more rational. Unlike the Ming, Qing officials did not take arbitrary measures like the sealing off of drainage routes because they disturbed the geomancy of the Emperor's ancestors' tombs.[10] Management of the water supply in the Qing was a race between inexorably increasing population and the ability of officials to postpone disaster.

ENCLOSURES AND SETTLEMENT IN HUNAN

Although the hydraulic cycle followed a similar course in Hunan and Hubei, the conditions of settlement around Dongting Lake differed significantly from those in Hubei near the Yangtze River. Peasants near the Yangtze were protected by a double row of dikes: the long straight dikes stretching along the Yangtze, and the individual dikes that surrounded their fields. The dikes along the Yangtze were closely supervised by officials, because of the potential danger of a disastrous river flood. A bureaucratic hierarchy of circuit intendants, prefects, and district magistrates divided up responsibility for the Yangtze dikes. In Hunan, settlers near the lake were protected only by round or rectangular enclosure dikes (called *yuan* or *wei*) from 200 or 300 *li* in circumference.[11] These dikes surrounded polder lands whose surface often lay below the level of the lake itself. The powerful local families who dominated these self-contained units kept them relatively free of official control. Although Hubei also had enclosure dikes, the heavier presence of official control on the Yangtze made them less independent than their neighbors to the south, but correspondingly more dependent on the effectiveness of imperial administration to protect their fields.

TABLE 19 The Surface Area of Dongting Lake

Year	Area (sq. km.)	Source
1825	6,000	Zhang Xiugui, p. 113
1850	5,220	Sun Ching-chih, p. 205
1896	5,400	Zhang Xiugui, p. 113
1906	5,000	Richthofen, *China* (at high water)
1932	4,700	Zhang Xiugui, p. 113
1940	3,700–5,000	Li Guoji (average-high water)
1949	4,350	*Renmin Ribao*, 1979/4/5; Zhang Xiugui, p. 113
1958	3,915	Sun Ching-chih, p. 205
1958	3,141	Zhang Xiugui, p. 113
1974	2,820	Zhang Xiugui, p. 113
1977	2,740	Zhang Xiugui, p. 113
1979	2,817	*Renmin Ribao*, 1979/4/5.

The threat of flooding in Hunan was less dramatic than in Hubei, because the slow rise of the lake allowed time for peasants to flee their fields. This meant that officials paid less attention to the lake, allowing the dominant landowners of the enclosures nearly free reign in determining the pattern of settlement. As early as the eleventh century, landowners had begun to "rob land from the lake" (*daohu weitian*).[12] This encroachment on the lake began the long-term reduction of the lake's surface area which has continued for eight centuries. In addition, by carrying 200 metric tons of silt per year into the lake, the Yangtze progressively reduced its water-holding capacity.[13] Figure 11 displays the disappearance of the lake that began in the Song and accelerated during the Qing. Table 18 shows this process of shrinkage during the last century, for which quantitative data are available. The settlement of the Dongting Lake region from the Song to the present day demonstrates the interaction of regional ecology, peasant cultivation, and official response.

FROM RESETTLEMENT TO
ENCROACHMENT: SONG TO MING

Dongting Lake was not hospitable to settlement in the Song dynasty. The swamps around the lake's edge were too vulnerable to inundation for permanent agriculture, and very few polder dikes were built. Hunan was often described in the Song as a "broad area" (*kuanxiang*) where "there was much land and little population."[14] For the Dongting settlers, fishing was a far more important source of livelihood than rice cultivation.[15] Beyond the lake, most of the sparse Han population settled in the uplands of the Xiang and Zi River Valleys, or in the mining camps of the southern hills. The rest of the province was dominated by non-Han tribespeople, who lived in small enclaves, practicing slash-and-burn agriculture. Still, landowners had already begun to create new land by enclosing parts of the lake. The Song state did nothing to stop them, and stressed only the dredging and clearing of drainage routes. Because most of the population did not live on the lake's edges, damaging floods were rare, but it was in the Song that the first state-sponsored encroachment on the lake began, when one large dike, the Nandi, was built in Xiangyin county to protect the lowlands against backflow from the lake.[16]

The Ming emperors began very early on to encourage widespread construction of irrigation works to promote agricultural recovery. In 1394, the Emperor sent students from the National Academy all over the country to supervise and encourage waterworks projects.[17] In 1404, the Yongle Emperor particularly ordered repair of dikes on the central and lower Yangtze. Forty-six dikes were repaired and strengthened after a severe flood in Huarong county. In 1438, one delegate was sent to each province to inspect irrigation, but two more were sent to Huguang, giving it particular importance.[18] These early efforts were followed by an increased tempo of dike-construction from the mid-fifteenth to mid-sixteenth centuries.[19] Although these projects constructed a ring of dikes around the entire lake area, they did not completely clear all available land. Nearly all the projects were concentrated in Baling and Huarong counties at the northern outlet of the lake, and at Longyang and Wuling counties on the southwestern end. The lowlands of Li *zhou* and Anxiang in the northwest, and Yuanjiang and Xiangyin in the southeast, would have to wait for the Qing period to be fully cleared.

Some of the early projects were huge, like the Yongji dike, built in 1484–1486 in Baling with a total labor force of 270,000 men who cleared a land area of "several ten thousands of *qing*." In this case, the motives for construction were more military and commercial than agricultural. The dike was built to protect boats passing by Chenglingji, north of Yuezhou's prefectural capital, at the time an important strategic post on the route to the southwest. It was said that "all imperial envoys with business in the southwest, barbarian chieftains, inspectors, corvée laborers, merchants and people, runners and officials come and go here."[20]

In the late Ming era, clearance of the lake borders advanced slowly. Xiangyin county, on the southern edge of Dongting Lake directly north of Changsha, illustrates the pattern of clearance, settlement, and flooding during this period. Low hills and some very steep mountains occupied the eastern half of the county, while swampy lands along the river mouths occupied the western half.[21] The entire western district formed only 1.5 *li* units and paid especially low tax rates.[22] Until the sixteenth century, social disorder in most of the county made life precarious. As the local gazetteer writer stated, "In the spring and summer, when the water rises, bandits everywhere take advantage of wind and sails to hide and occupy thickly reeded places and wildly commit plunder . . . When boats hide in the reeds, their traces are lost."[23] In 1561, when rebels from Jiangxi moved into the area, "the local people heard of this but did not know where to flee, as there was no fortified place to rely on for defense. This is like putting gold brocade in a large box and leaving it in the bazaar, or storing rice in a granary and destroying its bamboo fences."[24] The county capital had been a walled city since the Song dynasty, but it constantly shifted its location. In the Ming, officials selected a permanent site on the mouth of the Xiang River to protect the bandit-ridden swamplands. After the Jiangxi rebel incursion, they built a fortress northwest of the capital to protect the denser population in the south and east.[25] Only after the state had provided security could settlers begin to construct dikes and clear land.

Private construction of dikes in Ming Huguang took several forms.[26] Since newly cleared land around the lake was both highly fertile and exempt from taxation, the profits of land clearance could be great, but the capital investment required was large. In some cases, individual landlords contributed funds to create new polders: "After [Zhengtong (1436–1449)], local people frequently selected slightly higher ground and constructed [a dike] around it. These enclosures are found in over 100 districts."[27] Most of these individuals do not seem to have been members of the local elite. When a local landlord built his own dike, he maintained hereditary rights to the profits of the dike as well as the land.

Other waterworks were built jointly, sometimes with contributions by both gentry and non-gentry landlords, or with the cooperation of an entire lineage, as in Chaling *zhou:*

> Long Sheng came from Chaling. The Long family from way back owned Heshi reservoir. Lineage members took advantage of it to raise lawsuits incessantly. Sheng said: "To begrudge something is to be selfish and it is wrong not to be generous toward one's relatives. How can I begrudge one reservoir if it means being ungenerous to my relatives?" So he gave up his share and divided it among the others. Thus, the disputes ended and all were friendly as before.[28]

There are also examples of waterworks built by cooperation among villages, such as "One Hundred Family Dike," built in Shishou county. None of these private construction projects relied on any government aid, nor did they depend on the *lijia* organization. They represented collective efforts by a variety of local community groups, united around a landlord, a lineage, or a village, to solve pressing problems of flood control.

Nevertheless, waterworks had not progressed very far by the end of the Ming dynasty. The southeast portion of Dongting Lake lagged behind the development of the northeast and southwest areas (see Table 20). The lake continued to expand to the south in Yuanjiang, swallowing up cultivated fields and turning them into fishing ponds.[29] The state took little action to promote dike construction. A channel dredged to provide a smoother outlet for the Xiang River soon silted up.[30] Xiangyin built only four dikes during the Ming dynasty.[31]

TABLE 20 Dike-Building in Hunan in the Ming Dynasty

Reign		Year	Location	No.	Undated	No.
Zhengtong (1436–1449)	11	1446	Longyang	1	Huarong	48
Chenghua (1465–1487)	9	1473	Baling	1	Yuanjiang	1
	11	1475	Longyang	1		
	13	1477	Longyang	1		
	20	1484	Baling	1		
Hongzhi (1488–1505)	15	1502	Longyang	1		
Zhengde (1506–1521)	11	1516	Huarong	1	Huarong	1
	12	1517	Longyang	8	Wuling	5
	13	1518	Huarong	45		
	13	1518	Longyang	5		
	15	1520	Wuling	2		
	15	1520	Longyang	1		
Jiajing (1522–1566)	5	1526	Wuling	2		
	5	1526	Longyang	1	Lizhou	1
	10	1531	Baling	1		
	12	1533	Longyang	1		
	13	1534	Wuling	5		
	13	1534	Longyang	8		
	16	1537	Baling	1		
	22	1543	Huarong	a		
	30	1551	Huarong	1		
	33	1554	Longyang	1		
	39	1560	Wuling	7		
	41	1562	Baling	1		
	44	1565	Longyang	a		

TABLE 20 *(continued)*

Reign		Year	Location	No.	Undated	No.
Longqing (1567–1572)	1	1567	Baling	4		
	2	1568	Huarong	2		
	4	1570	Longyang	1		
	5	1571	Wuling			
Wanli (1573–1619)	1	1573	Anxiang	32	Huarong	a
	4	1576	Lizhou	1	Lizhou	1
	13	1585	Baling	1	Anxiang	3
	13	1585	Yuanjiang	2	Wuling	6
	14	1586	Wuling	1	Longyang	2
	14	1586	Yuanjiang	6	Yuanjiang	18
	15	1587	Huarong	a	Xiangyin	2
	16	1588	Huarong	a	Yiyang	29
	16	1588	Anxiang	15		
	16	1588	Wuling	1		
	17	1589	Yuanjiang	1		
	21	1593	Lizhou	1		
	24	1596	Anxiang	a		
	30	1602	Huarong	60		
	33	1605	Huarong	a		
	36	1608	Lizhou	3		
	36	1608	Wuling	1		
	37	1609	Huarong	a		
	41	1613	Longyang	1		
Tianqi (1621–1627)	1	1621	Longyang	1		
Chongzhen (1628–1644)	7	1634	Baling	1	Xiangyin	2

Note: a. Several (exact number not given). Undated projects are those for which only reign periods are given.
Source: Oh Keum-sung, "Myŏngmal Tongjŏngho Chubyŏn ŭi Wanjai ŭi Paltal," p. 121–122.

These dikes, built in the late Ming, indicated an incipient trend toward occupation of the lowlands, but the fall of the Ming dynasty cut this short.

Although the clearance of land in the Ming period began the settlement of the Dongting Lake region, it also increased the severity of flooding. The interconnected water flow between the Yangtze River and Dongting Lake aggravated the flood danger. Dongting Lake served as a regulator of the Yangtze, keeping its water level stable by accepting a net inflow when the Yangtze was high and providing an outflow when the Yangtze fell. The "backflow" (*daoyang*) from the Yangtze entered the lake through channels, after leaving the Yangtze along the southern bank in Hubei, beginning at Songci. Outlets on the north bank of the Yangtze leading to smaller lakes in Hubei similarly regulated water levels. These "nine holes and thirteen mouths" effectively prevented drastic flooding by draining off surplus water into the storage lakes.[32] Up to the Song dynasty, nearly all the mouths were open and floods were few, but some had already begun to silt up in the Tang as dikes were built to clear land along the channels. By the Yuan dynasty, most of them had become blocked, despite some efforts to clear them. The Jiajing reign (1522–1566) brought the first major floods to counties around the lake, when the blockage of these outlets caused the Yangtze to overflow its dikes.[33] In 1524, Ming officials intentionally blocked up one outlet in order to prevent flooding, but, in 1568, two outlets were reopened. These channels "not only divided the force of the Yangtze but also allowed a drainage route for Dongting Lake."[34] But in the Wanli reign (1573–1619), the large Huangtan dike was built at Jingzhou, "cutting off the throat" of the Dongting drainage route and "causing all the land near the lake to turn into mud and silt."[35] Proposals to reopen the outlets to the lake were blocked by local officials who claimed that there was inadequate local labor. In fact, they were protecting local power-holders (*haoyou*) who had cleared land over the channels.[36] By the late Ming era, there were only three drainage canals left, the Hudukou, Diaoxiankou, and Huangjinkou, and the last two could drain only in one direction, from the Yangtze into Dongting Lake. With all the north bank reservoirs blocked off, the Yangtze could pour its excess flood waters only into the lake.

As the channels grew fewer and the dikes higher, the Yangtze was directed into Hunan with even greater force, raising the water level of the lake and producing greater floods. Increased clearance aggravated the flood danger, while the decline of the *lijia* and *dizhang* reduced the effectiveness of repairs. Flooding and land abandonment preceded the downfall of the Ming. In Lizhou, for example, successive years of flooding began in 1586.[37] Then the chaos of the Ming-Qing transition completed the collapse of the dike network. Depopulation, wars, and destruction were the fate of the region for the next half-century. When district magistrate Tang Maochun arrived at Xiangyin in 1663, he found

> devastation everywhere. Everywhere inside the walls are shattered tiles and dilapidated walls with holes for squirrels and rabbits. On the south and east, the gates are eaten away. If the dike breaks, they will suffer flooding. I told the local people that, when the water rises in the spring, this area will be flooded, but they all think only of immediate gain. The expenses are several hundred *jin*, but the people are poor and the land is poor."[38]

DIKE-BUILDING IN THE QING DYNASTY

The recovery of Hunan dike-building in the Qing went through three distinct stages: "official dikes" (*guanwei*), "people's dikes" (*minwei*), and "private (illegal) dikes" (*siwei*)[39] (see Table 21). As in the early Ming, official dikes, promoted from the late Kangxi to the early Qianlong reign with subsidies from the state treasury, laid the basic framework. From the first decade of the Qianlong reign began the proliferation of the "people's dikes," which were almost completely financed by private contributions. They were more numerous but only about half as large in average length and in land area surrounded. The private dikes, the smallest of all, were built in defiance of an official prohibition on dike-building issued in 1747. Some of these were allowed to remain, but most were ordered destroyed. The official destruction campaign ran up against such entrenched local interest, however, that it achieved only partial success.

The late Kangxi and early Yongzheng reigns were the golden age of

TABLE 21 Dike-Building in Xiangyin County

No.	Name (weidi, guandi)	Date	Ln1	Ln2 (zhang)	Ln3	Ln4	Area 1 (mou)	Area 2 (mou)	Family (daxing)
Song									
1	Nan	Song							
Ming									
2	Jingtang	Wanli (1573–1619)	5,244	5,344			3,220	8,248	Zhang, Hu
3	Junmin	Chongzhen (1628–1644)	1,940	1,740			2,630	1,398	
4	Saizi	Wanli (1573–1619)	4,250	4,350			6,490		
5	Gutang	Chongzhen (1628–1644)	3,757	3,737			5,050		Lin
Qing (*Guanwei*)									
6	Shatian	1689	3,791				9,302		Ma
7	*Zhuangjia	1691	1,140				685		
8	*Huanggong	1691	1,020				657		
9	*Lujia	1691	1,500				1,284	1,184	
10	Yangliu	1693	1,350				677		

TABLE 21 (continued)

No.	Name (weidi, guandi)	Date	Ln1	Ln2	Ln3	Ln4	Area 1 (mou)	Area 2 (mou)	Family (daxing)
				(zhang)					
11	Putao	1693	1,549				960		
12	Jinpan	1694	3,345				3,320	3,120	
13	Wandou	1694	2,390	1,390			5,051	1,198	Huang
14	Hanwan	1694	5,840	5,804			7,186		Wang, Tian
15	Maima	1694	1,594	1,202	1,220		960	940	
16	*Shejia	1694	2,396	3,396			2,890		
17	Dongzhuang	1714	4,000				2,630		Sheng, Qin
	Total *Guanwei:*		45,286				52,992		
	Qing (*minwei*)								
18	*Lenggong	1734	300				9,000		
19	*Zhaojia	1734	400				6,000		
20	Sanhe	1735	2,180				7,000		
21	Linxing	1736	1,010				660		
22	Dayou	1737	1,000				800		
23	Fuxing	1737	3,780				7,000		Yi
24	Xifu	1737	4,750				7,100		Cai, Wang

TABLE 21 (continued)

No.	Name (weidi, guandi)	Date	Ln1	Ln2 (zhang)	Ln3	Ln4	Area 1 (mou)	Area 2 (mou)	Family (daxing)
25	Hexing	1737	900				1,210		
26	Sanyang	1737	1,700				2,700		
27	Ziao Sanyang	1737	200				400		
28	Mayan	1737	185	685			118	853	
29	Choutang	1739	3,380	2,645	1,750		8,800		
30	Pangshan	1739	1,900				300		
31	Banghu	1739	500				220		
32	Zhupo	1739	300				90		
33	Yangliuping	1739	299	478	1,100		730		
34	Huanjing	1739	1,790				1,660		
35	*Wangtong	1739	1,000				500		
36	Jincha	1739	400				190		
37	Dashun	1739	620				9,880	1,260	
38	Yihe	1740	4,000				6,000		
39	Renhe	1740	5,974	5,794			1,480	16,300	
40	Yaozui	1739	250	350			80		
41	Gongyue	1739	2,000	3,000			3,000		Yao
42	*Houjia	1739							destroyed 1763

TABLE 21 (continued)

No.	Name (weidi, guandi)	Date	Ln1	Ln2	Ln3	Ln4 (zhang)	Area 1 (mou)	Area 2 (mou)	Family (daxing)
43	Dihu	1739	1,300				3,000	900	
44	Ciyang	1739	800				400		
45	Luzi	1739	200				90		
46	Fuxing	1740	734				7,000	400	
47	Dongtuo	1740	100				50		
48	Tuntian	1740	800				400		
49	Qiaoshan	1740	1,900	1,750			1,260		
50	Yixing	1740	2,000	1,000			1,300		
51	Guangxing	1740	1,000				500		
52	Tuanshan	1740	640				440		
53	Zhenjiang	1743	630	405			479		
54	Wenzhou	1744	3,934	3,394			10,725		He, Li, Tan
55	*Yixing	1744	620	660			800		
56	Taihe	1744	5,860				5,700		
57	*Chenjia	1745	1,820						destroyed 1763
58	*Zhugong	1745	618	651			772		
59	Taoyuan	1745	820	863			536	526	
60	Donghe	1745	1,765				738		Zhou

TABLE 21 (continued)

No.	Name (weidi; guandi)	Date	Ln1	Ln2 (zhang)	Ln3	Ln4	Area 1 (mou)	Area 2 (mou)	Family (daxing)
61	Wangtu	1745	2,226	1,050	2,726	1,750	2,132		
62	Jincheng	1745	1,160	750	2,160	1,830	1,100		
63	Shunfeng	1745	1,305	1,654	1,500		1,480		
64	Nanyang	1745	2,280	1,700			690	1,754	
65	Dingfeng	1745	937	650			690		
66	Yongxing	1745	970	726			705		
67	Xiao Yongxin	1745	332	400			210		
68	Shamaochi	1745	807				530	520	
69	Dexing	1746	1,599	809			1,835		
70	Ju xian	1746	1,654	4,080	4,352		9,888		
71	*Wangjiazhai	1746							
72	Baofu	1746	1,654				1,002	1,102	
73	Xia Sanyang	1746	1,350				1,130		
	Total Minwei:		79,933				115,500		

Sources: *Hunan Tongzhi*, 1757, 1820, 1885.46.4a–7a; *Huguang Zongzhi* 1684; *Changsha Fuzhi*, 1747; *Xiangyin Xianzhi*, 1756, 1818; *Xiangyin Xiangtuzhi*, 1881.21. *indicates a family name in the name of the dike. Ln1, Ln2, Ln3, Ln4 refer to lengths, given in chronological order; Area 1, Area 2 refer to areas in chronological order. Although many names of *siwei* are provided, no consistent list of their dates or sizes is given in the source.

FIGURE 12 Dike-Building in Xiangyin County, 1570–1746

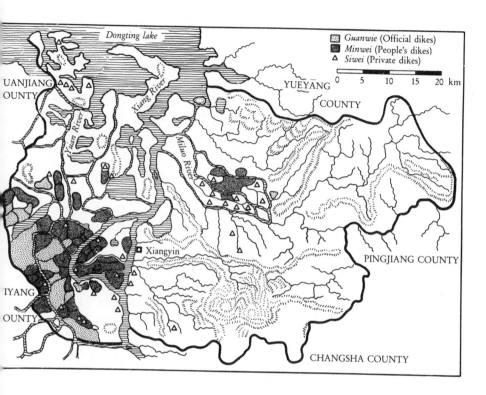

Source: Peter C. Perdue, "Water Control in the Dongting Lake Region," p. 755.

official dike-building in Hunan.[40] Since the stability of the government and the surplus in the treasury made it possible to subsidize dike works on an unprecedented scale, large grants promoted repair and construction projects. In 1718, the Kangxi Emperor had granted a total of 65,000 *taels* for repairs of dike works in Hubei and Hunan, 40,000 for Hubei and 25,000 for Hunan.[41] These grants were intended to encourage private dike-building as well as official repairs. These efforts were spurred on by severe floods, which occurred all around the lake in 1727. Heavy rains after the 5th month, which swelled the rivers flowing into the Yangtze and the lake, caused flooding of all the lowlands near the lake. Fortunately, certain areas, like most of

Changsha prefecture, had already gathered the early rice harvest in the 6th month before the floods hit, so grain supplies were adequate and prices remained level, but at least 20,000 *taels* had to be spent in supplementary relief money.[42] The Emperor, noticing the frequent flooding of areas near the lake, ordered the Governor General to take measures to repair the dikes. Four hundred and thirty breaks, requiring over 7,490 *taels* for immediate repairs, were discovered. Sixty thousand more *taels* were then allocated for further repairs. Governor Mai Gui reported that the common people "worked enthusiastically," completing the repair work by the end of 1728.[43] In 1748, an edict ordered that one-half of the repair costs in a year of flooding be borne by the government.[44]

In Xiangyin, the official dikes were concentrated on the western border of the county, spanning a total length of 45,040 *zhang* (144 km.).[45] The total land area encompassed was approximately 52,784 *mou* (3,243 *ha*) or 7.9 percent of the registered land acreage in the early Qing. Repairs were made in 1716 and 1728 from the 60,000 *taels* granted on each occasion by the Emperor's orders. Most of them were circular, serving to block off the river and its numerous branches and enclose land for cultivation.

The official backing for early projects touched off a brief blossoming of private contributions to "people's-dikes" projects built with private funds and official permission in the early decades of the Qianlong reign. Once state funds had provided the initial investment, private landowners found it profitable to contribute toward large dike projects. The private builders were encouraged by a 1740 edict exempting all newly diked land from taxation.[46] When the first private dike-builders found that they doubled their profits, many others joined in.[47] In Yiyang county, for example, 14 official dikes were built from 1717 to 1732, followed by 35 people's dikes from 1742 to 1765.[48]

The new wave of dike-building brought the area both commercial prosperity and greater security for harvests. Close as it was to the lake, Xiangyin still suffered from periodic droughts, particularly in the mountainous east. There were droughts in 1652, 1679, 1712, 1746, 1752, 1778, 1785, 1807, and 1835. But in 1751, when drought destroyed over half the harvest in the mountain lands, the diked regions of the west, or at least those areas near enough to the lake to use water pumps, were able to salvage up to 70 percent of the harvest.[49] The increase in agricultural prosperity, in turn, stimulated commercial development. Most of the new commerce was promoted by immigrants. Some of the local population became small peddlers, but most of the new merchant class were outsiders. Northerners brought in felt and skins from Shanxi and Shaanxi, while southerners traded in the silks of Soochow and Hangchow. Skilled artisans and builders were also attracted: "Whenever construction begins, many people come from Puqi in Jiangxi. Bamboo and iron artisans are mostly local people, but there are also skilled silver craftsmen."[50] Imperial policies supporting land clearance had, within fifty years, stimulated Hunan's development from devastation to prosperity.

DISCOURAGING EXCESSIVE DIKE-BUILDING: FROM YANG XIFU TO WEI YUAN

Yet, less than a decade later the official attitude had changed. In 1744, debate broke out between advocates of two opposing land policies, each based on a time-honored maxim. Advocates of further land clearance argued that one "could not abandon land for water," while their opponents insisted that "one cannot struggle with the water for land."[51] Junior Metropolitan Censor of the Board of War Hu Ding represented the advocates of further clearance. Concerned about a rapid rise in rice prices, he noted that there were still thousands of acres of uncleared wasteland around the lake. Allowing the people to build dikes on their own would increase rice production by several million *piculs*. He believed that rich households prevented people from clearing flooded lands because they profited from fishing rights in these lands. Clearance of the marshlands would benefit the state treasury by replacing the small fishing tax with a higher levy on paddy land. Hu Ding discounted the effects of clearance on the storage capacity of the lake, proclaiming his faith in the ability of local peasants to take a long-term view. He asked rhetorically, "How can the poor people be willing to waste their capital by failing to plan far in advance?"[52]

Hunan Governor Jiang Pu, on the other hand, directly connected the increasing settlement of the region with the increase in flooding.[53] He even argued that the early construction of official dikes had been a net loss to the state, costing it more in relief funds than it gained from taxes. The people's dikes that followed were built further out into the lake than the official dikes. They were less firmly built and even more vulnerable to floods. He concluded: "People only know about clearing the lake to become land; they do not know about returning land to the lake." In blaming the excess clearance on "outside wanderers and local people who like to cause trouble," he clearly recognized the role of immigrants in lake clearance. He also noticed the investment of entrepreneurial capital in lake lands, attacking the investors who "deceive the ignorant people by collecting funds to start dike works, then take land within the dikes and sell it." Jiang Pu called for severe restrictions under official supervision of all clearance around the lake, but he did still allow the construction of some polders in the mountain foothills, such as Wenzhouwei, surrounding 10,000 *mou*.

The issue was clearly joined between two opposing views of the local political economy. Both sides reacted to new trends in the eighteenth-century economy: the rise in grain prices, the growth of population, and the increasing strength of commercial capital. Traditionalists, like Hu Ding, maintained a faith in the ability of the people to look after their own affairs, as long as the state encouraged them to clear land for their own subsistence. Their opponents called for more active state intervention to meet the threat of aggressive commercial capital upsetting the local ecology. They saw the local peasants responding vigorously to market incentives, but they argued that the state needed to force people to look beyond short-term gain at the longer-term needs of the region.

This debate also implicitly represented a conflict between the view from the center and the view from the province. Many officials in Peking, like Hu Ding, focused on tax revenue and ignored the threat to the local ecology. Local officials, aware of the turbulent social transformation of their regions, were willing to sacrifice increased revenues in order to protect the region from flooding. Unlike their distant superiors, they foresaw potential conflict between the aggressive pursuit of private interest and long-range planning.

In 1746, the critics of land clearance won over the President of the Board of Finance, Liu Yuyi, who found lakes being turned into land "not only in Hunan, but in all the southern and eastern provinces."[54] He succeeded in getting the Grand Council to approve a ban on all land clearance that blocked water routes. In 1747, Governor Yang Xifu prohibited further building of new dikes, allowing only repairs to those which had already been built.[55] While Governor Yang Xifu was enthusiastic about waterworks projects in mountainous regions, he had already noticed the danger signs of excessive dike-building near Dongting Lake, although the situation had not yet reached the critical stage. He concluded that "now, because of the great population growth, dikes fill the view near the lake, and we cannot allow further dike-building."[56] He did not order the destruction of dikes already built, but, in 1747, he prohibited further construction of dikes on wasteland near the lake.

Other local officials began to realize the dangers of indiscriminate land clearance at about the same time. In 1748, district magistrate Xu Liangdong discovered that "ignorant fishermen," in 1745, had piled up sand into a dike along one of the rivers to block the current so as to catch fish in their nets.[57] This dike made the river impassable to boats in the winter and fall, thus harming trade. Xu arrested the fishermen, reopened the stream, and dredged out the sand, but he feared that the laws would soon be relaxed and the river blocked up again, so he requested the governor to set up a stele forbidding further dike-building along the river.

In 1756, Governor Chen Hongmou elaborated on the problem, saying: "In the last several decades there is no high land that has not had dikes built on it. Dikes on the lake border fill the view endlessly like fish scales, and there are cases of fighting with the water for land (*yushui zhengdi*)."[58] Further dike-building, he argued, would only cause the area of the lake to become narrower and produce huge floods. Even in areas far from lakes and streams, irrigation ponds were short-sightedly being turned into land:

Lands not close to rivers or lakes all depend on ponds and reservoirs for irrigation. If there is sufficient water in the reservoirs, then when there are long dry spells in summer and fall, there is still a sufficient supply of water.

> Now, since the population has begun to grow daily, all the wasteland has been cleared. The foolish people are blind about long-range plans and often abandon waterworks and plot to create more land. Not only the borders of the rivers and the great lake [Dongting], but other lakes several *li* and several *qing* in area gradually have dikes constructed along them to clear land, and in the end all trace of them disappears . . . People think that the reservoirs are useless, not realizing that if a drought or flood happens to come, what they have gained will not compensate for their loss.[59]

Filling in the upstream reservoirs not only made agriculture more insecure in the mountains but also aggravated the drainage problem downstream by eliminating storage areas for mountain rains. Provincial officials realized that effective management of flooding around the lake required equal attention to draining upstream watercourses and providing storage ponds in the mountains.[60]

Unfortunately, the prohibitions touched off a spate of lawsuits, and illegal dikes continued in defiance of official prohibitions. After 1747, owners of illegal dikes "each protected their private interests, led each other on to bribe and collude with clerks to report their dikes as destroyed, while they cultivated the land as before. All kinds of customary fees flourished. . . . From the late Qianlong to Jiaqing reigns, lawsuits, robberies, feuds, and violence did not cease for several decades."[61] There were "wicked people" who slandered rich households, falsely suing them for illegally clearing land in order to extort blackmail. "Strongmen" (*qiangmin*) secretly took over the shallow reed swamps on the lake border and sued each other for control. Although clearance of these lake lands was prohibited, there was profit in owning them, as landowners took mud from these areas to fertilize the fields and burned the reeds for fuel. "Pettifoggers falsely said that one place should build canals and destroy the land of those they don't like."[62]

Wei Yuan, writing his essay "On Irrigation in Huguang" about eighty years after Yang Xifu, revealed that the diking situation had become much worse.[63] While Yang had seen no conflict between officials and popular interest, Wei Yuan saw a direct clash. While Yang had called for improvement of irrigation, Wei Yuan now called for destruction of harmful dike works. Wei Yuan also provided a valuable historical survey of the development of Huguang in the Qing period which directly connected the rapid resettlement of the province with the growing crisis in dike-building. He stated that, while the people of Sichuan and Huguang were massacred by Zhang Xianzhong during the Ming-Qing transition, Jiangxi was hardly touched. After the Qing conquest, Jiangxi people moved into Huguang and Huguang people moved into Sichuan, so that a proverb appeared, "Jiangxi fills up Huguang, and Huguang fills up Sichuan." But, by Wei Yuan's time, people had built dikes and settled everywhere, and there was no more flat land or mountain land to be cleared. Sand brought down from the mountains produced sand bars, causing Dongting Lake to get shallower, while people around the lake created new polder lands. Illicit dikes flourished, blocking water routes and making the area more vulnerable to floods. Wei Yuan proposed the destruction of dikes that blocked vital water routes, preserving only those that protected city walls. Destruction of these dikes would protect not only Hunan from unexpected flooding but also Jiangxi, Jiangsu, and Anhui downstream.

Wei Yuan recognized that dike destruction faced formidable obstacles. Who would provide the money to destroy the dikes? What would happen to flooded grave sites? How would displaced people be resettled? While recognizing these problems, he insisted on the need to stop temporizing by local officials, to crack down on abuses of water rights, and to destroy dikes that interfered with the flow of water.

Wei Yuan's concern for supra-local interests, his awareness of the interrelation between irrigation problems in Hunan and flood control downstream in Jiangsu and Anhui, and his recognition of the rising strength of "private" illegal interests were characteristic of the attitudes of the statecraft school of his day.[64] As he put it, "Which is more important: protecting the fields of a few polders, or protecting the fields of four provinces along the Yangtze River?"[65] Higher-level officials, instead of enlisting local support in dike construction, now had to defy local interests in order to protect their broader jurisdiction, and they had to force local magistrates to pursue national goals. Here the later statecraft writers' views diverged from those of Gu

Yanwu, who saw local magistrates as outsiders who ignored local interests.[66] Gu had recommended a quasi-hereditary status for local officials in order to make them more concerned with their locality.

Yang Xifu and Wei Yuan, on the other hand, saw district magistrates as captives of local groups, unwilling to take strong action against illegal irrigation works. Both Yang Xifu and Wei Yuan aimed to motivate local landowners to look beyond their own "short-sighted interests" to consider the needs of the larger society. Yang still believed that, with sufficient official exhortation, the villagers could be persuaded to recognize their own best interests. Wei Yuan, though, had to admit that there was an open clash between the national need for properly regulated water supplies and the local compulsion to clear land whenever possible. Instead of persuasion, he called for coercive measures to destroy illegal dikes and to force local officials to follow orders from above. The urgency of the crisis Wei Yuan faced was ultimately a result of Hunan's eighteenth-century population boom. Our examination of the relationship between population growth and the long-term development of dike-works in Hunan explains why Yang Xifu and Wei Yuan could see irrigation in such a different light.

THE CAMPAIGN TO DESTROY ILLEGAL DIKES: OFFICIAL VS. LOCAL INTERESTS

The builders of illegal dikes fell into two classes. Many of those most intimately involved in defying the prohibition on dike-building around the lake were immigrant landlords from Jiangxi. Hunan Governor Kai Tai faced repeated requests by these "roving bullies" (*liugun*), who falsely requested permission to repair dikes around the lake as a pretext for illegally clearing land. His response was to cangue the violators and send them back to their home province.[67] These were people with substantial sums of capital to invest who looked for profit in developing polder lands to serve the expanding rice export market. Their dikes were firm enough to cause serious obstruction of water routes.

Other illegal dikes were built by poor tenants or landless immigrants who were unable to find open land within the legal polders and were thus forced to build small enclosures on the margins of the lake. Some were new immigrants, and some were originally seasonal settlers on the lake bottom exposed in the dry season who were now forced to build small dikes to protect themselves.[68] Their life was much like the original settlers of Hunan before the rice boom. Their dikes were only 1 or 2 *zhang* high, easily washed away by major floods. They lived in grass shacks, and each household owned a raft to allow them to escape the flood waters. They were still able to get a harvest by moving back to the flooded lands as the waters receded.[69] While numerous, their small, weak dikes were not much of a threat to the Dongting water supply.

Nevertheless, a policy of total destruction risked upsetting these small marginal settlers, who might cause unrest. Officials therefore made efforts to exempt from destruction those illegal dikes that did not block essential water routes, while they aimed to destroy the large-scale projects of "the power-holders" (*youlizhe*), which threatened the entire area.[70] Considering the influence of these "local bullies and evil gentry" and their ability to obstruct official policies, we may well wonder whether the dikes exempted from destruction did not belong to those with local influence rather than the marginal immigrants. As one magistrate put it, "The strong have much land and few dikes, and they are good at avoiding regulations; the weak have little land and many dikes, and bear extra burdens."[71] Illegal dike-building accentuated class divisions. The state's goal was to aid the poor and limit the damage caused by the rich, but in practice it had no way of enforcing these distinctions.

As the campaign against illegal dikes intensified, provincial governors were ordered to investigate annually and report on any additions to the dikes.[72] They recorded the names of landowners involved in illegal clearance. Governor Qiao Guangjie thought the task important enough to justify selecting his own deputy to fill the post of departmental police warden and jail warden (*limu*) in Lizhou. Although this was normally a Board-selected position, Governor Qiao asked for a capable man in this "important position for destroying dikes and draining the river."[73] In 1763, Qiao discovered a total of 77 illegal dikes, of which 10 either did not obstruct water routes or protected the city walls. These were to be preserved, but the other 67 were all to be destroyed. He also found that 60 to 70 percent of the illegal dike lands paid no tax. All of this land formerly qualified for exemption as wasteland, but now it was richly productive. Paradoxically, this land, which was supposed to be destroyed, also had to pay tax.[74] Apparently, the campaign succeeded for a while—by 1777 all the illegal dikes were reported to have been either totally destroyed or to exist only in remnants. Yearly inspections in 1781, 1782, 1783, 1784, and 1808 confirmed that there had been no further additions.[75] Nevertheless, there continued to be a basic conflict between local land hunger and official efforts to keep water routes cleared.

Ambiguities in official policy allowed representatives of local landed interests to argue against complete destruction of dikes. Kuang Minben, an influential eighteenth-century Hunanese statecraft writer, adeptly pointed out the difficulties in returning cultivated land to the lake. He noted that "the old, deep, wide water routes are now almost useless and have long since been blocked up." In response to a proposal to improve drainage by cutting a new channel from the Yangtze to Dongting Lake, he replied: "The idea is very good, the execution difficult ... Dikes and banks surround fields, gardens, and graves. If you want to dig a new channel you must destroy old dikes already built and add a large number of new dikes. Not only is the expense great, but people will lose their livelihood as land goes to waste."[76] There was a basic contradiction, he noted, between the two fundamental principles of water conservancy: "Do not struggle with the water for land," and "Do not throw away land into the water."[77]

While officials worried about the long-term threat of overbuilding, local elite members were more likely to play down the threat of flooding and stress the advantages of clearing land. An influential local gentryman, Jiang Changtai, had succeeded in leading local people to defy Governor Chen Hongmou's ban on dike construction.[78] In 1756, he boasted about the beneficial effects of dikes:

> New and old dikes (are) mixed together, strung together like stars or chess (*weiqi*) pieces, wriggling like millipedes . . . the water does not struggle with the land. If there is drought, the people cut openings in the polder and they open and close it from time to time, so the land is not silted up . . . In 1755, the prefect set up stone tampers and mounds of earth to prepare against the unexpected. Even if there is a fierce wind and heavy rain, the dikes are still strong, so land abandoned for two hundred years has become a fertile region.[79]

For Jiang, reflecting the sentiments of local landowners, the threat of flooding could be dealt with by reinforcing the dikes. It may also be true that, at this juncture, the immediate danger of floods was not great. A flood in Huarong in 1755 was not particularly damaging, because "households whose lands were flooded all had grain planted on high lands and did not solely rely upon [flooded lowlands]."[80] This was not true later on. Nevertheless, it was in Jiang's interest to defend clearance, since the dikes had too much importance to be abandoned lightly.

Given the support for land clearance shown by prominent local families like the Jiangs, it is not surprising that local officials tried to find ways to avoid embroiling themselves in the tangles that were sure to occur if they promoted dike destruction too intensely. In 1751, Governor Fan Shishou found that over 1,000 *qing* of land had been cleared in Yiyang and Xiangyin counties along the lake after the prohibition on new dikes, yet he memorialized to exempt this land from taxation as newly cleared wasteland. Most of it was of the most marginal kind, planted and harvested in the dry period and abandoned in flood time. Fan argued: "Every dry year people compete to occupy this land, but once just a little rain falls they abandon it. If this land is taxed, it will only be abandoned again and thus will be of no aid in tax revenues. Also, wicked people will take the pretext that tax is collected and expect relief in the future when the floods come."[81]

Taxation of newly cleared land, however, was likely to lead to abandonment only when it was in the stage of marginal, seasonal settlement. Once a strong dike had been built, people were likely to favor taxation in order to justify their tenure. In Longyang county, where 23,090 *mou* were cleared from 1730 to 1751, and a large polder 129 *li* long was constructed, "people were all willing to pay tax in order to make the land their permanent tenure (*yongshou shiye*)."[82] In either case, destruction or prohibition of clearance was ignored and the new tenants to some extent were officially protected. Fan Shishou was concerned about the blockage of drainage routes caused by private dikes, but he did not consider this land which was periodically cleared and abandoned to be such a danger. He was aware of the abuses of excess land clearance, but, in order to prevent lawsuits, he did not report them.[83]

Governor Ma Huiyu, on the other hand, realized that taxing newly cleared land offered the perfect loophole for evasion of the ban on dike construction. The only way to stop evasion of the ban was to confiscate all untaxed land as "official wilderness" (*guanhuang*) and prohibit all private clearance of it.[84] A hard-line policy, however, proved to be unenforceable. In 1763, when Chen Hongmou ordered the destruction of Yanglinzhai, a major illegal dike in Xiangyin county, he did not know that it was the protector of four other major dikes. As the destruction of Yanglinzhai meant "the ruination of several tens of households, lawsuits increased even further, and landowners put even more effort into protecting their private interests. Laws could not be carried out justly, people's feelings and customs became daily crueller . . . Even a good official like Chen Hongmou" was deceived by the rampant corruption of his underlings, who were "controlled by wicked people for profit."[85] Concern with tax avoidance, if pressed too far, completely undercut efforts to destroy illegal dikes.

Local interests were able to take advantage of such ambiguities, and they could enlist county officials on their side, particularly since the county magistrate always wanted to expand his tax base by reclaiming more land. In 1815, two censors, Sun Shengchang and Li Lisong, claimed that widespread concealment of taxes existed throughout the empire.[86] They called for reports on newly cleared land. Their primary concern was with Zhili and Guangdong provinces, but the counties around Dongting Lake immediately made this order a pretext to expand their land area and levy new taxes. Thus, private dikes continued to grow. The total increase in taxes was very small, but the new dikes, as before, obstructed water routes and caused increased flooding. Here again, the different levels of government demonstrated conflicting interests. County magistrates and court officials allied to promote clearance against provincial restrictions.

In 1825, Governor Kang Shaoyong was ordered to investigate and destroy these new private dikes, but he found that his only available military force was the Yuezhou water patrol, which had responsibility for the entire lake.[87] Since the swampy lake borders were notorious bandit lairs, the garrison was too busy protecting boats from piracy to have time to destroy dikes. Although local district magistrates should have been responsible for the inspection and destruction of dikes, Kang found, in 1828, that no patrols of the lake had been made for some time. In 1813, each county had been ordered to send its own troops to inspect the lake borders for bandits and illegal dikes, but this was stopped, because the yearly expense of several thousand *taels* was too great.[88] The Yuezhou garrison clearly was inadequate to the task of performing three functions simultaneously: protection of commerce, searching for illegal dikes, and stamping out bandits. Governor Kang had to depute the Chang-Bao circuit intendant and the salt circuit intendant to investigate and destroy 70 private dikes.

Seven years later, Governor Wu Rongguang had no better luck. Despite continual orders for destruction of dikes, he still heard of "small people only seeking profit" who took already destroyed dikes and repaired them, or who continued to clear land at the foot of mountains and river banks.[89] Official and illegal dikes were so closely intermingled that it was impossible to distinguish them. Deputies sent to investigate illegal dike-building pocketed fees in return for looking the other way.[90] In fact, of the 70 dikes ordered to be destroyed in the Qianlong reign, 18 still had not been destroyed by 1832. Ninety-six more were designated for destruction in the Jiaqing reign (1796–1820), but, by 1827, 143 had been built or added to. Forty-three of these blocked major water routes, while the rest were in mountainous areas along small streams far from the lake shore. These were allowed to remain, but no further repairs to them were permitted.

Perhaps the Hunanese officials had succeeded to some extent in shifting the main focus of land clearance away from the lake border and toward the mountainous regions. Yet, even Wu's efforts were compromised by the need for taxes. Governor Kang in 1827 had tried to encourage abandonment of these dikes by refusing to grant tax exemptions on them in case of flood, but this only encouraged further extension of dikes in an effort to make up for tax arrears.[91] The only solution was to admit that these illegal dikes in the mountains were not the same as other illegal dikes and to grant them tax exemptions along with the adjacent official dikes.

Even without the proliferation of illegal dikes, there were serious problems with maintaining effective repairs of "official" and "people's" dikes. Since both types of dikes were intermingled, it was very difficult to keep them at a uniform height. Official dikes could be controlled by regulations, but not all the households repairing people's dikes set aside sufficient heaps of earth and willow trees to keep their dikes repaired. In 1767, the circuit intendant attempted to establish uniform standards for the heights and materials used on official and people's dikes.[92] An alternative was to change the people's dikes into official dikes, but this risked eliminating all incentives for repair. Hence, the Yongzheng Emperor rejected changing people's dikes into official ones, knowing that, once a dike was designated "official," local people would avoid all responsibility for it.[93] On the other hand, officials tended to neglect all supervision of people's dikes. In 1805, a district magistrate and provincial treasurer were impeached for believing that they need not set any time limits for repairs of people's dikes.[94]

As predicted, deficiencies in dike repair, together with illegal dike-building, brought disaster in the nineteenth century. In Xiangyin, some dikes were damaged in 1816 and 1823, but the first major flood came in 1831. After that there were floods every year, but the worst were in 1834, 1838, 1839, 1844 ("thousands harmed"), 1848, 1849, ("boats floated inside the city walls"), 1860, 1861, 1863, 1865, 1868,

1869, 1871, 1872, 1873, 1875, and 1879.[95] The 1881 gazetteer reported that "not one single dike remains here, neither official, people's, nor illegal."[96] This was either an exaggeration or referred only to temporary damage, but 20 to 30 percent of the dikes were permanently abandoned, even though the tax registers still reported them as extant.[97] Apparently, given the decay of administration in the second half of the nineteenth century, almost nothing could be done about the situation. In 1865, Governor Yun Shilin discussed surveying the abandoned dikes and allowing people once again to clear the land, no matter if they were legal or illegal, with the unpaid taxes on these lands to be distributed over the extant dikes; nothing came of the proposal after he left his post.[98]

In the end, neither prohibitions nor local administrative reforms could stop the inexorable process that produced more dikes but fewer repairs, more land but greater vulnerability. Guo Songtao, reviewing the causes of disaster in his native county in 1881, concluded that prohibition of clearance only "robbed land from the people."[99] He argued that previous dynasties since the Song had laid equal stress on dike construction and dredging of water routes to allow drainage of surplus water. The Qing had neglected the drainage problem, to their cost. Guo found support in the words of Ji Wenchun, assistant district magistrate of Xiangyin in the Daoguang reign. Ji was in charge of the destruction of illegal dikes, but, as he found that "the wicked took advantage of the prohibitions to raise lawsuits," he proposed an alternative policy.[100] He stressed digging of several tens of drainage canals in lowland places, and he opposed the prohibition of clearance, as it "vainly burdened the people for no benefit."

Other officials, however, apparently considered the costs of large-scale dredging too high to be feasible. There was a limited amount of dredging of the lake at this time, carried out by "comb boats" with stakes attached to their hulls which moved around the lakes and rivers stirring up the mud. The option of thorough dredging of the lake and its channels, however, was not revived until the late nineteenth century, when the availability of Western technology prompted writers to consider the Yangtze and its paddy lands as analogous to the Mississippi River or the dikes of Holland.[101] Technological limitations had prevented earlier officials from considering extensive dredging, but the availability of steam and cement offered new possibilities for disposing of flood waters without running up against vested interests in preserving hard-won land. Under the Republic, several careful investigators devised ambitious plans for managing the lake waters, but the disorganization of the Republican government made large-scale planning impossible. Only after 1949 could extensive channeling and dredging of the lake begin.

The shrinking of Dongting Lake was only the most conspicuous example of a phenomenon occurring all over the densely settled parts of the empire. Yang Xifu himself had noticed that "not only Dongting Lake but other lakes several *li* or several *qing* in size have gradually had land cleared around them and disappeared."[102] The same process was going on throughout the part of Hubei between the lake and the Yangtze River. The shrinkage of the "nine holes and thirteen mouths" begun in the late Ming continued in the Qing, confining the Yangtze, like a caged beast, to ever more constricted outlets. Warnings about the need to provide drainage channels went unheeded.[103] By 1748, the Yangtze had only two channels leading to Dongting Lake.[104] In 1854, in the midst of the occupation of Wuchang by the Taiping rebels, the Yangtze itself, by breaking through its dikes at Ouchikou in Songci county, reopened the drainage channel into Dongting Lake that Qing officials had allowed to silt up. The silt carried into the lake by this flood produced a huge amount of new land, which in 1894 became part of a new independent sub-prefecture, Nanzhou *ting*.

In 1746, the Fuzhou prefect of Fujian province found that "wicked people" had cleared over one-quarter of a lake used for irrigation and evaded taxes on it. He, too, demanded that the land be returned to the lake.[105] In 1831, the Emperor delivered a stern edict to the governors of Anhui, Jiangxi, Hubei, and Hunan, attacking land occupation throughout the Yangtze River Basin. He demanded close investigation along all rivers and lakes and an end to "empty words" about prohibition of land clearance.[106] Nevertheless, illegal clearance persisted as population pressure intensified. Immigrants to the highlands of Sichuan and Shaanxi deforested the mountains, filling the streams with large quantities of silt which was eventually carried into the Yangtze River.[107] The "shack people" (*pengmin*) who settled the hills of Zhejiang, Anhui, Jiangxi, and Jiangsu indirectly aggravated flooding downstream by removing the ground cover and encouraging erosion.[108] The continual edicts and memorials attacking these practices indicate that Qing officials were aware of the ecological damage that oversettlement produced, but the ineffectiveness of their prohibitions demonstrates the loss of state control over an exploding population.

Like the other key components of agriculture discussed in this study, waterworks construction reflected the dialectical interplay between state policies and popular response. Official encouragement substantially aided the rehabilitation of Hunan in the seventeenth and early eighteenth centuries, but soon the local producers proved themselves able to construct waterworks independently. At least this was so in the lowland areas influenced by export demand. Yang Xifu's concern about neglect of waterworks was directed at the more remote districts, which lacked both the capital and incentives to invest in large reservoirs. By the mid-eighteenth century, the export boom and population upsurge of Hunan were well underway without any official intervention. By the end of the century, officials were desperately trying to put the brakes on the rush to clear land and build dikes before it led to disaster. But, by this time, the Qing government had lost a great deal of its effectiveness, and the weight of its bureaucracy in comparison with the flourishing commercial sector was far less than it had been in the early Ming. The severe floods of the nineteenth and twentieth centuries were the tragic outcome of the state's inability to halt the trends of land clearance and population growth which a century earlier it had done so much to promote.

EIGHT

Conclusion

We have described above the important, if limited, role that the bureaucratic state and its officials played in Qing socio-economic development. From the beginning of Qing rule, officials recognized the need to promote agricultural production in order to ensure peasant subsistence. They developed an array of policies—encouraging tax reform, granaries, land clearance, waterworks construction, and new technologies—in order to stimulate the agricultural economy. These policies had two fundamental goals: to provide the state with a reliable source of surplus extraction from the peasant farmers it ruled, and to maintain social order in the countryside. Qing officials had the same goals as their predecessors, and they drew from the same repertory of classical precedents, but they implemented these policies more extensively and they paid more attention to practical experience than most other dynasties. On the other hand, they faced problems of unprecedented magnitude. The demographic and commercial transformation of the early Qing decisively altered the balance of interests between officials and the peasant economy. Perceptive local officials demonstrated remarkable flexibility in applying inherited precedents to a changing environment.

The relationship between the Chinese state and the agricultural society it governed must be seen as a dynamic, dialectical one, influenced by the goals of state officials, the reactions of local communities to state policies, and the physical environment embracing both of them. This study has described three different phases of this relationship. At certain times, as in the late seventeenth and early eighteenth centuries, the state was aggressively committed to the restoration of the economy, local producers urgently needed outside assistance, and the local environment was one of sparse population and abundant land. In this situation, state effectiveness was at a maximum because its goals were in tune with what the local people needed, and officials who promoted immigration, land clearance, and waterworks were highly successful.

Later in the eighteenth century, officials took a more relaxed attitude. They let private investors build the dikes, allowed immigration without encouraging it, and tacitly permitted concealment of newly cleared tax-free land. In this period, state and local interests did not conflict, as there was still room for growth, but non-official initiatives clearly had the upper hand. By the end of the eighteenth century, it had become clear that private and official interests were increasingly coming into conflict. Around 1785, the famous Qing scholar Cui Shu (1740–1816) wrote a short essay, "On Struggle," in which he noted that litigation was on the rise, and the aggressive were competing for advancement. Rejecting the orthodox Confucian doctrine of "yielding," Cui Shu openly justified conflict: "It is inevitable that two people will struggle. The sage should understand this and not blame them." In another essay, "On Litigation," Cui Shu declared: "All living persons have struggle mentalities (*zhengxin*). If one person struggles and the other yields, then he who yields is finished. If he does not yield, then there must be litigation." Cui Shu went on to justify litigation as a means of defending the weak against the strong.[1]

Cui Shu's surprisingly modern attitude indicates a recognition that society in his time was becoming increasingly contentious. The type of conflict varied from place to place. In the remote mountains of Hunan, especially in the Miao territory, disputes were generally settled by bloodshed. In the lowlands, disputes could also lead to bloodshed, but more often they ended up in the magistrate's yamen. Lawsuits resulting from the rising value of land forced officials to establish new regulations over the land market. Lineages fought with each other over the right to clear land around the lake, while at the same time they defied official prohibitions against dike-building. In this third phase, official regulations were sometimes ignored (as in the case of rent deposits and dikes), and sometimes used by local interests for private purposes. The growing divergence of official and local interests in the late eighteenth and early nineteenth centuries foreshadowed the much larger conflicts that would dominate the nineteenth century.

The ultimate causes of this divergence are complex, but the two most basic factors were population growth and commercialization. In Hunan, these two trends reinforced each other in the eighteenth century. As the market spread, the fertile lands attracted immigrants, and the productivity of the newly cleared lands stimulated further market demand. Both developments made Hunan a much more prosperous and lively place than it had been two or three centuries earlier. But we should not ignore the negative side of the trend. China's ancient curse of too many people on too little land soon fell upon Hunan. Competition over smaller and smaller pieces of land increased the level of local conflict. At the same time, the inexorable progress of settlement posed the threat of ecological exhaustion in both lake and mountain regions.

Commerce, too, brought wealth and new goods to many people, but it also aroused resentment at the "foreigners" from Jiangxi who acquired a disproportionate share of the wealth. The new market also provided tenants with the opportunity and incentive to claim firmer rights to land from their landlords. Without denying the prosperity brought to many by the "rice boom" of the eighteenth century, we should recognize that such drastic social change also produced great conflicts.

STATE AND PEASANT IN THE LATE QING

The interaction of official initiative and peasant response continued to influence the development of the rural economy as long as the Qing empire survived. A complete account of developments in the province during the turbulent last half-century of Qing rule would require another study. Here I shall only highlight the continuities between the early Qing and the late nineteenth century. Despite the outbreak of major rebellions, the Western impact, reform programs, and the beginnings of modernization, the basic conditions of life for the Hunanese peasantry continued much as before, and the essential problems of agricultural production persisted.

After the mid-nineteenth century, the Hunanese rural population suffered intensely from the progressive breakdown of the Qing imperial state. The Taiping Rebellion and its suppression had a devastating impact on the province, but the Taipings drew support from the social tensions that had built up in the preceding centuries. In 1852, as the Taiping armies marched through the province on their way from Guangxi to Nanking, they drew in thousands of Hunanese followers. Jen Yu-wen claims that over 20,000 Hunanese responded to the Taiping proclamation issued at Daozhou condemning the crimes of the Manchus, but it is more likely that peasants were drawn to the Taiping cause by its promises of relief from landlord exploitation.[2] The Taipings appealed both to tenants victimized by landlords and to peasants dependent on the commercial export market. Taiping promises of rent reduction were welcomed in the lake districts, where for decades "stubborn tenants" had been battling landlords attempting to raise rent deposits. In mountainous districts, joining the Taiping army offered an escape for tenants from the tight control of local landlords.[3] Small owner-cultivators, heavily burdened by tax surcharges, took advantage of the Taiping arrival to resist tax payments, attracted by Taiping promises of three-year tax exemptions.[4] An uprising in Lizhou in 1856 both raised demands for rent reduction and focused attacks on the likin bureaus, because likin taxes harmed poor peasants living off cash crops.[5] A wave of attacks on moneychangers, rich households, and tax collectors followed the entrance of the Taiping army.[6] Others, however, probably joined to escape the turmoil in their locality. Those unwilling to join the Taiping often abandoned their fields, took all the grain they could carry, and moved to the mountains or fled to provinces near and far, including Jiangnan, Fujian, and Sichuan.[7]

When Hong Xiuquan besieged Changsha in 1852, he had amassed an army of 120,000 people.[8] Peasants fled to the mountains, and local banditry flourished.[9] Governor Luo Bingzhang was able to hold off the Taiping siege with loyal defenders of the city. When the Taiping returned to invade Hunan in 1854, Zeng Guofan's newly organized Xiang army proved its worth by driving the Taiping out of the province in a few months.[10] Many Hunanese joined the local militia simply to protect their homes and families.[11] When Shi Dakai moved into Hunan in 1859, he too found many local recruits, but, once again, the Xiang army forced him out. After the victory, however, the Hunanese suffered from pillaging by the Xiang army soldiers.[12]

The Taiping impact coincided with increasingly severe natural disasters. Drought, famine, and flood had struck Liling county in five of the fifteen years between 1828 and 1844. In 1849, a famine in the county forced uprooted peasants to wander on the roads in groups of 4,000 to 5,000 in search of food. The Taiping invasion stimulated the outbreak of local banditry in 1852, further damaging local production. Heavy rain in 1853 caused hundreds of thousands of piculs of grain to rot.[13]

More significant than the Taiping themselves were the host of local conflicts touched off by their incapacitation of the local government. The muted tensions building in the eighteenth and early nineteenth centuries burst out in innumerable varieties of open strife. Tax-resistance movements had broken out in Hunan and Hubei in the 1840s.[14] From the 1830s on, grain blockages had been conspicuous in southern Hunan, as localities fought to protect precarious local supplies against the demands of export merchants and military predators.[15] Secret society leaders took advantage of local demands for grain to turn local grain-blockage movements into anti-Manchu rebellions. The Daoguang Emperor had noted in 1835 the prevalence in Hunan and elsewhere of religious bandits carrying out "food equalization" (*junliang*).[16] Yao tribespeople also joined the rebellions out of resentment against Han domination.[17] The arrival of the Taiping facilitated the outbreak of new blockages of grain routes based on the same competition for local grain.

Districts like Wugang, which were relatively fertile exporting areas but located far up the riverine trade routes, were the most vulnerable to blockages. Earlier in the dynasty, provincial rulers had played an integrative role by responding to imperial edicts to keep localities open to market demands so that grain could flow freely. When the government lost its authority, local armed groups barricaded rivers at important posts to prevent grain supplies from being sent out.[18] Although official rhetoric condemned grain blockers as "bandits" and "local bullies," the prefect of Baoqing admitted that "the foolish people see [grain blockage] as protection of the local area's food and regard it as virtuous."[19]

The loss of security affected Dongting Lake as well. Pirates in light, fast boats infested the lake and river area, outrunning the desperate efforts of imperial patrol boats. Governors in the late eighteenth century had captured and executed thousands of pirates, but the nineteenth-century officials could not cope with them.[20]

Other signs of disorder that were sporadic in earlier times grew to serious threats in the 1850s. Waves of bandits moved in from Guangxi in the wake of the Taiping armies. Secret societies like the Heaven and Earth Society, which had seldom been prominent in the eighteenth century, proliferated under a variety of names.[21] Li Yuanfa, a Triad leader, led a rebellion in Xinning in the famine year of 1849, capturing the county seat with the help of yamen clerks and murdering the district magistrate.[22] Gentry-organized local militia besieged the city and drove Li out after twenty days. Salt smuggling and opium trading also increased in scale, and cattle rustling became endemic in peripheral districts.[23] These different forms of local conflict grew out of the competition for scarce resources which had intensified over the previous century, but, with the controlling hand of the state removed, the focus of these struggles shifted from the magistrate's courtroom to open violence.

To a certain extent, the Taiping period recapitulated the Ming-Qing

TABLE 22 Population Growth in Nineteenth-Century Hunan

County	Year	Kou
Qianzhou *ting*	1816	25,900
	1821	26,010
	1836	27,860
	1847	28,345
	1852	21,130
	1854	26,684
	1862	33,253
	1866	34,330
	1869	34,445
Cili *xian*	1815	140,236
	1866	149,272
Baojing *xian*	1816	96,840
	1860	92,284
Anfu *xian*	1815	91,008
	1837	116,332
	1845	116,908
	1848	117,154
	1849	114,927
	1850	115,022
	1856	118,459
	1860	136,491
	1865	164,424
	1866	173,395
Lizhou *benzhou*	1820	301,220
	1868	313,205
Shimen *xian*	1820	177,150
	1868	201,013

TABLE 22 *(continued)*

County	Year	Kou
Yongding *xian*	1820	128,940
	1869	135,370

Sources: Lizhou Zhi, 1874.5.5; *Anfu Xianzhi,* 1869.9 (only selected years listed); *Baojing Xianzhi,* 1871.3; *Cili Xianzhi,* 1869.4; *Qianzhou Tingzhi,* 1877.3.

transition. It too produced abandonment of the lowlands and flight to the hills, inverting the local demographic distribution. The collapse of local government forced peasants back to protective strategies, eliminating the incentives for opening up to market trade. Local power, which had earlier offered opportunities to farmers prospering from cash crops, reverted to military men: the gentry organizers of militia on the orthodox side, or the aggressive Triad leaders and bandits on the heterodox side. Serious damage was inflicted on the commercial economy. One of the most lasting effects of the rebellion was to reduce permanently the trade of Xiangtan, the dominant commercial city of the province, causing much of the rice export and processing trade to shift to Hankow.[24] The Taiping interlude, however, was much shorter than the Ming-Qing transition and its effects slighter, because the major battles of the Taiping took place downstream in the lower Yangtze region. By 1860, Hunan had begun to recover.

It has been argued that the Taiping devastation gave parts of China a temporary reprieve from Malthusian pressures.[25] This was in fact the case in some of the remoter districts of Hunan, like Rucheng county. The county suffered from severe land shortage by the end of the eighteenth century, but, in the 1850s, a local writer noted that there was now sufficient land to live on, because of the reduced population.[26] Still, Hunan's reprieve was brief. Provincial population figures show no decline in the 1850s and 1860s. Some local figures, which may be more reliable, show a drop in the 1850s, but recovery by 1862 (see Table 22). Major losses in population produced by the decade of turmoil were soon replenished by immigration from the five provinces downstream (Jiangsu, Anhui, Zhejiang, Jiangxi, Hubei).[27] Emigration from Hunan to the devastated lower Yangtze provinces indicates that overpopulation in Hunan persisted.[28]

After the rebellions ended, Hunan soon began to show signs of prosperity. The large country estates of rich landlords testified to the wealth of the province, which Baron Richthofen described as "one of the most favored landscapes of China."[29] The appearance of these landlords indicates growing land concentration in the province caused by urban capital flowing into the countryside.[30]

In fact, many Hunanese who had abandoned their fields to join the regional army under Zeng Guofan were able on their return to buy up large amounts of land with the money they had earned in military service.[31] Since much of the Hunan army was recruited from native tribespeople, these soldiers on their return brought capital into their remote districts.[32] The spread of wine shops and banqueting through the countryside indicated a new demand for luxuries.[33] Local officials, like their predecessors, denounced the waste of several million piculs of grain per year for making wine, but the export market in grain continued to grow.[34] By 1906, Xiangtan exported 1.5 million piculs and Changsha 1.0 million piculs of grain per year.[35]

Prosperity, however, was not unmixed. There still remained a sizable population of uprooted peasants, beggars, and landless poor. The inexorable growth of population increased the difficulties of making a living for peasants who could not produce for the export market. Several phenomena indicate increasing peasant poverty in the nineteenth century. Baling peasants who could no longer make a living from the soil were forced into seasonal migrant labor in Hubei, but, when floods struck Hubei, they had to return home.[36] By the 1870s, Wugang peasants had adopted the "little daughter-in-law" form of marriage, in which poor families avoided paying a bride price by bringing up a wife from childhood in their own household. This practice caused many disputes and unhappy marriages, but it had become an economic necessity in areas with dense populations on small amounts of land.[37]

The decline of effective local relief also increased peasant poverty. The local militia organized in the 1850s had provided a form of poor relief, substituting for soup kitchens and employment on public works.[38] Despite their attempts to drive out vagrants and "sturdy beggars" from the local militia, local officials themselves realized that the landless poor were an excellent source of recruits.[39] Demobilizing the militia left many poor Hunanese with no place to go. The collapse of local granaries also left them no food. A survey in 1861 discovered that, in 30 of the 75 *zhou* and *xian* of Hunan, the local granaries were completely empty.[40] Officials also noticed an increased reluctance of the local gentry to support local relief. The late nineteenth century saw a devolution of control over military, fiscal, and relief administration to local gentry, and the Tongzhi reform program encouraged gentry activism in restoring the local economy. Kui Lian, prefect of Baoqing, however, felt compelled to levy surcharges for relief on the gentry according to landholding because of the inadequacy of local contributions. He found that rich households and villages with good harvests had "still preserved a stubbornly localist view" and refused to give relief on behalf of outsiders.[41] Yet he and others continued to promote voluntary relief by urging lineages to take care of their own poor.[42]

Because of the decline of relief, peasants grew increasingly dependent on grain loans to get through the year. Baling peasants were regarded as being well off, because they pawned their clothes in the spring for loans from wealthy gentry at interest rates of only 30 percent per year![43] Wu Minshu attributed the heavy dependence on grain loans in Baling directly to the collapse of the community granary system which had functioned in the early Qing.[44] One of the reasons for the decline of the charitable granaries was that peasants were unable to repay the famine loans made by the granaries.[45]

Cooperative credit societies offered some peasants a way to avoid heavy interest rates. In Liling, seven people joined together to contribute capital, and each received a share in rotation at a 20-percent interest rate. These societies, however, were open only to peasants with some capital to begin with. No poor peasants could participate.[46]

The decline of granary stores in the nineteenth century left the state with far fewer resources for relief than in the eighteenth century, forcing it to depend even more heavily on private initiative.[47] After turning over important local administrative functions to gentry, however, local officials had great difficulty in preventing abuse. For example, after two Wugang gentry mobilized the militia successfully in 1858 to defend the local people against rebel attacks, they coercively collected contributions of over 100,000 strings of cash for their own use and misappropriated military supplies worth over 3,600 *taels*.[48] The local magistrate, forced to rely on these men for local defense, could do nothing to expose them. The military decline of state power exacerbated the struggle between local pursuit of gain and the state need to rely on upright gentry for local administration.

Tax inequalities also obstructed the recovery. In Baling county, taxes varied widely between villages and between mountain and lowland without any close relation to land productivity. Land which had been flooded and covered with water for years still failed to get exemptions.[49] The new likin tax burdened rural producers of textiles and cash crops and hindered exports.[50] In Hengyang and Qingquan counties, the *baojia* system, originally designed to capture bandits, was extended in 1835 to cover tax collection.[51] The results were strikingly analogous to the experience of the *lijia* in the Ming and the dike repair organizations in the Qing. Since the *baojia* head became responsible for tax arrears, the honest were driven out and the strongmen who took over colluded with yamen runners to extort surtaxes from taxpayers. They collected several times the official tax from the people and used their influence at the yamen to keep the surplus in their pockets. Even where the *baojia* did not take over tax collection, the household heads of *lijia* units were flogged for tax arrears. Naturally, they bribed yamen clerks to avoid this burden whenever possible.[52]

Hunan had seldom suffered tax arrears in the eighteenth century, but arrears began rising after 1830 when a series of bad floods struck the province.[53] Neglect of irrigation combined with the rising price of silver in terms of grain made it impossible for Hunanese peasants to pay taxes.[54] The combination of natural disaster and local peculation both damaged the province's prosperity and reduced its fiscal contribution to the state.

Governor Luo Bingzhang, one of the greatest of the Tongzhi Restoration leaders, did promote a comprehensive tax-reduction program in the province in 1855. By eliminating many surcharges, he claimed to have reduced total land-tax receipts in Xiangtan by one quarter, but this had no lasting effects.[55] In fact, by legalizing several informal surcharges and by delegating control over tax collection to local gentry, Governor Luo ensured that gentry interests and not the people would profit from the reform.[56] Inevitably, surcharges soon began to rise again, undermining the reforms. The Tongzhi reformers considered the reduction of the land tax to be the keystone of their program for rehabilitation of the agricultural economy, but their failure to deal with the causes of corruption and their deliberate neglect of rent reduction prevented resolution of the growing difficulties of Yangtze Valley peasants.[57] Tax equalization, which had been critical to the province's recovery in the early eighteenth century, was much less effective in the nineteenth.

Competition for control of water and land increasingly led to conflict. In the late nineteenth century, disputes over the allocation of water from mountain reservoirs led Wu Minshu to set up a stele clearly specifying the division of water rights according to landholding. He also selected one man from each village to be in charge of opening and closing sluice gates.[58] Once again, official intervention was the only method for resolving strife over water distribution. Land clearance also led to trouble, especially over newly silted-up land around the lake. After the breakthrough of the Yangtze River in Hubei had created the large sand-bar region of Nanzhou, an official survey in 1882 declared all the newly silted land to be government land, allotted the land to tenants, and drew up contracts. By 1890, immigrants were again flocking to the province to cultivate this fertile soil. "Bad gentry" (*diaosheng liejian*), however, grabbed the opportunity to take over land by deceptive means. Feuds and lawsuits proliferated; fatalities resulting from land disputes mounted.[59]

Besides disputes over land, the technological problems of preventing flooding around the lake continued to grow. The overflow of the Yangtze River through the Ouchikou channel into Dongting Lake caused major floods in 1868. Officials discussed blocking up this last outlet from the Yangtze into the lake, but the project was abandoned for lack of funds.[60] The availability of Western steamers, however, did offer the new possibility of comprehensive dredging of the lake, combined with blocking of the channels that filled it up with silt.[61] Dai Dancheng, citing the successes of the Netherlands and the Mississippi River levee dikes in controlling flooding, proposed a similar large-scale project for Dongting Lake.[62] In 1898, it was proposed to establish the Hunan Irrigation Bureau to install steam pumps in the countryside for pumping water to highland areas.[63] The basic conditions of agricultural production had not changed, but modern technology had begun to offer the promise of ameliorating age-old difficulties involving both water shortage and flood. The fiscal deterioration of the empire, however, prevented the implementation of any of these projects.

Under the Republic, too, the province continued to be plagued by flood. Major, disastrous floods struck in 1924, 1931, and 1935. Excessive clearance of land around the lake, silt deposits resulting from stripping of mountain hillsides, and neglect of waterworks repair were the basic causes, just as before. By 1936, the new migrants who had occupied Nan county in the 1880s could barely make a living even in a good year and had to take to begging in a famine year.[64] The warlord governments took little interest in protecting the agriculture of the region, but several excellent local surveys of landholding were conducted in the 1930s and 1940s.[65] All investigators realized that the difficulties of the Hunan peasantry arose fundamentally from the inadequacy of the land-registration system. They proposed detailed land surveys, followed by blocking of the silting and extensive dredging of the lake, but they had to recognize that the costs of such projects were prohibitive. A province-wide survey begun in 1932 foundered in maladministration, corruption, and lack of funds. Only four counties were ever surveyed, and concealed land persisted.[66] Only the powerful new administration of the People's Republic had the resources and dedication to undertake the extensive dredging required.

The most important development in agriculture in the nineteenth century was the widespread cultivation of non-grain cash crops. Evidence abounds of a wide variety of activities supplementing or even replacing rice monoculture. In Chengbu, nearly all the wealthy households grew bamboo for profit.[67] Poor peasants in Lingling burned down trees to make ash for sale on the market. Ash was an important source of fertilizer for mountain lands.[68] Paper-making from bamboo and commercial tea production also flourished.[69] Tobacco spread not only in the mountains but even near the lake. Rice paddies were turned into tobacco plantations in Shanhua, because the profit was several times greater. Production increased greatly in the forty years from 1830 to 1870.[70] One crop not widely grown in Hunan was opium, which in Sichuan and other provinces became one of the main cash crops of the hill country.[71] Another notable change was the rise of the porcelain industry in Liling.

Most important, however, was the spread of cotton and tea production.[72] Much of the newly silted sand-bar land around the lake was cleared for cotton, not grain.[73] The spread of cotton-planting furthered the penetration of the market into poor areas and stimulated the development of a local Hunanese merchant class engaging in rural trade. In this respect, Hunan, at a lag of several centuries, retraced the development of the Jiangnan region from grain to textiles and tea. Hunan, especially Anhua county, had been an abundant tea producer since the Song dynasty, but its tea had been of low quality. Only after the Opium War did Hunanese tea enter a new stage of high-quality production for a large export market. As Hankow rose to become the leading tea market of China in the twentieth century, its hinterland in Hunan and Hubei became the dominant tea producing area of China. In 1914, Maritime Customs reports put Hunan's tea exports at 2,219,917 piculs.[74] Tea was particularly valued in mountain regions where grain crops were insufficient. The attitude of the government toward tea production also changed. Earlier, few officials had encouraged tea production, because tea was regarded as a luxury that undermined grain, but they began to promote it after the 1850s when they realized that profits from tea production provided a reliable source of likin revenues.[75] Tea production, like cotton, permitted the formation of new merchant groups, who formed tea guilds to act as brokers between mountain household producers and export dealers. The boom in export production, however, did not basically transform social relations in the countryside, but was superimposed upon landlord-tenant production relations. Hired labor did increase in the tea districts, but tenant farmers and small holders continued to provide much of the crop.

In reaction to the increasing pressure on the land, intensification of rice production also appeared in the form of true double-cropping of rice. In Liling, late rice was planted between the rows of the early rice crop, to produce two crops of rice on the same plot (*erhe*). This method was used only where the soil temperature was too cold to allow planting of two rice crops in succession.[76] In the mountains, another response was to grow both sweet potatoes and rice, the rice to be sold on the market, the sweet potatoes to be consumed. These households were in a situation quite similar to Irish peasants in the nineteenth century—heavily dependent on a single potato crop for their own consumption while also subject to demands by outside powers for rice exports. When the sweet-potato crop failed, they could starve.[77]

The intensification of cultivation, like the development of cash crops, was in part a fulfillment of the early Qing officials' efforts to promote increased productivity in response to land shortage. These new crops ensured the livelihood of greater numbers of peasants, although they signified the abandonment of self-sufficiency and subjected the peasants to the new vulnerability of the market. The Chengbu magistrate warned the poor peasants of his locality not to abandon grain production for bamboo, noting that only rich households could afford the capital investments and the slow returns.[78] Complete conversion to cash-cropping could bring disturbing change to local areas. In Pingjiang, tens of thousands of tea pickers crowded the streets, causing local literati to worry about declining morals.[79] Intensification also damaged the local ecology. By the 1890s, officials realized that excess development of hill crops (*zaliang*) had stripped mountain forests and increased erosion.[80] The Liling porcelain industry also contributed to pollution, as waste from the kilns poured into the rivers, increasing their silt content.[81]

Recently, quite a few political scientists and historians have focused on long-term socio-economic change in the Asian countryside and its connection with peasant revolution.[82] They have approached the problem from a variety of perspectives. "Formalists" stress the rationality of peasant household economic behavior; "substantivists" emphasize risk avoidance and the subsistence ethic ensuring reciprocity between members of a moral community; and Marxists focus on the extractive relationship between landlord and tenant.[83] But, whatever their differences, in Philip Huang's words, "They share a common weakness in their neglect of the internal dynamics of change in peasant China before contact with the capitalist West."[84] This study has examined the interaction between the imperial state and peasant producers over a three-century period in one province. It provides evidence to support all three approaches. Population growth and market opportunity were important factors in innovation, as the formalists have claimed. Both officials and peasants responded rationally to the market, seeking the best return available under given conditions, but they also sought to insure against risk when possible. New crops or seed combinations succeeded best when they provided *both* higher return and lower risk. There are, however, signs that, by the nineteenth century, population pressure was forcing peasants into intensification and commercial cropping which damaged the local ecology and made them quite vulnerable to market fluctuations.

The laments of literati for the loss of harmony, which they saw as being undermined by incentives for profit, illustrate the decline of moral economy. On the other hand, it is questionable whether a unified moral community ever really existed in China outside the minds of nostalgic Confucians. In contrast to a widely held stereotype about traditional China, cooperation and restraint of individual interest for the welfare of a larger community were *not* easily enforced in the Hunanese countryside, despite the best official efforts.[85] The collapse of collective waterworks repair and the contention over land testify to an aggressive pursuit of gain, often at the cost of the wider society.

Class tensions, too, were not negligible in the countryside, although Marxists have exaggerated their dominance. Tenant disputes with landlords were one of a variety of foci of conflict, and the imperial state, although it was not merely a tool of the landlord class, did enforce landlord rights. Still, it is hard to claim that true class-consciousness opposing tenants *as a whole* to landlords *as a whole* was evolving in nineteenth-century Hunan, even during the Taiping incursion. Local conflicts always overrode broader movements. All these theories provide useful hypotheses for investigation, but ultimately abstract formulae must yield to the concrete realities of a particular place and time.

The imperial state was neither despotic nor laissez-faire, and its control over the agricultural economy was neither all-encompassing nor negligible. Imperial officials pursued policies of active intervention in the countryside, but their impact depended upon the state of the rural economy. As G. William Skinner puts it, "The dynastic cycle was *mediated* by regional developmental cycles."[86] Hunan's cycles of development in the Ming and Qing paralleled the dynastic cycle but were not identical with it. The best indicators of regional development in Hunan are waterworks construction, especially in the area around the lake, and population data, during the years for which it is available. Hunan experienced rapid growth in the early Ming but began to run into difficulties by the mid-sixteenth century. Decline set in, lasting beyond the establishment of the Qing until the end of the Wu Sangui Rebellion in the 1680s. The rapid recovery of the early eighteenth century was the period when state stimulation of the economy was most effective. As the private sector took over from state initiative in the second half of the eighteenth century, conflicts between official goals and local interests sharpened. The early nineteenth century, featuring illegal clearance, grain blockages, and tribal rebellion, set the stage for the decline into chaos of the late Qing.

On top of these cyclical processes, however, must be superimposed two major long-term trends: the halting but inexorable 10-fold rise in population from about 2 million in 1393 to over 20 million by 1850, and the progressive extension of market activity, both domestic and export-oriented. Both these trends incorporated Hunan into the heart of the empire by transforming it from a sparsely populated periphery into a major grain and cash-crop producer. The effect on the peasantry is complex and difficult to determine. There were those who profited from the new commercial opportunities, and there were those who lost their marginal footing on the land and were forced into rural labor or banditry. Throughout this great transformation, officials tried to adapt the agricultural policies inherited from the past to the changing socio-economic situation they faced. In this process, China had elements in common with eighteenth-century Europe. French physiocrats admired the Chinese bureaucrats precisely because they both shared the goal of wedding an authoritarian state to a market-oriented society.[87]

The fundamental problems of agriculture in Hunan, and the state's response to them, displayed great continuity over many centuries. Despite the political vicissitudes above them, Hunanese peasants continued to farm, feed their families, and sell their products. Officials continued to extract what they needed, cajole the peasants into improving production, and repress disorder. Taxes, famines, and overpopulation burdened the peasant producers, but increases in productivity, new crops, and access to the market offered opportunities for improvement. Officials drew upon a fixed repertory of policies explained in the Classics to apply those most appropriate to a given situation. The long-term trend from the Ming through the Republican period was toward declining state intervention in the processes of production. The state's ability to channel the direction of agricultural production became increasingly limited as production expanded and market forces came to the fore. In times of disaster, however, official relief was still critical to recovery, and state intervention aimed to restore the incentives needed to stimulate peasants to clear abandoned land. In Hunan, the eighteenth century deserves its reputation as China's Golden Age (*shengshi*), for state policies, at least for a short time, were in balance with local needs. Tax equalization, investment in the infrastructure of waterworks, and the promotion of new crops all were important stimulants to the local economy. Critical tensions began to appear, however, by the middle of the century. By 1800, natural disasters, defiance of imperial edicts, and rising local conflicts presaged the much-larger-scale disorders of the nineteenth century.

In the face of these changes, the Qing state had a mixed record. In general, the best officials of this period strike one as remarkably foresighted. They recognized the dangers as well as the potential of population growth well in advance. Nor were they bound by a purported

Confucian hostility to commerce. They took active measures to protect trade in the province against piracy and to promote it by building wharves. Tragically, those who foresaw the coming catastrophe were unable to forestall it. Perhaps their ultimate failure was not a lack of vision, but an inability to create a national consensus. The Hunanese saw themselves within a regional context that left little room for concerns of the nation as a whole. From their point of view, the state came to appear as a hostile force bent on frustrating their own immediate goals. As a result, official goals and local interests increasingly diverged as the Qing dynasty entered its last century.

Appendices
Notes
Bibliography
Glossary
Index

Appendix 1. Administrative Subdivisions
of Hunan in the Qing

During the Qing, Hunan was divided into a three-level hierarchy of discrete territorial units. On the first level below the province were the four *dao* (circuits) of Chang-Bao, Yue-Chang-Li, Chen-Yuan-Yong-Jing, and Heng-Yong-Chen-Gui. On the level below the *dao* were nine prefectures (*fu*), four independent departments (*zhilizhou*), and four independent sub-prefectures (*zhiliting*). (In 1891, a fifth *zhiliting* was created from the newly silted land around Dongting Lake at Nanzhou.) Unlike the prefectures, *zhiliting* contained no subordinate units and *zhilizhou* contained no separate county-level unit at the *zhou* capital. (Thus, the area governed by the capital of Lizhou, for example, is designated Lizhou *benzhou* to distinguish it from the entire territory of Lizhou). Prefectures and *zhilizhou* each contained subordinate units, which could be either districts (*xian*), departments (*zhou*), or sub-prefectures (*santing*). (In the text, the term "county" can refer to any one of these three units.) It is important to note the difference between the *zhou* and *santing*, which were each subordinate to prefecture-level units, on the one hand, and the *zhilizhou* and *zhiliting*, which were directly subordinate to the province, on the other. *Zhilizhou* and *zhiliting* tended to be located in peripheral regions of the province in order to assure closer strategic control. In Hunan they were found especially in the areas of the province where non-Han peoples, Miao and Yao, were prevalent.

The total number of lowest-level units is the sum of the *xian, zhou, zhiliting,* and the metropolitan areas of *zhilizhou*. During the Qing, Hunan contained 76 of these units (77 after 1891): 64 *xian*, 3 *zhou*, 4 *zhilizhou*, 4 *zhiliting*, and 1 *santing*.

For further discussion, see G. William Skinner, *The City in Late Imperial China*, pp. 275–352; H. S. Brunnert and V. V. Hagelstrom, *Present Day Political Organization of China; Hunan Shengzhi* (Hunan Provincial Gazetteer) II, 3; Zhao Quandeng, *Qingdai Dili Yange Biao* (Table of geographical changes in the Qing dynasty).

Administrative Units in Qing Hunan (before 1891)

(lowest level units are *xian* unless otherwise noted)

CHANGSHA *fu*
  Changsha
  Shanhua
  Xiangtan
  Xiangyin
  Xiangxiang
  Ningxiang
  Yiyang
  Liuyang
  Anhua
  Liling
  You
  Chaling *zhou*
BAOQING *fu*
  Shaoyang
  Xinhua
  Chengbu
  Xinning
  Wugang *zhou*
YUEZHOU *fu*
  Baling
  Linxiang
  Pingjiang
  Huarong
CHANGDE *fu*
  Wuling
  Taoyuan
  Longyang
  Yuanjiang
HENGZHOU *fu*
  Qingquan
  Hengyang
  Hengshan
  Leiyang
  Changning
  Anren
  Ling
YONGZHOU *fu*
  Lingling
  Qiyang
  Dongan
  Ningyuan
  Yongming
  Jianghua
  Xintian
  Dao *zhou*

CHENZHOU *fu*
  Yuanling
  Chenxi
  Xupu
  Lüxi
YUANZHOU *fu*
  Zhijiang
  Qianyang
  Mayang
YONGSHUN *fu*
  Yongshun
  Longshan
  Baojing
  Sangzhi
  Guzhangping *ting*
LIZHOU *zhilizhou*
  Lizhou *Benzhou*
  Anxiang
  Shimen
  Cili
  Anfu
  Yongding
JINGZHOU *zhilizhou*
  Jingzhou *Benzhou*
  Suining
  Huitong
  Tongdao
GUIYANG *zhilizhou*
  Guiyang *Benzhou*
  Linwu
  Lanshan
  Jiahe
CHHENZHOU *zhilizhou*
  Chhenzhou *Benzhou*
  Yongxing
  Yizhang
  Xingning
  Guidong
  Guiyang
HUANGZHOU *zhiliting*
QIANZHOU *zhiliting*
FENGHUANG *zhiliting*
YONGSUI *zhiliting*

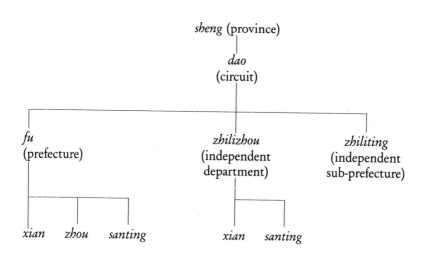

Appendix 2: Regulations for the Repair of the Wancheng Dike, Hubei, 1788

Source: *GZD-QL* 55016, 1788/9/16, Agui; *QSL-QL* 1315.1b

(1) Have a high-ranking official *manage* (*jingli*) the yearly repairs of the Wancheng dike. Give responsibility to the Jing-Yi-Shi circuit intendant to supervise. Each year in the fall high-water season, the assistant prefect in charge of water conservancy will investigate weak spots, estimate costs, draw up a register, send it to the Jingzhou intendant and inform the provincial treasurer. If costs are over 500 *taels,* report it to the Board of Finance and have funds loaned for the work. Inspect the work yearly before the spring high waters and impeach those who are negligent.

(2) Set a fixed time limit for completing repairs: one year for earthworks, three years for stone work. One repair project should last for ten years: if there is a break within this period, impeach the responsible officials.

(3) Heighten and widen dikes yearly.

(4) Hire strong laborers, record their names, drive away negligent ones. Let the assistant prefect supervise laborers personally. Do not rely on household servants and clerks.

(5) Plan ahead before lending funds for repair. Previously Wancheng dike had no funds prepared in advance. Henceforth, estimate expenses for each year and order the assistant prefect to prepare funds. Recover the loan by levying on each landowner in Jiangling county according to the amount of land held.

(6) Put three or four honest, public-spirited gentry in charge of all registers of expenses for earth and wages. Allow no yamen runners to interfere.

(7) Repair the new stone jetties from time to time. If roots grow on Jiaojinzhou, cut them down again. Follow the same principle for all new sand bars.

(8) On Wancheng, every 500 *zhang* is a work site; each work site has five administrators and overseers, three or four men each, rotated yearly. Henceforth all administrators and overseers are to be subordinated to the assistant prefect, but still rotated according to the old principle. Each work site needs four dike administrators and four overseers. Set up guardhouses on top of the dike to

report breaks. The administrators and overseers will cooperate to guard it night and day.

(9) Destroy people's houses on top of the dikes, as many now live on top of the dike. This tramples down the surface of the dike and lowers it so it cannot resist the high water. Have the prefect proclaim the destruction of all such houses and allow no one after this to build sheds on the dike. Also, at Shashi, from the head of West Street to the end of East Street, because the market is so dense, the old dike is used as a road. Here it is not convenient to destroy all the houses. If any houses collapse here, report them to the local official, who will investigate to see if they obstruct the dike surface.

(10) Divide up responsibility for the dike. The total length of Wancheng dike is over 200 *li;* one subprefect cannot investigate it closely. From Xiaoyaohu to Yulukou is over 60 *li,* and it is extremely strategic; have the district magistrate oversee it. From Yulukou to Huangjiachang, a distance of over 70 *li,* the Shashi sub-district military post is in charge. From Huangjiachang to Tuomaobu, a distance of 70 *li,* the Haojia sub-district military post is in charge. The above officials are responsible for inspection, recruiting labor, and materials. The assistant prefect will supervise yearly repairs and estimates of costs of earth and men. Do not let subordinate officials interfere.

(11) The yamen of the assistant prefect should be moved to the dike site. He used to be in Jingzhou city, but, since he is now solely responsible for waterworks, he should pick a spot at Zhonggangcheng or Lijiabu. This post is normally Board-selected, but we must have a man experienced in water-control work in it to be useful, and we fear a Board-selected man will not be acquainted with waterworks, so we request that the post be changed to be filled by the province as a transfer post.[1]

(12) Prepare piles of earth in advance at the prefectural city to stop floods.

---

1. On the importance of transfer posts, see Watt, *The District Magistrate in Late Imperial China,* pp. 46–47.

Abbreviations

GZD: *Gongzhongdang Zhupi Zouzhe*, Palace Museum, Taipei, Taiwan. *QL:* Qianlong, *JQ:* Jiaqing, *DG:* Daoguang

HCJSWB: He Changling, ed., *Huangchao Jingshi Wenbian*

HNSLCA: *Hunan Shengli Cheng'an*

QSL: *Daqing Lichao Shilu*

ZPZZ: *Zhupi Zhouzhe, Ming-Qing Archives,* Beijing.

An asterisk following a month in the notes indicates an intercalary month following that month.

Notes

ONE   *Introduction*

1. François Quesnay, *Le despotisme de la Chine*, in Lewis A. Maverick, *China a Model for Europe*, p. 141. The ideas of the physiocrats are analyzed in Elizabeth Fox-Genovese, *The Origins of Physiocracy: Economic Revolution and Social Order in Eighteenth-Century France*.

2. Montesquieu, *L'Esprit des lois*, in *Oeuvres complètes*, p. 576.

3. The history of the concept and its connection with Marx's "Asiatic Mode of Production" is traced in Perry Anderson, *Lineages of the Absolutist State*, Note B: 'The Asiatic Mode of Production,' pp. 462–549.

4. Raymond Aron, *Main Currents of Sociological Thought*, p. 25.

5. Shlomo Avineri, *Hegel's Theory of the Modern State*, pp. 223–229.

6. Max Weber, *The City*. Weber's arguments about the Chinese city are refuted by William T. Rowe, *Hankow: Commerce and Society in a Chinese City, 1796–1889*.

7. Karl Wittfogel, *Oriental Despotism*; Etienne Balazs, *Chinese Civilization and Bureaucracy*, p. 53.

8. Joseph Needham, "Science and Society in East and West," in *The Grand Titration*, pp. 190–217.

9. *The Grand Titration*, pp. 150–152, 175–179.

10. See, for example, Tanaka Masatoshi, "Chūgoku–Keizaishi"; Goi Naohiro. *Kindai Nihon to Tōyōshigaku*; Joshua A. Fogel, *Politics and Sinology: The Case of Naitō Konan*.

11. Wolfram Eberhard, *Conquerors and Rulers: Social Forces in Medieval China*, Chapter 3; Frederick Mote, "The Growth of Chinese Despotism: A Critique of Wittfogel's Theory of Oriental Despotism as Applied to China"; Edmund R. Leach, "Hydraulic Society in Ceylon"; S. N. Eisenstadt, "The Study of Oriental Despotisms as Systems of Total Power"; E. G. Pulleyblank, review of Wittfogel, *Oriental Despotism*; Maurice Meisner, "The Despotism of Concepts: Wittfogel and Marx on China."

12. Wei Qingyuan, "Lun Mingchu Dui Jiangnan Diqu Jingji Zhengce di Ruogan Wenti."

13. Evelyn Sakakida Rawski, *Agricultural Change and the Peasant Economy of South China;* Ping-ti Ho, *Studies on the Population of China, 1368–1953,* pp. 196–204.

14. Arif Dirlik, *Revolution and History: The Origins of Marxist Historiography in China, 1919–1937;* Benjamin Schwartz, "A Marxist Controversy on China." See, however, Joshua A. Fogel, "Debates on the Asiatic Mode of Production," for extensive discussion of the Asiatic mode by Chinese in the 1930s.

15. For example, *Zhongguo Lishixue Nianjian,* 1982, lists 29 articles on the subject published in 1981.

16. Bai Gang, ed., *Zhongguo Fengjian Shehui Changqi Yanxu Wenti Lunzhan di Youlai yu Fazhan,* 1984, summarizes different opinions on this issue from the 1930s through the 1980s. For one recent discussion, see Li Wenzhi, "Dizhu Jingjizhi yu Zhongguo Fengjian Shehui Changqi Yanxu Wenti Lungang." Also see William T. Rowe, "Approaches to Modern Chinese Social History."

17. Fu Yiling, "Ming-Qing Shidai Jieji Guanxi di Xintansuo."

18. Pang Zhuoheng, "Zhongxi Fengjian Zhuanzhi Zhidu di Bijiao Yanjiu."

19. Quesnay, p. 225.

20. Ibid., p. 182.

21. Ibid., p. 220.

22. Ibid., p. 261.

23. Ibid., p. 263.

24. Huan Kuan, *Discourses on Salt and Iron,* "Introduction," p. 6; Max Weber, *Economy and Society,* p. 1051.

25. T'ung-tsu Ch'ü, *Local Government in China Under the Ch'ing,* pp. 116–167, stresses the importance of tax collection and the administration of justice, and argues that other tasks, which did not affect the magistrate's career, were neglected.

26. Ramon H. Myers and Thomas A. Metzger, "Sinological Shadows: The State of Modern China Studies in the United States," p. 110.

27. Thomas Metzger, "On the Historical Roots of Economic Modernization in China: The Increasing Differentiation of the Economy from the Polity during late Ming and Early Ch'ing Times," pp. 33–44; Myers and Metzger, "Sinological Shadows."

28. Thomas Metzger, "The Organizational Capabilities of the Ch'ing State in the Field of Commerce: The Lianghuai Salt Monopoly, 1740–1840."

29. See Rowe, *Hankow,* for a recent discussion of merchant-official cooperation.

30. Peng Zeyi, "Qingdai Qianqi Shougongye di Fazhan," *Zhongguoshi Yanjiu;* Wei Qingyuan and Lu Su, *Qingdai Qianqi Shangban Kuangye he Zibenzhuyi Mengya,* summarized in William T. Rowe, "Recent Writing in the People's Republic on Early Ch'ing Economic History."

31. Myers and Metzger argue for a basic change in the state's relationship to the economy in the Ming-Qing period, but imply that this was a continuous long-

term change, without subdividing the period. Ramon H. Myers, "Transformation and Continuity in Chinese Economic and Social History."

32. See the discussion of famine-relief policies in R. Bin Wong and Peter C. Perdue, "Famine's Foes in Ch'ing China," pp. 313–315.

33. Zhang Shiyuan, "Nongtianyi (A discussion of agricultural land)," *HCJSWB juan* 36.2b–3a.

34. Matteo Ricci's memory image for *li* was "a farmer holding a sickle, ready to cut the crops in the field"; Jonathan Spence, *The Memory Palace of Matteo Ricci*, p. 162; L. Wieger, *Chinese Characters: Their Origin, Etymology, History*, p. 143.

35. Qiao Guanglie, "Tongzhou-fu Huangdi Ququan Yi" (A discussion of canals and springs on wasteland in Tongzhou prefecture), *HCJSWB juan* 38.9a.

36. Zhang Shiyuan, "Nongtianyi."

37. Zhang Lüxiang, "Nongshu" (Agricultural handbook), *HCJSWB juan* 36.27b.

38. Chen Hongmou, "Guangxing Shancan Jiao (1757)" (Spreading cultivation of mountain silkworms), *HCJSWB juan* 37.12; Timothy Brook, "The Spread of Rice Cultivation and Rice Technology into the Hebei Region in the Ming and Qing."

39. Amano Motonosuke, *Chūgoku Nōgyōshi Kenkyū*, pp. 278–389, on Ming-Qing rice technology.

40. He Changling, "Quanmin Kaigou Chulao Shi (1822)" (A proclamation urging the people to open ditches to eliminate flooding), *HCJSWB juan* 38.23–24.

41. Guo Qiyuan, "Lun Minsheng Wuben Jieyong Shu" (A treatise on practicing agriculture and thrift in Fujian), *HCJSWB juan* 36.20a.

42. Described for Jiangsu in Amano, *Chūgoku Nōgyōshi Kenkyū*, pp. 364–370; Sun Zhaikui, "Qutianshuo" (Explanation of *qutian*), *HCJSWB juan* 36.33–34; Wang Xinjing, "Qutian Putian Shuo" (Explanation of *qutian* and *putian*), *HCJSWB juan* 36.35–36; Lu Shiyi, "Lun Qutian" (On the *qutian*), *HCJSWB juan* 36.37–41.

43. Sun Zhaikui, *HCJSWB*, p. 34b.

44. Amano, *Chūgoku Nōgyōshi Kenkyū*, p. 369.

45. Wang Xinjing, *HCJSWB*, p. 35b.

46. Ouyang Xuefeng, "Zhong hanhe shu."

47. Zhang Yunsui, "Quannong Sance Shu (1737)" (Three policies for promoting agriculture), *HCJSWB juan* 36.17; Chen Hongmou, "Zhong Zaliang Guang-shuzhi Zhuang" (A letter on planting miscellaneous crops and trees), *HCJSWB juan* 36.37.

48. Thomas Metzger, *The Internal Organization of Ch'ing Bureaucracy*, pp. 74–80; Metzger, *Escape from Predicament*, pp. 154–158, 188–190.

49. Metzger, *Escape from Predicament*, pp. 155–156.

50. Ibid., p. 156.

51. Huang Dan, "Xiantian Shuo" (A proposal to limit landholdings), in Luo Ruhuai, ed., *Hunan Wenzheng: Guochaowen, juan* 18.25.

52. Alexander B. Woodside, "The Ch'ien-lung Reign," draft chapter for the *Cambridge History of China* IX, 10.

53. Cf. Ramon H. Myers, *The Chinese Peasant Economy: Agricultural Development in Hopei and Shantung, 1890–1949*, pp. 14–15, for discussion of two similar theories about Chinese agriculture in the twentieth century.

54. Woodside, p. 95; *Huangchao Wenxian Tongkao* 4.8–8b.

55. Dwight Perkins, ed., *China's Economic Development in Historical Perspective.*

56. Pierre-Etienne Will, *Bureaucratie et famine en Chine au 18e siècle;* R. Bin Wong, "The Political Economy of Food Supplies in Qing China"; R. Bin Wong et al., *Nourish the People;* Lillian Li, ed., "Food, Famine, and the Chinese State—A Symposium"; James Lee, unpublished ms. "State and Economy in Southwest China, 1250 to 1850," Chapter 7.

57. Han-sheng Chuan and Richard A. Kraus, *Mid-Ch'ing Rice Markets and Trade*, p. 70.

58. R. Bin Wong, "Food Riots in the Qing Dynasty."

59. Mark Elvin, *The Pattern of the Chinese Past.*

60. Vaclav Smil, *The Bad Earth.*

TWO   *Geography and Population*

1. The figure for provincial area is from Joint Publications Research Service, *Hunan Provincial Gazetteer*, Vol. II (1961). *Hunan Nongye*, p. 3, gives 204,000 sq. km. Other basic sources for this section: Fu Jiaojin, *Hunan Dilizhi;* Yang Renzhang, "Xiangjiang Liuyu Shuiwen Dili"; Sun Ching-chih, ed., *Economic Geography of Central China: Hunan*, pp. 199–358; Kanda Masao, *Konanshō Sōran;* Yasui Shōtarō, *Konan.*

2. See table in *Hunan Nongye*, p. 33.

3. See, for example, *GZD-JQ* 1801.12.4.

4. *Hunan Nongye*, p. 41.

5. Yang Renzhang, p. 168.

6. James Thorp, *Geography of the Soils of China*, pp. 274–350.

7. Sun Ching-chih, p. 20.

8. Yang Renzhang, p. 166.

9. *Hunan Nongye*, pp. 398–401, describes one such reforestation project.

10. G. William Skinner, ed., *The City in Late Imperial China*, p. 287, describes this process. See also Tuan Yi-fu, *China*, pp. 29–41.

11. Skinner, *City in Late Imperial China*, p. 215.

12. "Kaihe tongshang yi" (A discussion of opening a river to promote commerce), *Changsha Fuzhi* 1685.15.61; *Changsha Xianzhi Xuji* 1747.1.8a; *Changsha*

Xianzhi 1817.14.10b describe Changsha's disadvantages for trade and unsuccessful official efforts to build a port in the Qing. Gilbert Rozman, *Urban Networks in Ch'ing China and Tokugawa Japan,* pp. 232–234, implies that Changsha was a larger city than Xiangtan in the mid-nineteenth century. He puts Changsha's population at 200,000 to 300,000 and Xiangtan's at over 100,000, but it should be noted that his figure for Hunan's total population is too high: 25 instead of the actual 20 million in 1850.

13. The following description is drawn from Yang Renzhang.

14. See graphs in Yang Renzhang, p. 170.

15. Ibid.

16. Rawski, p. 106.

17. For the following information, the main sources are, Sun Ching-Chih, p. 205, and *Hunan Nongye,* pp. 6–13.

18. Joint Publication Research Service, *Hunan Provincial Gazetteer,* p. 227.

19. On the Miao territory, see Susan Mann Jones and Philip A. Kuhn, "Dynastic Decline and the Roots of Rebellion," pp. 132–133; Ma Shaoqiao, *Qingdai Miaomin Qiyi;* Xie Hua, *Xiangxi Tusi Jilue;* Jeffrey C. Kinkley, "Shen Ts'ung-wen's Vision of Republican China."

20. *Huarong Xianzhi* 1882.1.15.

21. *Yongzhou Fuzhi* 1828.5.7b, 12b.

22. Li Zongyun, "Liuyang Tuchan Biao," (Table of the local products of Liuyang), *Nong Xuebao* 3, 1897.5, cited in Li Wenzhi, ed., *Zhongguo Jindai Nongyeshi Ziliao* I, 916.

23. *Pingjiang Xianzhi* Qing, 5a.

24. *Changde Fuzhi* 1813.18.1; *Shanhua Xianzhi* 1818.23.8b.

25. *Taoyuan Xianzhi* 1821.3.14; *Huarong Xianzhi* 1882.1.15.

26. *Yongxing Xiangtuzhi* 1906.1.58a; *Yuezhou Fuzhi* 1746.12.1.

27. *Changde Fuzhi* 1813.13.1.

28. *Yongzhou Fuzhi* 1828.5.18; *Yuanzhou Fuzhi* 1790.19.8b.

29. *Qianyang Xianzhi* 1874.16.2; Li Wenzhi, ed., *Zhongguo Jindai Nongyeshi Ziliao,* p. 527. On the importance of wood ash, see *Yongzhou Fuzhi* 1828.5.18; *Baling Xianzhi* 1873.11.8b; *Lingling Xianzhi* 1876.5.17; *Yongxing Xianzhi,* 1870.6.2b.

30. *Yongzhou Fuzhi* 1828.7a.12.

31. *Fenghuang Tingzhi* 1758.20.17a.

32. *Qiyang Xianzhi* 1870.22.6.

33. *Hengyang Xianzhi* 1872.11.5b–6a.

34. *Chenzhou Fuzhi* 1685.3.46a.

35. Morita Akira, "Shindai Kokō Chihō ni Okeru Teikishi ni Tsuite"; Shigeta Atsushi, *Shindai Shakaikeizaishi Kenkyū,* pp. 207–293, on tea.

36. *Hengyang Xianzhi* 1872.11.5b; *Lingling Xianzhi* 1876.5.17b.

37. Cf. Ester Boserup, *The Conditions of Agricultural Growth: The Economics of*

Agrarian Change under Population Pressure, on the succession of agricultural forms according to intensity of labor. The list given here, however, differs considerably from hers.

38. The statement "The Chu people engage in hunting and fishing" is quoted in many gazetteeers, e.g. *Xiangyin Xianzhi* 1565, *fengsu,* citing an earlier edition.

39. Sun Ching-chih, p. 356.

40. *Taoyuan Xianzhi* 1821.3.7; *Wugang Zhouzhi* 1817.18.18; *Chenzhou Fuzhi* 1765.14.5b, 28b; *Hunan Tongzhi* 1820.49.23–25, 174.24–25 (citing the Song text *Laoxuean biji*).

41. *Baling Xianzhi* 1873.11.8b; *Yuanjiang Xianzhi* 1810.18.2.

42. *Hengyang Xianzhi* 1872.11.5b.

43. *Chengbu Xianzhi* 1867.10.35b.

44. Ping-ti Ho, *Studies on the Population of China, 1368–1953,* pp. 147–150, 182–195; Ho Ping-ti, "Meizhou Zuowu di Yinjin Zhuanbo Jiqi dui Zhongguo Liangshi Shengchan di Yingxiang"; Ping-ti Ho, "The Introduction of American Food Plants into China."

45. *Changde Fuzhi* 1813.13.1, citing "an old gazetteer"; *Linxiang Xianzhi* 1892.2.; *Huguang Tongzhi* 1684.6.4b; *Hengshan Xianzhi* 1488.1.2.

46. *Huarong Xianzhi* 1760.10.29.

47. *Huarong Xianzhi* 1882.1.15; *Baling Xianzhi* 1873.11.8b; *Yuanjiang Xianzhi* 1810.18.2.

48. *Hengshan Xianzhi* 1823.18.7a.

49. *Hengshan Xianzhi* 1774.4.19a.

50. *Lingling Xianzhi* 1876.5.17.

51. Dwight Perkins, *Agricultural Development in China, 1368–1968,* p. 200.

52. Ping-ti Ho, *Population of China,* p. 9; Perkins, *Agricultural Development,* pp. 200–201.

53. Hans Bielenstein has recently argued that the early-Ming population figures indicate far too large and uniform a decline in population from the Song and must thus be very incomplete (talk at Premodern China Seminar, Harvard University, 7 October 1985). He has not, however, provided any method of estimating the true population. Robert Hartwell's method of computing regional population relies on the assumption that the percentage of the total regional population occupied by sample prefectures (Tan and Heng in Hunan) remained the same from A.D. 1080 to A.D. 1948. ("Demographic, Political, and Social Transformations of China, 750–1550"). Applying this method to Hunan in 1393 yields a population of 1.44 million, which is far too low. The early-Ming census figures remain the best available, despite their limitations.

54. Cf. Hartwell's estimate of 40.8 persons per square mile in the West Core Region of the Middle Yangtze, and 13.1 in the West Periphery; Hartwell, p. 384.

55. Calculated from data in Perkins, *Agricultural Development,* p. 200.

56. If the very high population figure given for Linwu county in fact refers to all of Guiyang *zhou,* the density drops to a more reasonable level of 4.5.

57. Fujii Hiroshi, "Mindai Dendo Tōkei ni Kansuru Ichi Kōsatsu"; Perkins, *Agricultural Development*, p. 225.

58. Perkins, *Agricultural Development*, p. 225. For similar overcrowding in southwest China, see James Lee, "State and Economy," Chapter 4.

59. Yeh-chien Wang, *Land Taxation in Imperial China*, p. 23. Ray Huang, on the other hand, points out many deficiencies in the survey, but admits that "the failure was mainly at the national level," implying that local figures may be more accurate than the national totals; Ray Huang, *Taxation and Governmental Finance in Sixteenth-Century Ming China*, pp. 300–301. Cf. Kawakatsu Mamoru, "Chō Kyōsei Jōryō Saku no Tenkai–Toku ni Minmatsu Kōnan ni Okeru Jinushisei no Hatten ni Tsuite." James Lee, "State and Economy," Chapter 5, also argues that that cultivated acreage increased in proportion to population.

60. Xie Zhaozhe, *Wuzazu*, p. 165.

61. Oh Keum-sung, "Myŏngmal Tongjŏngho Chubyŏu ŭi Suri Kaebal Kwa Nongch'on Sahoe"; Iwami Hiroshi, "Kokōjuku Tenka Zoku"; Yasuno Shōzō, "Kokō Juku Sureba Tenka Zokusuru Kō."

62. Ping-ti Ho, *Population of China*, pp. 36–62.

63. Ibid., pp. 65–73.

64. Chart in James Lee, "State and Economy," Figure 4-1; cf. Michel Cartier "La croissance démographique chinoise di XVIIIe siècle et l'enregistrement des *paochia*," pp. 20–21; James Lee, "Food Supply and Population Growth in Southwest China, 1250–1850."

THREE   *The Resettlement of Hunan*

1. Michel Cartier and Rémi Mathieu, "Les conceptions démographiques de l'antiquité chinoise: quelques réflections."

2. James Lee, "Migration and Expansion in Chinese History"; Lee, "Settlement of China's Southwest Frontier."

3. Joanne Meskill, *A Chinese Pioneer Family*, describes this process of settlement in Taiwan.

4. Lai Jiadu, "Mingdai Nongmin di Kenhuang Yundong"; Lai Jiadu, *Mingdai Yunyang Nongmin Qiyi*.

5. Lai Jiadu, *Mingdai Yunyang*, pp. 25–32.

6. There is, however, reference to a prohibited mountain area in Yongming county, Hunan, in 1836. Otake Fumio, *Kinsei Shina Keizaishi Kenkyū*, p. 212.

7. Robert H. G. Lee, *The Manchurian Frontier in Ch'ing History*. On Manchu policies of racial segregation, see Frederic Wakeman, *The Great Enterprise*, p. 826.

8. Hung's essay was written in 1793. It is summarized in C. F. Lung, "A Note on Hung Liangchi: The Chinese Malthus," and in Ping-ti Ho, *Population of China*, pp. 271–272.

9. See below, Chapter 4.

10. Dwight Perkins, *Agricultural Development*, p. 225.

11. *Xiangyin Xianzhi* 1818.27.7b.

12. See Chapter 7.

13. *Huguang Zongzhi* 1591.4.7b.

14. Shimizu Taiji, "Chō Kyōsei no Tochi Jōryō ni Tsuite"; Liang Fang-chung, *The Single Whip Method of Taxation in China*, tr. Wang Yü-ch'uan; Wei Qingyuan, *Mingdai Huangce Zhidu*; Ray Huang, *Taxation and Governmental Finance*; Gu Yanwu, *Tianxia Junguo Libingshu, juan* 35. In addition, the Wanli Emperor expropriated land in Huquang and elsewhere for the Prince of Fu and burdened the peasant population with heavy rents; Wakeman, *The Great Enterprise*, pp. 337–338.

15. Hong Maode, "Dingliang Huowen" (Someone's questions on taxation), *Xiangxiang Xianzhi* 1673.9.29. *Xiangyin Xianzhi* 1565, Preface, also notes abandonment of land due to unequal taxes.

16. Hong Maode, "Dingliang Huowen."

17. Ibid., p. 32.

18. Nan Qifeng, "Qing Huoduiliang Xiangwen" (A request to reduce taxes), *Changsha Fuzhi* 1685.15.41–2.

19. *Xiangtan Xianzhi* 1781.8.15–23.

20. *Changsha Fuzhi* 1685.15.44a; *Liuyang Xianzhi* 1733.4.26.

21. Wu Daoliang, "Fuyi Siyi" (A private discussion of tax and corvée), *Changsha Fuzhi* 1685.15.58–9.

22. *Huarong Xianzhi* 1611/1685.3.16.

23. Mei E, "Qing Tili Zhengtianfu Shenwen" (A request to equalize land taxes), *Lizhou Zhilizhou Zhi* 1821.20.28b.

24. He Mengchun, *Yudong Xulu*, cited in Iwami Hiroshi, "Kokōjuku Tenka Zoku."

25. Li Wenzhi, *Wanming Minbian*, p. 186; Wakeman, *The Great Enterprise*, p. 233.

26. James B. Parsons, *The Peasant Rebellions of the Ming Dynasty*, pp. 151–154.

27. Li Wenzhi, *Wanming Minbian*, p. 88.

28. *Changsha Xianzhi Xuji* 1747.8.14a; *Xiangyin Xianzhi* 1818.22.

29. *Changsha Fuzhi* 1685.1.44b.

30. Luo Ruhuai, 1.6,1.7.

31. *Dongting Huzhi* 1825.7.

32. *Wugang Zhouzhi* 1873.20.19a.

33. *Huguang Tongzhi* 1684.53.61.

34. Jin Tingxian, "Qing Shuzen Shu" (A memorial requesting famine relief), *Changsha Fuzhi* 1685.14.82.

35. Guo Songyi, "Qingchu Fengjian Guojia Kenhuang Zhengce Fenxi."

36. *Xiangxiang Xianzhi* 1673.4.17b.

37. *Guiyang Zhili Zhouzhi* 1868.9.78b.

38. *Chenzhou Fuzhi* 1685.53.

39. For example, *Changsha Fuzhi* 1685.14.76a; Wakeman, *The Great Enterprise,* p. 227.

40. *Leiyang Xianzhi* 1725.3.8b.

41. *Changsha Fuzhi* 1685.15.37a; *Baoqing Fuzhi* 1685.13.5a.

42. *Xiangxiang Xianzhi* 1673.3.39; *Changde Fuzhi* 1671.1.28; *Hengyang Xianzhi* 1872.11.5.

43. On Wu Sangui's revolt, see Arthur W. Hummel, ed., *Eminent Chinese of the Ch'ing Period,* pp. 877–880; Lawrence D. Kessler, *K'ang-hsi and the Consolidation of Ch'ing Rule, 1661–1684,* pp. 81–90; Wakeman, *The Great Enterprise,* pp. 1101–1104, 1119.

44. *Ningxiang Xianzhi* 1748, preface.

45. Luo Ruhuai, 1.15a.

46. *Xiangxiang Xianzhi* 1673.10.25. (Supplement added in 1686.)

47. *Chenzhou Fuzhi* 1685.6.54b.

48. *Linxiang Xianzhi* 1685.3.4a.

49. *Ningxiang Xianzhi* 1682.3.4a.

50. *Changde Fuzhi* 1671.10.13b and *Xiangyin Xianzhi* 1818.27.8b give examples of such efforts.

51. *Ningxiang Xianzhi* 1748.2.20b.

52. Guo Songyi, pp. 127–130; Wakeman, *The Great Enterprise,* p. 918, notes the dual goals of resettling refugees and raising taxes.

53. *Ningxiang Xianzhi,* 1682.3.24–32.

54. *Xiangtan Xianzhi* 1889.11.1–2.

55. *Liuyang Xianzhi* 1733.4.29a.

56. *Daqing Huidian, Qianlong* 10.11–12; *Daqing Lüli* 1795.7.

57. Liu Cuirong, "Qingchu Shunzhi-Kangxi Nianjian Jianmian Fushui di Guocheng."

58. Ray Huang, pp. 1–2.

59. *Liuyang Xianzhi* 1733.4.3a; *Xiangxiang Xianzhi* 1673.3 *ben.*1a, 3 *mo.*29,35; *Ningxiang Xianzhi* 1748.2.23b.

60. *Chaling Zhouzhi* 1817.8.10,8.49.

61. *Liuyang Xianzhi* 1733.4.33a.

62. *Ningxiang Xianzhi* 1682.3.5a.

63. *Chaling Zhouzhi* 1817.8.49.

64. *Chaling Zhouzhi* 1817.45–47.

65. *Hengyang Xianzhi* 1761.3.36. The late-Ming surtaxes were theoretically abolished in 1644 but persisted in fact in Hunan at least until 1654; Wakeman, *The Great Enterprise,* pp. 455–456.

66. Nishimura Genshō, "Shinsho no Tochi Jōryō ni Tsuite."

67. Zhou Zhaonan, "Qing Ting Zhangliang Shu" (A memorial requesting that the land survey be stopped), *Changsha Fuzhi* 1685.14.99. In 1660–1661, the Shunzhi Emperor did attack tax evasion by Jiangnan gentry, in order to eliminate

government deficits, but this did not extend to other provinces; Wakeman, *The Great Enterprise,* pp. 1058–1073.

68. Chen Dengyuan, *Zhongguo Tianfu Shi;* Wang Yeh-chien, *Land Taxation;* Dai Yi, *Jianming Qingshi;* Nishimura; Ping-ti Ho, *Population of China,* pp. 101–135.

69. Yeh-chien Wang, *Land Taxation,* p. 26.

70. Madeleine Zelin, *The Magistrate's Tael,* describes the Yongzheng Emperor's reform effort.

71. Charles Tilley, ed., *The Formation of National States in Western Europe,* p. 54.

72. Rudolf Braun, "Taxation, Sociopolitical Structure, and State Building: Great Britain and Brandenburg-Prussia," in Tilly, ed., *Formation of National States,* pp. 243–328; Wakeman, *The Great Enterprise,* pp. 1125–1126.

73. Braun, p. 280.

74. Shigeta Atsushi, *Shindai Shakaikeizaishi Kenkyū,* pp. 98–154.

75. *Huarong Xianzhi* 1760.10.34–5.

76. *HNSLCA hu* 7.9a.

77. Ding Sikong, "Qing Zhangtianliang Zi" (A request to conduct a land survey), *Lizhou Zhilin* 1750.20.17–8. Ding was Governor General of Hubei and Hunan from 1683 to 1688.

78. *Huarong Xianzhi* 1760.3.6b.

79. Chen Changzhen, "Qingli Chunan Qianliang Ce" (Policies for clearing up Hunan's taxes), in Luo Ruhuai, 9.10–14. Chen received his *jinshi* degree in 1748; *Hunan Wenzheng,* Biographies, 4.8. Kung-chuan Hsiao describes the trend of the *baojia* taking over tax collection functions; *Rural China,* pp. 60–61.

80. Otake, pp. 177–178; Guo Songyi, p. 123.

81. *Hengshan Xianzhi* 1774.7.32b; *Yuanling Xianzhi* 1708.7.24b; Lu Zhen, "Shenchi Niebao Kenhuangbei" (A stele giving orders about wasteland falsely reported as cleared), *Changsha Fuzhi* 1685.15.20a, and *Anfu Xianzhi* 1869.30.37b; Hu Erkai, "Zhichen Hunan Libi Shu" (A memorial outlining abuses in Hunan), *Changsha Fuzhi* 1685.14.76a, and Luo Ruhuai, 1.7–9.

82. *Huarong Xianzhi* 1760.10.35.

83. *Ningxiang Xianzhi* 1748.2.24.

84. *Xiangxiang Xianzhi* 1673.3.42.

85. Guo Songyi, p. 125.

86. *Xiangxiang Xianzhi* 1673.3.49.

87. Guo Songyi, pp. 115–120.

88. See edict of 1662 from *Wenxian Tongkao,* cited in Otake, pp. 184–185.

89. Zhongguo Renmin Daxue, ed., *KangYongQian,* p. 330.

90. Zhao Shenqiao, *Zhao Gongyigong Zizhi Guanshu,* 1.1.

91. For examples of murder cases, see Zhao Shenqiao, *Zizhi Quanshu,* 5.9, 5.16, 5.21, 5.28, 5.39, 5.41, 5.43, 5.46, 5.48, 5.65, 5.69, 5.71, 5.82, 5.126.

92. Ibid., 17.27.

93. Ibid., 11.54,56a.

94. Ibid., 7.24–6.

95. Ibid., 1.31b, 5.126–127; *Zhao Gongyigong Shenggao*, 1.18a, 1.24a.

96. Zhao Shenqiao, *Zizhi Guanshu*, 3.26a.

97. Ibid., 4.30a.

98. Ibid., 7.20a.

99. Ibid., 5.32, 14.15, 14.77; *Shenggao*, 1.36a.

100. Zhao Shenqiao, *Zizhi Guanshu*, 11.46b.

101. Ibid., 11.57.

102. Ibid., 8.9a, 8.24a, 11.57, 14.77.

103. R. Bin Wong, "Food Distribution Crises: Markets, Granaries, and Food Riots in the Qing Period." R. Bin Wong, "Les émeutes de subsistances en Chine et en Europe occidentale."

104. Zhao Shenqiao, *Zizhi Guanshu*, 5.101–104.

105. Ibid., 5.108.

106. Ibid., 9.40.

107. Ibid., 6.86.

108. Ibid., 4.46a.

109. Ibid., 11.39a.

110. Ibid., 9.42.

111. Ibid., 9.114a.

112. Philip A. Kuhn, "Local Taxation and Finance in Republican China," in Susan Mann Jones, ed., *Select Papers from the Center for Far Eastern Studies*, The University of Chicago, No. 3, 1978–79, pp. 100–136; Nishimura; Wei Qingyuan, *Mingdai Huangce Zhidu*.

113. Zhao Shenqiao, *Zizhi Guanshu*, 13.47b.

114. Obata Tatsuo, "Kōnan ni Okeru Rikō no Hensei ni Tsuite"; Kuhn, "Local Taxation," pp. 105–107; Kuribayashi Nobuo, *Rikōsei no Kenkyū*, pp. 210–215.

115. Zhao Shenqiao, *Zizhi Guanshu*, 12.35–47. Other proposals for tax equalization are found in *Changsha Fuzhi* 1685.14.97a, 15.63–67; Guo Xiu, *Shugao*, 3.12–16 (Guo was Huguang Governor General in 1699); *Xiangxiang Xianzhi* 1673.9.47.

116. Zhao Shenqiao, *Zizhi Guanshu*, 16.20–23.

117. Kung-chuan Hsiao, pp. 84–143.

118. Ibid., p. 102.

119. Guo Songyi, p. 134.

120. *Lizhou Zhilizhou Zhi* 1821.28.45a.

121. Otake, p. 192.

122. *Chaling Zhouzhi* 1817.8.45b; Otake, p. 203; Yeh-chien Wang, *Land Taxation*, p. 29.

123. *Hunan Tongzhi* 1757.49.15; *Changsha Xianzhi* 1817.14.7.

124. *Ningxiang Xianzhi* 1748.1.32; *Sangzhi Xianzhi* 1764.4.24.

125. *Huarong Xianzhi* 1760.10.35b; *Hengyang Xianzhi* 1761.3.41; *Yiyang Xianzhi* 1874.23, reporting all barren land cleared by 1714.

126. *Sangzhi Xianzhi* 1764.4.25a.

127. *Xiangyin Xianzhi* 1818.27.49a.

128. Wei Yuan, *Guweitang Neiwaiji, waiji,* 6.5a.

129. *Hengyang Xianzhi* 1872.11.5b.

130. *Yiyang Xianzhi* 1874.2.12; *Qiyang Xianzhi* 1870.22.5b; *Dao Zhouzhi* 1878.10.12; Luo Ruhuai, 97.19b.

131. Cited in Yasui Shōtarō, *Konan,* p. 665.

132. *Yuezhou Fuzhi* 1746.9.5a; *Chengbu Xianzhi* 1867.10.33, cited in Li Wenzhi, *Zhongguo Jindai Nongyeshi Ziliao,* p. 919.

133. Zhao Shenqiao, *Zizhi Guanshu,* 5.32.

134. Cited in *Hunan Tongzhi* 1885, *shou* 1.18a.

135. *Ningxiang Xianzhi* 1748.2.24b.

136. *Yuanzhou Fuzhi* 1790.19.8; *Qiyang Xianzhi* 1765.1.15a; *Mayang Xianzhi* 1873.5b.2b.

137. Memorial dated 1746, cited in *Hunan Tongzhi* 1885.47.27a.

138. *Baling Xianzhi* 1892.7; cf. Wei Yuan, 6.5b.

139. Zhao Shenqiao, *Zizhi Guanshu,* 7.18a.

140. Ibid., 16.52.

141. *Ningxiang Xianzhi* 1748.2.20.

142. Gu Jiantian, "Yi Wenzhouwei Yuhuang Gui Yixue Die" (A letter proposing that wasteland in Wenzhou polder be allocated to the charity school) (1748), *Xiangyin Xianzhi* 1818.27.25.

143. Case described in Kang Shaoyong, "Kang Shaoyong Zougao: Hunan Rennei," 5.2–11, dated 1829/8/17.

144. Ibid., 5.16–26.

FOUR   *Immigration and Agricultural Productivity*

1. Tan Qixiang, "Zhongguo Neidi Yiminshi–Hunan Bian."

2. Ibid., p. 80; *Pingjiang Xianzhi* 1875, preface by Ma Weixu.

3. *Hunan Tongzhi* 1820.54.8b.

4. Luo Xianglin, *Zhongguo Zupu Yanjiu,* Chapter 4. The pattern of military colonization in the Ming, followed by voluntary immigration in the Qing, follows that of the southwest, where, however, the military impact was much greater; cf. James Lee, "State and Economy," Chapter 2.

5. *Huguang Zongzhi* 1591.35.15b–16; *Shimen Xianzhi* 1889.6.1.

6. *Xiangyin Xiangtuzhi* 1881.22.10b; *Ningxiang Xianzhi* 1748.4.

7. *Liling Xianzhi* 1744.4.44a; cf. *Changsha Xianzhi* 1703.2, "Fengsu."

8. Deng Yao, *Shuangwu Shanguan Wenchao,* 4.1–2b.

9. *Changsha Fuzhi* 1747.22.82b–83a.

10. *Xiangtan Xianzhi* 1889.6.

11. *Huarong Xianzhi* 1882.1.15a.

12. *Liuyang Xianzhi* 1733.1. Other discussions of "shack people," primarily focusing on Jiangxi, are: Morita Akira, "Minmatsu Shindai no 'Hōmin' ni Tsuite"; Stephen C. Averill, "The Shed People and the Opening of the Yangtze Highlands"; Lü Xisheng, "Ming-Qing Shiqi Shezu dui Zhenan Shanqu di Kaifa."

13. *Wugang Zhouzhi* 1817. 12.7.

14. *Yongzhou Fuzhi* 1828.7.13b.

15. *Yuezhou Fuzhi* 1746.12.4b. Similar evidence for immigrants planting new crops is found in *Yongzhou Fuzhi* 1828.7a.3b.

16. *You Xianzhi* 1871. 6b.

17. *Changsha Xianzhi* 1703, "Fengsu"; also *Baoqing Fuzhi* 1685.13.5b.

18. *Xiangtan Xianzhi* 1553. xia. 6a.

19. Qian Kuangzhi, "Yitian Ji" (A record of charitable land), *Xiangyin Xianzhi* 1818.35b.22b.

20. Zhao Shenqiao, *Zizhi Guanshu* 12.71a; *GZD-QL* #30129 (1774.9.29).

21. *Hengzhou Fuzhi* 1593.2.13b.

22. Zhang Wenda, "Sizhinian Zhengguan Mianqin Shu," *Fuchu Shuchao*, 3.121.

23. *Leiyang Xianzhi* 1725.1.57b, 3.104a, 106b; *Yongding Xianzhi* 1870.6.1b.

24. Zhao Shenqiao, *Zizhi Guanshu* 6.34a.

25. *Shanhua Xianzhi* 1818.4.3.

26. *Dongan Xianzhi* 1752.4.25; *Yongshun Fuzhi* 1763. shou. 10b.

27. *Huarong Xianzhi* 1760.1.15b; *Changde Fuzhi* 1671.1.28a.

28. *Ningyuan Xianzhi* 1811.2.6.

29. *Fenghuang Tingzhi* 1758.14.4; *Yongzhou Fuzhi* 1828.5.19; *Chenzhou Fuzhi* 1765.14.6b; *Yuanzhou Fuzhi* 1790.19.9; *Yongshun Xianzhi* 1874.6.2b; *Xinning Xianzhi* 1893.39.4a.

30. *Xiangtan Xianzhi* 1818.39.4a.

31. *Yongzhou Fuzhi* 1828.5.19.

32. *Yongzhou Fuzhi* 1828.5.19; *Chenzhou Fuzhi* 1765.14.6b; *Yongshun Xianzhi* 1874.6.2b; *Yuanzhou Fuzhi* 1790.19.9; *Anfu Xianzhi* 1869.24.4b, states that *now* many local people practice artisanry, implying that it was not done before.

33. E.g. *Hengzhou Fuzhi* 1593.2.41a.

34. *Huarong Xianzhi* 1760.1.15b; Rawski, pp. 101–139.

35. *Chenzhou Fuzhi* 1765.14.6b; *Changde Fuzhi* 1671.1.28; *Xinning Xianzhi* 1893.19.2a.

36. *Ningyuan Xianzhi* 1811.2.7b.

37. *Changde Fuzhi* 1813.13.2b.

38. *Yuanzhou Fuzhi* 1790.19.9; this indicates that the influence of merchants was more pervasive than the abstractly conceived "market." Cf. *Anhua Xianzhi* 1872.24.4b, for another example of outside-merchant dominance in a relatively uncommercialized area.

39. *Huarong Xianzhi* 1760.1.15b; *Shanhua Xianzhi*, 1818.22.

40. *Shanhua Xianzhi* 1818.22.11a.

41. See, for example, the genealogical references in *Xiangyin Xiangtuzhi* 1881.17–18.

42. His biography is given in L. Carrington Goodrich and Chaoying Fang, eds., *Dictionary of Ming Biography* I, 249–252.

43. *Huangming Jingshi Wenbian*, 72.1608.

44. Ferdinand Richthofen, *China: Ergebnisse eigener Reisen* II, 39. Yunnanese made similar remarks about commercial dominance of their province by immigrants from Jiangxi, Sichuan, or Hunan; James Lee, "State and Economy," p. 44.

45. Tan Qixiang, "Zhongguo Neidi."

46. Ping-ti Ho, *Population of China*, pp. 143–145.

47. *Yuanling Xianzhi* 1708. mo; *Liuyang Xianzhi* 1680.14; *Yongshun Xianzhi*, 1930.15; all cited in Tan Qixiang, p. 75n5.

48. Tan Qixiang, p. 93; *Wugang Zhou Xiangtuzhi*, 1908, preface to *Shizuzhi*.

49. *Yizhang Xianzhi* 1756.4.

50. Wei Yuan, 6.5–7.

51. *Xinning Xianzhi* 1893.22.50a–51b.

52. Rawski, p. 119; Ping-ti Ho, *Population of China*, p. 173.

53. Rawski, p. 161.

54. John Watt, *The District Magistrate in Late Imperial China*, p. 215.

55. For example, *Baoqing Fuzhi* 1685.13.7 draws a connection between the rise in lawsuits and the increase of commerce; *Liuyang Xianzhi* 1733.1, and *Dao Zhouzhi* 1878.3.5a specifically blame immigrants for causing lawsuits.

56. *Dao Zhouzhi*, 1878.3.5a.

57. Deng Yao, 4.1–2b.

58. *Huarong Xianzhi* 1760.16a.

59. *Huarong Xianzhi* 1882.1.15a.

60. Peter C. Perdue, "Outsiders and Insiders: The Xiangtan Riot of 1819 and Collective Action in Hunan."

61. Liu Yan, "Guanyu Jiefangqian Liangshan Yizu Shehui Xingzhi di Jige Wenti," citing Wei Yuan, *Shengwuji*. On Hunanese in the southwest, see James Lee, "State and Economy," Chapter 2, passim.

62. *Ningxiang Xianzhi* 1748. shou. 19b. Imperial policy on emigration is discussed in Peter C. Perdue, "*Liumin* and Famine Relief in Eighteenth-Century China."

63. *Guolu* is probably derived from the Tibetan word *goluk*, for "bandit"; Joseph Fletcher, verbal communication.

64. *GZD-QL* #39130 (1781.9.26), Liu Yong.

65. *Guofei* are discussed in Suzuki Chūsei, *Shinchō Chūkishi Kenkyū*, pp. 68–69, 82–85, and Cheng-yun Liu, "Kuo-lu: A Sworn Brotherhood Organization in Szechuan."

66. Edict cited in Otake, p. 205.

67. *Baling Xianzhi* 1873.11.16b; *Xiangyin Xianzhi,* 1818.17.2b; *Liling Xianzhi* 1871.1.24; Yasuno.

68. *Hunan Nongye* p. 149; Li Zhen, *Hunan Binhu Gexian Shixi Diaocha Riji,* p. 93; this includes Chaling, Xiangxiang, Xiangtan, Liling, Liuyang, and You counties.

69. Yasuno, pp. 302, 306.

70. *Daqing Lichao Shilu,* Qianlong, 1743/7/16, cited in Yasuno, p. 302.

71. *Hunan Nongye,* p. 146.

72. Ping-ti Ho, "Early Ripening Rice in Chinese History."

73. Richard von Glahn, "The Country of Streams and Grottoes: Geography, Settlement, and the Civilizing of China's Southwestern Frontier, 1000–1250."

74. *Xinning Xianzhi* 1823.30. Nearly all the local gazetteers cited in the Bibliography contain lists of rice seeds in the chapter on "local products" (*wuchan*). These seed lists are the sources for Figure 10.

75. *GZD-QL* #16001.

76. *Baoqing Fuzhi* 1685.13.25.

77. *Changde Fuzhi* 1813.18.3,7.2.

78. *Yongzhou Fuzhi* 1694.4.21.

79. *Yongming Xianzhi* 1716.2.6b; *Jianghua Xianzhi* 1729.4.10a.

80. *Hunan Tongzhi* 1757.49.15.

81. *Changsha Xianzhi* 1817.14; *You Xianzhi* 1871.8.2.

82. Ping-ti Ho, "Early Ripening Rice"; *Population of China,* pp. 169–176; Rawski, pp. 40–43, 118–120; Perkins, *Agricultural Development,* pp. 38–41.

83. *Chunan Miaozhi* 1758.1.50.

84. *Hengzhou Fuzhi* 1593.2.26a; *Ningxiang Xianzhi* 1682.3.6.

85. Late rice was sometimes grown on mountain lands as a winter crop, but only in small quantities; *Hengyang Xianzhi* 1761.3.

86. *Hunan Tongzhi* 1757.49.15; *Baoqing Fuzhi* 1685.13.25; *Xiangyin Xianzhi* 1818.18.1; *Lingling Xianzhi* 1876.5.16; *Anhua Xianzhi* 1872.10.

87. On granaries, see R. Bin Wong, "The Political Economy of Food Supplies"; Chaun and Kraus, pp. 28–39; Will, *Bureaucratie.* Much more detailed information on local price history will soon be available from analysis of price memorials in the Ming-Qing archives. The comments here are based on the small sample available to me in Taiwan. Cf. Chuan and Kraus, pp. 132–136, for Hunan prices from 1723–1735.

88. *GZD-QL* #1267; Yang Xifu, "Chenming Migui Zhi Youshu" (A report explaining the causes of high rice prices), *HCJSWB juan* 39.21–25.

89. *Chengbu Xianzhi* 1867.10.35; Li Wenzhi, *Zhongguo Jindai Nongyeshi Ziliao* I, 538. For another statement on the impending shortage of food due to population growth, see *Baling Xianzhi* 1892.7, citing an earlier edition.

90. *Hunan Tongzhi* 1757.50.1b; *Changde Fuzhi* 1813.18.4.

91. *GZD-QL* #7247 (1754.7.16); *HNSCLA hu,* 7.13a.

92. *GZD-QL* #1869 (1752.5.26), #9496 (1755.5.29); *JQ* #10774 (1808.5.15); *DG* #861 (1837.5.2).

93. *GZD-DG* #1551 (1838.4*.18).

94. *GZD-QL* #1267 (1752.3.24).

95. *GZD-DG* #1758 (1838.7.4).

96. *Qianzhou Tingzhi* 1877.13.

97. *Baoqing Fuzhi* 1849.4a; *Lizhou Zhilizhou Zhi* 1821.8.1b; *Yongzhou Fuzhi* 1828.7a.3b.

98. *Chenzhou Fuzhi* 1765.15.5.

99. *Qianzhou Xianzhi* 1739.2.52b; *Xinhua Xianzhi* 1759.13.1, 1872.7.45; *Xinning Xianzhi* 1823.29.5; *Dongan Xianzhi* 1752.4.22; *Yuanzhou Fuzhi* 1790.20.2b; *Yongshun Xianzhi* 1793.1.49b; *Baoqing Fuzhi* 1849. Appendix 2.4a.

100. *Ningyuan Xianzhi* 1876.3.3, on Yao planting sweet potato; 1811.12 notes that Yao tribespeople were also the first to plant maize there; *Yuezhou Fuzhi* 1746.12.1b. Cf. James Lee, "State and Economy," Chapter 5.

101. *You Xianzhi* 1871.54.6b.

102. *Xiangxiang Xianzhi* 1673.1.10.

103. E.g. district magistrate Zhong Renwen of Sangzhi county: "Quanmin Zhutang Zhiche Shi" (A proclamation urging the people to build reservoirs and run pumps), 1756, in *Yongshun Fuzhi* 1763.11.42a.

104. *Lingling Xianzhi* 1876.5.17.

105. *Yongxing Xiangtuzhi* 1906.2.42a; *Xinhua Xianzhi* 1549.1.16b–17a; *Ningxiang Xianzhi* 1816.8.8.

106. *Liuyang Xianzhi* 1873.14.20, cited in Li Wenzhi, *Zhongguo Jindai Nongyeshi Ziliao* I, 588.

107. *Zhijiang Xianzhi* 1839.7.11.

108. *Chenzhou Fuzhi* 1765.45.47.

109. *Huguang Tongzhi* 1684.18.9.

110. Liu Yingzhong, "Ping Miao Xu" (On pacifying the Miao), *Qianzhou Zhi* 1739.3.13a.

111. *Yuanling Xianzhi* 1708.2.16.

112. *Yuanzhou Fuzhi* 1790.19.8b.

113. *Mayang Xianzhi* 1873.5b.2b.

114. von Glahn, p. 417.

115. *HNSLCA hu* 7.19.

116. *Yongxing Xianzhi* 1762.5.

117. Yang Xifu *Sizhitang Wenji*; *Hunan Tongzhi* 1885.47.27 (dated 1746); Fan Shishou: *GZD-QL* #1872, 1752.5.26.

118. Luo Ruhuai, *Hunan Wenzheng: Guochaowen*, 4.41.

119. *HNSLCA hu* 7.6.

120. *HNSLCA hu* 7.31.

121. Kui Lian, *Qianhou Shoubaolu*, 1.16; 2.4 (1851.9.16).

122. *Leiyang Xianzhi* 1725.2.47.

123. *Dao Zhouzhi* 1878.10.12.

124. *Xiangtan Xianzhi* 1756.13.5a.

125. *Hunan Nongye,* p. 150.

126. *Xiangtan Xianzhi* 1889.6.8b.

127. *HNSLCA hu* 8.6.

128. *Changde Fuzhi* 1813.13.

129. *Chengbu Xianzhi* 1867.10.33b; *GZD-QL* 7247 (1754.7.16); *Liling Xianzhi* 1871.1.24. Cf. Boserup.

130. *Chengbu Xianzhi* 1867.10.33b; *Qiyang Xianzhi* 1870.22.5b; *HNSLCA hu* 8.22b, 7.11a.

131. *HNSLCA hu* 8.8a.

132. *Qiyang Xianzhi* 1765.4.

133. *HNSLCA hu* 7.20b.

134. Cf. Douglass C. North, *Structure and Change in Economic History.*

135. *GZD-JQ* #17650 (1815.1.28).

136. *Yuanzhou Fuzhi* 1790.19.8b.

FIVE   *Property Rights and Social Relations*

1. Rawski; Shigeta; Yeh-chien Wang, "Agricultural Development and Peasant Economy in Hunan during the Ch'ing Period (1644–1911)"; cf. Ramon Myers and Chang Fu-mei Ch'en, "Customary Law and the Economic Growth of China during the Ch'ing Period."

2. This discussion is based on Niida Noboru, *Chūgoku Hōseishi Kenkyū* II, 329–374.

3. Niida Noboru, ed., *Chūgoku Nōson Kankō Chōsa,* cited in Niida, *Hōseishi,* p. 334.

4. H. Franz Schurmann, "Traditional Property Concepts in China"; Li Wenzhi, "Lun Qingchao Qianqi di Tudi Zhanyou Guanxi."

5. Yang Guozhen, "Shilun Qingdai Minbei Minjian di Tudi Maimai"; Yang Guozhen, "Qingdai Minbei Tudi Wenshu Xuanbian."

6. Pierre Hoang, "Notions techniques sur la propriété en Chine."

7. These practices are discussed in detail in Henry MacAleavy, "*Dien* in China and Vietnam"; Peter Hoang, "A Practical Treatise on Legal Ownership."

8. Yang Guozhen, "Shilun Qingdai Minbei," p. 33.

9. *Hengshan Xianzhi* 1774.4.21.

10. Yang Guozhen, "Shilun Qingdai Minbei," p. 33.

11. See *Chūgoku Tochi Keiyaku Bunshoshū;* Rinji Taiwan Kyūkan Chōsakai, *Shindai Keiyaku Bunsho, Shoken Bunruishū.*

12. Jones and Kuhn; James H. Cole, *Shaohsing: Competition and Cooperation in Nineteenth-Century China.*

13. *HNSLCA hu* 9.5b; *Qingquan Xianzhi* 1869.5.12.

14. *Huarong Xianzhi* 1760.1.16b; *Nigxiang Xianzhi* 1748.3.51b; *Hengyang Xianzhi* 1761.5.15.

15. Watt, pp. 210–224.

16. *Changsha Fuzhi* 1747.22.85.

17. *HNSLCA hu,* 5.18.

18. *HNSLCA hu* 5.7a–9a, 5.19, 9.5a, 19b, 22a.

19. *Neige Sanfasi Dang'an,* Zhong Bao, 1734.

20. *GZD-JQ* #12223, Jing An, 1808.10.16.

21. *Yongshun Xianzhi* 1874.13a.

22. *HNSLCA hu,* 9.19b.

23. *HNSLCA hu* 9.26.

24. George Jamieson, et al., eds., "Tenure of Land and Conditions of the Rural Population," pp. 69–74.

25. *HNSLCA hu* 5.2.

26. Hoang, "Notions techniques," p. 11.

27. *HNSLCA hu* 5.31–32b, 35b, 37; 6.6a, 9b.

28. *Baling Xianzhi* 1873.11.8.

29. *HNSLCA hu* 6.15.

30. *HNSLCA hu* 6.19, 40. P. Hoang, "Notions techniques," p. 13.

31. *HNSLCA hu* 6.19.

32. *HNSLCA hu* 6.39.

33. *HNSLCA hu* 5.47.

34. *HNSLCA* 5.45a.

35. *HNSLCA hu* 5.45b.

36. *HNSLCA hu* 5.39a–43b.

37. *GZD-JQ* #9879, Jing An 1808.2.4.

38. Peng Yangzhong, *Guxiangshanguan Cungao,* 4.11b, 8.10b–11a.

39. Ramon Myers, "Customary Law, Markets, and Resource Transactions in Late Imperial China"; Ramon Myers and Chang Fu-mei Ch'en.

40. Douglass C. North and Robert Paul Thomas, *The Rise of the Western World: A New Economic History,* pp. 91–101.

41. Shigeta Atsushi, "Shinritsu ni Okeru Kokō to Denko: 'Shuboku no Bun' o Meguru Ichi Kōsatsu" (Hired labor and tenants in Qing law: An examination of 'the distinction of master and servant'), in Shigeta, *Shindai Shakaikeizaishi Kenkyū,* pp. 81–97.

42. Sudō Yoshiyuki, *Chūgoku Tochi Seidoshi Kenkyū,* pp. 107–172; von Glahn.

43. *Changsha Xianzhi* 1870.20.21, cited in Li Wenzhi, *Zhongguo Jindai Nongyeshi Ziliao,* p. 80; cf. Yang Yi, "Qingchao Qianqi di Tudi Zhidu," p. 38.

44. *Sangzhi Xianzhi* 1764.4.31b.

45. *HNSLCA hu* 5.11a.

46. See Jing Junjian, "Shilun Qingdai Dengji Zhidu"; Liu Yongcheng, "Qingdai Qianqi di Nongye Zudian Guanxi," for examples of such subjection.

47. Cf. Jing Junjian, p. 160.

48. See *Shangyudang* 1819.12.12, p. 121, for an example of rent reduction on official lands in Hunan.

49. *Shanhua Xianzhi* 1747.5.32; *Ningxiang Xianzhi* 1748.*shou*.35b; Zhao Shenqiao, *Zhao Gongyigong Zizhi Guanshu* 9.114a (see Chapter 3).

50. *GZD-QL* #55366, 1788.10.24.

51. Shigeta Atsushi, "Chichōgin no Seiritsu to Nōmin" (The establishment of the *diding* tax and the peasantry), in Shigeta, *Shindai Shakaikeizaishi Kenkyū*, pp. 137–154.

52. *Xiangyin Xianzhi* 1818.24.14a; Jamieson notes that landlords were expected to give tenants three-tenths of tax remissions but were not compelled to do so; see "Tenure of Land in China," p. 78.

53. *Pingjiang Xianzhi* 1875.9.

54. Kuang Minben, *Goulou Wencao Zazhuo*, p. 38b.

55. *HNSLCA hu* 5.12, 20b.

56. Mori Masao, "Min-Shin Jidai no Tochi Seido."

57. Liu Yongcheng, p. 73.

58. Mori, p. 268.

59. *HNSLCA hu* 5.12, 5.21, 5.25.

60. *HNSLCA hu* 5.21b. This saying is roughly equivalent to "Give them an inch and they'll take a mile."

61. *Pingjiang Xianzhi* 1875.9.

62. *Huarong Xianzhi* 1760.1.16; *Ningxiang Xianzhi* 1816.5.80.

63 *Ningxiang Xianzhi* 1867.13.95.

64. Liu Yongcheng, p. 87.

65. Peng Wenhe, *Hunan Hutian Wenti*, p. 380.

66. Shiraishi Hirō, "Shindai Konan no Nōsonshakai–Kaso Kankō to Kōso Keikō." However, Zelin, "The Rights of Tenants in Mid-Qing Sichuan," gives examples of rent deposits used with share rents (p. 510).

67. Rawski, pp. 112–133; Yeh-chien Wang, "Agricultural Development."

68. *Chhenzhou Zongzhi* 1820.21, cited in Zhongguo Renmin Daxue Qingshi Yanjiusuo, p. 73.

69. See tables in Yeh-chien Wang, "Agricultural Development," pp. 37–38.

70. *Liuyang Xianzhi* 1873.8.35; Li Wenzhi, *Zhongguo Jindai Nongyeshi Ziliao* I, 257; *Liuyang Xianzhi* 1818.16.

71. *Hengyang Xianzhi* 1761.5.27b–28a.

72. *Baling Xianzhi* 1873.11.8.

73. *Liuyang Xianzhi* 1733.1.

74. *HNSLCA xing* 9.26.

75. *HNSLCA gong* 1.33; Liu Yongcheng, p. 69.

76. *HNSLCA hu* 5.20b.

77. *HNSLCA xing* 9.26; Shiraishi, p. 8; Minchiu Chu, "The Evolution of Rent Deposit"; Imahori Seiji, *Chūgoku no Shakai Kōzō*, p. 60.

78. *HNSCLA hu* 7.4b.

79. "Huang Dan Xiantian Shuo" (Huang Dan's discussion of limiting landholdings), in Luo Ruhuai, p. 18.

80. *HNSLCA gong* 1.32–34; Rawski, p. 93 n.49.

81. Cf. similar discussion of arrears in *Hengyang Xianzhi* 1761.4.85b.

82. Shigeta, pp. 66–80.

83. *Chhenzhou Zongzhi* 1820, *fukao*, 11a; *Changning Xianzhi* 1799.4; *Hengyang Xianzhi* 1761.4.85b; *Shanhua Xianzhi* 1747.4.3.

84. *Leiyang Xianzhi* 1725.1.79.

85. Peng Wenhe, p. 501.

86. Zelin, "Rights of Tenants."

87. *Chhenzhou Zongzhi* 1820, *fukao*, 11a, Yang Cang, "Jin Edian Zhantian Shi" (A prohibition against wicked tenants occupying land), (my italics); also excerpted in Zhongguo Renmin Daxue Qinshi Yanjiusuo, *KangYongQian Shiqi Chengxiang Renmin Fankang Douzheng Ziliao,* p. 74.

88. *Baling Xianzhi* 1892.52.5, cited in Li Wenzhi, *Zhongguo Jindai Nongyeshi Ziliao* I, 78.

89. Song Tingdan, "Zoujin Fuhu Weijin Guli Bei (1733)" (A memorial to prohibit wealthy households from defying prohibitions on taking profits), *Xiangyin Xianzhi* 1818.27.19.

90. *Xingke Tiben* 1753.6.12, Fan Shishou, cited in Zhongguo Renmin Daxue Qingshi Yanjiusuo, ed., *KangYongQian Shiqi,* p. 72.

91. *Shangyudang* 1771.10.17; 1771.8.11; 1771.8.20; 1771.8.24.

92. Kojina Shinji, "Taihei Tengoku to Nōmin."

SIX   *Waterworks Construction*

1. *Ningxiang Xianzhi* 1816.8.20; according to legend, Xu Sun controlled the flood dragon by binding him to an iron tree.

2. One such organization is described in Ramon Myers, "Economic Organization and Cooperation in Modern China: Irrigation Management in Hsing-tai County, Hopei Province."

3. Yang Xifu served as Governor of Hunan for the following dates: 1745/4–1748/10, 1750/10–1751/10, 1753/9–1753/10, 1755/2–1755/9. These are the dates confirmed by his actual submission of memorials contained in the Palace Museum Archives in Taiwan. Other dates given in *Hunan Tongzhi, juan* 121, or *Qingshigao* can not be considered accurate. His essay is summarized in Madeleine Zelin, *The Magistrate's Tael: Rationalizing Fiscal Reform in Eighteenth-Century Ch'ing China,* pp. 295–298.

4. Yang Xifu, "Chen Migui Zhi You Shu" (A memorial stating the causes of high grain prices), *HCJSWB, juan* 39.21; also in Yang Xifu, *Sizhitang Wenji,* 10.1. Here the essay is dated as 1748/2/24.

5. Yang, "Chen Migui."

6. Yang, "Chen Migui."

7. Mancur Olson, *The Logic of Collective Action*, p. 2. Italics are in the original.

8. Samuel Popkin, *The Rational Peasant*.

9. Denis Twitchett, "The Fan Clan's Charitable Estate."

10. Olson, p. 15.

11. Ibid., pp. 3, 29; Popkin, pp. 254–255.

12. Olson, pp. 15–16.

13. See Table 18.

14. Contributions and rewards are discussed in Xu Daling, *Qingdai Juanna Zhidu*.

15. North, *Structure and Change*, pp. 45–59.

16. Ibid., p. 53.

17. Yang, "Chen Migui."

18. Morita Akira, *Shindai Suirishi Kenkyū*; Amano Motonosuke, "Chūgoku ni Okeru Suiri Kankō"; Kung-chuan Hsiao, pp. 282–287; Mark Elvin, "On Water Control and Management during the Ming and Ch'ing Periods: A Review Article"; Ramon Myers, "Economic Organization and Cooperation."

19. Morita, *Shindai Suirishi*, pp. 139–170.

20. Amano, "Suiri Kankō," pp. 124–128.

21. Mark Elvin, "Market Towns and Waterways: The County of Shanghai from 1480 to 1910," pp. 456, 462–467.

22. Ch'ang-tu Hu, "The Yellow River Administration in the Ch'ing Dynasty"; Rinji Taiwan Kyūkan Chōsakai, *Shinkoku Gyōseihō, zhang* 7, *jie* 5, "Zhishui."

23. Elvin, "Market Towns," p. 473.

24. It might be argued that many of these names are actually names of settlements that were transferred to the polders and thence to the lineages, but, on examining the 1:50,000-scale Japanese army maps of this region, I have found no settlements with names equivalent to those of the polders.

25. Frederic Wakeman, Jr., *Strangers at the Gate*, p. 153, citing Sasaki Masaya, "Shunde Xian Kyōshin to Tōkai Jūroku-sa." Note, however, that the *kung-t'ung-ti* organization referred to by Wakeman is an invention of Sasaki and not a native Chinese institution.

26. *Huarong Xianzhi* 1882.1.15.

27. Li Zhen, p. 165.

28. *HNSLCA*, 5.7.

29. Fei Hsiao-t'ung, *Peasant Life in China*, p. 158; Hamashima Atsutoshi, "The Organization of Water Control in the Kiangnan Delta", pp. 75, 80.

30. Ts'ui-jung Liu, "Dike Construction in Ching-chou: A Study Based on the *Ti-fang chih* Section of the *Ching-chou fu-chih*," pp. 1–28; Morita, *Shindai Suirishi Kenkyū*, pp. 56–57.

31. *Zhupi Yuzhi*, 6.4.40 (Wang Guodong).

32. Peng Wenhe, p. 377.

33. Yanagida Setsuko, "Kyōsonsei no Tenkai," p. 332.

34. Peng Wenhe, p. 378.

35. *Xiangyin Xianzhi* 1818, 27.53.

36. Li Zhaoxi, "Zhisheng Shuili," p. 1749.

37. Kuang Minben, p. 28a.

38. See, for example, memorials on floods in Hunan and Hubei in the *GZD*, e.g. *GZD-QL* #6398 (1754.4*.3), #6586 (1754.4*27) on Hunan; #6981 (1754.6.15) on Hubei.

39. Ferdinand Richthofen, *Letter from Hunan*, p. 10.

40. E.g. *GZD-QL* #6586.

41. Hamashima Atsutoshi, "Mindai Kōnan no Suiri no Ichi Kōsatsu."

42. Ibid., p. 13; Hamashima, "The Organization of Water Control."

43. Jin Zao, "Sanjiang Shuixue Huowen" (Some questions on the hydrology of the Three Rivers) in Yao Wenhao, *Zhexi Shuilishu*, cited in Hamashima, "Mindai Kōnan," p. 13.

44. Hamashima, "Mindai Kōnan"; Oyama Masaaki, "Minmatsu Shinsho no Daitochi Shoyū"; Kitamura Hirotada, "Minmatsu Shinsho ni Okeru Jinushi ni Tsuite."

45. Recent descriptions in English of this process are found in Liang Fang-chung; Ray Huang, pp. 36, 110. See also Wei Qingyuan, *Mingdai Huangce Zhidu*; Wakeman, *The Great Enterprise*, pp. 606–612.

46. *Changshu Shuili Quanshu*. Geng Ju obtained the *jinshi* degree in 1601; Goodrich and Fang, p. 703.

47. Hamashima, "Mindai Kōnan," pp. 22–29, lists projects in Soochow and Songjiang prefectures.

48. Hamashima, "Mindai Kōnan," p. 20.

49. Kawakatsu Mamoru, "Minmatsu Shinsho Kōnan no *Uchō* ni Tsuite,"

50. Hamashima, "Water Control," pp. 69–92.

51. The broader context of reforms in Sung-chiang county in the early Ch'ing is described in Jerry Dennerline, "Fiscal Reform and Local Control: The Gentry-Bureaucratic Alliance Survives the Conquest."

52. Cf. Oyama, pp. 62–64; Hamashima, "Water Control," pp. 79–80; Kawakatsu Mamoru, "Minmatsu Chōkō Deruta Chitai ni Okeru Suiri Kankō no Hen-shitsu"; Kawakatsu Mamoru, "Minmatsu Shinsho Soshū Kakyō Ryōfu ni Okeru Uchō no Shokumu to Junten Yakuhō no Tenkai."

53. Hamashima, "Mindai Kōnan," p. 55.

54. During the Ming dynasty, the single province of Huguang comprised the present-day provinces of Hunan and Hubei.

55. Oh Keum-sung, "Myŏngmal Tongjŏngho Chubyŏn ŭi Suri Kaebal Kwa Nongch'on Sahoe," p. 131.

56. Chen Siyu, "Zhuanghou Xiu Shangxia Qiongdi Bing Qiao Ji" (A record of Mr. Zhuang's repair work on the upper and lower basins and bridges), *Changde Wenzheng* 8.16a.

57. Oh Keum-sung, Myŏngmal Tongjŏngho ŭi Suri, p. 132.

58. "Jingzhou Fudi Kaolue" (Considerations on dike repair in Jingzhou), *Huguang Tongzhi* 1684.9.24b.

59. There was, however, rapid growth of a cotton industry from the mid-Qing on. See Morita Akira, "Shindai Kokō Chihō ni Okeru Teikishi ni Tsuite," pp. 65–69.

60. *Jiangling Xianzhi* 1877,8.13a; cited in Oh Keum-sung, "Myŏngmal Tŏng-jongho ŭi Suri," p. 133n29.

61. *Huarong Xianzhi* 1760.10.20.

62. Peng Zongmeng, *Chutai Shulue* 8.7b.

63. *Changde Fuzhi* 1671.9.68b; Zhao Shenqiao, *Zizhi Guanshu* 7.24a.

64. Guo Xiu, 3.23.

65. *HNSLCA gong* 2.2a; *Hunan Tongzhi* 1885.47.25a.

66. *HNSLCA gong* 2.53b.

67. *HNSLCA gong* 2.16a; *Huarong Xianzhi* 1760.3.8a.

68. *HNSLCA gong* 2.29a.

69. *Changde Fuzhi* 1671.9.68a.

70. Yang Xifu, *Sizhitang* 10.10–11b; Li Zhaoxi, "Zhisheng Shuili."

71. Yang Xifu, 9.11a.

72. Ibid. 7.6a.

73. Ibid. 7.8a.

74. The importance of all local administrative units in the empire was described by one to four of the characters for "frequented," "troublesome," "wearisome," and "difficult" (*chong-fan-bi-nan*). The "most important posts" (*zuiyaoque*) had all four characters. H. S. Brunnert & V. V. Hagelstrom, *Present Day Political Organization of China*, pp. 426–427; T'ung-tsu Ch'ü, p. 15; Skinner, *The City*, p.314. "Metropolitan counties" are those counties (*xian*) that also contain a prefectural capital.

75. *HNSLCA gong* 1.37–55.

76. *HNSLCA gong* 1.41–44.

77. *HNSLCA gong* 1.41–44.

78. *HNSLCA gong* 1.44a.

79. *HNSLCA gong* 1.45b.

80. Quotation from Yang in Perdue, "Water Control in the Dongting Lake Region during the Ming and Qing Periods," p. 750.

81. *HNSLCA gong* 2.29a.

82. *HNSLCA gong* 2.29a–30a.

83. *HNSLCA gong* 1.27.

84. *HNSLCA gong* 2.31.

85. *HNSLCA gong* 2.31a.

86. *HNSLCA gong* 2.37a.

87. *HNSLCA gong* 2.2a.

88. *HNSLCA gong* 2.30b, 34.

89. *HNSLCA gong* 2.52.

90. *HNSLCA gong* 2.23a, 2.27a.
91. *HNSLCA gong* 2.47a.
92. *HNSLCA gong* 2.23a, 34, 47a.
93. Chen Hongmou, *Peiyuantang Oucungao juan* 37.28 (dated 1755/11).
94. *Xiangyin Xianzhi* 1818.27.18a.
95. Li Zhaoxi, "Zhisheng Shuili" *juan* 25; similar criticism by the Emperor in 1789: Li Zhaoxi, *juan* 38.
96. *Xiangtan Xianzhi* 1781.9.3b.
97. Li Zhaoxi, "Zhisheng Shuili" *juan* 51, 1833.11.
98. *Huidian Shili juan* 704, cited in Rinji Taiwan Kyūkan Chōsakai, *Shinkoku Gyōseihō* 3.244.
99. Further discussion of the 1788 flood is found in Perdue, "Water Control," pp. 757–761.
100. *Shinkoku Gyōseihō* 3.241; cf. Wakeman, *The Great Enterprise*, p. 1065, on *guandu minban* management of local waterworks.

SEVEN   *Transformation of Dongting Lake Economy*

1. Zhang Xiugui, "Dongtinghu Yanbian di Lishi Guocheng"; Yang Renzhang, "Xiangjiang Liuyu Shuiwen Dili."
2. Zhang Xiugui, p. 105.
3. Richthofen, *China* III, 467; W. Dickson, "Narrative of an Overland Trip through Hunan from Canton to Hankow," p. 171.
4. Richthofen, *China* III, 467.
5. *Xiangyin Xiangtuzhi* 1881.22.9b.
6. Pierre-Etienne Will, "Un cycle hydraulique en Chine; la province du Hubei du 16ème au 19ème siècles."
7. G. W. Skinner, "Presidential Address: The Structure of Chinese History." See Pierre-Etienne Will, "State Intervention in the Administration of a Hydraulic Infrastructure," for a discussion of the cycle in Jiangnan.
8. Mira Mihelich, "Polders and the Politics of Land Reclamation in Southeast China during the Northern Sung Dynasty (960–1126)."
9. C. S. Liang, "Three Types of Agricultural Water Use in the Yangtze Basin," p. 51.
10. Will, "Un cycle hydraulique en Chine," p. 274.
11. Perdue, "Water Control in the Dongting Lake Region," p. 749.
12. *Xiangyin Xiangtuzhi* 1881.22.1.
13. Sun Ching-chih, p. 207.
14. Yanagida Setsuko, "Sōdai Tochi Shoyūsei ni Mirareru Futatsu no Katachi—Senshin to Henkyō"; Yanagida Setsuko, "Sōdai no Kyakko ni Tsuite"; Morita, *Shindai Suirishi*, pp. 29–31; von Glahn, Chapters 7, 8.
15. *Yueyang Fengtuji*, cited in Zhang Xiugui, p. 106.

16. *Xiangyin Xiangtuzhi* 1881.22.1.

17. Oh Keum-sung, "Myŏngmal Tongjŏngho Chubyŏn ŭi Wanjae ŭi Paltal," p. 115; *Xiangyin Xiangtuzhi* 1881.22.1.

18. Oh Keum-sung, "Myŏngmal Tongjŏngho Chubyŏn ŭi Wanjae ŭi Paltel," p. 116.

19. Ibid., p. 121, Table 2. Note the striking parallels with extensive state sponsorship of irrigation projects around Dian lake in Yunnan; James Lee, "State and Economy," Table 5-5.

20. Ibid., p. 120. Text in *Hunan Tongzhi* 1885.46.26a, and *Huangming Jingshi Wenbian*. There are some discrepancies between the two texts.

21. *Xiangyin Xianzhi* 1565.6b.

22. *Xiangyin Xiangtuzhi* 1881.5.1.

23. *Xiangyin Xianzhi* 1565 *shang* 1–6b.

24. *Xiangyin Xianzhi* 1565 *shang* 9b.

25. *Xiangyin Xianzhi* 1565 *shang*, 9b.

26. Oh Keum-sung, "Myŏngmal Tongjŏngho, Chubyŏn ŭi Suri Kaebal Kwa Nongch'on Sahoe," pp. 135–139.

27. Chen Shiyuan, "Shuili Lun," *Yuezhou Fuzhi*, 1567–1672 *juan* 12; cited in Oh Keum-sung, "Myŏngmal Tongjŏngho Suri Kaebal Kwa Nongch'on Sahoe," p. 136.

28. Oh Keum-sung, "Myŏngmal Tongjŏngho Suri Kaebal Kwa Nonch'on Sahoe," p. 138; *Changsha Fuzhi* 1534. c.6, Xiaoyishu, Long Sheng.

29. *Yuanjiang Xianzhi (Jiajing)*, cited in Zhang Xiugui, p. 108.

30. *Xiangyin Xiangtuzhi* 1881.22.7b.

31. *Xiangyin Xiangtuzhi* 1881.5.1.

32. "Chuanjiang Difang Kaolue" (A study of dikes on Huguang's rivers), *Huguang Tongzhi* 1684.9.24a.

33. Wei Guoyu, "Wang Hou Tianfu Wen" (An essay on the land and taxes of Dr. Wang), *Huarong Xianzhi* 1760.10.33.

34. *Xiangyin Xiangtuzhi* 1881.22.10a.

35. *Xiangyin Xianzhi* 1818.35.61b–63a.

36. *Huguang Zongzhi* 1591.34.33a.

37. *Lizhou Zhilizhou Zhi* 1821.20.24.

38. *Xiangyin Xianzhi* 1818.35b.37a, dated 1664. Tang's biography is given in *Xiangyin Xiangtuzhi* 1881.31.9b–10a.

39. The names and dates of *guanwei* and *minwei* are given in the *shuili* (water control) chapters of many local gazetteers, e.g. *Hunan Tongzhi* 1757, 1820, and 1885 editions; *Changsha Fuzhi* 1747; *Xiangyin Xianzhi* 1756 and 1818; and *Xiangyin Xiantuzhi* 1881. A table of the dikes in Xiangyin is given in Morita, *Shindai Suirishi*, pp. 32–33, and Quan Hansheng, "Qingchao Zhongye Suzhou di Miliang Maoyi," II, 567–582. Both Morita and Quan's lists are based only on *Hunan Tongzhi* 1885. Table 21 collates the data from all editions available in the United States, Japan, and Taiwan. There are significant discrepancies between different editions, which may indicate an increase in dikes in the time period between editions.

40. *Xiangyin Xiangtuzhi* 1881.5.1, 31.11b. describes the period up to the end of Qianlong as "extremely flourishing," but notes that lawsuits began in the Qianlong period. Cf. Rawski, pp. 101–138, which discusses the "rice boom" in Hunan.

41. *Zhupi Yuzhi* 6.4.40a, Wang Guodong; *Xiangyin Xianzhi* 1818.9.1; *Xiangyin Xiangtuzhi* 1881.22.2a.

42. *Hunan Tongzhi* 1885. *shou* (1), 34b–35.

43. Ibid.

44. *Daqing Huidian Shili; juan* 931; Morita, *Shindai Suirishi*, p. 38.

45. *Hunan Tongzhi* 1885.46.4a–7b.

46. *Xiangyin Xiangtuzhi* 1881.22.8a; *Hunan Tongzhi* 1885.4; Yan Youxi, "Chaken Binhu Huangtu Yixiang" (A report on clearance of wasteland near the lake), *Lizhou Zhilizhou Zhi* 1821.20.23a.

47. *Hunan Tongzhi* 1885.47.

48. *Hunan Tongzhi* 1885.46.11a–13a.

49. *Xiangyin Xiangtuzhi* 1881.29.8b; *Xiangyin Xianzhi* 1818.27.31a.

50. *Xiangyin Xianzhi* 1818.17.4b, 17.3a.

51. *Qingshigao: Hequzhi* 4.514c.

52. *ZPZZ: tunken gengzuo* 1744.2.20.

53. *ZPZZ: tunken gengzuo* 1744.7.28; 1744.11.12.

54. *ZPZZ: tunken gengzuo* 1746.2.9.

55. Yang Xifu, 7.19.

56. Ibid., 9.12b.

57. *Xiangyin Xianzhi* 1818.27.28a. *GZD-QL* #58741 (1789.11.9) has a report from Huguang Governor General Bi Yuan on fishermen blocking the Yangtze River current.

58. *GZD-QL* #14984 (1763.5.22), Chen Hongmou.

59. Yang Xifu, 7.19; *HCJSWB* 38.29.

60. *GZD-QL* #1872 (1752.2.26), Fan Shishou.

61. *Xiangyin Xiangtuzhi* 1881.31.11b–12a.

62. *Xiangyin Xianzhi* 1818.27.52a.

63. Wei Yuan, "Huguang Shuili Lun" (A discussion of water conservancy in Huguang), *Guweitang Neiwaiji* 1878, *waiji*, 6.5a–7b.

64. Jones and Kuhn, pp. 148–154, 161–162.

65. Wei Yuan, "Huguang Shuili Lun," 6.7b.

66. Gu Yanwu, "Junxianlun" (A discussion of counties and prefectures), in *Tinglin Wenji*. Partial English translation in W. Theodore de Bary, et al., eds., *Sources of Chinese Tradition*, pp. 556–557; complete Japanese translation and notes in Gotō Motomi and Yamanoi Yū, eds., *Minmatsu Shinsho Seiji Hyōronshū*, pp. 115–122; Cf. Philip Kuhn, "Local Self-Government under the Republic: Problems of Control, Autonomy, and Mobilization."

67. Li Zhaoxi, "Zhisheng Shuili" *juan* 12, 1749.

68. *GZD-QL* #5773 (1754.1.29), Fan Shishou.

69. Kang Shaoyong III, 55.

70. Morita, *Shindai Suirishi*, p. 40.

71. Fan Yuanlin, "Sheli Digong Dongshi Shi" (A proclamation establishing supervisors for dike work) (1755), *Xiangyin Xianzhi* 1818.27.47.

72. *GZD-QL* #15445 (1763.7.12) Qiao Guanglie.

73. *GZD-QL* #15697 (1763.8.21) Qiao Guanglie.

74. *GZD-QL* #16260 (1763.11.9) Qiao Guanglie.

75. *GZD-QL* #40336 (1781.22.16) Liu Yong; #41192 (1782.3.29) Li Shijie; #44588 (1783.4.18) Yixang-a; *GZD-JQ* #12354 (1808.11.1) Jing-an. There may have been inspections in other years, but these are the only dates confirmed by memorial reports in the Archives in Taipei.

76. Kuang Minben, 9.26b. Kuang's biography is given in Luo Ruhuai, *juan* 1.

77. Kuang Minben, 9.26b–27b.

78. Perdue, "Water Control," p. 756.

79. *Xiangyin Xianzhi* 1818.35.61.

80. *GZD-QL* #9938 (1755.7.7) Yang Xifu.

81. *GZD-QL* #5774 (1754.1.29) Fan Shishou.

82. Yang Xifu, 10.30–31b.

83. *Xiangyin Xiangtuzhi* 1881.22.8b.

84. *GZD-JQ* #8017 (1802.5.5); *Dongting Huzhi* 1825.1.10b.

85. *Xiangyin Xiangtuzhi* 1881.22.9a.

86. Kang Shaoyong I,35–36.

87. Ibid. III,53a.

88. Kang Shaoyong II,16a–17b.

89. Wu Rongguang, *Shiyun Shanren Ji: Zougao*, Daoguang, 4.1a–4a.

90. Li Zhaoxi; *Zhisheng Shuili Zhaoxi juan* 48, 1825.

91. Wu Rongguang, *Shiyun Shanren Ji: zougao*, 5.10a–11b.

92. *HNSLCA gong* 2.63.

93. *Zhupi Yuzhi* 4.1.56 (vol.19).

94. *Shangyudang*, 1804.7.2.

95. *Xiangyin Xiangtuzhi* 1881.29.4b–6a.

96. *Xiangyin Xiangtuzhi* 1881.22.2b,11a.

97. *Xiangyin Xiangtuzhi* 1881.22.10b.

98. Ibid.

99. *Xiangyin Xiangtuzhi* 1881.22.11a.

100. *Xiangyin Xiangtuzhi* 1881.31.13b, 22.10b–11a.

101. Yang Renjun, "Dongtinghu Chuangshe Jianshui Shanglun Youyi Wusun Shuo."

102. Yang Xifu, 7.19.

103. Wan Benduan, "Hequzhi: Zhisheng Shuili," 1748.

104. Li Zhaoxi, "Zhisheng Shuili" *juan* 26, 1748.11.

105. Ibid., *juan* 10, 1746.1.

106. Ibid., *juan* 50, 1831.12.
107. Ibid., *juan* 54, 1851.12.
108. Ibid., *juan* 56, 1850.10.

EIGHT *Conclusion*

1. Cui Shu, quoted in Qin Shangzhi, *Zhongguo Fazhi Ji Falü Sixiang Shi Jianghua*, p. 143.
2. Yu-wen Jen, *The Taiping Revolutionary Movement*, pp. 93-97.
3. Kojima Shinji, part 2, *Shichō*, 96, pp. 10-17.
4. Kung-chuan Hsiao, p. 142.
5. Kojima Shinji, part 3, *Shichō*, 97, pp. 85-88.
6. Kojima Shinji, part 3, p. 90.
7. *Pingjiang Xianzhi* 1875, preface.
8. Philip A. Kuhn, "The Taiping Rebellion," p. 275.
9. *Ningxiang Xianzhi* 1941, *juan* 4.
10. Jen Yu-wen, pp. 216, 220, 234.
11. Kung-chuan Hsiao, p. 301.
12. Ibid., p. 310.
13. *Liling Xianzhi* 1948, *dashiji*, p. 13.
14. Philip A. Kuhn, *Rebellion and Its Enemies in Late Imperial China: Militarization and Social Structure*, pp. 98-99; Jones and Kuhn, p. 131; Kung-chuan Hsiao, pp. 136, 442.
15. R. Bin Wong, "Food Riots"; Kojima Shinji, part 2, pp. 24-30.
16. Kung-chuan Hsiao, pp. 200, 447.
17. Kojima Shinji, part 2, p. 26; Kuhn, "Taiping Rebellion," p. 265.
18. Kui Lian, *Qian Shoubaolu, juan* 1.11,2.8,5.1,4.13.
19. Kui Lian, *Hou Shoubaolu, juan* 4.13.
20. Ibid., *juan* 4.10b.
21. Ibid., *juan* 4.12b.
22. *Xinning Xianzhi* 1893.6.9a; Kuhn, *Rebellion and Its Enemies*, pp. 106-112.
23. Kui Lian, *Hou Shoubaolu, juan* 4.13, 14.3; *Qian Shoubaolu, juan* 1.4, 2.6, 4.6
24. Yasui Shōtarō, p. 642.
25. Ping-ti Ho, *Population of China*, pp. 275-278; Perkins, *Agricultural Development*, pp. 29, 185.
26. *Rucheng Xianzhi* 1932.18.4b.
27. Perkins, *Agricultural Development*, p. 210.
28. Ping-ti Ho, *Population of China*, p. 244.
29. Richthofen, *Letter from Hunan*, p. 9; *China* II, 39.
30. Kung-chuan Hsiao, p. 407.
31. *Liling Xiangtuzhi* 1926.4.15b.
32. Richthofen, *China* II, 39.

33. *Liuyang Xianzhi* 1873.8.37, cited in Li Wenzhi, *Zhongguo Jindai Nongyeshi Ziliao* I, 931.

34. *Changsha Xianzhi* 1870.20.36, in Li Wenzhi, *Zhongguo Jindai Nongyeshi Ziliao* I, 478.

35. *Shibao* 1906.12.26, in Li Wenzhi, ibid. I, 471.

36. *Baling Xianzhi* 1892, *juan* 52.6, cited in Kung-chuan Hsiao, p. 401.

37. *Wugang Zhouzhi* 1873.28.4. The reasons for this type of marriage are discussed in G. William Skinner, "Regional Systems in Late Imperial China," pp. 12–18; Arthur P. Wolf and Chieh-shan Huang, *Marriage and Adoption in China, 1845–1945*.

38. Kuhn, *Rebellion and Its Enemies*, p. 137.

39. Kui Lian, *Hou Shoubaolu, juan* 5, 1851.12.11; *juan* 6.7a,17.10b; 2.13a.

40. Kung-chuan Hsiao, p. 155.

41. Kui Lian, *Qian Shoubaolu, juan* 3.17b; 5.2b, 4.13b; *Hou Shoubaolu, juan* 15.20b. Similar evidence of compulsory contributions in Kung-chuan Hsiao, p. 160.

42. *Hou Shoubaolu, juan* 3.17; *Liling Xianzhi*, 1948.13.

43. *Baling Xianzhi* 1873.11.9b.

44. Wu Minshu, "Baling Jizhou Shuo" (A discussion of granaries in Baling), *Panhu Wenji, juan* 2.10a.

45. Kung-chuan Hsiao, p. 166.

46. *Liling Xianzhi* 1948.5.98.

47. R. Bin Wong, et al., eds., *Nourish the People*.

48. *Wugang Zhouzhi* 1873.20.28b.

49. Wu Minshu, *Panhu Wenji, juan* 2.8b.

50. *Liling Xiangtuzhi* 1926, *juan* 6.24.

51. Zeng Guofan, "Zeng Wenzhenggong Quanji, Zougao," *juan* 2.30, in Li Wenzhi, *Zhongguo Jindai Nongyeshi Ziliao* I, 335; Kung-chuan Hsiao, pp. 60–61.

52. Kung-chuan Hsiao, p. 102.

53. *GZD-DG* #8291 (1845.9.30).

54. Hsia Nai, "The Land Tax in the Yangtse Provinces before and after the Taiping Rebellion," p. 367.

55. K. C. Liu, "The Ch'ing Restoration," p. 445; Hsia Nai, pp. 373, 381.

56. Kojima Shinji, part 3, pp. 98–102.

57. Mary Clabaugh Wright, *The Last Stand of Chinese Conservatism: The T'ung-chih Restoration, 1862–1874*, pp. 163–167.

58. Wu Minshu, *Panhu Wenji, juan* 2, 9a.

59. Zhang Zhidong, *Zhang Wenxianggong Dugao*, pp. 5–6, and *Shibao* (1906.1.15), in Li Wenzhi, *Zhongguo Jindai Nongyeshi Ziliao* I, 231.

60. Cai Zhongjian, "Dongting Yusai yu Changde You he Sunyi Shuo."

61. Yang Renjun, *juan* 5, p. 50a.

62. Dai Dancheng, "Dongtinghu Yusai yu Changde You he Sunyi Shuo."

63. *Nongxuebao* 1898.7, in Li Wenzhi, *Zhongguo Jindai Nongyeshi Ziliao* I, 879.

64. Li Zhen, p. 61.

65. Li Zhen; Zhou Yikui, *Hunansheng Shuizai Chakan Baogaoshu; Hunansheng Shuili Gaikuang.*

66. Li Zhen, p. 54.

67. *Chengbu Xianzhi* 1867.10.35b.

68. *Qianyang Xianzhi* 1874.16.2, in Li Wenzhi, *Zhongguo Jindai Nongyeshi Ziliao* I, 527.

69. *Lingling Xianzhi* 1876.5.17b.

70. *Shanhua Xianzhi* 1877.16.23, in Li Wenzhi, *Zhonguo Jindai Nongyeshi Ziliao* I, 441.

71. Richthofen, *Letter from Hunan,* p. 4.

72. Morita, "Shindai Kokō," pp. 49–73; Shigeta, "Shinmatsu ni Okeru Konan Cha no Shin Tenkai" (New developments in Hunan tea in the late Qing), "Shinmatsu ni Okeru Konan Cha no Seisan Kōzō" (The structure of Hunan tea production in the late Qing), in Shigeta, *Shindai Shakaikeizaishi Kenkyū,* pp. 207–293.

73. *Guangxu Zhengyao, Shiye* 8,1908.14.13, in Li Wenzhi, *Zhongguo Jindai Nongyeshi Ziliao* I, 422.

74. Shigeta, "Shinmatsu ni Okeru Konan Cha no Seisan Kōzō," p. 246.

75. Ibid., pp. 261–262.

76. *Liling Xiangtuzhi* 1926.6.24.

77. Li Zongyun, *Liuyang Tuchan Biao, Nongxuebao* 1897.5, in Li Wenzhi, *Zhongguo Jindai Nongyeshi Ziliao* I, 916.

78. *Chengbu Xianzhi* 1867.10.35b.

79. *Pingjiang Xianzhi* 1875.20.4b.

80. *Baling Xianzhi* 1892.7; *Yiyang Xianzhi,* 1874.2.12.

81. *Liling Xianzhi* 1948.5.

82. For example, James Scott, *The Moral Economy of the Peasant: Rebellion and Subsistence in Southeast Asia;* Popkin, *The Rational Peasant;* Joel Migdal, *Peasants, Politics, and Revolution: Pressures toward Political and Social Change in the Third World;* and the symposium on Scott's book in *Journal of Asian Studies* 42.4 (August 1983).

83. These perspectives are outlined in Philip C. C. Huang, *The Peasant Economy and Social Change in North China,* pp. 3–32.

84. Philip Huang, p. 22.

85. Restraint of individual interest for the benefit of *family* goals is, however, a different question, not addressed here.

86. Skinner, "Presidential Address," p. 284. Italics in original.

87. Fox-Genovese.

Bibliography

Gazetteers are listed with edition and place consulted, as follows: LC, Library of Congress; ND, National Diet Library, Tokyo; NB, Naikaku Bunko, Tokyo; TB, Tōyō Bunko, Tokyo; YC, Harvard-Yenching Library, Cambridge; SK, Sonkeikaku Bunko, Tokyo; UC, Far Eastern Library, University of Chicago; GG, Palace Museum, Taipei; SY, Lishi Yuyan Yenjiusuo, Academica Sinica, Taipei. For consistency, dates of editions follow the dates given in Zhu Shijia, *Zhongguo Difangzhi Zonglu Zengding* (Shanghai, 1958), or the Japanese Library Catalogue, *Nihon Shuyō Toshokan Kenkyūjo Shozō Chūgoku Chihōshi Sōgō Mokuroku* (Tokyo, 1969), even though these are not always correct. Chhenzhou is spelled with two h's to distinguish it from its homophone Chenzhou. 郴州，辰州。

Amano Motonosuke 天野元之助. "Chūgoku ni Okeru Suiri Kankō" 中国における水利慣行(Irrigation customs in China), *Shirin* 38.6:123–149 (1955).

———. *Chūgoku Nōgyōshi Kenkyū* 中国農業史研究 (Studies on Chinese agricultural history). Tokyo, Nōgyō Sōgō Kenkyūjo, 1962.

Anderson, Perry. *Lineages of the Absolutist State.* London, Verso, 1979.

Anfu Xianzhi 安福县志 1869.LC.

Anhua Xianzhi 安化 1545.LC.

Anhua Xianzhi. 1872.ND.

Anxiang Xianzhi 安乡 1748.YC.

Aron, Raymond. *Main Currents of Sociological Thought.* Garden City, Doubleday, 1968.

Averill, Stephen C. "The Shed People and the Opening of the Yangtze Highlands," *Modern China* 9.1:84–126 (January 1983).

Avineri, Shlomo. *Hegel's Theory of the Modern State.* Cambridge, Cambridge University Press, 1972.

Bai Gang 白纲, ed. *Zhongguo Fengjian Shehui Changqi Yanxu Wenti Lunzhan di Youlai yu Fazhan* 中国封建社会长期延续问题论战的由来与发展 (The origin and development of the debate over the prolonged period of Chinese feudalism). Beijing, Zhongguo Shehui Kexue Chubanshe, 1984.

Balazs, Etienne. *Chinese Civilization and Bureaucracy.* Tr. H. M. Wright. New Haven, Yale University Press, 1964.

Baling Xianzhi 巴陵县志 1873.NB.YC.

Baling Xianzhi 1892.YC.

Baojing Xianzhi 宝庆县志 1871.LC.

Baoqing Fuzhi 宝庆府志 1685.NB.

Baoqing Fuzhi 1849.YC.

Boserup, Ester. *The Conditions of Agricultural Growth: The Economics of Agrarian Change under Population Pressure.* Chicago, Aldine, 1973.

Brook, Timothy. "The Spread of Rice Cultivation and Rice Technology into the Hebei Region in the Ming and Qing." In Li Guohao, Zhang Mengwen, Cao Tianqin, eds., *Explorations in the History of Science and Technology in China.* Shanghai, Chinese Classics Publishing House, 1982.

Brunnert, H. S., and V. V. Hagelstrom. *Present Day Political Organization of China.* Tr. A. Beltchenko and E. E. Moran. Peking, 1910.

Cai Zhongjian 蔡仲潛. "Dongting hu Yusai Yu Changde You he Sunyi Shuo" 洞庭湖淤塞於常德有何損益説 (A proposal on the advantages and disadvantages of the silting of Dongting Lake at Changde). In Jiang Biao, ed., *Yuanxiang Tongysliu* 沅湘通埶錄 (Literary collection of the Yuan and Xiang Rivers). Changsha, 1897.

Cartier, Michel. "La croissance démographique chinoise du XVIIIe siècle et l'enregistrement des *pao-chia,*" *Annales de démographie historique,* 1979. pp. 9–24.

Cartier, Michel, and Rémi Mathieu. "Les conceptions démographiques de l'antiquité chinoise: quelques reflections," *Annales de démographie historique,* 1974, pp. 375–89.

Cartier, Michel, and Pierre-Etienne Will. "Démographie et institutions en Chine: contribution à l'analyse des recensements de l'époque imperiale (2 A.D.–1750)," *Annales de démographie historique* (1971), pp. 161–245.

Chaling Zhouzhi 茶陵州志 1817.TB.

Chang Chung-li. *The Chinese Gentry.* Seattle, University of Washington, 1955.

Changde Fuzhi 常德府志 1671.NB. (Preface dated 1671 but contains material from later periods.)

Changde Fuzhi 1809–1813.YC.

Changde Wenzheng 常德文徵 (Changde Literary Collection).

Changning Xianzhi 常宁县志 1799.YC.

Changsha Fuzhi 常沙府志 1534.

Changsha Fuzhi 1685.NB.

Changsha Fuzhi 1747.YC.

Changsha Xianzhi 常沙县志 1703.NB.

Changsha Xianzhi 1817.YC.

Changsha Xianzhi 1870.YC.

Changsha Xianzhi Xuji 長沙县志續紀 1747.NB.

Chen Dengyuan. 陳登原 . *Zhongguo Tianfu Shi* 中国田賦史 (History of land taxation in China). Shanghai, 1936.

Chen Hongmou 陳宏謀 . *Peiyuantang Oucungao* 培遠堂偶存稿 (Collected writings). 1763.

Chengbu Xianzhi 城步县志 1867.YC.

Chenzhou Fuzhi 辰州府志 1685.NB.

Chenzhou Fuzhi 1765.LC.

Chhenzhou Zongzhi 郴州绕志. 1772.ND.

Chhenzhou Zongzhi 1820.LC.

Chu Minchiu. "The Evolution of Rent Deposit." In Institute of Pacific Relations, ed., *Agrarian China*. Chicago, University of Chicago Press, 1938.

Ch'ü T'ung-tsu. *Local Government in China under the Ch'ing*. Stanford, Stanford University Press, 1969.

Chuan Han-sheng and Richard A. Kraus. *Mid-Ching Rice Markets and Trade: An Essay in Price History*. Cambridge, East Asian Research Center, Harvard University, 1975.

Chūgoku Tochi Keiyaku Bunshoshū 中国土地契約文書集 (Collection of Chinese land contracts), Tokyo, Tōyō Bunko Mindaishi Kenkyūshitsu, 1975.

Chunan Miaozhi 楚南苗志 (Gazetteer of the Miaio people of southern Hunan). 1758.

Cili Xianzhi 1869.YC.

Cole, James H. *Shaohsing: Competition and Cooperation in Nineteenth-Century China*. Tucson, University of Arizona Press, 1986.

Dai Dancheng 戴丹誠. "Dongtinghu Yusai Yu Changde You He Sunyi Shuo" 洞庭湖淤塞於常德有何損益説(The advantages and disadvantages of the silting of Dongting Lake at Changde). In Jiang Biao, ed., *Yuanxiang Tongyilu*. Changsha, 1897.

Dai Yi 戴逸. *Jianming Qingshi* 簡明清史 (Concise history of the Qing dynasty), Vol. I. Beijing, Renmin Chubanshe, 1980.

Dao Zhouzhi 道州志 1878.YC.

Daqing Huidian 大清會典 (Statutes of the Qing dynasty). 1818.

Daqing Huidian Shili 大清會典事例 (Statutes and cases of the Qing dynasty). 1818.

Daqing Lichao Shilu 大清歷朝實錄 (Veritable records of successive reigns of the Qing dynasty). Taipei, Huawen shuju, 1964.

Daqing Lüli 大清律例 (Law code of the Qing dynasty). 1870.

de Bary, Wm. Theodore, et al., eds. *Sources of Chinese Tradition*. New York, Columbia University Press, 1968.

Deng Yao 鄧瑤. *Shuangwu Shanguan Wenchao* 雙梧山館文鈔 (Collected writings). 1860.

Dennerline, Jerry. "Fiscal Reform and Local Control: The Gentry-Bureaucratic Alliance Survives the Conquest." In Frederic Wakeman, Jr., and Carolyn Grant, eds., *Conflict and Control in Imperial China.* Berkeley, University of California Press, 1975.

Dickson, W. "Narrative of an Overland Trip through Hunan from Canton to Hankow," *Journal of the North China Branch of the Royal Asiatic Society* 1:159–173 (1864).

Dirlik, Arif. *Revolution and History: The Origins of Marxist Historiography in China, 1919–1937.* Berkeley, University of California Press, 1978.

Dongan Xianzhi 東安县志 1752.LC.

Dongting Huzhi 洞庭湖志 1825.YC.

Durand, John. "Population Statistics of China, A.D. 2–1953," *Population Studies* 13:209–256 (March 1960).

Eberhard, Wolfram. *Conquerors and Rulers: Social Forces in Medieval China.* Leiden, E. J. Brill, 1970.

Eisenstadt, S. N. "The Study of Oriental Despotisms as Systems of Total Power," *Journal of Asian Studies* 17.3:435–446 (May 1958).

Elvin, Mark. *The Pattern of the Chinese Past.* Stanford, Stanford University Press, 1973.

——. "On Water Control and Management during the Ming and Ch'ing Periods: A Review Article," *Ch'ing-shih wen-t'i* 1975. 3:82–103.

——. "Market Towns and Waterways: The County of Shanghai from 1480 to 1910." In G. William Skinner, ed., *The City in Late Imperial China.* Stanford, Stanford University Press, 1977.

Fei Hsiao-t'ung. *Peasant Life in China.* London, G. Routledge & Sons, 1939.

Fenghuang Tingzhi 凤凰厅志 1758.LC.

Feuerwerker, Albert. *State and Society in Eighteenth-Century China: The Ch'ing Empire in Its Glory.* Ann Arbor, Center for Chinese Studies, University of Michigan. 1976.

Fogel, Joshua A. *Politics and Sinology: The Case of Naitō Konan.* Cambridge, Council on East Asian Studies, Harvard University, 1984.

——. "Debates on the Asiatic Mode of Production in the Soviet Union, China, and Japan." Unpublished ms., 1986.

Fox-Genovese, Elizabeth. *The Origins of Physiocracy: Economic Revolution and Social Order in Eighteenth-Century France.* Ithaca, Cornell University Press, 1976.

Fu Jiaojin 傅角今. *Hunan Dilizhi* 湖南地理志 (Gazetteer of the geography of Hunan). Changsha, 1933.

Fu Yiling 傳衣凌 . "Ming-Qing Shidai Jieji Guanxi di Xintansuo" 明清時代階級关系的新探索 (New considerations of class relations in the Ming-Qing period), *Zhongguoshi Yanjiu* 1979.4:65–74.

Fujii Hiroshi 藤井宏 . "Mindai Dendo Tōkei ni Kansuru Ichi Kōsatsu" 明代田土統計に関する一考察 (A consideration of Ming dynasty land statistics), *Tōyō Gakuhō* 30.3:90–123 (August 1943).

Geng Ju 耿橘 . *Changshu Shuili Quanshu* 常熟水利全書 (Complete record of water conservancy in Changshu). Ca. 1620.

Goi Naohiro 五井直弘 . *Kindai Nihon to Tōyōshigaku* 近代日本と東洋史學 (Modern Japan and Sinology). Tokyo, Aoki Shoten, 1976.

Gongzhongdang Kangxichao Zouzhe 宮中档康熙朝奏摺 (Secret palace memorials of the Kangxi reign). Taipei, Guoli Gugong Bowuyuan (Palace Museum), 1976–present.

Gongzhongdang Qianlongchao Zouzhe 宮中档乾隆朝奏摺 (Secret palace memorials of the Qianlong reign). Taipei, Guoli Gugong Bowuyuan (Palace Museum), 1976–present.

Gongzhongdang Yongzhengchao Zouzhe 宮中档雍正朝奏摺 (Secret palace memorials of the Yongzheng reign). Taipei, Guoli Gugong Bowuyuan (Palace Museum), 1976–present.

Gongzhongdang Zhupi Zouzhe 宮中档硃批奏摺 (Secret palace memorials with vermilion endorsements). Palace Museum Archives, Taipei, Taiwan. Cited by reign period (QL: Qianlong, JQ: Jiaqing, DG: Daoguang), accession number, date (Western year/lunar month/day. *Indicates intercalary month following the numbered month.)

Goodrich, L. Carrington, and Chaoying Fang, eds. *Dictionary of Ming Biography*. New York, Columbia University Press, 1976.

Gotō Motomi 後藤基巳 and Yamanoi Yū 山井湧 , eds. *Minmatsu Shinsho Seiji Hyōronshū* 明末清初政治評論集 (Collection of late Ming and early Qing political theory). Tokyo, Heibonsha, 1971.

Gu Yanwu 顧炎武 . *Tianxia Junguo Libingshu* 天下郡国利病書 (Essays on the advantages and disadvantages of the districts of the empire). 1879.

——. *Tinglin Wenji* 亭林文集 (Collected writings). Shanghai, 1929.

Guiyang Zhili Zhouzhi 桂陽直隶州志 1868.YC.

Guo Songyi 郭松义 . "Qingchu Fengjian Guojia Kenhuang Zhengce Fenxi" 清初封建国家星荒政策分析 (An analysis of the policy toward clearance of wasteland of the early Qing feudal state), *Qingshi Luncong* II, 112. 1980.

Guo Xiu 郭秀 . *Shugao* 疏稿 (Memorials). 1699.

Hamashima Atsutoshi 浜島敦俊 . "Mindai Kōnan no Suiri no Ichi Kōsatsu" 明代江南の水利の一考察 (A consideration of irrigation in Ming Jiangnan), *Tōyō Bunka Kenkyūjo Kiyō* 47:1–62 (February 1969).

Hamashima Atsutoshi. "Gyoshokudenryoku kō" 業食佃力考 (A study of *yeshi dianli*), *Tōyōshi Kenkyū* 39.1:118–155 (1980).

——. "The Organization of Water Control in the Kiangnan Delta in the Ming Period," *Acta Asiatica* 1980. 38:69–92.

Hartwell, Robert. "Demographic, Political, and Social Transformations of China, 750–1550," *Harvard Journal of Asiatic Studies* 42.2:365–342 (December 1982).

He Changling 賀長齡 , ed. *Huangchao Jingshi Wenbian* 皇朝経世 文編 (Qing dynasty collected essays on statecraft). Guofeng reprint of Sibulou edition, 1887.

Hengshan Xianzhi 衡山县志 1488 (1924 reprint).YC.

Hengshan Xianzhi 1774.GG.

Hengshan Xianzhi 1823.YC.

Hengyang Xianzhi 衡陽县志 1761.GG.

Hengyang Xianzhi 1872–1874.YC.

Hengzhou Fuzhi 衡州府志 1593.TB.

Ho Ping-ti. "The Introduction of American Food Plants into China," *American Anthropologist.* April 1955.

——. "Early Ripening Rice in Chinese History," *Economic History Review*, 2nd series, 9.2:200–218 (1956).

——. *Studies on the Population of China 1368–1953*, Cambridge, Harvard University Press, 1959.

Ho Ping-ti 何炳棣 . "Meizhou Zuowu di Yinjin Zhuanbo Jiqi dui Zhongguo Liangshi Shengchan di Yingxiang" 美洲作物的引進傳播及其 对中国糧食生产的影響 (The introduction of American plants and their effect on the growth of China's food production). In *Dagongbao Zaigang Fukan Sanshizhouji Jinian Wenji.* Hong Kong, Da Gongbao, 1978. II, 673–731.

Hoang, Peter. "A Practical Treatise on Legal Ownership." In George Jamieson, et al., eds., "Tenure of Land and Conditions of the Rural Population," *Journal of the North China Branch of the Royal Asiatic Society* n.s. 1888.23:118–174.

Hoang, Pierre. "Notions techniques sur la propriété en Chine," *Variétés Sinologiques* 1897.11:9.

Hsia Nai. "The Land Tax in the Yangtse Provinces before and after the Taiping Rebellion." In E-tu Zen Sun and John De Francis, eds., *Chinese Social History.* Washington, American Council of Learned Societies, 1956.

Hsiao Kung-chuan. *Rural China: Imperial Control in the Nineteenth Century.* Seattle, University of Washington Press, 1972.

Hu Ch'ang-tu. "The Yellow River Administration in the Ch'ing Dynasty," *Far Eastern Quarterly* 14 (1955).

Huan Kuan. *Discourses on Salt and Iron.* Tr. Esson Gale. Taipei, Ch'eng-wen, 1967.

Huang, Philip C. C. *The Peasant Economy and Social Change in North China.* Stanford, Stanford University Press, 1985.

Huang, Ray. *Taxation and Governmental Finance in Sixteenth-Century Ming*

China. Cambridge, Cambridge University Press, 1974.

Huangchao Wenxian Tongkao (Collection of Qing dynasty documents). 1785.

Huangming Jingshi Wenbian 皇明経世文編 (Ming dynasty essays on statecraft). Taipei reprint, 1977.

Huarong Xianzhi 華容县志 1685 (contains material from 1611 edition also).NB.

Huarong Xianzhi 1760.TB.

Huarong Xianzhi 1882.YC.

Huguang Tongzhi 湖廣統志 1684.LC.

Huguang Zongzhi 湖廣総志 1591.UC.

Hummel, Arthur W., ed. *Eminent Chinese of the Ch'ing Period*. Washington, D.C., 1943–1944.

Hunan Jinbainian Dashi Jishu 湖南近百年大事紀述 (History of great events in Hunan in the last hundred years). Hunan, Xinhua Shudian, 1980.

Hunan Nongye Xueyuan, ed. *Hunan Nongye* 湖南農業 (Agriculture in Hunan). Beijing, Beijing Gaodeng Jiaoyu Chubanshe, 1959.

Hunan Shengli Cheng'an 湖南省例成案 (Collected legal cases from Hunan). Changsha, 1820.

Hunan Tongzhi 湖南統志 1757.YC.

Hunan Tongzhi 1820.YC.

Hunan Tongzhi 1885.YC.

Hunansheng Shuili Gaikuang 湖南省水利概况 (Outline of water conservancy in Hunan). 1946.

Imahori Seiji 今堀誠二. *Chūgoku no Shakai Kōzō: Ancien Regime ni Okeru Kyōdōtai* 中国の社会構造アンシァンレジレに おける共同体 (The social structure of China: Community in the ancien regime). Tokyo, Yūhikaku, 1953.

Institute of Pacific Relations. *Agrarian China*. Chicago, University of Chicago Press, 1938.

Iwami Hiroshi 岩見宏. "Kokōjuku Tenka Zoku" 湖廣熟天下足 (When Huguang has a good harvest, the empire has sufficient grain), *Tōyōshi Kenkyū* 20.4:175 (March 1962).

Jamieson, George, et al., eds. "Tenure of Land and Conditions of the Rural Population," *Journal of the North China Branch of the Royal Asiatic Society* n.s. 1888.23:59–174.

Jen Yu-wen. *The Taiping Revolutionary Movement*. New Haven, Yale University Press, 1973.

Jianghua Xianzhi 江华县志 1729.GG.

Jing Junjian 经君健. "Shilun Qingdai Dengji Zhidu" 试论清代等级制度 (On the status system of the Qing dynasty), *Zhongguo Shehui Kexue* 1980.6:149–172.

Joint Publications Research Service, tr. *Hunan Provincial Gazetteer*, Vol. II. Translation of *Hunan Shengzhi*. Changsha, 1961.

Jones, Susan Mann, and Philip A. Kuhn. "Dynastic Decline and the Roots of Rebellion." In John K. Fairbank, ed., *The Cambridge History of China Vol. X, Late Ch'ing, 1800–1911*, Part 1, pp. 107–162. Cambridge, Cambridge University Press, 1978.

Junjichu Dang 軍機處档 (Grand Council archives), Palace Museum Archives. Same citation as *Gongzhongdang*. Date indicates date of submission of memorial.

Kanda Masao 神田正雄. *Konanshō Sōran* 湖南省綜覧 (Overview of Hunan). Tokyo, Shinpōsha, 1943.

Kang Shaoyong 康紹鏞. "Kang Shaoyong Zougao: Hunan Rennei" 康紹鏞奏稿湖南任内 (Memorials of Kang Shaoyong concerning Hunan). A collection of unpublished draft memorials held in the Tōyō Bunko. 1829.

Kawakatsu Mamoru 川勝守. "Chō Kyosei Jōryō Saku no Tenkai–Toku ni Minmatsu Kōnan ni Okeru Jinushisei no Hatten ni Tsuite" 張居正丈量策の展開－特に明末江南における地主制の發展について (On Zhang Juzheng's land survey, especially the development of the landlord system in Jiangnan in the late Ming), *Shigaku Zasshi* 80.3:1–38 (March 1971); 80.4:40–59 (April 1971).

——. "Minmatsu Shinsho Kōnan no Uchō ni Tsuite" 明末清初江南の圩長について (On the polder chieftain in Jiangnan in the late Ming and early Qing), *Tōyō Gakuhō* 55.4:18–19 (March 1973).

——. "Minmatsu Chōkō Deruta Chitai ni Okeru Suiri Kankō no Henshitsu" 明末長江デルタ地帯における水利慣行の変質 (The transformation of water-conservancy customs in the Yangtze Delta region in the late Ming), *Shien* 1974.111:65–112.

——. "Minmatsu Shinsho Soshū Kakyō Ryōfu ni Okeru Uchō no Shokumu to Junten Yakuhō no Tenkai" 明末清初蘇州嘉興兩府における圩長の職物と均田役法の展開 (The duties of the polder chieftain and the development of land and corvée equalization in Suzhou and Jiaxing prefectures in the late Ming and early Qing). In *Enoki Hakase Kanreki Kinen Tōyōshi Ronsō* (Essays on East Asian history in honor of the sixty-first birthday of Dr. Enoki). Tokyo, 1976.

Kessler, Lawrence D. *K'ang-hsi and the Consolidation of Ch'ing Rule, 1661–1684*. Chicago, University of Chicago Press, 1976.

Kinkley, Jeffrey C. "Shen Ts'ung-wen's Vision of Republican China." PhD dissertation, Harvard University, 1977.

Kitamura Hirotada 北村敬道. "Minmatsu Shinsho ni Okeru Jinushi ni Tsuite" 明末清初における地主について (On landlords in the late Ming and early Qing), *Rekishigaku Kenkyū* 1949. 140:13–26.

Kojima Shinji 古島晋治 . "Taihei Tengoku to Nōmin" 太平天国と
農民 (The Taiping Heavenly Kingdom and the peasantry), *Shichō* 93:44–77
(October 1965); 96:1–30 (August 1966); 97:85–102 (November 1966).

Kuang Minben 曠敏本 . *Goulou Wencao Zazhuo; shanyu wencaoji* 岣嶁
文草雜著删餘文草集　　　 (Collected writings). 1775.

Kuhn, Philip A. *Rebellion and its Enemies in Late Imperial China: Militarization
and Social Structure.* Cambridge, Harvard University Press, 1970.

———. "Local Self-Government under the Republic: Problems of Control
Autonomy, and Mobilization." In Frederic Wakeman, Jr., and Carolyn Grant,
eds., *Conflict and Control in Late Imperial China.* Berkeley, University of California Press, 1975.

———. "The Taiping Rebellion." In John K. Fairbank, ed., *The Cambridge History
of China, Vol. X, Late Ch'ing, 1800–1911,* Part I. Cambridge, Cambridge University Press, 1978.

———. "Local Taxation and Finance in Republican China." In Susan Mann Jones,
ed., *Select Papers from the Center for Far Eastern Studies,* The University of
Chicago, No. 3, 1978–1979.

Kui Lian 魁聯　. *Qianhou Shoubaolu* 前後守寶錄 (A record of
government in Baoqing prefecture). 1874.

Kuribayashi Nobuo 粟林宣夫. *Rikōsei no Kenkyū* 里甲制の研究
(Studies on the *lijia* system). Tokyo, Bunri Shoin, 1971.

Lai Jiadu 賴家度 . "Mingdai Nongmin di Kenhuang Yundong" 明代農民
的墾荒运動　　 (The movement to clear wasteland by the peasants in the
Ming dynasty), *Lishi Jiaoxue* 3.10–12 1952.

———. *Mingdai Yunyang Nongmin Qiyi* 明代鄖陽農民起義 (The
peasant uprising in Yunyang in the Ming dynasty). Wuhan, 1956.

Leach, Edmund R. "Hydraulic Society in Ceylon," *Past and Present* 15:2–26
(April 1959).

Lee, James. "Migration and Expansion in Chinese History." In William McNeill,
ed., *Human Migration: Patterns and Policies.* Bloomington, University of
Indiana Press, 1979.

———. "The Settlement of China's Southwest Frontier, 316 B.C.–1850 A.D." PhD
dissertation, University of Chicago, 1981.

———. "Food Supply and Population Growth in Southwest China, 1250–1850,"
Journal of Asian Studies 41.4:723 (August 1982).

———. "State and Economy in Southwest China, 1250–1850." Unpublished
manuscript. 1986.

Lee, Robert, H. G. *The Manchurian Frontier in Ch'ing History.* Cambridge,
Harvard University Press, 1970.

Leiyang Xianzhi 耒陽县志　 1725.GG.

Leiyang Xianzhi 1885.YC.

Li, Lillian, ed. "Food, Famine, and the Chinese State – A Symposium," *Journal of Asian Studies* 41.4:685–797 (August 1982).

Li Wenzhi 李文治. *Wanming Minbian* 晚明民变 (Rebellions in the late Ming dynasty). Shanghai, 1948.

——. "Lun Qingchao Qianqi di Tudi Zhanyou Guanxi" 論清朝前期的土地占有关係 (A discussion of landowning relations in the early Qing), *Lishi Yanjiu*, 1963.5. In *Zhongguo Jinsanbainian Shehui Jingjishi Lunji* 中国近三百年社会经济史论集 (Collection of articles on Chinese socio-economic history during the last three hundred years). Hong Kong, Cuncui Xueshe, 1979.

——. "Dizhu Jingjizhi yu Zhongguo Fengjian Shehui Changqi Yanxu Wenti Lungang" 地主經濟与中国封建社会長期延續問題论綱 (A discussion of the landlord economic system and the prolonged period of Chinese feudal society), *Zhongguoshi Yanjiu* 1983, Vol. I.

——, ed. *Zhongguo Jindai Nongyeshi Ziliao* 中国近代農業史資料 (Materials on the agricultural history of modern China). Vol. I. Peking, 1957.

Li Zhaoxi 李肇錫 , "Zhisheng Shuili" 直省水利 (Water conservancy in various provinces). Unpublished draft in Palace Museum, Taipei, Taiwan.

Li Zhen 李振. *Hunan Binhu Gexian Shixi Diaocha Riji* 湖南濱湖各县实習調查日記 (Diary of an investigation of the water system around Dongting Lake, Hunan). In *Minguo Ershiniandai Zhongguo Dalu Tudi Wenti Ziliao* 民国二十年代中国大陸土地問題資料 (Materials on the land problem in mainland China in the 1930s), no. 150, 1977.

Liang, C. S. "Three Types of Agricultural Water Use in the Yangtze Basin," *Chung Chi Journal* 1965. 1:40–59.

Liang Fang-chung. *The Single Whip Method of Taxation in China.* Tr. Wang Yu-ch'üan. Cambridge, East Asian Research Center, Harvard University, 1970.

Liling Xiangtuzhi 醴陵鄉土志   1926.YC.

Liling Xianzhi 醴陵县志 1744.NB.

Liling Xianzhi 1871.YC.

Liling Xianzhi 1948. Beijing National Library.

Lingling Xianzhi 零陵县志 1684.NB.

Lingling Xianzhi 1876.YC.

Linwu xianzhi 臨武县志 1817.GG.

Linxiang Xianzhi 临湘县志 1685.NB.

Linxiang Xianzhi 1892.YC.

Liu Cheng-yun. "Kuo-lu: A Sworn Brotherhood Organization in Szechuan," *Late Imperial China* 6.1:56–82 (June 1985).

Liu Cuirong 劉翠溶 . "Qingchu Shunzhi-Kangxi Nianjian Jianmian Fushui di Guocheng" 清初順治康熙年間減免賦税的過程 (The process of reducing and remitting taxes in the early Qing dynasty), *Zhongyang Yanjiuyuan Lishiyuyan Yanjiuso Jikan* 37.2: Table 1 (June 1967).

Liu, K. C. "The Ch'ing Restoration." In John K. Fairbank, ed., *The Cambridge History of China Vol. X, Late Ch'ing, 1800–1911*, Part I. Cambridge, Cambridge University Press, 1978.

Liu Ts'ui-jung, "Dike Construction in Ching-chou. A Study Based on the *Ti-fang chih* Section of the *Ching-chou fu-chih*". *Papers on China*, No. 23. 1970.

Liu Yan 刘炎 . "Guanyu Jiefangqian Liangshan Yizu Shehui Xingzhi di Jige Wenti" 关于解放前凉山彝族社会性质的几个问题 (On several problems concerning the social formation of the Yi tribe of Liangshan before Liberation), *Wenshizhe* 1962.4.58.

Liu Yongcheng 刘永成 . "Qingdai Qianqi di Nongye Zudian Guanxi" 清代前期的农业租佃关係 (Tenancy relationships in early Qing agriculture). In *Qingshi Luncong* II, 56–88 (1980).

Liuyang Xianzhi 浏阳县志 1561.TB.

Liuyang Xianzhi 1680. Beijing National Library.

Liuyang Xianzhi 1733.TB.

Liuyang Xianzhi 1818.YC.

Liuyang Xianzhi 1873.YC.

Liuyang Xianzhi 1967 (Copy of original manuscript from late Qing or Republican period). YC.

Lizhou Zhi 澧州志 1874.YC.

Lizhou Zhilin 澧州志林 1750.NB.

Lizhou Zhilizhou Zhi 澧州直隶州志 1821. Seikadō.

Longyang Xianzhi 龍陽县志 1875.LC.

Lung, C. F. "A Note on Hung Liangchi: The Chinese Malthus," *T'ien Hsia Monthly*, October 1935.

Luo Ruhuai 罗汝怀 , ed. *Hunan Wenzheng* 湖南文徵 (Essays from Hunan). 1872.

Luo Xianglin 罗香林 , ed. *Zhongguo Zupu Yanjiu* 中国族譜研究 (Studies in Chinese genealogies). Hongkong, 1971.

Lü Xisheng 吕錫生 , "Ming-Qing Shiqi Shezu dui Zhenan Shanqu di Kaifa" 明清時期畬族对浙南山区的开发 (The opening of southern Zhejiang by the She people), *Zhongyang Minzu Xueyuan Xuebao* 1982.2:90–91.

Ma Shaoqiao 馬少僑 . *Qingdai Miaomin Qiyi* 清代苗民起義 (The uprising of the Miao people in the Qing dynasty). Hankow, 1956.

MacAleavy, Henry, "Dien in China and Vietnam," *Journal of Asian Studies* 17.3: 403–415 (May 1958).

Mayang Xianzhi 麻陽县志 1873.

Meisner, Maurice. "The Despotism of Concepts: Wittfogel and Marx on China," *China Quarterly* 16:99–112 (November–December 1963).

Meskill, Johanna. *A Chinese Pioneer Family: The Lins of Wu-feng, Taiwan, 1729–1895.* Princeton, Princeton University Press, 1979.

Metzger, Thomas. "The Organizational Capabilities of the Ch'ing State in the Field of Commerce: The Lianghuai Salt Monopoly, 1740–1840." In W. E. Willmott, ed., *Economic Organization in Chinese Society.* Stanford, Stanford University Press, 1972.

——. *The Internal Organization of Ch'ing Bureaucracy: Legal, Normative, and Communication Aspects.* Cambridge, Harvard University Press, 1973.

——. *Escape from Predicament: Neo-Confucianism and China's Evolving Political Culture.* New York, Columbia University Press, 1977.

——. "On the Historical Roots of Economic Modernization in China: The Increasing Differentiation of the Economy from the Polity during Late Ming and Early Ch'ing Times." In Institute of Economics, Academia Sinica, *Conference on Modern Chinese Economic History.* Taipei, 1977.

Migdal, Joel. *Peasants, Politics, and Revolution: Pressures toward Political and Social Change in the Third World.* Princeton, Princeton University Press, 1974.

Mihelich, Mira. "Polders and the Politics of Land Reclamation in Southeast China during the Northern Sung Dynasty (960–1126)." PhD dissertation, Cornell University, 1979.

Montesquieu, Charles. *L'Esprit des lois.* In *Oeuvres complètes.* Paris, Editions du Seuil, 1964.

Mori Masao 森正夫 . "Min-Shin Jidai no Tochi Seido" 明清時代の土地制度 (The land system in the Ming-Qing period). In *Iwanami Kōza Sekai Rekishi* (Iwanami lectures on world history) Tokyo, Iwanami Shoten, 1971, XII, 260–271.

Morita Akira. "Shindai Kokō Chihō ni Okeru Teikishi ni Tsuite" 清代江南地方における定期市について (On the history of periodic markets in Hunan in the Qing dynasty), *Kyūshū Sangyō Daigaku Shōkei Ronsō* 5.1:49–73 (1964).

——. *Shindai Suirishi Kenkyū* 清代水利史研究 (Studies on water control in the Qing dynasty). Tokyo, Aki Shobo, 1974.

——. "Minmatsu Shindai no 'Hōmin' ni Tsuite" 明末清代の棚民について (On the "shack people" of the late Ming and early Qing), *Jimbun Kenkyū* (Osaka University) 28.9 (December 1976).

Mote, Frederick. "The Growth of Chinese Despotism: A Critique of Wittfogel's Theory of Oriental Despotism as Applied to China," *Oriens Extremus* 8.1:1–41 (1961).

Myers, Ramon H. *The Chinese Peasant Economy: Agricultural Development in Hopei and Shantung, 1890–1949.* Cambridge, Harvard University Press, 1970.

——. "Economic Organization and Cooperation in Modern China: Irrigation Management in Hsing-tai County, Hopei Province." In *Ko-Muramatsu Yūji Kyōju Tsuitō Rombunshi: Chūgoku no Seiji to Keizai* (Politics and economics in

China: Memorial volume for the late Muramatsu Yūji). Tokyo, Tokyo Keizai Shimposha, 1975.

———. "Transformation and Continuity in Chinese Economic and Social History" (Review article on Mark Elvin, *The Pattern of the Chinese Past*), *Journal of Asian Studies* 33.2:165–277 (February 1979).

———. "Customary Law, Markets, and Resource Transactions in Late Imperial China." *Explorations in the New Economic History.* Academic Press, 1983.

Myers, Ramon, and Chang Fu-mei Ch'en. "Customary Law and the Economic Growth of China during the Ch'ing Period," *Ch'ing-shih Wen-t'i* 3.5:1–32 (November 1976); 3.10:4–27 (December 1978).

Myers, Ramon, and Thomas Metzger. "Sinological Shadows: The State of Modern China Studies in the United States," *Washington Quarterly,* Spring 1980.

Needham, Joseph. *The Grand Titration.* Toronto, University of Toronto Press, 1969.

Neige Sanfasi Dang'an 内閣三法司档案 (Archives of the Three High Courts). Taipei, Academia Sinica. Cited by author and date of memorial.

Niida Noboru 仁井田陞. *Chūgoku Hōseishi Kenkyū* 中国法制史研究 (Studies in Chinese legal history). Vol. II, *Tochihō* (Land law). Tokyo, 1960.

———, ed. *Chūgoku Nōson Kankō Chōsa* 中国農村慣行調査 (Investigation of Chinese peasant customs). Tokyo, 1953–1958.

Ningxiang Xianzhi 寧鄉县志 1682.NB.

Ningxiang Xianzhi 1748.GG.

Ningxiang Xianzhi 1816. Beijing National Library.

Ningxiang Xianzhi 1867.

Ningxiang Xianzhi 1941. Beijing National Library.

Ningyuan Xianzhi 寧遠县志 1811.YC.

Ningyuan Xianzhi 1876.YC.

Nishimura Genshō 西村元照. "Shinsho no Tochi Jōryō ni Tsuite" 清初の土地丈量について (On the land surveys in the early Qing), *Tōyōshi Kenkyū* 33.3:102–155 (December 1974).

North, Douglass C. *Structure and Change in Economic History.* New York, Norton, 1981.

North, Douglass C., and Robert Paul Thomas. *The Rise of the Western World: A New Economic History.* Cambridge, Cambridge University Press, 1973.

Obata Tatsuo 小畑龍雄. "Kōnan ni Okeru Rikō no Hensei ni Tsuite" 江南における里甲の編成について (On the changes in the *lijia* in Jiangnan), *Shirin* 39.2:1–35 (March 1956).

Oh Keum-sung 吳金成. "Myŏngmal Tongjŏngho Chubyŏn ŭi Wanjae ŭi Paltal" 明末洞庭湖周边斗垸堤斗發達 (The development of dikes on the borders of Dongting Lake in the late Ming),

Yŏksa Kyoyuk 21:101–129 (May 1977). Japanese translation in *Shihō* 10:22–41 (April 1979).

——. "Myŏngmal Tongjŏngho Chubyŏn ŭi Suri Kaebal Kwa Nongch'on Sahoe" 明末洞庭湖 周边斗 水利開 發 外農村社会 (Peasant society and the development of water control on the borders of Dongting Lake in the late Ming), *Yŏksa Hakpo* 77:127–154 (March 1978).

Olson, Mancur. *The Logic of Collective Action: Public Goods and the Theory of Groups.* Cambridge, Harvard University Press, 1974.

Otake Fumio 小·竹文夫. *Kinsei Shina Keizaishi Kenkyū* 近世支那经济史研究 (Studies in modern Chinese economic history). Tokyo, 1946.

Ouyang Xuefeng 欧阳学风. "Zhong hanhe shu" 种旱禾書 (A treatise on planting drought grain), *Hunan Lishi Ziliao* 1959.4:162–179.

Oyama Masaaki 小·山正明. "Minmatsu Shinsho no Daitochi Shoyū," 明末清初の大土地所有 (Large landholding in the late Ming and early Qing), *Shigaku Zasshi* 66.12:1–30 (1957); 67.1:50–72 (1958).

Pang Zhuoheng. 庞卓恆 "Zhongxi Fengjian Zhuanzhi Zhidu di Bijiao Yanjiu" 中西封建专制制度的比较研究(A comparative study of Chinese and Western European feudal autocracy), *Lishi Yanjiu* 1981.2:1–13.

Parsons, James B. *The Peasant Rebellions of the Ming Dynasty.* Tucson, University of Arizona Press, 1969.

Peng Wenhe 彭文和. *Hunan Hutian Wenti* 湖南湖田問题 (Problems of lake land in Hunan). *Minguo Ershiniandai Zhongguo Dalu Tudi Wenti Ziliao* (Materials on the land problem in mainland China in the 1930s), No. 75. 1977.

Peng Yangzhong 彭洋中. *Guxiangshanguan Cungao* 古香山館存稿 (Collected writings). 1874.

Peng Zeyi 彭泽益. "Qingdai qianqi shougongye di fazhan" 清代前期手工業的發展 (The development of handicraft industry in the early Qing), *Zhongguoshi Yanjiu* 1981.1.

Peng Zongmeng 彭宗孟. *Chutai Shulue* 楚台疏略 (Memorials on Huguang). 1601.

Perdue, Peter C. "*Liumin* and Famine Relief in Eighteenth-Century China." Unpublished manuscript. 1974.

——. "Water Control in the Dongting Lake Region during the Ming and Qing Periods," *Journal of Asian Studies* 41.4:747–765 (August 1982).

——. "Outsiders and Insiders: The Xiangtan Riot of 1819 and Collective Action in Hunan," *Modern China* 12.2:166–201 (April 1986).

Perkins, Dwight. *Agricultural Development in China, 1368–1968.* Chicago, Aldine, 1969.

——, ed. *China's Economic Development in Historical Perspective.* Stanford, Stanford University Press, 1975.

Pingjiang Xianzhi 平江县志 1875.YC.

Pingjiang Xianzhi Qing.NB.

Popkin, Samuel. *The Rational Peasant: The Political Economy of Rural Society in Vietnam.* Berkeley, University of California Press, 1979.

Pulleyblank, E. G. Review of Wittfogel, *Oriental Despotism, Bulletin of the London School of Oriental and African Studies* 21:657 (1958).

Qianyang Xianzhi 黔陽县志 1874.YC.

Qianzhou Zhi 乾州志 1739.GG.

Qianzhou Tingzhi 乾州厅志 1877.TB.

Qin Shangzhi 秦尚志. *Zhongguo Fazhi ji Falü Sixiang Shi Jianghua* 中国法制及法律思想史講話 (Lectures on legal institutions and legal thought in China). Taipei, 1966.

Qingquan Xianzhi 清泉县志 1869.YC.

Qingshigao 清史稿 (Draft history of the Qing dynasty). Beijing, Qingshiguan, 1928.

Qiyang Xianzhi 祁陽县志 1765.GG.

Qiyang Xianzhi 1870.YC.

Quan Hansheng 全漢昇. "Qingchao Zhongye Suzhou di Miliang Maoyi" 清朝中葉苏州的米糧貿易 (Rice trade in Soochow in the Ch'ing dynasty). In Quan Hansheng, *Zhongguo Jingjishi Luncong* (Collection of articles on Chinese economic history). Vol. II. Hong Kong, 1972.

Quanguo Minshu Gushu Qingce 全国民数谷数清册 (National population and grain-supply registers), *Huangce* Record Group, *wen* 497, 965–1006. Ming-Qing Archives, Beijing, China.

Quesnay, François. *Le despotisme de la Chine.* Tr. Lewis A. Maverick. In *China a Model for Europe.* San Antonio, P. Anderson Co., 1946.

Rawski, Evelyn Sakakida. *Agricultural Change and the Peasant Economy of South China.* Cambridge, Harvard University Press, 1972.

Richthofen, Ferdinand Freiherr von. *Letter from Hunan.* Shanghai, 1870.

——. *China: Ergebnisse eigener Reisen. . . .* Berlin, 1912.

Rinji Taiwan Kyūkan Chōsakai 臨時台湾旧慣調査会. *Shindai Keiyaku Bunsho: Shoken Bunruishū* 清代契約文書書簡文類集 (Qing dynasty land contracts and documents). Tokyo, Kyuko Shoin, 1973.

——. *Shinkoku Gyōseihō* 清国行政法 (Administration of the Qing dynasty). 1967 Daian reprint.

Rowe, William T. "Recent Writing in the People's Republic on Early Ch'ing Economic History," *Ch'ing-shih Wen-t'i* 4.7:73–90 (June 1982).

——. *Hankow: Commerce and Society in a Chinese City.* Stanford, Stanford University Press, 1984.

——. "Approaches to Modern Chinese Social History." In Olivier Zunz, ed.,

Reliving the Past: The Worlds of Social History. Chapel Hill, University of North Carolina Press, 1985.

Rozman, Gilbert. *Urban Networks in Ch'ing China and Tokugawa Japan.* Princeton, Princeton University Press, 1973.

Rucheng Xianzhi 汝城县志 1932.YC.

Sangzhi Xianzhi 桑植县志 1764.GG.

Sasaki Masaya 佐々木正哉 . "Shunde Xian Kyōshin to Tōkai Jūroku-sa" 川順德鄉紳と東海十六沙 (The gentry of Shunde district and the sixteen delta lands of the Eastern Sea), *Kindai Chūgoku Kenkyū* 3:163–232 (1959).

Schurmann, H. Franz. "Traditional Property Concepts in China," *Far Eastern Quarterly* 15.4:507–516 (August 1956).

Schwartz, Benjamin. "A Marxist Controversy on China," *Far Eastern Quarterly* 13.2:143–155 (February 1954).

Scott, James. *The Moral Economy of the Peasant: Rebellion and Subsistence in Southeast Asia.* New Haven, Yale University Press, 1976.

Shangyudang 上諭档 (Imperial Edict record books). Palace Museum Archives, Taipei, Taiwan.

Shanhua Xianzhi 善化县志 1747. Beijing National Library.

Shanhua Xianzhi 1818.TB.

Shanhua Xianzhi 1877.YC.

Shigeta Atsushi 重田德 . *Shindai Shakaikeizaishi Kenkyū* 清代社会经济史研究 (Studies in Qing social and economic history). Tokyo, Iwanami Shoten, 1975.

Shimen Xianzhi 石門县志 1889.TB.

Shimizu Taiji 清水泰次. "Chō Kyosei no Tochi Jōryō ni Tsuite" 張居正の土地丈量について (On the land survey of Zhang Juzheng), *Tōyō Gakuhō* 29.2:167–198 (May 1942).

Shiraishi Hirō 白石博男 . "Shindai Konan no Nōsonshakai—Kaso Kankō to Kōso Keikō" 清代湖南の農村社会—加租慣行と抗租傾向 (Agricultural society in Hunan—the custom of rent deposit and the trend toward rent resistance). In *Chūgoku Kindaika no Shakai Kōzō* (The social structure of Chinese modernization). Tokyo, Tōkyō Kyōiku Daigaku, 1960.

Skinner, G. William. "Regional Systems in Late Imperial China." Paper prepared for the second annual meeting of the Social Science History Association, Ann Arbor, Michigan, 1977.

——. "Presidential Address: The Structure of Chinese History," *Journal of Asian Studies* 44.2 (February 1985).

——, ed. *The City in Late Imperial China.* Stanford, Stanford University Press, 1977.

Smil, Vaclav. *The Bad Earth: Environmental Degradation in China.* Armonk, N.Y., M. E. Sharpe, 1984.

Spence, Jonathan. *The Memory Palace of Matteo Ricci.* New York, Viking, 1984.

Sudō Yoshiyuki 周藤吉之 . *Chūgoku Tochi Seidoshi Kenkyū,* 中国土地 制度史研究 (Studies in the Chinese land system). Tokyo, Tōkyō Daigaku Shuppansha, 1971.

Sun Ching-chih, ed. *Economic Geography of Central China.* Tr. Joint Publications Research Service. Washington, D.C., 1960.

Suzuki Chūsei 鈴木中正 . *Shinchō Chūkishi Kenkyū,* 清朝中期 史研究 (Studies in the history of the mid-Qing dynasty). Aichi, Aichi University, 1952.

Tan Qixiang 譚其驤 . "Zhongguo Neidi Yiminshi–Hunan Bian" 中 国内地移民史 – 湖南編 (A history of migration in China– Hunan), *Shixue Nianbao* 1.4:47–104 (1932).

Tanaka Masatoshi 田中正俊 . "Chūgoku–Keizaishi," 中国 – 经济 史, *Ajia Keizai* 19.1–2:41–51 (February 1978).

Taoyuan Xianzhi 桃源县志 1821.LC.

Thorp, James. *Geography of the Soils of China.* Peking, 1939.

Tilly, Charles, ed. *The Formation of National States in Western Europe.* Princeton, Princeton University Press, 1975.

Tuan Yi-fu. *China.* London, Longman, 1970.

Twitchett, Denis. "The Fan Clan's Charitable Estate." In A. F. Wright and David Nivison, eds., *Confucianism in Action.* Palo Alto, Stanford University Press, 1959.

——. "Some Remarks on Irrigation under the T'ang," *T'oung Pao* 48.1–3: 175–194 (1960).

van der Sprenkel, O. B. "Population Statistics of Ming China," *Bulletin of the School of Oriental and Asian Studies* 15.2:289–326 (1953).

von Glahn, Richard. "The Country of Streams and Grottoes: Geography, Settlement, and the Civilizing of China's Southwestern Frontier, 1000–1250." PhD dissertation, Yale University, 1983.

Wakeman, Frederic, Jr. *Strangers at the Gate: Social Disorder in South China, 1838–1861.* Berkeley, University of California Press, 1966.

——. *The Great Enterprise: The Manchu Reconstruction of Imperial Order in Seventeenth-Century China.* Berkeley, University of California Press, 1985.

Wan Benduan 萬本端 . "Hequzhi: Zhisheng Shuili" 河渠志 : 直省水 利 (Rivers and canals: Water conservancy in various provinces). Unpublished draft in Palace Museum, Taipei, unpaginated; cited by year of entry.

Wang Yeh-chien. *Land Taxation in Imperial China.* Cambridge, Harvard University Press, 1973.

——. "Agricultural Development and Peasant Economy in Hunan during the

Ch'ing Period (1644–1911)." Unpublished manuscript.

Watt, John. *The District Magistrate in Late Imperial China.* New York, Columbia University Press, 1972.

Weber, Max. *The City.* Tr. Don Martindale and Gertrud Neuwirth. New York, Free Press, 1958.

——. *Economy and Society.* Berkeley, University of California Press, 1978.

Wei Qingyuan 韦庆远 . *Mingdai Huangce Zhidu* 明代黄册制度 (The Yellow Register system in the Ming dynasty). Beijing, Zhonghua Shuju, 1961.

——. "Lun Mingchu Dui Jiangnan Diqu Jingji Zhengce di Ruogan Wenti" 论明初对江南地区经济政策的若干问题 (A discussion of several problems concerning early Ming economic policy toward the Jiangnan region). Beijing, Zhongguo Renmin Daxue Danganxi Zhongguo Zhengzhi Zhidushi Yanjiushi, 1983.

Wei Qingyuan and Lu Su 鲁素 . *Qingdai Qianqi Shangban Kuangye he Zibenzhuyi Mengya* 清代前期商辩矿业和资本主义萌芽 (Merchant mining industry and the sprouts of capitalism in the early Qing). Beijing, Renmin Daxue, 1981.

Wei Yuan 魏源.. *Guweitang Neiwaiji* 古微堂内外集 (Collected writings). 1878.

Wieger, L., S. J. *Chinese Characters: Their Origin, Etymology, History, Classification and Signification.* New York, Dover, 1965.

Will, Pierre-Etienne. *Bureaucratie et famine en Chine au 18e siècle.* Paris, Mouton, 1980.

——. "Un cycle hydraulique en Chine: la province du Hubei du 16ème au 19ème siècles," *Bulletin de l'école française d'extrême orient* 1980. 68:261–287.

——. "State Intervention in the Administration of a Hydraulic Infrastructure: The Example of Hubei Province in Late Imperial Times." In Stuart Schram, ed., *The Scope of State Power in China.* Hong Kong, The Chinese University Press, 1985.

Wittfogel, Karl. *Oriental Despotism.* New Haven, Yale University Press, 1953.

Wolf, Arthur P., and Chieh-shan Huang. *Marriage and Adoption in China, 1845–1945.* Stanford, Stanford University Press, 1980.

Wong, R. Bin. "Food Distribution Crises: Markets, Granaries, and Food Riots in the Qing Period." Paper presented to workshop on Food and Famine in Chinese History, Harvard University, 4–25 August 1980.

——. "Food Riots in the Qing Dynasty," *Journal of Asian Studies* 41.4:774–780 (August 1982).

——. "Les émeutes de subsistances en Chine et en Europe occidentale," *Annales: Economies, Sociétés, Civilisations,* Mars-Avril 1983, pp. 234–258.

——. "The Political Economy of Food Supplies in Qing China." PhD dissertation, Harvard University, 1983.

Wong, R. Bin, Pierre Etienne Will, James Lee, Peter C. Perdue, and Jean Oi. *Nourish the People: The State Civilian Granary System in China, 1650–1850.* Ann Arbor, Center for Chinese Studies, University of Michigan, in press.

Wong, R. Bin, and Peter C. Perdue. "Famine's Foes in Ch'ing China," *Harvard Journal of Asiatic Studies* 43.1:291–332 (June 1983).

Wong, R. Bin, and James Lee, eds. *Civilian Granary Supplies in Qing China.* Ann Arbor, Center for Chinese Studies, University of Michigan, forthcoming.

Woodside, Alexander B. "The Ch'ien-lung Reign." Draft chapter for *The Cambridge History of China*, Vol. IX.

Wright, Mary Clabaugh. *The Last Stand of Chinese Conservatism: The T'ung-chih Restoration, 1862–1874.* Stanford, Stanford University Press, 1957.

Wu Minshu 吳敏樹 . *Panhu Wenji* 柈湖文集 (Collected Works). 1893.

Wu Rongguang 吳荣光 . *Shiyun Shanren Ji: Zougao* 石雲山人集 – 奏稿 (Collected memorials and writings). 1841.

Wugang Zhouzhi 武岡州志 1817.TB.

Wugang Zhouzhi 1873.SY.

Wugang Zhou Xiangtuzhi 武岡州鄉土志 1908.TB.

Wuling Xianzhi 武陵县志 1868.YC.

Xiangtan Xianzhi 湘潭县志 1553.LC.

Xiangtan Xianzhi 1756.YC.

Xiangtan Xianzhi 1781.NB.

Xiangtan Xianzhi 1818.YC.

Xiangtan Xianzhi 1889.YC.

Xiangxiang Xianzhi 湘鄉县志 1673.NB.

Xiangxiang Xianzhi 1825.LC.

Xiangyin Xiangtuzhi 湘陰鄉土志 1881.YC.

Xiangyin Xianzhi 湘陰县志 1565.TB.

Xiangyin Xianzhi 1756.LC.

Xiangyin Xianzhi 1818.

Xie Hua 謝華 . *Xiangxi Tusi Jilue* 湘西土司輯略 (Collection of materials on tribal chiefs in western Hunan). Shanghai, 1956.

Xie Zhaozhe 謝肇淛 . *Wuzazu* 五雜俎 (Miscellaneous writings), Guoxuezhenben wenku edition, 1935, 1.13.

Xingke Tiben 1753. In #1 Archives, Bejing.

Xinhua Xianzhi 新化县志 1549.LC.

Xinhua Xianzhi 1759.NB.

Xinning Xianzhi 新宁县志 1823.TB.

Xinning Xianzhi 1893.LC.

Xu Daling 許大齡 . *Qingdai Juanna Zhidu* 清代捐納制度 (The system of contributions in the Qing dynasty). Taipei, 1977 reprint.

Xupu Xianzhi 溆浦县志 1921.TB.

Yan Zhongping 严中平 , ed. *Zhongguo Jindai Jingjishi Tongji Ziliao Xuanji* 中国近代经济史统计资料选集 (Selected statistical materials on Chinese economic history). Beijing, 1953.

Yanagida Setsuko 柳田節子. "Sōdai no Kyakko ni Tsuite" 宋代の客戸 について (On the guest households of the Song dynasty), *Shigaku Zasshi* 68.4:1–39 (April 1959).

——. "Sōdai Tochi Shoyūsei ni Mirareru Futatsu no Katachi–Senshin to Henkyō" 宋代土地所有制に見うれる二つの形 —先進と辺境 (Two forms of landholding in the Song dynasty: Advanced areas and border regions), *Tōyō Bunka Kenkyūjo Kiyō* 1963. 29:95–130.

——. "Kyōsonsei no Tenkai" 郷村制の展開 (The development of the village control system). In *Iwanami Kōza Sekai Rekishi* (Iwanami Lectures on world history), Vol. IX, *Chūsei* (Middle Ages). Tokyo Iwanami Shoten, 1970.

Yang Guozhen 杨国桢 . "Shilun Qingdai Minbei Minjian di Tudi Maimai" 试论清代闽北民间的土地买卖 (A discussion of private land sales in northern Fujian in the Qing), *Zhongguoshi Yanjiu* 1981. 1:29–42.

——. "Qingdai Minbei Tudi Wenshu Xuanbian" 清代闽北土地文书选编 (A selection of land documents from northern Fujian in the Qing), *Zhongguo Shehui Jingjishi Yanjiu* 1982. 1:111–121.

Yang Renjun 楊仁俊. "Dongtinghu Chuangshe Jianshui Shanglun Youyi Wusun Shuo" 洞庭湖創設浅水商輪有益無損说 (The establishment of steamships on Dongting Lake has advantages and no harm). In Jiang Biao, ed., *Yuanxiang Tongyilu*. Shanghai, 1935.

Yang Renzhang 楊紉章 . "Xiangjiang Liuyu Shuiwen Dili" 湘江流域水文地理 (Hydrological geography of the Xiang River Basin), *Dili Xuebao* 23.2:161–181 (May 1957).

Yang Xifu 楊錫綬. *Sizhitang Wentji* 四知堂文集 (Collected writings). 1805.

Yang Yi 楊儀. "Qingchao Qianqi di Tudi Zhidu", 清朝前期的土地制度 (The land system in the early Qing), *Shixue Yuekan*, 1958.7. In *Zhongguo Jinsanbainian Shehui Jingjishi Lunji*. Hong Kong, Cuncui Xueshe, 1979.

Yasui Shōtarō 安井肴太郎 . *Konan* 湖南 (Hunan). Tokyo, 1905.

Yasuno Shōzō 安野省三 , "Kokō Juku Sureba Tenka Zokusuru Kō" 湖廣熟すれば天下足する考 (An examination of "When Huguang has a good harvest, the empire has enough grain"). In *Kimura Masao Sensei Taikan Kinen Tōyōshi Ronshū*, 1976, pp. 301–309.

Yiyang Xianzhi 益陽县志 1874.YC.

Yizhang Xianzhi 宜章县志 1756.TB.

Yongding Xianzhi 永定县志 1870.TB.

Yongming Xianzhi 永明县志 1716.GG.

Yongming Xianzhi 1907.TB.

Yongshun Fuzhi 永順府志 1763.LC.

Yongshun Xianzhi 永順县志 1793.LC.

Yongshun Xianzhi 1874.TB.

Yongshun Xianzhi 1930.TB.

Yongxing Xiangtuzhi 永兴鄉土志 1906.TB.

Yongxing Xianzhi 永兴县志 1762.GG.

Yongxing Xianzhi 1883.LC.

Yongzhou Fuzhi 永州府志 1495.TB.

Yongzhou Fuzhi 1670.UC.

Yongzhou Fuzhi 1694.GG.

Yongzhou Fuzhi 1828.YC.

You Xianzhi 攸县志 1871.YC.

Yuanjiang Xianzhi 沅江县志 1810.YC.

Yuanling Xianzhi 沅陵县志 1708.GG.

Yuanzhou Fuzhi 沅州府志 1790.LC.

Yuezhou Fuzhi 岳州府志 1567–1572.LC.

Yuezhou Fuzhi 1746.YC.

Zelin, Madeleine. *The Magistrate's Tael: Rationalizing Fiscal Reform in Eighteenth-Century Ch'ing China.* Berkeley, University of California Press, 1984.

——. "The Rights of Tenants in Mid-Qing Sichuan: A Study of Land-Related Lawsuits in the Baxian Archives," *Journal of Asian Studies* 45.3:499–526 (May 1986).

Zhang Pengyuan 張朋園. "Jindai Hunan di Renkou yu Dushi Fazhan 近代湖南的人口與都市發展 (The development of population and cities in modern Hunan), *Guoli Shifan Daxue Lishi Xuebao*, Vol. IV (1977).

Zhang Wenda 張問達. *Fuchu Shuchao* 撫楚疏抄 (Memorials on the pacification of Hunan). 1612.

Zhang Xiugui 張修桂. "Dongtinghu Yanbian di Lishi Guocheng" 洞庭湖演变的历史过程 (The historical process of the changes in Dongting Lake), *Lishi Dili* 1981.1:99–116.

Zhang Yun-ao 張雲璈. "Xiangtan Shuiliji" 湘潭水利記 (Record of irrigation in Xiangtan), *Jiansong caotang wenji*, 簡松草堂文集 (Collected writings). 1941, 10b–11b.

Zhao Shenqiao 趙申喬. *Zhao Gongyigong Zizhi Guanshu* 趙恭毅公自治官書 (Materials on government). Hunan, 1849.

——. *Zhao Gongyigong Shenggao* 趙恭毅公剩藁 (Collected memorials). 1741.

Zheng Zhaojing 鄭肇経. *Zhongguo Shuilishi* 中国水利史 (History of water control in China). Taipei, Shangwu Yinshuguan, 1976.

Zhijiang Xianzhi 芷江县志 1839.SY.

Zhongguo Lishixue Nianjian 中国历史学年鑑 (Yearbook of Chinese historical studies). Beijing, Renmin Chubanshe, 1982.

Zhongguo Renmin Daxue Qingshi Yanjiusuo, Danganxi Zhongguo Zhengzhi Zhidushi Jiaoyanshi 中国人民大学清史研究所档案係. 中国政治制度史教研室 , eds. *KangYongQian Shiqi Chengxiang Renmin Fankang Douzheng Ziliao,* 康雍乾時期城鄉人民反抗斗争资料 (Materials on the resistance struggles of urban and rural people in the Kangxi, Yongzheng, and Qianlong reigns). Beijing, Zhonghua Shuju, 1979.

Zhou Yikui 周一夔 . *Huansheng Shuizai Chakan Baogaoshu* 湖南省水災查看報告書 (Report on an investigation of the flood in Hunan). 1931.

Zhupi Yuzhi 硃批諭旨 (The Yongzheng Emperor's vermilion endorsements and edicts). 1738.

Zhupi Zouzhe 硃批奏摺 (Palace memorials with vermilion endorsements) Number One (Ming-Qing) Historical Archives. Beijing.

Glossary

anchatian 安插田
anmou paifu 桉畝排夫
anmou zhengfei 桉畝徵費
Antu 安圖

ba 壩
baogu 宝谷
baojia 保甲
baolan 包攬
baopei 包賠
bazhang 壩長
benzhou 本州
biaochan 標產
Boyanghu 潘陽湖
Bulaichao 布平朝

Cao Zongqi 曹宗奇
Cao Zongshu 曹宗書
chang 場
changfu 場夫
Changshu 常熟
Chen Changzhen 陳長鎮
Chen Jiuchang 陳九長
Chen Weizhi 陳為之
Chen Youliang 陳友諒
Chendingli 辰鼎澧
Chenglingji 城陵機

chong 衝
chongyang nuo 重陽糯
Chu 楚
chuangzei 闖賊
chushu 处署
Cui Shu 崔述

Dai Dancheng 戴丹誠
Daming Huidian 大明会典
Danbage 檐壩歌
Dangying 当陽
dao 道
Dangyang 道光
daohu weitian 盜湖為田
daosun 稻孫
daotai 道台
daoyang 倒洋
dapengche 大輣車
daxie 大写
daxing 大姓
daxiu 大修
Daxue Yanyibu 大学衍義補
Deng Chaoqun 鄧超群
di (land) 地
dian 典
dianli 佃力
diaosheng liejian 刁生劣監

315

Diaoxiankou 調弦口

difu 堤夫

dijia 堤甲

dilao 堤老

ding 丁

Ding Chang 定長

dizhang 堤長

dizong 堤總

dongshi 董士

Dongting 洞庭

dou 斗

du 都

duan 垻

Duan Rulin 段汝霖

Duan Xingbang 段興邦

duanmai 斷賣

duanqi 斷契

duchai 都差

dui 隊

duxiu 督修

duzheng yi lisu 杜爭以厲俗

erhe 二禾

fa qi shanxin 發其善心

Fan Shengzhi 范勝之

Fan Shishou 范時綬

Fan Zhongyan 范仲淹

fengjinshan 封禁山

fu 府

gaitu guiliu 改土归流

Gao Qizhuo 高其倬

gaotian 高田

ge 箇

Geng Ju 耿橘

gengmingtian 更明田

gongjuan yicang 公捐義倉

gongsheng 貢生

Gu Yanwu 顧炎武

guandu minxiu 官督民修

guanggun 光棍

guanhuang 官荒

guanwei 官圍

Guo Songtao 郭嵩燾

guofei 囯匪

guoge 過割

guolu 囯嚕

Guzong 顧琮

haomi 耗米

haoxian 耗羨

haoyou 豪右

He Mengchun 何夢春

hebosuo 河泊所

hemai 合買

Heshi 賀石

Hong Liangji 洪亮吉

Hong Maode 洪懋德

Hong Xiuquan 洪秀全

Hongwu 洪武

hu 戶

Hu Ding 胡定

Hu Mingshan 胡明山

Hu Yuanshen 胡源深

Hu Yuling 胡愈靈

Huang Dafu 黃大富

Huang Dan 黃炎

Huang Jueci 黃爵滋

Huangchao Jingshi Wenbian 皇朝經世文編

Huangjinkou 黃金口

Huangtan 黃檀

Hucheng 護城

Hudukou 虎渡口

huigu 灰谷

huiguan 会館

huohao 火耗

hutian 湖田

Ji Wenchun 秬文醇

Jiang Changtai 蔣常泰

Jiang Pu 蔣溥

Jiangxi zao 江西早
Jianli 監利
jiansheng 監生
Jiaojinzhou 窖金洲
jiazu 加租
jin 金
jindili 盡地力
jingli 經理
Jinshazhou 金沙洲
jinshi 進士
jinzhuangyin 進庄銀
jiudian shengjian 久佃生奸
jiuhuangzao 救荒早
jiuli 九釐
jiuqiongliang 救窮糧
jue 蕨
juemai 絕賣
junliang 均糧
juren 舉人
juzuo 踞坐

Kai Tai 開泰
kou 口
Kuang Minben 曠敏本
kuanxiang 寬鄉

li (distance) 里
li (profit) 利
Li (river) 澧
Li (surname) 李
Li Lisong 李隸頌
Li Tengfang 李騰芳
Li Weijun 李維鈞
Li Xiuxi 李修禊
Li Yuanfa 李沅發
Li Zicheng 李自成
liangmin 良民
liangzhang 粮長
lijia 里甲
limu 吏目
Lin Zexu 林則徐
ling 領

Liu Laoshi 刘老十
Liu Yingzhong 劉應中
Liu Yuyi 劉於義
Liu Zhongwei 劉重偉
liugun 流棍
liumin 流民
lizhang 里長
Long Sheng 龍晟
Lu Ban 魯班
Lu Shiyi 陸世儀
Luo Bingzhang 駱秉章
Luo Tianfu 羅添福

Ma Huiyu 馬慧裕
Ma Jinzhong 馬進忠
mai 賣
Mai Gui 邁桂
maizhu 買主
mangzhong 忙中
Mianyang 沔陽
Ming Taizu 明太祖
minwei 民圍
mou 畝
mu-er 木耳

Nandi 南堤
Nanzhou 南洲
ning 寧
Nongshu 農書
Nongzheng Quanshu 農政全書
nupu 奴仆

Ouchikou 藕池口

Pan Zengqi 潘曾沂
Peng Yangzhong 彭洋中
pengmin 棚民
pi 陂
pingtian 平田
pu 僕
Pu Lin 浦霖

qian 欠
Qian Baochen 钱宝琛
qiangmin 强民
Qiao Guanglie 喬光烈
qing 頃
qinghuang bujie 青黃不接
qingming 清明
Qingshilu 清實錄
qingyi zhi jiao 情誼之交
Qiu Jun 邱濬
qu (canal) 渠
qu (district) 區
qutianfa 區田法

renman 人滿

Sangyuanwei 桑園圍
shang 上
shangtian 上田
shantian 山田
shanxiang 山鄉
shen 紳
sheng 升
shengshi 盛世
shengyuan 生員
shi 石
Shi Dakai 石達開
Shi Jingguo 石經幗
shihao 勢豪
shu 贖
sidang 死党
simai 死賣
simai huotou 死賣活頭
siwei 私圍
sixiang gengti 私相更替
Song (surname) 宋
Songci 松滋
songshi 訟师
Sun Shengchang 孫升長

Taihu 太湖
tang 塘

Tang Maochun 唐懋淳
tangfu 塘夫
tangzhang 塘長
tanqi 嘆契
teitairon 停滯論
tian 田
tiangen 田根
tianpi 田皮
tiantou 田頭
tianzhu 田主
tie 貼
tong 桐
tongche 筒車
Tonggu 銅鼓
tuanlianju 团練局
tuishou 推收
tuntian 屯田
tusi 土司

waidi 外堤
Wancheng 万城
Wang Anshi 王安石
Wang Bolan 王伯蘭
Wang Boshi 王伯仕
Wang Bozhen 王伯畛
Wang Guodong 王國棟
Wang Mang 王莽
Wang Xinjing 王心敬
Wang Yuandong 王原凍
Wang Zhen 王楨
Wanzi 萬子
wei 圍
weidi 圍堤
weiqi 圍棋
Wenzhouwei 文洲圍
Wu Daoing 吳道行
Wu Sangui 吳三桂

xiancheng 縣丞
xia 下
xian 縣
Xiang 湘

xiangong 險工
Xiangyang 襄陽
xianzei 獻賊
xiaoxie 小寫
xiatian 下田
xinhuang 新荒
Xu Guangqi 徐光啟
Xu Guoru 許幗儒
Xu Liangdong 徐梁棟
xunjiansi 巡檢司

yabao 押保
yan 堰
Yan Sisheng 晏斯盛
Yan Youxi 嚴有禧
Yang Cang 楊藏
Yanglinzhai 楊林寨
yanzhang 堰長
yeshi dianli 業食佃力
yitian liangzhu 一田兩主
yizhidan 易知單
Yongji 永濟
yongshou shiye 永收世業
youlizhe 有力者
yourenjie 遊人街
Yu Wanjun 于文駿
Yuan (River) 沅
yuan 垸
yuanzong 垸總
yujia 圩甲
Yun Shilin 惲世臨

yushui zhengdi 与水争地

zaliang 雜糧
zeguo 澤国
zeng 增
Zeng Guofan 曾國藩
zhang 丈
Zhang Can 張璨
Zhang Juzheng 張居正
Zhang Maoxi 張懋熺
Zhang Rongchang 張荣常
Zhang Xianzhong 張獻忠
zhao 找
Zhao Hongen 趙弘恩
zhaojia 找價
zhaotian paiyi 照田排役
zhen 圳
zhengxin 争心
zhilizhou 直隶州
zhishi 執事
zhongtian 衝田
zhou 州
Zhou Dexian 周德先
Zhou Zhaonan 周召南
Zhu Xi 朱熹
zhuandian 轉典
Zhuang 莊
zhubin zhi fen 主賓之分
zhubo 主簿
Zi 資
Zou 鄒

Index

Harvard East Asian Monographs

46. W. P. J. Hall, *A Bibliographical Guide to Japanese Research on the Chinese Economy, 1958-1970*

47. Jack J. Gerson, *Horatio Nelson Lay and Sino-British Relations, 1854-1864*

48. Paul Richard Bohr, *Famine and the Missionary: Timothy Richard as Relief Administrator and Advocate of National Reform*

49. Endymion Wilkinson, *The History of Imperial China: A Research Guide*

50. Britten Dean, *China and Great Britain: The Diplomacy of Commerical Relations, 1860-1864*

51. Ellsworth C. Carlson, *The Foochow Missionaries, 1847-1880*

52. Yeh-chien Wang, *An Estimate of the Land-Tax Collection in China, 1753 and 1908*

53. Richard M. Pfeffer, *Understanding Business Contracts in China, 1949-1963*

54. Han-sheng Chuan and Richard Kraus, *Mid-Ch'ing Rice Markets and Trade, An Essay in Price History*

55. Ranbir Vohra, *Lao She and the Chinese Revolution*

56. Liang-lin Hsiao, *China's Foreign Trade Statistics, 1864-1949*

57. Lee-hsia Hsu Ting, *Government Control of the Press in Modern China, 1900-1949*

58. Edward W. Wagner, *The Literati Purges: Political Conflict in Early Yi Korea*

59. Joungwon A. Kim, *Divided Korea: The Politics of Development, 1945-1972*

60. Noriko Kamachi, John K. Fairbank, and Chūzō Ichiko, *Japanese Studies of Modern China Since 1953: A Bibliographical Guide to Historical and Social-Science Research on the Nineteenth and Twentieth Centuries, Supplementary Volume for 1953-1969*

61. Donald A. Gibbs and Yun-chen Li, *A Bibliography of Studies and Translations of Modern Chinese Literature, 1918-1942*

62. Robert H. Silin, *Leadership and Values: The Organization of Large-Scale Taiwanese Enterprises*

63. David Pong, *A Critical Guide to the Kwangtung Provincial Archives Deposited at the Public Record Office of London*

64. Fred W. Drake, *China Charts the World: Hsu Chi-yü and His Geography of 1848*

65. William A. Brown and Urgunge Onon, translators and annotators, *History of the Mongolian People's Republic*

66. Edward L. Farmer, *Early Ming Government: The Evolution of Dual Capitals*

67. Ralph C. Croizier, *Koxinga and Chinese Nationalism: History, Myth, and the Hero*

68. William J. Tyler, tr., *The Psychological World of Natsumi Sōseki*, by Doi Takeo

STUDIES IN THE MODERNIZATION OF THE REPUBLIC OF KOREA: 1945–1975

90. Noel F. McGinn, Donald R. Snodgrass, Yung Bong Kim, Shin-Bok Kim, and Quee-Young Kim, *Education and Development in Korea*

91. Leroy P. Jones and Il SaKong, *Government, Business and Entrepreneurship in Economic Development: The Korean Case*

92. Edward S. Mason, Dwight H. Perkins, Kwang Suk Kim, David C. Cole, Mahn Je Kim, et al., *The Economic and Social Modernization of the Republic of Korea*

93. Robert Repetto, Tai Hwan Kwon, Son-Ung Kim, Dae Young Kim, John E. Sloboda, and Peter J. Donaldson, *Economic Development, Population Policy, and Demographic Transition in the Republic of Korea*

106. David C. Cole and Yung Chul Park, *Financial Development in Korea, 1945-1978*

107. Roy Bahl, Chuk Kyo Kim, and Chong Kee Park, *Public Finances during the Korean Modernization Process*

94. Parks M. Coble, *The Shanghai Capitalists and the Nationalist Government, 1927-1937*

95. Noriko Kamachi, *Reform in China: Huang Tsun-hsien and the Japanese Model*

96. Richard Wich, *Sino-Soviet Crisis Politics: A Study of Political Change and Communication*

97. Lillian M. Li, *China's Silk Trade: Traditional Industry in the Modern World, 1842-1937*

98. R. David Arkush, *Fei Xiaotong and Sociology in Revolutionary China*

99. Kenneth Alan Grossberg, *Japan's Renaissance: The Politics of the Muromachi Bakufu*

100. James Reeve Pusey, *China and Charles Darwin*

101. Hoyt Cleveland Tillman, *Utilitarian Confucianism: Ch'en Liang's Challenge to Chu Hsi*

102. Thomas A. Stanley, *Ōsugi Sakae, Anarchist in Taishō Japan: The Creativity of the Ego*

103. Jonathan K. Ocko, *Bureaucratic Reform in Provincial China: Ting Jih-ch'ang in Restoration Kiangsu, 1867-1870*

104. James Reed, *The Missionary Mind and American East Asia Policy, 1911-1915*

105. Neil L. Waters, *Japan's Local Pragmatists: The Transition from Bakumatsu to Meiji in the Kawasaki Region*

108. William D. Wray, *Mitsubishi and the N.Y.K., 1870-1914: Business Strategy in the Japanese Shipping Industry*

109. Ralph William Huenemann, *The Dragon and the Iron Horse: The Economics of Railroads in China, 1876-1937*